Allan D. Burdick, CPA
838 S.W. First Ave., Suite 300
Portland, Oregon 97204

Oral History Series
Book No. 2
Swiftwater People

Front cover picture is a McGoldrick Lbr. Co. log jam on Slate Creek 1913. — Courtesy of Mrs. Dave Nelson

Back cover is Sourdough Bob Corby and his wife on their way from a cooking and flunkey job in Marble Creek. Detail in the story of Marble Creek Jerry Broderick.

CORRECTIONS TO HARDSHIPS AND HAPPY TIMES

While we try to accurately report oral accounts we inevitably make mistakes or omissions. Herewith, in Book 2 of our series of oral histories we offer corrections to Book 1, **Hardships And Happy Times**:

Contents page and cut lines, pages 228 and 233 mistakenly spell Ernie Bel as Ernie Bell.

Page 1. Wash Applegate went trapping the fall of 1917 — not 1920 and his trapline did **not** go down on the St. Joe side.

Page 52. Pete Johnson says, where the white pine grew around the bunk beds the tent camp belonged to Francis O'Keefe and burned in 1923 — **not** 1922. They were logging the 1922 burn.

The 1923 fire started when an O'Keefe man was heating chute grease of animal fat that stunk like hell, down below the tent camp. The grease caught fire and took the camp. The flash fire also went downhill and across to the other side of Marble and travelled up to Freezeout in the fire killed stuff of the fire of 1922.

Page 53. Smokechasers from Jug Camp walked over Black Dome to Indian Dip **not** Indian Henry Ridge, and back — 14 miles.

Page 145. Andy Porterfield was born 1882 **not** 1812 (a typo error).

P. 175 — planting crew picture. 1st man in the back row listed as unknown has been identified as Earl Moore by Stan Kreshel of Spokane, a nephew.

Page 228. Boat load 110 lbs. should be 1,000 lbs.

Page 236. The name Burleigh was misspelled Burley.

SWIFTWATER

PEOPLE

Lives of Old Timers

on the upper St. Joe & St. Maries rivers

Tape Recorded and Edited
by
BERT RUSSELL

Library of Congress Catalog Card Number: 79-92395
ISBN 0-930344-02-2

Lacon Publishers
Bert Russell
Harrison, Idaho
83833

FIRST EDITION

Composition by Marie Russell

With Gratitude for the help of the Gazette-Record's
Robert Hammes
Sharon Blackburn
Sandra Ragsdale
Sheryl McPherson

I regret that space limitations make it impossble to include the histories of hundreds of other old timers as unique as the ones randomly
presented here. In these unsettling times we need to draw from the
reservoir of fortitude, humor and inventiveness handed down by river
drivers and horse loggers, and by women and men homesteaders who
made-do with what tools and food life offered and took their satisfactions
and happiness in the accomplishments of hard work.

CONTENTS

ILLUSTRATIONS

Chute Builder

John Akerstrom

Promised Not To Tell

John Akerstrom 1974

I was born northeast of Arvika, Sweden in 1887.

TOO MANY GIRLS

How I left Sweden, I started to dance when I was very young, you know. I started to go home with girls right along. I was nice looking and a good dancer. I used to take too many home. I was young and awful curious to learn the truth about everything.

PROMISED NOT TO TELL

I guess I was foolish. If they didn't want to tell me I'd keep trying till finally they told me if I promise I'll never tell that to anyone. I got them to tell me everything that she didn't want to tell, you know, and we could be together towards morning. I got maybe 12 girls to tell everything like that and I kept my word. I never said one word they ever told me.

NEVER TOLD

Years went by and not one of them knew any other girl had told me anything. And it got so when no word came back, they wanted to tell me more things. That's the way it went on.

NEVER INTENDED TO GO TO U.S.

In 1910 one of my boy friends, Pete Westman, wrote me he wanted to go to America and he wanted me to go with him. I told him I would think it over. But I never intended to go. He got a permit to leave Sweden and he was after me to get a permit too. So I did get a permit but I still tried to talk him out of it.

We was hauling timber all winter and got through in the early part of April.

They had a dance and Pete come there and said he is going to America inside of two weeks. He expected me to go with him.

I felt like I could sink through the floor. I told him I had to ask at home.

I asked when they were all at the breakfast table. I asked my mother first and she said, "It's up to you."

Then I asked my brother and my sister and they said the same. My father was dead. The reason so many men left Sweden was wages were awfully low at that time. There was not too much work, either. So I decided I would go. But I was coming back before the summer was over.

FAREWELL PARTY

Friends and neighbors on each side of the small lake come over to our home for a dance and farewell party.

John Akerstrom 23 years old in the old country.

The one that come first, she was one that had told me everything that way. I danced with her first and she started crying and wanted to go out.

We went outside and she kept on crying. She couldn't stop.

I tried to tell her to forget me and find someone else.

She said she will never forget. Never! It will never be the same here again!.

She squeezed me every way she could and I held her hand and she couldn't say anything for crying. So finally she wanted to go home and I took her a long ways home.

I COULDN'T SLEEP

After that they had more dances and I saw more of these girls I had been with so much. The same things happen with them. I couldn't sleep nothin'.

When the time come I was ready to go. My brother took me to the railroad station with three others. And just as I left, I said to myself, "No! I can never go back home again. If I come back I'll be the one that's cryin' because I love too many."

TIE JOB IN WYOMING

I was 23 years old when I got my first job in a tie camp at Elk Mountain, Wyoming. It was a nice town not too far below timberline with 5 or 6 feet of snow. No dams there, we had to wait till the afternoon when the melting snow sent water down. The creek was only 8 feet wide so it was hard to turn the ties around. We had to stand in the cold water with a pickaroon and drag those ties to keep one going downstream after the other. The water was swift and your legs stayed numb. Sometimes the ties hit your leg and that hurt somethin' awful. If you climbed up the bank to stand in the snow it hurt worse than ever.

LETTERS FROM HOME

I wrote a letter home and I got so many letters because those girls got my address that I decided I couldn't write home any more. I was heartbroken.

The kind of work I followed took me up into the mountains and logging camps where there were only men. It would have been impossible to get married anyhow. It was 35 miles into that first camp and you had to carry your own bedding and clothes. It was the same everywhere I went. No women in camp.

So I never did go back to Sweden. And it wasn't because I got any girl in trouble. The girls at that time they didn't want to do anything before they were married because they learned that if you let the man have anything, you couldn't get the man you wanted. It was very seldom then that a girl got knocked up.

But if a boy got a girl in the family way, he'd leave and come to the United States. That was another reason the girls were scared of doing anything. They'd get the worst of it.

The man who came with me stayed two years and went back and got married, Pete Westman. It hurt me that I could never go back or get married.

THE GIRL WAS 17

At Fort Steele, Wyoming in 1911 a man wanted me to go with him to the sporting house down by the railroad station. 20 men boarded there and there was 10 or 12 girls. We was sittin' in the saloon room that night in chairs along the wall. About 8 o'clock a fellow come in with this young girl. I'm sure she was not much over 17 years old. Little bit of a thing and she was so drunk that if he hadn't held her up she would fall down. She was so little she couldn't hardly get her elbow up on the bar. I don't remember if she had a beer or whiskey but she stood there awhile and then walked out again.

In the morning we went in there again and bought a drink.

THE LANDLADY GAVE HER HELL

The landlady was there, a big woman, and this girl had a room alongside the dining room and the old lady pounded on the door and yelled, "Get up! Get up!"

Finally she came out, sick as any person could be. White as a ghost. And she sat on a chair in front of us with the old lady bawling her out because she got drunk and didn't make any money. But she never said nothin'. She just sit there.

I told my partner, "Let's get out of here."

We went to the railroad station, sitting there on the platform.

And here the girl come and walked by on the street and into a drug store. She never looked at us as she went past and the same coming back. She went into her room and locked the door and drank poison. After awhile they began to wonder what she was doing in there and when she wouldn't answer they knocked down the door and she was dead.

LEARNED CHUTE BUILDING
I worked for the Canadian Pacific Railroad making ties at Bull River, British Columbia. In this camp was a foreman who knew chute building and he showed us how to do it. We built the chutes of long saplings, cutting them up to 4 inch tops. The jackpines were skidded to the chutes, hewed and cut to length and shot down to the river. Lots of places were awfully steep and the ties really travelled.

BUGS
When I worked at Bull River it didn't do much good to wash your clothes and your blankets.

The bugs would come right back. We had a 5 gallon can to boil our clothes and the bugs would float up on the water. The bunks were double, 2 men sleeping together and double decked. You could sit and watch the bugs crawl up on the bunks.

Near Saratoga, Wyoming, in 1916, I worked building a bridge and on Saturday night we'd go up to Encampment. At Encampment they had a sporting house with 6 or 7 young girls. That was about the only place the young fellows could go.

LAPFULL OF GIRLS
The girls would sit down on your lap and tell you they love you.

I knowed different because I felt awful bad about that girl that killed herself. So when the girl sat on my lap, I said, "You can't tell me that. You say that to everybody. That's your business. Why are you here?"

That did it. She took me to her room and told how she was betrayed when she was young and her friends turned against her and the man that done it, left her. How she tried to get as far away as she could from people she knew. She tried to work. They didn't pay her nothin'. The men would give her whiskey or drinks but she couldn't get anything to eat. So pretty soon she had no choice but to get into a place like this.

It got so every time I come there, there was another one wanted to tell me. Even the landlady. She was maybe 55 and the worse for wear and she told me all about it and we were both cryin'.

After that they didn't want to take my money and if they took it they would wait and stick it in the pocket of my coat when nobody seen.

LOW PAY. SMOKE AND BUGS

It was like depression in 1912. I went on a railroad construction job out beyond Davenport, Washington. The bunkhouse was an old box car with layers of double bunks so close together that you had to bend low to slide in.

No light inside. A man rolled into the lower bunk clear over and I was supposed to roll in on my side after him.

I said to him, "What do we get here?"

He said, "$2 a day and they charge 75 cents board."

All night long somebody was getting up to go out and take a leak in the grass and the man in front had to get up and let the man in back out.

The cookstove was a hole in the ground next to the boxcar with some 6 inch pipe stuck in it and a piece of iron across. The smoke came into the bunkhouse till everybody coughed.

The bugs kept you awake anyhow, so we built a big bonfire outside and stood around that till we got tired out.

I said to my partner, "If I have to work under these conditions, I'm going to quit."

So we pulled out and went around the country some more till we found a post making job up by Sandpoint, Idaho.

EMERALD AND 2 NICE GIRLS

I built log chute at Emerald Creek with Louie Peterson in 1920. A couple of nice girls came up there to work as flunkies in the camp. There was an old girl there working that was raised on a farm around Clarkia. She got jealous of these girls because the men paid them a lot of attention. She began to whisper at the table and tell fellows them two girls was laying up with some of the men and she said it loud enough that people next to them could hear.

Finally the girls couldn't take it any longer and they quit. The engineer named Randall and the conductor Hewett went into the office and drawed some money and gave it to the girls. The girls rode in the railroad engine with the men when they went out to St. Maries. The next week the men went into St. Maries and married the girls.

SLEEP SINGING

At Emerald Creek I knew one fellow, a Norwegian who used to sing in his sleep in Norwegian. We used to tell him about it daytimes. And there was a Swede that would talk in his sleep and say, "Did they tell you that? Did they tell you that?"

When it was early spring and sunny this big, husky Norwegian got word that he could come back home at Davenport and start farming work. I quit at the same time and we went into Spokane.

AIRPLANE RIDE

We wanted to celebrate. There was an airplane at Felt's field taking up passengers and we took a taxi out there.

The plane was a two passenger job with open cockpit. I sat beside the pilot and my Norwegian friend sat behind. It was a clear day. We circled over the city and saw Natatorium Park and the river and all the buildings

Then the pilot climbed to 4,000 feet and all of a sudden turned its nose down toward the field. We went faster and faster and it was fun. I saw the ground pretty soon only 500 feet away and I knew this was it. Only seconds and we'd hit.

SAW PICTURES LIKE MOVIE

I was just as calm as I am right now. Not scared at all. But in a second or two I saw pictures like in a movie, plain as could be, every detail, one after the other. Things I had seen back in Sweden when I was little. The meadow, the house where I was born, the cattle grazing, my father.

The engine roared and the plane tipped up level and we landed.

I climbed out onto the ground. It was a weedy field. I was still thinking about the pictures I had seen so real. I turned around and my Norwegian friend was getting out and his face was white as snow. He took one step in the weeds and fainted.

After we fanned my friend conscious the pilot told us we were his first passengers. He had just learned to fly by himself.

Two years later I met this same Norwegian in the Steinhaus in Spokane. He had just come in from Marble Creek after a winter's work with $2400. He was all excited and happy. He had made up his mind to go up in another airplane and have him do all the stunts he could do.

Afterward, he said, "I liked it. But I wouldn't advise anybody to do that unless he is prepared for it."

CHUTE BUILDING PAID GOOD

I began to do a lot of chute building and made good money. In 1922 I got acquainted with top chute builders like Pete Peterson and Alex Smith, at Falls Creek, a branch of Big Creek of the Coeur d'Alene

River now called Shoshone Creek. Pete was a Dane. He has been dead a long time.

I saw a chute on Carpenter Creek out of Santa which the original Chute Smith built. It was old at the time. He was one of the earliest chute builders.

LOG DRIVE ON MARBLE
I worked on one log drive on Marble Creek in 1923 for Dunc Mc-Donald at the Camp 7 dam and built chute above there for him. That was the next year after that big fire and there was an awful lot of camps in there to save the timber. Lavigne had a camp across from McDonald's upper camp. He had a fast running chute and it killed 4 or 5 men. One man was at a phone 200 feet up the hill from the chute and a log jumped and came end over end and killed him. The government shut Lavigne down on account of it.

INVESTED IN OIL
I got contact with an outfit out of Denver that had leases on Texas oil ground. I dreamed of getting rich. I invested all my excess income in it. If I made it big I was going to marry a good woman and live the life of travelling. But I never planned to go back to Sweden. It made me hurt to think of it.

BOND CREEK FOR O'NEIL
In 1928 and '29, O'Neil built a little mill up Bond Creek at Camp 1, two miles from the river, to cut lumber for a flume. I built chutes to bring logs to the mill and after the mill finished cutting flume lumber I extended the chutes to the flume pond.

Some chute men like to see logs come down off the hill like a streak and hit the water so it goes 50 feet in the air. The trouble is that the logs come in so fast they gouge chunks out of the others already there and big logs can hit hard enough to break smaller logs in two in the middle. It wastes a lot of good white pine. This was big, clean stuff.

CONTROLLING A LIVE CHUTE
When the chute was dry they didn't go so fast but when it got wet from rain or snow they went like a bat. I bored holes in the bottom of the chute and then chiselled them out square so they fit the goose neck spikes. Then when I didn't need the spikes to slow down the logs, the spikes could be taken out with your fingers.

Another thing, some chute men let the 2 inch wide heads of the goose necks stick up so far they peeled deep strips of wood out of the logs. I drove them into the chute so they just peeled out a little more than the bark. I set them at an angle too, so it would throw the slivers out of the chute.

At the pond I put in a fender that caught the head end of the log and shoved it over so the logs came in alongside one another and rolled easy into the water.

They took out 30,000 cedar poles there, too. Poles up to 75 feet. That required a fairly straight chute. The only way they could get them out was to truck them over to that first chute I built.

The next year they went up another one half-mile and set up Camp 2 and a dam. At Camp 2 the flume branched. I built two chutes on the right hand fork. The upper one that came in above Camp 3 went way back up onto a flat and was trail chute till it came to the edge of the hill and then it was steep and fast.

CAMP 2 AND CEDAR POLES

At Camp 2, Anderson, the superintendent for O'Neil, wanted to bring in a lot more cedar poles, so I made the chute so it would send them into the pond underwater, then they'd float up to the surface. That still broke up some of 'em so I ran the chute alongside the pond on a turn, just above water level so they almost came to a stop and rolled into the water.

O'Neil went broke several times but I don't think any working man lost a cent. He was an awful nice fellow and common. But I don't think he had ever done any woods work himself. He had some good men there workin' for him though, like Earling and Oscar Moe and Lee Carpenter.

ALLOWING FOR HUMPS

I learned a lot from earlier chute builders by asking them questions and looking at old chutes. I knew one chute builder that would build a nicely graded chute into a hump or hollow without ever allowing ahead for it. He couldn't seem to get the feel. It's simple. I used 26 foot sticks of tamrack for chute timbers and laid the next two cross ties ahead of the three already laid down we were spiking the chute timber to. They can be easily lined up with the eye only and that way you can see ahead and allow for the humps and hollows.

OIL DIDN'T PAN OUT

By 1934 I found out the outfit in Denver that claimed to own oil leases didn't own anything but sucker lists and kept changing the names of their ownings just to keep the money coming in. So I didn't get rich after all.

Interviewed 4-3-73 Riverside Hotel, Spokane, Washington.

I'd rather drive logs than eat

Wash Applegate

Wash Applegate at 81

I rode a freight train in from Cincinnati, Ohio in June, 1913, when I was 15. I stayed with Wolfes a year and a half. He was my uncle.

I was fair sized for my age. I first worked for the Forest Service planting redwood up on Bohl's Spur. Most of them winter killed.

SLATE CREEK AND BEAR

One of the first times I ever worked in the woods was for Wallace Lavigne up on Slate Creek in about 1915. They had a flume on the West Fork.

There were a lot of bear up Slate. Another lad and I went huckleberrying up on the West Fork and when we came down there were 2 big bear standing up in the trail.

We walked 'way up the sidehill around 'em, I'm telling you.

One fellow went out of the bunkhouse in the dark to take a leak and an old bear slapped him flat. A fellow named George Burroughs, later a blacksmith in St. Maries, rigged up a live trap and caught some bear.

Then one evening we set a quarter inch cable decking line so it slid over a cub's head when he went into a live trap to get some bait. We had a great time playing with him.

WORKED FOR DAVE DOLLAR ON MARBLE

I think the first drive came out of Marble for Stack & Gibbs. Dave Dollar did the logging, in about 1915.

I saw Oscar Blake at the mouth of Homestead Creek in '16. He was workin' for Dollar. Dollar's camp was above the mouth of Homestead a half mile or so and up on the hill.

DONKEYS MOVED INTO MARBLE

I helped move eight donkeys in on Marble from Clarkia about February, 1918. You set your cable for one and as he pulled ahead he stretched the cable for the next donkey. We had to take them over in the winter time so we could get water to keep up steam. We had to shovel snow in them water tanks.

DRIVING LOGS IS FUN

I'd rather drive logs than eat. I would! You've got to learn to make the current do the work, like maybe hang onto one end of the log with your peavy and let the current catch the other end and roll it over a rock.

Our main river camp had some good sized buildings. It was a half mile below the mouth of Duplex Creek. We drove from there to the mouth of Marble.

DELYEA AND MARQUETTE DROWNED

I seen two men drown at Camp 7 dam. One was the father of Bill Delyea that became World Champion at log rolling and the other was Ben Marquette.

One of 8 donkeys moving into Marble Creek 1918

There was a big wing of logs built up on one side of the river below the dam. The crew had been working through one flood and flattened it all out. There are always some who show a little more bravery while the rest hang back. When the gates opened this old man Delyea was plumb out in the middle of the Marble and Marquette was with him.

The splash carried Delyea away.

Marquette made it close enough to shore to grab for a bush but he slipped and went down between the logs.

When they saw what happened they lowered the gates and cut off the water but it was too late. They found Delyea's body in the big hole just below Boulder Creek but Marquette was never found.

Another man drowned down by what we call Homestead Flats between Homestead Creek and Hobo.

Looking downstream at Camp 7 Dam where Delyea and Marquette drowned. Dam is 5.3 miles from mouth of Marble.

Here are some of the others that didn't make it. Ed.

CAREY & HARPER LOGGING CONTRACTORS

Mr. Olson Deputy Sheriff:

On May 30th 4P.M. a man drowned on our drive.We are still looking for the body. James Flanigan.The only Information I can get is that He came from Ireland when boy with an aunt & has no known Relatives in this country. J.Flanigan was about 5 foot 10 inch tall weight about 175 lbs had dark brown hair and rather sandy complected and should say about 32 or 33 years of age. He was working in front on a jam on some loose logs and when the flood struck the logs he was on he lost his footing and was carried down the river. The current seemed to hold him to the centre of stream so it was impossible to reach him. (signed) W.D. Colburn

Clarkia, Idaho June 8, 1916
P.S. His beddin & clothing I will send down on pack train. Am sending you a check for balance due him here for labor.

Aug. 10, 1916 — L.M. Young 40, Relatives-unknown. Effects — $700 in Exchange Bank in Cda. Buried at St. Maries. Drowned in Marble Cr. while driving logs.

Dec. 4, 1916 — Albert Corwin 31, Struck and killed by log at Rutledge Camp in Marble Cr. Buried at St. Maries.

CEDAR POLES SMASHED TO HELL

We put some cedar poles out one time from just above Camp 3. We kept them back behind the rear of the drive. Poles are valuable and cedar is easily shattered. Right at the end when they came out of the Marble into the Joe river the poles hit the tail end of the log rear and smashed to hell.

Going back to camp I took the high trail around Marble Mt., went down the ridge and crossed the mouth of Homestead and up the river trail. I beat the rest of the crew back to the River camp by 2 hours.

THE BUMBLEBEE

The Bumblebee was a wood burning donkey on a barge that we used in 1919 after I come back from the army to work the drive from the mouth of Marble down to St. Joe. We'd skid the Bumblebee onto a railroad car, go up to Marble station and unload it and back into the river. At first they had a little American donkey on it but then they taken it out and put in the Dave Dollar donkey, old Betsy, that Oscar Blake first run up to Homestead in '16.

Where the water went down and left a bunch of big logs we'd skid 'em off the bars. Logs too big for teams to handle. It was big timber that came out of Bussel Creek, too big for the Bussel flume. They had a lot of trouble with that flume. Six miles of it without a feeder in it. A feeder was a trough coming in from the side to replenish water that got splashed overboard or leaked out. And it was too steep where it went down to empty in Camp 11 dam.

TAKING THE BOSS FOR A RIDE

At the time of the Bumblebee, Clarence Graue was purchasing agent for the Rutledge outfit. When the cook ordered supplies he ordered canned pineapple. Graue wouldn't send it. Maybe he thought it was too damn good for riverpigs.

We were just below the mouth of Marble one day and he came up and wanted to go out on the Bumblebee. It was a wading chance and he had on a suit and store shoes.

I said, "Get on my back. I'll take you out."

When we got out just above that deep hole I said, "Graue! If there's no pineapple you're going in this hole head first. I mean it!"

He said, "Did you order pineapple?"

I said, "You bet we ordered pineapple."

He said, "I'll get it up to you right away."

"You're sure?"

"Yes! I'm sure."

They had a wholesale house down at 10th Street in St. Maries. He sent us 3 or 4 cases up next morning. The boys got a great kick out of that.

BIG DECK

I saw 7 million feet of logs decked where Lavigne logged out all of Davies Creek around 1921 and 1922

LAZY DAYS

Billy Lyons and I had the drive from Mica Creek where the logs come out of the flume, down to Calder, one summer. At first it was for O'Neil & Irvine and then Herrick bought out timber, flume and all.

Old Mica Flume last used in the 1930s

We fixed up the wings all the way down as the water fell and we had shear booms at the eddies so the logs wouldn't go aground. John Neff lived up on the hill above the Johnny Frances place which is across from the mouth of Mica. He was a veteran driver so when we needed help we could get him.

Once it was all channeled we'd walk up from Calder to the Mica flume and start a few logs off. Then we'd stop at the flat at the mouth of Elk Creek where there's a big spring and there we'd eat our lunch and smoke and B.S. About 2 o'clock we'd hop a log and ride down the river to Calder. We got $7 a day. It was a nice life.

Just at the end, maybe about 1926, times were getting hard in the lumber industry and money was scarce but we got our pay, although once Ernie McLaughlin paid us.

Herrick's empire was getting in hard financial shape about then. Ernie McLaughlin was manager for Herrick's store over in milltown at St. Maries and through him Herrick often advanced supplies and sometimes money to logging outfits. Hundreds of Herrick's workers stayed loyal to him, carrying his uncashable paychecks around for months in hopes his luck would change. Ed.

Gazette-Record Oct. 18, 1928 — Fred Herrick, owner of 2 mills in St. Maries, one in Harrison, one in Coeur d'Alene and one in Alabama, meets with creditors and asks time to liquidate assets worth an estimated 9 million dollars to meet creditor claims of 2 million dollars.

Herrick places his entire assets except for home, car, etc. and small notes, in the hands of the Spokane Merchants Association to meet liabilities of 4 million dollars.

Jan. 3, 1929 — Involuntary bankruptcy proceedings are filed against Herrick with a listing of his properties.

Jan. 24, 1929 — The Exchange National Bank of Spokane which held $418,000 worth of Herrick paper, closes its doors. Also closing are the First Exchange National Bank of Coeur d'Alene, and banks at Northport, Farmington and Rockford.

MICA FLUME
Kroll put the first logs out of the Mica Flume in about '18. Kroll was the first to run the St. Maries mill. He didn't build it but he bought it after it was built. Kroll logged Mica for years. They had trouble with the logs bunching up on this flume so they put in another dam about a mile and a half above Engstrom Creek. The whole flume was 10 or 11 miles long.

They first started hauling logs from Engstrom Creek on a narrow gauge railroad and unloaded at the dam. That's where Camp 3 was. Later when Blackwells got to logging up on the Hump above Crystal Creek, the Mica people brought a wide gauge engine around on the Blackwell railroad, built a track down the hill and lowered it into Mica Creek.

YOU'RE JUST THE MAN
My partner and I went to Clarky in 1921 lookin' for work. Just got in town and Gaffney seen me and hollered, "Just the man I'm lookin' for.

Sourdough Smith has been a'wantin' to come out from the dam. He's been there all summer. He's stakey— money burning his pockets. I need somebody to send out to take charge of the dam."

"But Ed," I says. "There's two of us." My partner, Hip Lindsey had a bad leg, shot in the first world war.

Gaffney says, "I'll take the second one, too."

OVER THE HUMP TO DUPLEX DAM
We walked over the hump into the Marble and up to the Carey & Harper dam below the mouth of Duplex Cr.

There was a fella named Montana Red workin' with Sourdough. He had a still there and was makin' whisky in the cabin and workin' at the dam.

So I told Sourdough Smith I come up to take the dam.

He says, "I'm glad you come."

I said, "Gaffney didn't say anything about another man bein' here."

Montana Red says, "Well I ain't gonna go away."

I says, "I dont blame you, Red. If I had known two of you was here I wouldn't have come in. We don't want to take anybody's job. We can make more money gypoin'."

MESSAGE TO MONTANA RED
Anyhow we went up to Camp 15 on Delaney Creek and Tommy Stevens was running camp. He was finally made assistant superintendent under Gaffney.

Tommy says, "We been tryin' to get rid of Montana Red. I'll write him a note and you give him his checks."

I took 'em down to the dam and says, "Here you are, Montana. Tommy said they didn't want you."

MONTANA RED GAVE ME THE STILL
"Fine!" he says. "You took my job. I'll give you my still, too."

He had the damndest still you ever seen. Great big boiler, it was. He had a pan to put on top it.

My partner, Hip Lindsey says, "We sure hit it lucky, by Gum!"

Hip never got out of the cabin except when I went down to sluice, he'd go with me. I packed the chuck down and I packed horse feed, hay and oats down from Camp 15. The cook baked cookies, cakes and pies for us. Plenty of sugar, too. I did run off a coupla little batches of moonshine.

The season was late and they couldn't get enough head of water to sluice oftener than once every two days. Logs came down the flume

Duplex Dam with sluices open to flush logs down Marble. About 1919.

from Camp 15 into the flowage of the dam at the mouth of Freezeout and they'd sluice 'em out and when I seen the flood coming, I'd open our gate and sluice 'em on down.

THE HORSE WALKED A CIRCLE

It was a two gate dam with gates that lifted straight up. To lift the gate you had a windlass with a sweep fastened to it so the horse could walk around in a circle. You'd make the old horse go fast so you wouldn't waste the water. After you got it up, there was a trip that fastened it.

Puttin' logs through the dam didn't take five minutes, four or five logs going through the gate at once.

We taken the horse and singletree off the sweep. When you wanted the gate to drop you just tripped it and got out of the way. That old sweep would go round and round.

STOPPIN' LEAKS WITH GUNNYSACKS AND MANURE

Them long gates was made out of logs and wore out from logs gouging the sides. You had to throw in gunnysacks and manure to hold the water from leaking out between sluicings.

That was the easiest job I ever had in my life.

HANDLOGGING

In 1923 I had an Indian and a Frenchman with me logging into the Marble across from the mouth of Hobo. We'd go up the hill a half mile and fall a half dozen of the fire blackened white pine, and handlog them down to the creek, tree length. To handlog you use your peavies to roll, pry and hunch logs down a steep slope. Hardly a log less than 2 feet in diameter and they'd pop open when they'd hit the creek. Averaged 3 logs to the thousand board feet.

Next year I had 5 new partners on the same job. A trail came from Camp 3 up to Camp 5 on Hobo Creek with a fork to Camp 9 at the mouth of Hobo. This bunch of saddle horses came down that trail and we had fell a tree across it. The only man I knew in the bunch was Ed Gaffney, a Potlatch push. They had to wait for me to saw out the tree.

OLD WEYERHAEUSER

One of these fellows with Gaffney had on a brown suit and a little derby hat. He says, "You got another handle for that saw?"

I said, "I sure have."

"Just a minute," he says. "I'll help you cut that log."

Couple weeks later Gaffney come up and he laughed and says, "Do you know who that old guy was that helped you cut that log? That's old Weyerhaeuser hisself."

It was old Frederic or George — I don't know which.

Anyway the summer was hot and dry.

FIRE DANGER

I said, "We'd better move out of here. This woods could go up anytime."

This timber had burned in '23.

My partners said, "After it's been burned once, you couldn't burn this place with gasoline."

We finished skidding, got settled up and went out to St. Maries Saturday night and the whole damn country burned up Sunday. A hellish hot fire. The trees were dry and ready to go. Everything burned, camp 9 and all.

But the logs we'd skidded got flooded down the creek so they weren't lost and we'd already got paid.

HENRY ST. PETER AND SNOOSE

Henry St. Peter wasn't very tall. His pants were stagged off they hung down eight inches below his crotch. He was a tough son of a bitch and a good top loader. I knew him well. In town he'd stuff so much snoose in his face it would make him dizzy.

I met Henry in front of the bank in St. Maries and he started across the street toward the C & M Cafe. Next door to the C & M, between it and the Hardware, Mrs. Crandall had a jewelry shop and a little lawn in front.

Henry went down in the middle of the street on his face.

I ran out and grabbed him up and skidded him over to the lawn. I said, "What's the matter? You drunk?"

He said, "No! It's the snoose. I have these quite often."

I worked with a big fellow on the drive. He thought he was tough and one time he set out to rob Henry. Henry damn near killed him with his calked boots. Tore his face all to pieces.

SKIDDING ON DUPLEX CREEK
Along maybe 1924 I looked over a skidding strip at Camp 8 up Duplex Creek. The foreman, Sullivan had bossed all over the country for Rutledge. The chute ran past 10 feet higher than where this draw for our strip came out and everybody that skidded into that chute up above hadn't been able to figure a landing out. With horses it was impossible to skid uphill. We needed a spot not only level but at the same height as the chute in order to roll the logs into the chute.

AN INDIAN PARTNER
Sullivan said, "I got a man, awful good man, Indian and he'd like to make some money. He's been working here all summer by the day."

I said, "I'll be glad to have him."

Some of the trees were fire killed red fir and some was white pine. You could lay your finger right down in the cracks where it had dried and checked.

I said, "The fire killed stuff ain't worth skidding. It's all checked."

"It's no deduct for checks," he said. And the scaler was there and heard him.

I went down a little ways and a ledge came across the creek.

Me and the Indian took the team and skidded big rocks down to this ledge and dammed it so the water level came up to the chute and it was about 4 foot deep. Just below that ledge the chute broke off steep and logs went down to a roll dam.   A roll dam has no gates. It just holds water so the logs don't bust up when they hit in it. Every time there's a flood from upstream it rolls the logs over the top of it. The Duplex dam was above there.

Anyhow we had a place to skid and land our logs and hold them till the scaler came.

THE LOGS TAKEN OFF LIKE A SHOT
So we skidded a coupla days and we were putting 18 to 20 thousand (board feet) a day into that chute. The logs taken off like a shot. We was getting five and a half dollars a thousand — and that was 50 cents more than any of the others got because the boss thought this was a harder chance. That was $90 to $110 a day less rent and maybe $5 feed for the team. That was $45 to $52.50 apiece, compared to $4 regular day wages.

THE BOSS TRIES TO WELCH

Sullivan came out and "Say, Wash! I'm gonna have to cut you on account of the checks."

I said, "No you don't cut me on no checks. That's not our agreement."

The scaler spoke up, "No! You don't cut him. I heard you make that agreement and that's how I'm gonna scale (measure) it."

My partner's name was John Barnaby. When we finished the strip he says to me, "If you ever get another job, look me up. I made more money here working with you than I did all summer."

TOO OLD TO MAKE A FRESH START

At the bunkhouse in the evening I talked a lot with Spike Clifton, a guy I'd worked with at Camp 15. He worked the year around in the woods. He told me he had a wife and a daughter or two and a couple of sons.

He said, "I can't go to Coeur d'Alene today but what people will holler across the street to me to come in and pay my debts. All I do is work here and send my check to my wife. They don't pay the bills. They just spend it. I've stood it as long as I can."

I said, "Spike! Damn it! If you can't get along with 'em why don't you pick up and leave? That's what I'd do. To hell with 'em if they're doing that."

"No, Wash!" he says. "I'm too old a man. Too old to make a fresh start. I'd be better off dead."

I said, "What's the matter with you? You're too good a man."

He said, "I'm going to do it."

Spike Clifton went on a year or two. Then at the mouth of Duplex in that two gate dam where I had worked, he left his hat and gloves on the

Duplex Dam 1977, where in 1919 Spike Clifton drowned himself. X right center is the rock where he left his hat and gloves.

bank and his body lay in the bottom of the deep pool. I never said anything to anybody about him talking suicide.

CRANBERRY FLOOD

Everett & Kelso were contractors for Herrick. Their camp was about a mile up the road from Rutledge Camp 3 on Jack Stevenson's Claim. I think they used Stevenson's cabin as part of their camp. Ole O'Dean had a cabin up there, too.

They built a dam a coupla miles up Cranberrry.

They had skidded a lot of logs below the dam and the first time they turned loose the flood she washed logs and stumps and windfalls and brush past Camp 3 so close that everybody thought the camp was a goner.

Camp 4 Dam below the mouth of Cornwall Creek 1975

CORNWALL WAS STEEP

I think Camp 4 dam just below the mouth of Cornwall was the last dam built on Marble. The camp was above the dam on the north side. They had a splash dam about three quarters of a mile up Cornwall.

Ross and Doran had a highline donkey up Cornwall. We'd skid the logs with teams, maybe a quarter of a mile. The stumps had been cut off so then we could let them roll down into the side canyons and main canyon into big decks. They'd put a highline from the donkey over these decks and pull the logs where they could be flooded down.

It was too steep and too dangerous to skid with horses after the snow came. I remember bringing horses out of Cornwall, taking them to Clarkia and we brought them up over a ridge and when we went down the other side they'd slide a hundred feet on those big shoes before they could stop.

I drove some awfully good Company teams. A team — a good one — went for $500.

CALKED BOOTS AND THE BULLDOG

I saw Gus Saugstad pretty mad once. He used to meet the passenger train in the evening when it pulled into Marble Station and the lumberjacks got off. Gus had a great, big bulldog.

I got off the train with a shepherd bitch and that bulldog grabbed her by the front leg. He pinned her down and she was pawing and squealing and couldn't get loose.

I said, "Gus! Make your dog get off my bitch. He's hurtin' her."

He says, "I can't do anything with him."

I says, "You'd better!"

CALKING A DOG

He didn't make a move to stop his dog so I bent its head around so the gums was exposed. I brought my calked boots right down across his gums. You talk about a dog lettin' loose! Blood spurtin'. He let go right now.

Gus didn't say a word.

I seen guys fight a few times with calked boots but they didn't get far enough along that much damage was done. People separated them.

RUN OVER BY THE TRAIN

The Indian I had hand logged with at Hobo Creek went down to catch a ride on the freight where it stopped above Marble Station at Tank Creek to take on water. He laid down drunk on the track and the train ran over him. His name was Hardy.

HARRY BURNS — BOOTLEGGER

Up above Marble Station on the main river, Harry Burns had a still and bootlegged. He had a good thing going with Gibbs, the deputy sheriff. Gibbs had spotters working for him in Montana and they'd let him know. He'd stop the train and confiscate the booze.

Then Gibbs, the deputy, would turn one case in to the county and turn over the rest to Harry Burns to bootleg.

Upper end of Herrick upper tunnel 2.7 miles from mouth of Marble. A short distance above this point is the clump of dirt and trees where Herrick's railroad was brought to a halt.

HERRICK'S RAILROAD GRADE AND LOWER TUNNEL

Uncle Jim Peters was the other main bootlegger around there. When Herrick made his railroad grade he went from the bridge at the mouth of Marble and stayed alongside the water on the west side for a couple hundred yards, then cut across Marble to the east side and went up around a point past Uncle Jim's house. Then the railroad was to cross again to the east side and enter the lower tunnel. A cable bridge was anchored in the rock right beside the tunnel for use of packtrains.

Jim Peters, he was whiskers all over, hid his whiskey in the tunnel.

HERRICK'S UPPER RAILROAD TUNNEL

Proceeding through the tunnel, Herrick's grade went on up a couple of miles into the upper tunnel.

Herrick's upper tunnel is exactly 2.7 miles from the mouth of Marble by road. Ed.

Charley Kelso told me, "I know for a fact that those two tunnels only cost Herrick $22,000. The reason was that the man who took the contract to build the tunnels figured on getting the contract to build the whole railroad."

Just above the second tunnel Rutledge chopped him. Later Rutledge built a flume all the way down to here and Herrick chopped them off.

At a clump of rocks and trees a short distance up the present road above the upper tunnel is the point where Rutledge — Potlatch subsidiary — stopped Herrick and his logging railroad from going further up the Marble. The railroad would have been able to bring out millions of feet of the finest white pine butt logs and second cuts which had some center rot. Such logs would be shattered into matchwood by the turbulent Marble and had to be left in the woods. Even solid logs were cut an extra 6 inches longer to allow for the destructive pounding on the rocks which left them broom ended and largely debarked.

At this point also was destroyed Rutledge's dream of carrying logs down the main Marble by flume. The Rutledge attempt to build a flume out of Bussel Creek for its big donkey logs had been unsuccessful because of lack of water to feed a six mile length and also because the flume ended up too high on the mountainside to empty into the Camp 11 dam on the main Marble without changing the end of it into a chute. Rutledge then built Dam 18 on Bussel at the mouth of Bear Creek and splashed its logs into Camp 11 dam on the main Marble. From the Camp 11 dam it was their intention to flume the logs the rest of the way down the main Marble.

But Herrick gave notice by force and lawsuit that the flume could go no further than the same spot where Rutledge had stopped his railroad.

The upstart Herrick, had challenged the mighty Weyerhaeuser empire and given it a slight wound. He managed to buy various scattered homesteads in the Marble area and drove his own timber out in the floods along with the Rutledge timber, for a time shoving his own ahead of theirs so they had to drive his logs to bring down their own. Ed.

Wash Applegate continues: So Herrick's railroad grade and tunnels became the main trail 4 miles up Marble. Dick Talbot packed over this for years.

CABLE CROSSING
About a quarter mile above the end of Herrick's railroad grade the trail went across another cable bridge to the east side of the creek. The trail zigzagged up the draw and on the ridge to the right. You clumb a quarter or half mile and the trail forked.

RIVER TRAIL
The one to the right was the River Trail up Marble. Around rock points, mules walked on poles 7 or maybe 8 feet in the air, supported by rocks and braces. To get money to maintain the trails the county used to collect poll tax from the lumberjacks paychecks till one time Huntington Taylor — Rutledge Big Wheel — was up there and he seen the sign in the Camp 7 office and he asked the clerk, "Who put that sign up?"

The clerk said, "The county road man."

"Tear that down and tell that bird to keep outa here!"

DAM 5.3 MILES UP MARBLE
The River Trail dropped into Camp 7 just above the flowage of Camp 7 dam and continued on upriver. At Daviggeo Creek it started climbing way up around the hill and came down to Camp 3 across the St. Joe crossing the log bridge that Oscar Blake and the crew of the Ol' Betsy donkey built in the summer of 1916.

HIGH TRAIL PAST MARBLE MT.
The other fork continued up from the cable bridge above the tunnel to the High Trail. It swung around the west side of Marble Mountain. The Fire Association used to always have a lookout on Marble Mountain and there was a good trail running from the Association cabin, which is on a ridge running out below Marble Mt. down to Homestead Creek.

BRANCH TO CAMP 3 AND ST. JOE CROSSING
Another branch headed down to Camp 3 and the St. Joe Crossing above the mouth of Bussel Creek. These were the main pack trails coming from Marble Station .

CLARKIA-GRANDMOTHER MT.-FREEZEOUT TRAIL
The dam at the mouth of Freezeout on upper Marble was for Carey &

Harper. Their supplies came in from Clarkia to a Halfway House on the south side of Grandmother Mt. In later years Rutledge built a road up to the Halfway House and then packed down Freezeout Creek and up the steep flume to Camp 15 on Delaney and into Cucumber Mike Mahoney's Camp 22 on upper Delaney. Camp 10 was in there too with a flume coming down from toward Crater Lake.

CLARKIA TO BUSSEL CR. ROAD

The old road to Bussel Cr. didn't run through Davis Pass like now. It started at Rutledge Ranch out of Clarkia, went right up back of the barns and up a draw, over the hill and around and crossed the West Fork of Merry Cr. and went up the main Merry to a place called Trout Foot Hill and it swung right and started climbing until it reached the divide east of the Incline. It went around a ways and dropped straight down the hill to Camp 1.

CAMP 1 BUSSEL CREEK

I helped build Camp 1 at the head of Bussel Creek. The dam was below it where the two creeks came together. You can still find the footings of the dam. Camp 2 was on the other creek with a flume that came down to empty into the Camp 1 dam. In winter you didn't worry about the 7 or 8 feet of snow in the flume but the big chunks that hung alongside. Those great, big gobs settlin' down could break down the flume. Half a ton of snow or more in each. We'd take shovels and break them off.

FREIGHT WAGON ROAD CAMP 1 TO CAMP 3

From Camp 1 the road continued along the sidehill and to the ridge and Camp 20, then it pased Everett & Kelso's Camp at the Stevenson cabin and down to Camp 3. Rutledge freight wagoned supplies from Clarkia into Camp 3 to be packed to other camps up Marble like on Hobo, Cornwall, Homestead and Duplex.

HOMESTEAD TRAIL AND BECKY

After the trail crossed the mouth of Homestead it zigzagged up the sidehill on the north side a half mile. The packer had a little mule, Becky, packing two bales of hay up this steep trail in 1921 and after she got almost to the top of the steep slope she lost her footing and went over backwards. She rolled end over end clear to the bottom. The packer went down to see if she was dead and she was standing there, wasn't hurt at all but she'd lost the 2 bales of hay. The boys on the drive made a pet of Becky. They fed her cake and cookies out of their lunches.

THE OLD TRAIL

The old trail did not follow along the upper hillside like today but swung back to the creek, crossed on the Carey & Harper Dam below the mouth of Duplex then stayed on the south side going up till below the Carey & Harper Dam near Freezeout where it crossed again to the north side and went up to Camp 15 on Delaney.

LOG CHUTE ON EAGLE

I worked for Louie Larson and Frank Fremault in 1927 and got 30 cents a thousand for rolling logs into the chute. I done all the trailing down and rolling in.

After the log was rolled into the chute the jig team hooked tongs on it and kicked it ahead to make up the trails. It was so nearly level that we had to trail the logs a ways. We didn't cut any cedar logs. Most all the cedar on the Marble had ring rot.

Louie Larson used the same camp as Carey & Harper there in the split of the Eagle Road where a branch turns up to Huckleberry Mountain.

Eagle Creek Dam 11.2 miles from mouth of Marble. 1975

CHUTE BUILDING

That was one fine chute system there. It ran almost level to the breaks and then dived down a mile of steep, crooked canyon to Eagle Creek. It took a master chute builder to flatten out where you had to trail them and steepen the edges where the chute went steep and the logs began to run. He knew the tricks of how much to tip the curves. He'd have 5 or 6 good men with him, skidding in timber, spiking them down on the crossers.

Then the chute builder laid out the chalkline and snapped it. His double bit axemen scored down not quite to the mark. Then the hewer he'd come with the broadaxe. He didn't have to be the man that was head of it but lots of times he was. There was not too many knew how to use a broadaxe real good and an ordinary man would play out in just a little while.

Some used the broadaxe left handed and some chopped right so a man had to be able to work either downhill or uphill.

The crew that built the chute I skidded into at Camp 8 got $2.00 a running foot. They furnished the teams and it was a long ways to skid the timbers. Chute builders got different prices but a lot of it run about a dollar and a quarter a foot. Corduroy which often had to be built alongside so the horses could trail was about 60 cents a foot.

ROLLING LOGS OFF BOULEY'S GRAVE

When I worked for Larson & Fremault in 1927 on Eagle Creek I rolled the logs off Bouley's grave because I didn't want to skid over him. At that time the horse bones was still on the grave.

Interviewed Nov. 28, 1972

Dirty John Pounded The Counter!

Good Samaritan

Genevieve Avery

Genevieve Avery 1979

I was born Genevieve Maher, March 17, 1904 at Ledgerwood, North Dakota. When I was about 6 years old we moved to Billings, Montana where Dad was salesman for the Minneapolis Thrashing Machine Co. He then had a hardware store in Redmond, Oregon which burned. Then we lived in Medford and then in Spokane.

In 1917 Dad decided to try homesteading. He bought a relinquishment from some people at Clarkia. In those days a settler could legally relinquish all his homestead rights to someone else and the buyer could then carry on the homesteading and receive a patent.

A GO-DEVIL

We were city people and had never so much as lived on a farm. Our homestead was in the Gold Center area where there was no road. Dad pulled our stuff up there on a go-devil — a rough sled with log runners pulled over the ground by horses. Dad left my mother and we three kids at the Griffin homestead cabin which they generously allowed us to use — they were gone someplace — while he and my brother went on up Flewsie Creek to camp in a lean-to to build our log cabin.

PACKRATS

When darkness came the packrats started running around inside the Griffin cabin. Mother was so very frightened. We sat up all night listening to them patter around the eaves and push dishes and cans off the shelves.

Next morning, Mother said, "House finished or not finished, we'll go up with your father and stay in that lean-to or outdoors. We're not staying here any longer!"

While the cabin building was going on my father let us wander around on our horses so long as Josie Gunderson went with us. She knew the woods and was older.

LOST TEETH

I don't know how many days Josie taught me how to pack a horse. I practiced and practiced. This one morning I packed and unpacked the horse three times and I finally realized Josie was looking for something.

I said, "Josie! I'm not going to unpack again till you tell me what you've lost."

Josie said, "I've lost my false teeth."

So I took the packs off the horse, laid them out on the ground and we started going methodically through everything. When we unrolled the blankets, there were her teeth.

Land Rush days at Clarkia

CLARKIA — BUSY AND WILD

Clarkia was a rough place: saloons, O'Brien's place, drinks plus gay ladies, the Idaho Hotel — just across the bridge as you go into town on the opposite side of the St. Maries River from the depot. The first store and post office, built of logs was in that end of town.

It was my understanding that the post office was in at least two other places before it ended up in Clarkia — one of them was at the McPeak place at the mouth of Olson Creek — Van Brunt owned it in later years.

A man named Young who ran the log store in the early days told me when he came later to Clarkia on a visit, "If you think Clarkia was busy during the logging days you should have seen it during the rush for homesteads and timber claims. There would be as many as 500 horses out there in the street."

The Wilson that later owned the Pea and Seed Company in Moscow also ran the log store at one time. He had a homestead over on Cranberry Creek, a branch of Marble. He used to bring out all his friends to show them where he got his start.

Along in the 1930s Oral and I made a trip to Calgary and visited with the Anderson brothers who had homesteaded in the St. Joe country. They told Oral about some shootings that took place in the early days over Milwaukee right-of-way up the river.

In the other end of Clarkia beyond the corner where you turn right to Merry Creek was the Elk Hotel. Before we came Mrs. Ina Fertiz, Oral Avery's sister operated it. After we came the Schuberts ran it. There was a little butcher shop run by Hopkins and a drugstore operated by Agnes Gallagher, a little barber shop, Bill Leonard's saloon with meals and rooms and then Connolly & McGovern came in and built a general store.

TWO YEAR HIGH SCHOOL
I had finished grade school when we moved to Clarkia and there was no high school so I returned to Spokane for my first year of high school. Next year, 1918, a two year high school started in Clarkia and so I attended my second year there and finished my last two years at Holy Names Academy in Spokane.

My brother went to the grade school in the Gold Center area. The schoolhouse was close to the Sweitzer place at the mouth of Flewsie Creek and set just beyond the Sweitzer barn beside the St. Maries River.

STRAND KILLING
In the early 1920s this man Strand wanted to marry this fellow's daughter at Santa and the father would have none of it. So Strand shot the father and hid out in the woods. He came down to the Martin cabin at Gold Center for food and shelter and threatened them if they told. They finally got word to the posse and a member of the posse named Cox killed Strand.

STORE OWNER ORAL AVERY
When we moved to Clarkia in 1917 Oral Avery had the former Ross store down by the river just after you cross the bridge going into town. Oral Avery's dad, William came originally from England and homesteaded in Kimball, Minnesota where Oral was born in 1894. Then the father came to Idaho bringing Oral and his brother Glenn.

How Oral got his start: he was working in the store for Bill Ross. Ross lived in St. Maries. Ross took an absence and left Oral to take care of the store. Then one day he phoned Oral and said he wasn't coming back — that Oral could have the store. Whether their agreement over the phone was later put into writing I don't know.

LUMBERJACKS AND HOMESTEADERS

I worked at the river store summers for Oral during my high school years. Besides working himself Oral hired a man and two of us girls. With the logging in the upper St. Maries River and Marble Creek and the building of the Incline railroad, Clarkia was really booming. Hundreds of lumberjacks poured through. Homesteaders came in for groceries. Rutledge mechanics and office workers made their homes in town. There wasn't a U. S. Forest Service there then but out of the store we'd load up packtrains of mules for the Clearwater Protective Association and logging camps with two and three thousand dollar orders at a time. Oral told how he worked for the Clearwater Protective Association away back in 1910 and how he almost lost his whole crew fighting the great fire.

BRAWLS, GAMBLING, WOMEN

On the surface, the town seemed quiet but you heard about lots of brawls and fighting.

There was lots of drinking and women. George McDonald had a place right across the street from the store. He had two beautiful blondes working for him. One of them named Mary came running over and told us to get a doctor quick. She had cut her "husband's" throat with a butcher knife. Although it took the doctor hours to arrive the man lived.

There was usually a deputy sheriff around just in case — but Shoshone County had the reputation of overlooking bootlegging, gambling, prostitution and fights so long as no one was killed.

SELLING VANILLA EXTRACT

On their way to pick huckleberries and dig camas the Indians used to camp in the meadow. The store had vanilla extract in bottles of all sizes. I was doing a great business by the time Oral saw what I was doing and warned me that it was illegal to sell alcohol to the Indians.

He reminded me that anyhow we had an enterprising bootlegger in Clarkia that for a long time was hiding his whiskey behind the altar of the Catholic Church.

My dad found living at Clarkia a new kind of life, different from anything he had ever done. He took out cedar and attempted to make a living but it didn't work out. So he moved to a little farm at North Point, Oregon.

ORAL WAS FREE HANDED

About 1924 Oral bought the Connolly and McGovern store which is still operating in the same location after several owners.

I was early attracted to Oral. He was a very kind and generous individual, always willing to help someone in hard luck with a gift of groceries or candy for the kids.

After I finished high school I attended Northwest Business College in Spokane a short time. I tried working as receptionist in a doctor's office. Then I worked in Minneapolis for a year.

Oral and I had been corresponding. I came back and we were married in the Catholic Church in Potlatch, March 1, 1927.

Oral and I had 3 daughters Donna, Oralee and Janice Ann and a son, Glenn. We hired a woman to help with the children and housework and I worked in the store and post office with Oral. As soon as the children were high school age, they helped summers in the store, too.

Oral and Genevieve Avery 1947

DECENT LUMBERJACKS

I never knew an oldtime lumberjack saying a word out of the way to me no matter how drunk he was. They were certainly honest. You could fit him up with wool underwear and wool shirts and heavy pants and calked boots and he'd always pay when he came back to town again. The prostitutes paid their bills, too. It was a honor with them not to owe people.

DIRTY JOHN

I had one unpleasant confrontation, though.

Dirty John Sodahl was just an old man living up the river alone. In later years he thought everyone was working against him. He came to the post office window and accused me of tearing up his letters. So far as I know he had never had a letter.

He was a huge man. I was afraid. Oral happened to be gone so I put a pipe wrench under the counter to protect myself.

Next day Dirty John came in. He pounded on the counter top till everything jumped.

I put my hand under the counter, feeling for the pipe wrench.

He stood glaring at me. Then suddenly he said, "You pistol packing mama. You got a gun under there."

Then he turned around and went out.

OPEN LONG HOURS

One time Oral had quite a surprise. We kept the store open till 9 o'clock every night in summer. But no matter how late the store stayed open, often there were people who hadn't been able to get into town before we closed.

This particular night several people had been at our house wanting things from the store. Oral rolled out each time, unlocked the store and waited on them.

About 4 o'clock in the morning a man knocked and wanted to borrow a quarter.

Oral told him to run along.

He came back two more times wanting to borrow the quarter.

Oral finally got tired of listening to his babblings and pushed him off the porch and told him not to come back.

Then just before 6 o'clock there came another knock.

Oral wasn't in the mood to hear any more pleadings for a quarter. He leaped out and swung open the door ready for fight.

But it was only my inoffensive brother arrived for a visit.

MIDWIFING

Being the store owner's wife and easy to find I was always the first one called on in family emergencies like the birth of a baby or child sickness.

I realized in later years how inept my own mother must have felt when handling other people's problems and yet how homesteaders in our Gold Center neighborhood had always called on her for help.

There was a barefoot southern family named Justite, very poor and the woman was expecting a child and lost her mind. She wouldn't let any of the family come near her. Mother had to go to their house and sit up all night with those crazy eyes staring at her while they waited for the wagon to come and take her away.

DREADED WHOOPING COUGH

During the Depression Clarkia had an epidemic of whooping cough. At that time there weren't immunization shots or antibiotics and kids were sick for days. This sick three months old baby was one I had delivered. It was about the same age as one of my own and mine was in the hospital in Spokane. Her parents lived down in the old Anthony place but they had left the baby in someone's care in town, thinking it would be nearer aid.

It was also during the Christmas to New Year period of the flood of 1933 and Dr.Platt hadn't arrived because he got stuck in the mud somewhere between St. Maries and Clarkia.

I stopped in to see the baby.

Josie Benscotter said, "She's getting much better. She doesn't cough or anything."

And of course, that's when you worry. They stop coughing when their lungs get too full to cough. I hurried into the bedroom.

I said, "Oh Josie! This baby is dying!"

Josie fainted and I was alone with it.

I picked it up and spooned a little whiskey into its mouth to see if I could make it choke and cough up the phlegm. But it couldn't.

This baby I'd delivered only a few months before died right there in my arms.

EVERYONE WAS KIND
Then the mother and father came and were going to take it out and bury it under a tree in the front yard.

I said, "You can't do that! There are certain formalities. You must get a death certificate."

I knew nothing about preparing the baby for burial. A woman told me to rub the skin with camphor to keep the little body from discoloring.

It is strange. There are times in a small town when everyone is kind. People may have strong differences about some trifling matter and then the next day something happens and everyone helps.

It was depression time. The parents had no money. But men out of work had plenty of time and men of the town built a coffin. Then the women got together and lined it and padded it.

There was a short service. And people brought food to the family.

Then there was Mrs. Smith. Her husband was head mechanic for Potlatch. She went to peoples' houses all around the community and helped anyone who was ill. A really good Samaritan!

BOY WITH LUNG TROUBLE
In another family where the parents had no money a little boy had lung trouble. Oral took it upon himself to send the boy to doctors in Spokane. One was a child specialist and one was a nerve specialist. They refused to take pay for the treatment. Doctors Codd and E. J. Barnett. The boy recovered.

STORE CREDIT AND DEPRESSION
In those days it was customary for stores in communities like Clarkia to extend credit. And of course there was always some loss but that was the way business was carried on.

Then the Depression came and people had no jobs. Many people had been good customers and you hate to say, "No." Others who were hard-up and hungry, Oral took boxes of groceries to.

Well, (laughing) I'm not so sure that I continued feeling charitable toward some. The Depression was changing peoples' attitudes toward paying their bills. And as jobs became more available again a more floating lumberjack population often with cars and trucks moved out overnight and left their bills behind.

In later years we learned to watch credit very carefully.

Then Oral died April 27, 1957.

When I sold the store in 1960 I still had quite a few old outstanding accounts. Some people who did quite well for themselves came around afterwards and said, "Well! I'll pay you half." when they could well have afforded to pay it all.

But after so many years the bills become outlawed anyway and I had no choice but to accept whatever they offered.

RETIREMENT AND TRAVEL
In the nineteen years since I came to Spokane I've kept busy. With another woman I joined a bus tour through the southern states. We were gone five weeks. I had always hesitated about a bus trip because I thought it would be tiring — they'd need to go so many miles a day. But it was a bus with an elastic schedule that stopped at many interesting places. A delightful trip.

Then I spent a couple of months in Mexico.

VOLUNTEER RED CROSS
During this time I did volunteer work, health care for the Red Cross in Spokane along with my niece. We decided to travel to Asia and signed up for an independent tour — at our own expense, of course.

The Spokane Red Cross people said they had never had any of their volunteer people visit Asia. They knew people there and made arrangements for us to visit a hospital in the Phillipines. We didn't want to be rushed so we made hotel reservations giving us plenty of time — we thought — in the Phillipines, Thailand, Malaysia, Hong Kong, Taiwan and Japan.

PHILLIPINE HOSPITAL
We hardly got into the hotel in Manila — all tired out from the long flight from day into day and the jet lag — we hadn't had time to get our clothes changed and this nice Filipino lady had a meeting set up for us with all the doctors and a wonderful lunch and a tour of the Red Cross units.

V.I.P. TREATMENT IN TOKYO

Then no matter where we went from there we met people who referred us to somebody else.They made arrangements for us to visit a sister hospital in Japan. In Tokyo they picked us up and took us to the hospital 60 miles out.

I can't believe the day we spent out there. This Col. Wells was in charge. He told us how these hospitals are organized and how long they kept the boys — if they were going to be sent home or sent back to the front.

We visited all the wards. Our boys from Vietnam were flown into these hospitals just wrapped in a sheet, you know, and needed many personal things furnished by the Red Cross. Some pitiful cases.

They had a wonderful luncheon for us all.

I said, "But we're nobodies. We're not used to the Very Important Person treatment."

He said, "Well! You really are V.I.P.s. Because everyone else we get here is an inspection outfit!"

SINGAPORE AND A CHAUFFEUR

From then on things seemed to fall into our laps. I knew people in Singapore that had a sawmill.

This businessman said, "My chauffeur and limousine are at your disposal. They'll take you up to the Malaysian peninsula."

Then we flew over the other area of Malaysia. Everywhere we went, the Asiatic people were friendly and planned things for us. Somebody here knew somebody there who would do something for us. What delightful people!

Interviewed at Spokane, 1977

Four bears up a tree

Annetta Bellows

Annetta Bellows at 83

Homesteading

I was born Annetta Kellom at Mondovi, Wisconsin, April 2, 1896. In 1897 my father, Frank Kellom, moved my mother, whose maiden name was Sarah Hill and myself to Spokane and then to Springston, Idaho where Dad worked on the railroad.

In 1898 my sister Marie was born.

Dad bought two high chairs so Marie and I could sit and look out the window at the passing trains. Then a year later, Marie died at 13 months. My parents thought I was going to die and had my picture taken.

They left me at the Springston station house with an old man and went off to bury her in the Harrison cemetery. I looked out the window at the passing trains and cried.

A peculiar thing. I had cousins back East and one in Post Falls that caught meningitis at the same time. One of my cousins died. One became completely deaf. I was the only one to come out of it whole.

The high chairs came in handy later when the twins were born.

Annetta at age 3

That same year, 1899, we moved to Harrison where Dad worked in a sawmill and my twin brothers, George and Edgar Kellom were born. Dr. Busby delivered them.

ST. JOE AND NO SCHOOL
In 1901 we moved to the Dighton Ranch — now part of the Scott Ranch at St. Joe. Another year and I was school age but there was no school in St. Joe. In 1905 Dad moved us to Coeur d'Alene so I could go to school. For 2 years he worked outside of town in the woods and I completed the 1st and 2nd grades.

MOTHER DIED
Then in 1907 my mother died of a heart attack. She was only 32 but she had suffered with heart trouble ever since having rheumatic fever when she was a girl.

My brothers and I went to stay with our grandmother in Spokane. I was 11 years old and so big I stuck out like a lummox over the other kids in the 3rd grade. My teacher saw that I was embarrassed and couldn't study. She told me if I'd take the arithmetic book home at night and memorize the multiplication tables for times 6 and times 7 she'd put me in the 4th grade. Then I started doing well in school.

My grandmother was old. Running a rooming house and keeping three grandkids was too much for her. Before I could finish the 4th grade a Mrs. Peter Harrison, who had previously roomed at Grandmother's while taking nurses training in Spokane, agreed to take me to live with her at Boyd, Washington. They had 3 small children and needed someone to look after them. That stopped my schooling.

BY THE GREAT HORN SPOON!
Finally in 1909 when I was 13 Dad was able to buy a home for us in Bovill where he had found a job as crosscut saw filer for the camps. Dad was a kind and patient man and he never had to paddle us to enforce obedience. I'd dawdle sometimes because I hated doing dishes.

But when he said, "By the Great Horn Spoon!" I knew that meant business. I moved!

I missed another year of school when Dad and another man he had hired took a winter job cutting wood and needed a cook — me. But later, I managed to attend the brick schoolhouse in Bovill under a couple of good teachers, Mr. and Mrs. Taylor. He later became Latah County Assessor. In 1912 at age 16 I graduated there from the 8th grade.

MARRIED AT 16
Then that same year I married Harris Bellows. He was 24 and worked at logging. He had been born at Brenton, Michigan in 1888.

About a year and a half later, when I was 18, we went back to Michigan where Harris was to farm his father's place.

I wanted to travel on the daylight Columbian so I could see the mountains. We left St. Maries at 10:30 on a January morning in 1914. We went up over the Bitterroots and down into a howling blizzard in Montana. I had brought a basket of fried chicken and sandwiches and preserves and cake. We sat in the warm pullman car and looked out at the flying snow and ate. There was a little coal stove in the end of the car where we heated water for coffee.

BUMPY TRAIN

When darkness came we shared the same berth. Going down the curves of the Rockies I woke up Harris and said, "Why is it so bumpy? Are there rocks on the track?"

He laughed and said, "That jerk is when they throw on the brakes."

Our basket of food lasted till we reached Chicago about 3 days later. We stayed a day there to rest up and took another train to Grand Rapids. This was my first time to eat in a dining car. They featured mackinaw trout from Lake Michigan and the menu was much like in an ordinary restaurant.

The whole trip took us the better part of a week.

SCARLET FEVER AND ASTHMA

Thelma and Ned were born in Michigan. Thelma in 1918 and Ned in 1923. When I was young I had most of the childhood diseases except one. After Thelma was born I had scarlet fever. She had it, too, and couldn't walk for awhile.

We were all quarantined, including my husband, with a SCARLET FEVER placard tacked to the front door. His dad brought groceries and set them down in the yard so we could get them.

We had chickens on that farm and sold eggs and by Golly! Harris couldn't stand it in the chicken coop. Chickens were always scratching and stirring up a dust. As a child Harris had asthma. Now the hen coop choked him up so bad he couldn't breathe. That last year in Michigan Harris couldn't lie down at all. He slept sitting up in a chair.

The doctor told him, "If you were free of asthma out West, get back there as quick as you can."

A CLASSY MODEL T

We went to a sale. A man had died. Harris bid two or three hundred dollars on a good, used 1923 Ford and got it. Then he paid to have a hard top built on it so we had a sedan. It carried a spare tire on the back and had running boards so you could step into it. It had balloon tires which were a new thing then — much like the tires today. The older tires were narrow and inflated hard. They cut into the earth and were a lot harder riding. They also had lots of flats.

WEST TO BOVILL

So in 1925 we drove the Ford all the way west and had only one flat tire in all that distance.

Back in Bovill Harris' asthma wore off except one time. He was working in the woods and came home on a week end.

He said to me, "You know! I felt fine in camp but this week end at home I've been smelling that geranium. I wonder if that could be what's chokin' me up?"

I said, "We won't have that geranium when you come home next time."

And sure enough, that's what had been doing it.

But I've never had a sense of smell. As a child I might get a whiff from an especially strong flower. I had my tonsils and adenoids out when I was a child. I've never asked a doctor but that might be what caused it.

I had lost a first baby by miscarriage in 1914 before we went to Michigan. Now I lost another. Back in those days people had more trouble losing babies than now.

Old Montgomery house. Left is the barn where the cattle drowned in the '33 flood. Harris Bellows tore down the house and used the doors, windows and lumber in the new log house 1934.

MONTGOMERY MURDER

Harris was a natural born farmer and I liked it, too. In fact when he left Michigan people told us they hated to lose a good farmer like him from the community. Then too, working in the woods kept him away except week-ends and in those days they worked 6 days.

We were staying with my father in Bovill and looking for a place of our own to farm.

Dad read in the paper about the murder of Montgomery near Calder.

Dad said he had worked with Mr. Montgomery and liked him and suggested we might buy his place from the heirs.

St. Maries-Gazette-Record 12-31-25 reported the disappearance of James Montgomery, 54, and finding of Morris Hanson at the ranch. Hanson had in his possession an overcoat, watch chain and fob known to belong to Montgomery. Hanson claimed he bought these from Montgomery and that Montgomery left to make a visit to Ezel, Kentucky, leaving him, Hanson, in charge of the ranch near Herrick.

St. Maries-Gazette-Record 1-7-26 reported the finding of Montgomery's body in the base of a cedar stump on the farm concealed by trash and found to have been killed by a .38 revolver bullet in the head.

St. Maries-Gazette-Record 1-14-26 reported a charge of murder entered against Lee Foyte, alias Morris Hanson.

St. Maries-Gazette-Record 3-4-26 — The Jury found Lee Foyte guilty of murder.

HAROLD THERIAULT, 82, of Avery knew Montgomery.

Bart Chamberlain was the original homesteader and Montgomery bought from him and logged the place. Montgomery was a man about 5 feet 10 inches from Kentucky. I think his wife had died before he came here. I knew his daughter, Nora when she attended the Academy in Tekoa.

Montgomery was living alone and made the mistake of befriending a drifter.

In the early days Montgomery was logging partner to Billy Stone. They both owned good logging teams. Stone was a little shorter than Montgomery and a little heavier and bowlegged. He was always clean shaven. Billy Stone had homesteaded a good farm that Greene later bought up on the hill above Pyle's Ranch below the mouth of Big Creek. River Driver Johnny Frances, when he was an old man, lived there.

JOHN DENNIS says: Jaffe was the fellow that killed Montgomery. He come off a fence gang for the railroad. Fall brought the close down of the season so he went to work for Montgomery for the winter.

When Montgomery didn't show up to get his mail at the Calder store, they asked Jaffe and Jaffe said, "He's gone back east and I'm looking after the place while he's gone."

Then Jaffe came over town wearing Montgomery's best suit and a 10 or 20 dollar goldpiece watch charm they knew was Montgomery's.

So the deputies came and took Jaffe up to the Montgomery place and searched all over blue hell for Montgomery and finally one of the deputies took a look into that cedar stump and found him.

MRS. BELLOWS continues: After we offered our bid on the Montgomery place, the only heir, his daughter Nora, came up from some place in the south to look it over. She said the place wasn't worth fussing about and accepted our offer. I wonder what she'd think today if she could see that green meadow and mile of frontage on the river and land selling for sky high prices.

THE GOAT TRAIL

On July 15, 1927 when we came up to take possession of the Montgomery place we had to drive our overloaded Model T Ford over the old Milwaukee Tote Road from Little Falls through Calder. We always called it the Goat Trail. It had been built about 1907 for teams and wagons to haul supplies to the construction crews building the railroad.

Tote road crossing the mountainside above the highway bridge east of Falls Creek.

It was a scary trip for us and our kids. Dad had come along to help and live with us.

The Goat Trail had been blasted along the almost straight up and down mountainside and dipped from one rock point to another. It was so narrow in spots they had wedged logs into rocks on the outer edge so the wheels would have something to run on.

Over the years — By Golly! — I've wondered when some of those logs would cave away and let some car dive down 200 feet on the Milwaukee railroad track but they never did.

END OF THE ROAD

After we passed through Calder and its little mill and store, another 6 miles brought us to the mouth of Big Creek. We forded across and that was as far as the road went.

We carried our supplies to the railroad crossing at the little station Herrick, a short distance and then a half mile up the track. Montgomery had bought a house in St. Joe and moved it upriver — I can't guess how he did it — and set it up near the edge of the river bank on the other side of the river.

A rowboat came with the place. We had paid a good lump sum down and borrowed the rest from the bank at 7 per cent interest. We paddled across the river and we were home.

THE MOONSHINERS

The moonshiners used our rowboat, too. It seemed like a lot of people were bootlegging: Harry Burns and Jim Peters at Marble Creek, the

Benton Boys up Big Creek. A good profit in it and not much work to it, I guess.

We had a bachelor neighbor, Paul Roland, who made moonshine just for his own use, I think. A cousin of Harris worked as a mechanic on airplanes for the Forest Service at Felts Field in Spokane. This mechanic told the pilot of the airplane that flew over the St. Joe National Forest that he'd like him to circle our farm and take a picture. The mechanic wanted to enlarge it and give it to us as a Christmas present.

So (laughing) when this pilot circled low over our neighborhood several swings, our neighbor Paul Roland thought it was government agents spying on his still. He dumped his barrel of mash and destroyed everything!

HAY CROP FOR DYNAMITE

Our flat along the river was full of stumps and limbs and tops. My dad and Harris set to work clearing it. Some of the big cedars had been cut off so high that Harris could use the high parts to make fenceposts. One cedar was hollow and as high as a house ceiling inside and large enough for a room. Harris said he'd like to have made a playhouse out of it.

They dynamited the stumps to split them and loosen the roots, then used the team and block and tackle to pull them out piece by piece. Harris borrowed a stump puller from Black Joe Finef that was stronger than a block and tackle. It was a geared thing with a cable that hooked to the stump and horse power pulled the stump out. We knew the clearing would take years. To get money to live and buy dynamite we planted a hay crop. My dad was quite adept at using a hand scythe to cut the hay around the stumps. We never hired any help. When the hay was cured they hauled it by wagon to a stationary baler.

I WIRED THE BALER

My father pitched hay off the wagon. Harris fed hay into the baler. Then I'd put in the board that separated the bales and thread wire around. We had this one horse that would go 'round and 'round at the end of a pole maybe 20 feet long, tightening down the baler and compressing the hay into bales. Most of our bales weighed from 85 to 100 pounds. One time we had some damp, damp hay and the bale weighed 155.

Harris said, "That's too heavy. We don't want to handle bales that heavy!"

When we finished a load the men weighed the bales and rolled them out of the way. Those days each bale had a little piece of wood shoved under one of the wires with the weight pencilled on it.

Then they'd go back after another load of hay while I'd go into the house and cook or wash or make preserves. The children were very good about washing dishes and other chores in the house while I was working out on the baler. But (laughing) I had to buy a new set of dishes after they helped about so long.

TIMOTHY FOR HORSE FEED

Our hay was mostly timothy. They tried alfalfa but the meadow was too wet and alfalfa would drown out or freeze out. Often in the spring the water would overflow the lower spots of our meadow and deposit a layer of silt and make timothy grow even better. Of course, the same high water sometimes brought driftwood like stumps and logs which Harris had to skid off before the hay grew too high so we wouldn't run into them with the mower.

Harris asked the Potlatch buyer at Bovill if they wanted to buy some horse hay for their logging camps.

The buyer said, "No! We don't want any of that St. Joe slough grass."

Harris said, "Ours is not marsh hay. I'll tell you what I'll do. I'll ship you a carload and if you don't like it you don't need to pay me for it."

And by Golly! Potlatch got that carload and bought the rest of what we had. Timothy was a favored hay for hard working draft horses. It didn't overheat them.

I think we got $25 a ton for it. A good price at that time and it gave us enough money to pay off our mortgage. When the '32 Depression hit we didn't owe a thing. Lucky for us!

FLAGGING THE TRAIN.

Our Ford car stayed at the end of the road where we left it except for an occasional trip to the outside. Some years we didn't even license it. Harris built a shed over it so it wouldn't depreciate.

When we wanted to get our mail we used to walk 6 miles down the track to Calder and come back riding the Columbian. It cost 10 cents. It was a local and could be flagged at any of the little stations like Finef or Marble or Zane. Or maybe we'd flag the Columbian at Herrick and ride down to Calder for mail and groceries and walk back. The Olympian was a Limited train and wouldn't stop. Each train went through each way every 24 hours.

It always thrilled me when whistles echoed through the mountains. From our home at night we could see the headlight of the locomotive flashing down the canyon followed by the long train of lighted pullman cars.

CABLE BRIDGE

A year after we arrived — 1928 — Harris bought some used cable from Potlatch and had it shipped over on the railroad. He built a cable bridge 325 feet long across the river and anchored the cables at each end in the ground. He split cedar boards 5 feet long and 2 inches thick to make the floor of the bridge and put cables on the sides with meshed wire fastened to them to make it safe for the children. Harris used the stump puller borrowed from Joe Finef to tighten the cables.

SUPPLIES BY PUSH CAR

After that it was a lot easier to bring supplies. They'd be freighted on the railroad to Herrick. Harris would borrow the handcar left at Big Creek. First he'd phone the railroad agent at Avery and see if any trains were coming. Then he'd load the pushcar and push it up the track to the cable bridge and unload and get the pushcar back to Big Creek or out of the way of a train.

Then my dad and Harris would put in a day carrying the supplies by hand over the cable bridge to the house. Our house was about 50 feet east of the end of the bridge.

Later, we were able to bring supplies over the railroad crossing at Herrick and up a road between the railroad track and the river to the approach of our bridge. That relieved them of needing to push a car up the track and worrying about trains.

And of course, we didn't take horses over the cable bridge. The men forded the river with them.

FISHING BOOTS

I always loved fishing. We were always busy but when Harris said, "Let's go fishing!" he didn't have to twist my arm. There's nothing much tastier than trout so fresh they curl up in a frying pan over a wood fire. On the main river I once caught a Dolly Varden 22½ inches long.

I liked to wade as I fished. I had to be careful on the main river and not take chances but on Marble Creek when the water was low, I didn't have to watch out. Many a time I found myself bobbing through a pool.

But I'd wear out a pair of hiking boots every year from wading.

One day in about 1930, we were walking past White's Shoe Shop in Spokane and Harris said, "Come on in here for a minute."

Ned, Annetta and Harris Bellows fishing Marble Cr. 1930

So he told them to take my foot measurements and custom make a pair of calked boots like loggers wear. Those were the most comfortable shoes I ever owned. A pair would last 3 years and then I'd have them re-soled and wear them another 3 years.

Whites kept a file of your name and measurements. When I needed a new pair I had only to write or phone them and here would come a new pair exactly like the first.

The calked boots were good for working on the baler, too. They wouldn't slip on slick hay.

CHICKENS, EGGS AND CREAM

I used to get around 150 chicks each spring. Harris built a little house with an old wood stove for heat so the baby chicks could run around during the day. But because of the cool nights they could get chilled and die when the fire went out. I'd put them in boxes lined with old clothes and carry them into the house. In the morning I'd rebuild the fire in their house and put 'em back out. I don't think I ever lost more than ten or a dozen. Rhode Island Reds. Good for meat as well as eggs.

We had one mean rooster.

Our little boy Ned said, "Every time that rooster sees me he takes after me and he pecks hard, I'll tell you that!"

The rooster wasn't old enough to have spurs but he was really mean.

Holsteins give lots of milk but their milk is not rich. We crossed them with milking shorthorns for greater richness. That cross also built strength in the critters and made better beef to market.

It was my job to clean the cream cans and the cream separator. We put cream in five and ten gallon cans and shipped it on the train to a Spokane creamery.

I made cottage cheese with the extra milk.

We leased some pasture ground from the Milwaukee Land Co. and raised steers for market.

APPENDICITIS AND BLOOD POISON

Living so far from town we were lucky we didn't often need a doctor. But one spring our boy, Ned, had to have his tonsils and adenoids removed and the next spring he had appendicitis.

Then we had a pet sheep and Harris went to run her out to shear her. He slipped and fell on his right thumb so hard it bent back and the bone came out. He put the bone back in place and came to the house and I done it up. But he kept on using his hand and got blood poisoning.

By the time we got him to Dr. Cornwall and in the St. Maries hospital, the thumb was so infected it had to be split all the way down and a tube put in to drain the pus. Harris was terribly worried that he'd lose the thumb and be unable to milk — in fact he'd be handicapped from doing almost any of his work if he had no right thumb.

Dr. Cornwall told me privately that it would probably have to be cut off.

There was also the danger the blood poison might spread through his body. There were no antibiotics then. Blood poison could kill within a few hours.

Luckily the blood poison did not spread but the thumb stayed swelled and didn't seem to heal. Cornwall released Harris from the hospital and told me it was up to me to look after that hand and dress it each day. There was nothing else a doctor could do.

One day after Harris came home I was looking at his hand and I said, "That looks like a sliver of bone in there." I sterilized a pair of tweezers and took out a sliver. Next day I done the same thing. Another sliver.

Then the hand got well.

FLOOD OF '33

We were still living in the old Montgomery house. It had a lean-to kitchen, a living room and bedroom downstairs and two bedrooms upstairs with windows in the gable ends.

It was the 22nd day of November, 1933. There had been heavy snowfalls in the higher elevations but we had only about an inch at the ranch. The temperature had risen to 54 degrees with a chinook wind blowing and a warm rain that was cutting the snow clear to the tops of the mountains.

This was Depression time and there was a 200 man CCC camp at Herrick.

Harris had been over to the CC camp to borrow a gasoline lantern for the Christmas program at the school.

He came in the house and said, "You'd better go over to the school and get the kids out. The water is coming up fast! I'm going after our rowboat and bring it here to the house."

I walked from the house to the approach of the bridge on boards we had laid down on the muddy ground. It was 6 o'clock in the evening and already dark. I went across the bridge and dropped into the school yard — the school was between the river and the railroad track. I think there were 8 kids in the school rehearsing for the Christmas program. Our daughter Thelma had come home from St. Maries high school and was there. Other people were already gathering.

The teacher was Agnes Tierney — not yet 21. Her name now is Hutchins. She and her husband live in Cottonwood, Idaho and had a store there. We still correspond.

I said, "Harris thinks you'd better not try to have the Christmas program tonight. The river is coming up terribly fast."

His kids were all grown up and gone but the elder Hibblen had come

—44—

down from his homestead just east of the Huckleberry road to see the program.

He said, "I think that's the wisest idea. Don't put on your program tonight."

WADING HOME
I walked back in the rain over the bridge with Thelma and Ned and the boards I had walked on from the house to the approach had already floated away. In pitch dark we slopped through ankle deep water to the house.

Harris had already waded across the meadow leading the rowboat and tied it to the porch.   When we came into the house he said, "I'm going over to the school and get that gasoline lantern. If we have to get out of here during the night we'll need something better than a coal oil lantern."

WATER UNDER THE DOOR
Our house set three feet off the ground. In a short time after Harris returned, water was pouring under the door and covering the floor.

Harris said, "I tied the rowboat higher up — this time on the railing."

We went upstairs to the bedrooms and took off our wet shoes and stockings and hung up our wet, outside clothing. We laid down. The children went to sleep.

Now and then we could hear debris hit the enclosed porch. At eleven o'clock we went downstairs. The water was already up over the mopboards.

Next morning, from the upstairs window the whole flat over to the hill was river with logs and stumps and brush floating down. Now and then some tin cans and boxes came floating and once a dead cow.

Our enclosed porch had been smashed in. But the water was sub-siding a little. Through the day it kept falling and we felt the peak might be past.

MILKED COWS IN THE WATER
At four o'clock in the afternoon Harris and my father went out to the barn to milk the cows in the water and relieve their bags. The cows were still in their stanchions. The water was too deep to take them across the flat to the hill.

When he went out, Harris had said, "The water is coming in from the river and digging a gully under your clothesline between here and the barn. I anchored some planks there so we can walk across. It's digging deeper by the minute."

I kept going downstairs with the coal oil lamp to check the water. All of a sudden it was higher on the stairs.

I ran back upstairs and yelled out the window. "Harris! Harris! It's rising real fast. Hurry back!"

We didn't take time to put any bedding in the rowboat. We just grabbed the first thing to eat and that happened to be a 5 pound box of chocolates we had bought for Christmas. We took that and our outer clothing.

Thelma sat in the bow holding the gas lantern up so we could see our way through the stream of debris coming down what had been the meadow. I sat in the stern. Ned and my dad sat in the middle and Harris stood near the bow so he could see further. Harris and I paddled for the hill.

The only dry place on higher ground was the old Bart Chamberlain homestead cabin with a lot of dynamite boxes piled inside. At that time the CCs of the camp at Herrick were punching a road up the south side of the river across from Calder. They had been walking back and forth across our cable bridge to the job. But when the flood came most of them were gone home for Christmas.

ROOMING WITH DYNAMITE

Harris and Dad piled the dynamite against the walls and over the holes where the windows had been. They built a warm fire in the middle of the dirt floor. A lot of people told me afterward they would be scared to death to stay with that dynamite and a fire. But there was no danger. It takes a cap to set it off.

The next day in the afternoon the water started going down. We went back to our house in the boat and when we waded inside we found the high water mark 42 inches above the floor. But it was falling so rapidly that Harris and my father and I went to sweeping mud out of the house by stirring it up in the water and pushing it out the door.

The men checked the barn. The horses, Sadie and Bill, had come through the night all right. They were big horses and were able to hold their heads out. There were chips on their backs that had floated there. Sadie, the mare, was oldest and was always kind of stiff after that from standing in cold water 2 days and nights.

MILK COWS DROWNED

The two heifers and a little bull may have survived by climbing up on some baled hay in the barn. But the 6 milk cows had drownded. The stanchions had prevented them from raising their heads above water. So there went our cash income for groceries. And we lost 3 steers, too — 9 head altogether.

We still couldn't take any of the surviving stock across the flat. The water was still 6 feet deep and deeper in spots. But Harris fed so they could keep their strength.

CABLE BRIDGE WRECKED

A jam of logs and stumps and trees had formed against the cable bridge and tore out the abutment on our side of the river. The cables still remained anchored to the other side but the bridge floor was swept away and the cable and mesh wire twisted and unusable.

The CC camp at Herrick had flooded and some of the buildings shoved off their foundations. The ones at Little Falls and Calder, and Finef and Hoyt's Flats and Marble Creek had been flooded, too. When the CC boys came back from the Christmas vacation they had plenty of work cut out for them.

CCC Camp at Herrick during the flood Dec. 1933. Notice how some of the buildings have already shifted.

REBUILT CABLE BRIDGE AND HERD

The CCs depended on our cable bridge to get across the river — there was still no bridge at Calder, so they furnished man power and everything to rebuild the bridge, including bigger cable. They made Harris overseer and built it in the same place.

We had quite a lot of silt on the meadow when the water went down but most of the debris had floated on through. The silt was so fine and lots of times I remember a fencepost falling out and I'd see a streak of these rubies the current had brought in. Just tiny little red rubies.

We had to buy a new cow to get some milk and from that cow and the 2 little heifers we built a new herd.

After the flood Harris had to build a bulkhead and fill in the gully that the current had dug between the house and the barn so the next flood wouldn't deepen it and form another path for the river through our field.

Harris also sloped the bank all along next to the river and riprapped it with rocks and planted brush to hold it because every year the river had been eating away at our land.

The little building which sets today near the riverbank was a blacksmith and repair shop Harris built. The log walls still standing near it was the original barn where the cattle drownded and where in front of it stood the half burned out stump into which the murderer shoved Montgomery's body and covered it with manure.

I think it was the Mountain Queen who first suspicioned something about Montgomery being killed. She came up from St. Maries to visit him and she asked this fellow where Montgomery was and he said Montgomery went East.

When she asked him, "How come?" he gave her a vague answer.

ONCE IN A LIFETIME

Harris was a hard worker. He wasn't tall, maybe 5 foot 7 but he was husky built with heavy shoulders. After the flood he started building a log house and barn on the hillside. We took the windows and doors out of the old Montgomery house to use in the new log house and used the lumber from it wherever we could. Harris and Dad didn't have time to cut green trees and peel them. They went out and brought in dry timber, mostly white pine. They cut them nearly all the same size and stained them.

People came along and said, "Why are you building up on this hill? A flood like that only happens once in a lifetime."

Harris said, "Once in a lifetime is enough for me."

Once he finished with the house he started on the barn. Along in October I could hear him pounding nails late one night.

He come in and he says, "You know! I was nailing shakes in the moonlight. It's that bright."

And he wasn't satisfied till he had built another and bigger barn up on the hill. From that time on the men had to haul hay from the meadow uphill to the barns — but he never regretted it.

Bellows log cabin built 1934. Picture taken 1979

THE MILK RUN

We started delivering milk to Avery in 1938. When Thelma came home from college she liked to drive our pickup from the log house downriver, cross the now completed steel bridge to Calder and then down over the Goat Trail to St. Maries to haul back a ton of grain. And she liked to drive the milk run, too.

I was scared for her but Harris would say, "Oh! She'll make it."

Years before this I had learned to drive our Ford sedan most any place. But later we were in a wreck on the highway west of Spokane. Harris was driving and a man swung his car directly across the highway in front of us. There was the man and his wife and his father and mother and 4 kids. The highway police were laying them out on the pavement and those kids were crying.

I said, "We've got to help them." But I couldn't move. I had a crushed chest and spent two weeks in the hospital. Being in that wreck frightened me so much I didn't have courage to tackle driving the pickup with its stick gearshift.

COWS SPOOKED

We milked by coal oil lanterns. One night the cow Ned was milking she just hauled off and kicked the seat out from under him and knocked it against the barn wall. Then she walloped him and kicked him against the wall. And she started bawling!

Then the cow Harris was milking did the same thing. My Golly! Harris jumped up out of there.

Come to find out what was wrong, our old shepherd dog had come into the feeding alley in front of the cows' noses and the green glow of the dog's eyes in the lantern light spooked the cows.

PANIC OF THE CATS

Alongside Harris the cats were gathered around a pan waiting for their warm milk. By Golly! When the cows kicked up it scared the cats and they made a run for the east end of the barn to get out the cat hole. The cat hole was only big enough for one cat at a time. Running hard, the cats all hit the cat hole at once and couldn't go through. That scared them even more. They turned into the feeding alley and ran the other way the full length of the barn and out the west door.

Harris laughed and laughed about that.

DOING DISHES

Then we put in a Delco system with direct current powered by a gasoline engine and Harris bought 32 volt milking machines. He did the milking and ran the separator. We didn't use electricity for stuff like ironing and we didn't have a refrigerator.

We had a good, cold spring. I don't remember our milk or cream spoiling even once. My job was to wash the 150 to 200 bottles twice a week and every morning and evening to wash the separator and all the milk pails and the cooler and the milkers.

I have always hated doing dishes. My mother would yell, "'Netta! The dishes aren't done." And here I had the job of washing all that stuff.

Harris delivered the milk Mondays and Fridays. Along with the milk we sold hens and eggs and potatoes and what garden truck we didn't need for ourselves. Our eggs were always fresh and I cleaned them well. Some people complained the yolks were too yellow when the hens ate grass in summer and there were other people who didn't like to eat eggs if they came wrapped in brown shells.

Harris and my dad did the gardening. My part was to gather the vegetables and clean and cook or can them.

MEASLES EPIDEMIC

During a general measles epidemic a girl died in Avery. Somebody suggested the measles might be caused by our milk. So they sent a bottle into the health department in Spokane. We were told about it later and that it was sent under unfair conditions but still the bacteria count in it was less than the dairy milk in Spokane.

Mr. Wilcox, the electrical engineer in Avery said, "That did more for the Bellows milk than anything in the world."

THE SANITARY INSPECTOR

One time I expected company and while Harris was gone on the milk delivery I thought, I'd better wash all that bedding."

And by Gollys! I was right in the midst of the washing when the milk inspector came.

Well, (laughing) I wouldn't have been washing I can assure you, if I'd known he was coming.

But everything inspected just fine.

THE FLOOD OF '38

It came the 18th of April. Harris was already plowing the ground to plant potatoes. The flood was 18 inches higher than it had been in 1933. If we had been still living in the Montgomery house on the flat, the river would have taken the house and everything we had. It was a comfort to look down the flooded meadow and be able to think, "And we're not in it!"

After the water went down there was a lot of drift on the meadow. Harris skidded it into piles and burned it. However, the lower part of the meadow was open and a lot of the debris went straight through. It was when the water level was falling that drift hung up on our ground.

There was 2 to 18 inches of silt on the meadow. Harris' mind was working all the time to figure a way out with all that silt. He went and bought oats and seeded it with a cyclone hand seeder and the oats produced good hay that summer.

GIANT POTATOES

Where he had plowed earlier to plant potatoes there was 12 to 18 inches of silt. So he planted potatoes in the silt and my Golly! The soil was rich and they grew fast. Those potatoes, OH! They were huge. But they had grown too fast. You could eat them but they had great hollows in them and people don't like to buy hollow potatoes.

But the oat hay helped pull us out financially and we had our cows up on the hill still giving milk.

A PECULIAR NOISE

Harris and I used to do a lot of fishing in the Coeur d'Alene lake. We come home one night along in September about 9 o'clock. As he opened the gate at the barn — our road up from the highway runs past the barn to reach the house — I heard a most peculiar noise.

I said, "What in the world is that?"

Harris listened and he said, "Oh! I don't know. Maybe a bird. And how come the cat isn't here to meet us?"

We drove on up to the house and as we went to get out of the car, I said, "Harris! I still hear that. That isn't a bird. And there's something wrong or that cat would be here meowing for her supper."

He said, "Well, take the flashlight and see if you can locate it."

So I followed the sound out to the corner of the yard. I thought maybe the noise was Flicka, my granddaughter Sidney's mare. She had been lame and I thought she had gotten down and couldn't get up.

GROWLING OVERHEAD

I was right under this big pine tree and all at once I heard the awfulest growling above me. I called to Harris, "Hurry up here! I'm scared."

He took the flashlight from my hand and flashed it up the tree and there was a bear.

He said, "Shall I kill it?"

I said, "Well, Golly, Harris! We got all these fish to clean and we haven't eaten supper yet. Let it go."

We went in the house and the dog kept barking and barking.

When it got daylight Harris took the gun out and here the dog had kept that bear up that tree all night. So he shot the bear.

And you know what? There were 3 more bear up in that tree — an old mother and 3 cubs. There had been 4 bear up that tree!

So we kept the one he had shot. Then Harris called a neighbor to ask if she wanted one and they said they did so he killed one of the little cubs for them. Then we called off the dog and let the others go.

THE DOG THAT UNDERSTOOD WORDS

We always kept a dog. But in about 1936 we got one named Mike — the smartest dog I ever saw. He was out of a shepherd we had and a sheep dog that came into the country along with the big bands that pastured the Joe river country in summers. You talk to him and he would turn his head sideways and listen like he understood what you were saying.

Mornings we put the milk cows down on the meadow to pasture. Every day when we opened the gates, Mike was always there to round them up and drive them down.

One day when they reached the meadow, Harris missed one of the cows and he come back and found her in the back shed where we had a watering trough.

Harris said, "Mike! You missed this one cow. Now, next time you want to watch. There might be a cow hiding in here."

And do you believe it! That dog, from then on always went back to look in that shed.

One day the bull came into the barnyard and was bellering.

Harris said, "Mike! Go put that bull in a corner and shut him up."

And Mike drove the bull to one corner of the corral and made him stand right there. That took the bull's mind off bellering.

Mike was a good watch dog, too — you bet! Harris fixed a box on the porch and lined it so it was warm.

BIRD DOG, TOO
When Mike was about a year old Harris went fishing down over the hill. Mike always went with him. And on the way back up the hill Mike put 3 grouse up in a tree and was barking at them.

That surprised Harris because we hadn't trained Mike for birds.

Harris said, "Mike! You stay here and watch them. I'll go get the gun ."

And that dog set there and barked till he came back.

Later we had some friends visiting and when Harris walked them down over the hill he wanted to show off Mike.

He said, "Mike! Do you suppose you could scare us up a bird?"

Well, Mike found a grouse and sent it up a tree and was barking at it.

Harris didn't want to kill the bird so he said, "That's fine. You've impressed our company. Now, let's go home."

But Mike didn't want to leave.

Harris said, "Mike! Come on now!" He had a hard time getting Mike to come home.

DOG ALARM CLOCK

We loved Mike like one of the family. In fact, we allowed him in the house part of the time — not all the time.

I'd say, "Mike! Thelma came home last night from college. Go wake her up!"

He'd go upstairs and lay a paw against the side of her bed and look at her.

When he came down I'd say, "You didn't wake her up. Go back and talk to her."

He'd go back up and sit beside the bed and look at her and, "Boo! Woo! Woo!"

Mike wouldn't chase chickens either but after we told him he'd keep watch and haze them slowly away from the garden.

DOGS AND DOES

We had a couple of mule deer that stayed around spring and summers. One doe had the tip of her tail taken off-we called her Tippy. The other had lost her entire tail and we called her Bobby. They'd bring their spotted babies with them and leave them a ways back laying down. Then they'd lay around the barnyard and let the chickens pick flies off them.

Mike never bothered either the does or their fawns.

But if Harris would holler, "Mike! Bobby's in the garden!" he'd go herd her out.

The deer came every year till that below zero winter and deep snow when so many died. Bobby and Tippy never came back after that.

SEVEN YEARS — SO SHORT

When Mike was seven years old in 1943 we lost him. They put out poisoned pellets for coyotes and I think he got hold of one of those pellets. A dog doesn't live long enough anyway and a dog like Mike was just once in a lifetime.

There wasn't a dry eye in the family.

My father stood there with tears running down his cheeks.

He said, "Why couldn't it have been me? I'm old and ready to go."

And we never had another Mike.

THE NATURAL MEADOW

By about 1941 Harris and my dad had all the stumps and litter cleared off the part of the meadow we owned. We paid the Milwaukee Land Co. $500 for the other 15 acres and Harris and Dad tore into it and soon had that cleaned up, too. Then we owned all the meadow.

Some of the people who want to keep the river natural are under the impression that the long 70 acre green meadow has always been there. They should have seen the hundreds of stumps and the mess when we started in 1927.

80th birthday party for Jim Peters in early 1940s.
Black Joe Finef, Dooley Cramp, Harris Bellows, Gus Saugstad, Jim Peters holding the cake, Frank Kellom, Dorothy Saugstad, Annetta Bellows, Cy Perkins and Sylvester "Hutch" Hutchison.

Work is what made it. People used to ask me, "Don't you ever get lonely living on that farm and not seeing other women?" But I didn't. I loved to knit and loved to sew quilts. I always liked to be busy. I never cared to join women's groups.

My dad was a hard worker, too. He lived with us till his heart wore out in 1950. He died the 17th of May. He would have been 82 the 8th of June.

In 1953 we were able to hook up to alternating electricity.

We carried on the milk run to Avery 19 years till 1957.

Harris died in 1973, Nov. 3rd at the age of 85.

And I'm 83 and still like to fish.

Interviewed June, 1979 at Avery, Idaho

Stella Bottrell

Waitress

I was kinda flirty

Stella Bottrell 1979

I was born Stella Patterson, June 8, 1907 on a ranch 7 miles upriver from St. Maries.

My dad, James Patterson was Scotch-Irish and born, 1864 in New York state and moved to Lodi, Wisconsin. His mother and father died when he was young and his uncle raised him. But he told me they were not too good to him so he and another kid ran away and came to Tekoa, Washington.

From their camp spot outside of Tekoa, they saw Indians and a lot of tepees. They didn't know how well they'd be received by the Indians so they got out of there.

Dad came up to the St. Joe Valley and did odd jobs to get along. He had a little house in that draw where the Sam Jacot place is.

Seven miles upriver from St. Maries some guy had homesteaded a ranch across the river from where the abandoned school is now. Dad bought the ranch from him.

DAD DRAFTED 1898

Then the Spanish-American War broke out in April of 1898 and Dad at age 34 was drafted. He stayed in the service 2 years in the Phillipines and then volunteered and stayed another 2 years.

The other soldiers were dropping over with cholera.

Another soldier poked him in the ribs and said, "How are you feeling?"

Dad said, "Not so good. I'm getting the chills."

They were bathing their feet in soapy water because they were so sore from marching.

The soldier said, "Me, too. Let's pick up our foot bath and drink it!"

They did that and somehow it washed them out. They didn't get cholera.

One of my brothers said to him, "Why didn't you run away, Dad?"

Dad said, "If you deserted and got caught you went before the firing squad. No questions. No excuses. Just the firing squad."

Then Dad got malaria. For the rest of his life he'd get spells of the fever and chills.

Dad came home with a Spanish-American War pension.

MOTHER — SWISS SEAMSTRESS

Mother was born Olga Bel in Payerne, Switzerland, June 16, 1877. She studied to be a school teacher but kids made her nervous so she took up the profession of seamstress. In Switzerland, people hired a seamstress to stay in their homes and sew for the whole family.

Some friends in Switzerland sent her to sew for some rich people in England and they in turn sent her to some of their relatives in St. Paul, Minnesota.

Porrets, who had homesteaded up river from St. Maries, were my mother's first cousins. In 1903, she wrote Charlie Porret that she was getting ready to go back to Switzerland but wanted to come and visit them first.

When Mother came to the Porrets, Dad met her.

They were married in Porret's house, Nov. 24, 1903. Mother was 26. Dad was 39.

Olga Bel, about 16 in
Payerne, Switzerland

My mother was a tiny woman, smaller than I am. They had nine kids, the first one stillborn but the other 8 are living yet: Maude Lecoultre, then me, then Bob, Yvonne, Betty Good, Olga Anderson, Agnes Studer then Walt Patterson who now has the ranch. My brother, Bob lives in a little house over there, too. He's retired from the railroad now.

My accent came from my mother who came from the part of Switzerland that is next to France. When my dad wasn't around Mother talked only French so all of us kids learned French.

When Dad was around, my mother and all of us spoke English so we grew up speaking both languages.

At 74 Mother broke her hip. It took the life out of her — she was never worth a ding dong after that.

Gazette-Record, 1962 — Olga Patterson, 85 died yesterday at the home of her daughter, Mrs. Maude Lecoultre.

NEW MILWAUKEE RAILROAD

In 1908 and '09 my sister, Maude and I were watching Dad hay and the freight train would go by with flatcars loaded with rails and ties and gandy dancers to lay the new Milwaukee railroad. They'd wave and holler and us little girls would wave back.

Patterson Ranch looking downriver. In the foreground upper end of the field was site of the 1909 Milwaukee railroad camp.

Dad had rented ground to the railroad for a big camp on the upper end of our place where the cut used to be.

The railroad hired a lot of laborers to clear out the brush, hand drill and blast the rock cliffs and team and fresno the dirt and rocks off the right-of-way and set the ties and rails.

They'd have a big feed and invite Mother and Dad to come up.

There were hundreds of Chinese and Italians and others. They had built a round platform. I was a little bitty thing, a year and a half or two years old. They lifted me up on the platform and I danced for 'em while they played accordions — the ones with the buttons. I doubt if I sang and probably I just lifted my feet in time to the music but they laughed and cheered and threw money up on the platform.

After a dance or two Dad would take me down from the platform and we'd go home.

Years afterward, Dad had a bellows up above the woodshed that must have come from this camp. The bellows were 6 feet long and 3 or 5 feet wide — probably for a forge big enough to heat and bend rails.

Up on the celler there was also a collection of whisky bottles about 8 feet deep from that camp.

THE WAY IT WAS, compiled by Robert M. Hammes and E. Mark Justice contains pictures of the track being laid in St. Maries, August 8, 1908 and of the first transcontinental train passing through from Chicago to Tacoma, April, 1909.

THE BIG FIRE

During the 1910 fire my dad and Uncle Ernie Bel and my Uncle Emil used ropes to pull up buckets of water to douse the embers lighting on the roof of the barn and the house. The wind was so intense that the burning treetops came floating through the air like an inferno. My aunt was standing beside me out in the yard, watching. I was only 3 years old but it shows how a little kid can remember something that impresses them. And we was scared!

NO SCHOOL BUSES

When I was about 5 years old Dad bought a house from Grandpa Pentland and moved Mother up to St. Joe. My oldest sister Maude was school age and he didn't want her to have to walk all that way down from the ranch to the Omega school.

Mother stayed there one year but she and Dad couldn't make ends meet living in both places so she moved back on the farm.

The next year we crossed the river in a rowboat and walked two and a half miles to the school down on Charley Porret's ranch. In winter the road was unplowed and unbroken. Rochats walked down from their place, too, 3 miles.

CHORES NIGHT AND MORNING

We had no time to study when we got home. Maude and I put 7 to 10 cows in the barn and milked them. Then we separated the milk and took the skim milk back to feed the calves. At 6 o'clock in the morning we milked again and fed the calves.

We changed clothes and went to school. We didn't smell of perfume — we smelled of cow manure. But then, the other kids smelled the same way.

But the reason we had to do all this work was because Dad had a night job patrolling the railroad track for slides from our cut to Martin's Gulch. He carried a kerosene lantern to flag down trains. So naturally he slept daytimes and couldn't do the chores.

When we took a bath on Saturday night we heated water on the wood range and poured it into a washtub — used to wash clothes with a washboard — and we bathed in the middle of the floor. Nowadays, taking so many baths I think is what causes allergies. It takes the top layer of oil off. You don't need so many baths — so long as you don't get cruddy.

Then when I was about 16 young Lee Lowry and Lee Carpenter and the others used to come down to get me to go to dances up at St. Joe.

But my dad put a stop to that. He said they drank and he didn't think....

WORKED FOR BOARD

When I attended high school in St. Maries I boarded with Mrs. Nevins. She belonged to the Nazarene Church and was very religious. I had to go up the hill every day with the horse and milk the cows and strain the milk and let the cows out and come down the hill and peddle the milk as I come through town. That's how I paid my board.

I wore a pair of bib overalls and a cowboy hat. One time some people saw me and wanted to adopt me. I must have looked pretty ragged. They thought I was an orphan.

I attended high school two years. Then I decided I needed money more than I needed an education. That's when I went to work at the Irish restaurant.

PONY AND BUGGY

Dad had a boat maybe 16 feet long with a fringed surrey top. He had trouble with the engine so he got disgusted and sold the boat for enough to buy a buggy and a nice pony. He kept the buggy across the river in the draw and when we wanted to go to town we'd ferry the pony across the river on a raft.

WORKING FOR IRISH CAFE

I don't remember it had any name except just "CAFE". It was

somewhere toward the river on First Street. It was owned by Vanderveers. She had a terrible Irish brogue.

I was about 17. I started out washing dishes then I learned to make change.

I sang as I worked and some fellow wanted me to go to Hollywood and get in the movies.

I called up my dad and he said, "Don't you have a thing to do with it."

So I was scairt to go.

I also learned about insurance. A slickeroo young fellow come in and sold me insurance — health and accident. About 6 months later I was skating on the river and playing hockey and I fell and hurt my knee. I was laid up for a couple of weeks so I put in my bid for this insurance.

He said, "It doesn't cover that!"

I said, "O.K. Forget it!"

From that time on I made it a practice to put a certain amount into a savings account every payday. I never again patronized insurance.

TIPS
Then I got to be the waitress, making tips hand over fist. I was five-feet-two and weighed 105 pounds and was kinda flirty.

My Irish lady boss saw I was making all this money.

She said, "You got to share your tips with us."

I said, "Nothin' doin'!"

She said, "You are!"

One night she said, "All right, Stella! Come on back here and let's settle them tips!"

I said, "I'm quittin'!"

Mrs. Anita Paris was running the Midway Cafe 2 or 3 blocks away. She hired me.

The Midway was real modern, crabs and clams — a big restaurant. All the customers I had at the Irish Cafe came up to the Midway.

Mrs. Vanderveer came up to hire me back.

I said, "Nothin' doin! Mrs. Paris pays more wages and don't ask for my tips."

Those old lumberjacks had been out in camps 30, 40, 60 days when they come into town. They were all cruddy and they stunk, but I liked 'em.

In those days rib steak cost 75 cents. T-bone steak was a dollar — and no tax. They'd pay for the meal with a $5 bill and give me the change. "You keep it, honey. You're my friend!"

I'm not kiddin'. I used to make 25, 30 and sometimes 40 dollars a day in tips.

If I had saved that money, I'd sure be well off. But I bought me a Ford Bug. No top on it. I run that steady and never, never remember putting oil in it.

CHAPERON — BILL SCHELL

Bill Schell cruised timber and surveyed. He lived in the old Midway Hotel over the restaurant and had a room across from mine. He used to watch me like a hawk. If I'd go out with some guy — Bill never came in my room — never! But when I came up the stairs he'd holler, "Come over here! Don't let me catch you goin' out with that guy again. He's no good!"

He didn't like Rusty Johnson, either. He said, "It ain't none of my business but that boy is gonna cause you a lot of God damn trouble."

MARRIAGE

But I married Rusty Johnson in 1927 and we moved to Potlatch where Rusty had a job in the mill.

I had a baby in 1929. I couldn't hardly wait till little Don was old enough so I could go back to work. I never was happy unless I could work and was out meeting people.

DEPRESSION

Then nobody had a job in Potlatch and we moved back to St. Maries with our baby boy. No jobs in St. Maries, either. The Midway had closed. Mrs. Paris had started a restaurant in Kellogg.

I heard that Mansfield Shepherd — he was game warden — found a man up in the woods with a fresh killed deer out of season.

Mansfield knew the man was poor and had a bunch of kids.

Mansfield said, "Don't be scared. Just take it home and cook it."

We lived in one of Mrs. LaPlante's little houses on about First and Jefferson. We only paid $6 a month for a bedroom, front room and kitchen.

I had lost $350 in my savings account when the Lumberman's Bank went broke in the Depression. It was about where the Midway Cafe is now on Second and College. You were supposed to get back a certain percentage but I never got a cent.

Dad brought meat and vegetables from the farm and he told me, "In a bind you and the baby can always come home. I won't take your husband because he's a man and can look after himself."

But I never done that. I suffered.

In 1931 our light bill was about 75 cents a month.

SELLING WOOD
Rusty and I had an old pickup and we'd go out and saw wood with a crosscut saw and deliver it to people for $4 a cord. We never refused to leave it if they couldn't pay us. Then we run out of a pickup license which was only about a buck and a tire blew out and we had no money to buy an inner tube so we were out of business.

Beer was illegal but you could buy the makings in most stores. I made a 5 gallon crock of beer and evenings we had friends in to play cards. First thing you know they brought their friends and their friends brought their friends and we had no money to make more home brew.

So I told 'em, "From now on you gotta pay me two bits a quart and 15 cents a pint."

BOOTLEGGING
Then I started making homebrew and I sold it to all my friends and to the Lafferty boat crew and to Josie and Nellie's boathouses. I got $5 a case. If I'd delivered it to the boathouses I'd have got a bad reputation so I left it under a bush on shore and they paid me by pinning a five dollar bill to the same bush.

So I became a bootlegger and if I'd been caught they could have put me in jail.

CATS KILL BIRDS
Harry Glidden's boy, Herb used to come over to play with Don. They were 6 or 7 years old. I liked young Herb.

Harry Glidden never drank or smoked but he had the reputation of hating cats and I had two white cats. Harry had a bird dog, brown with little spots. He come over to our house one day. Harry was a quiet talking man.

He scratched his neck and said, "Them your cats?"

I said, "Yep."

He said, "You know cats are an awful bad thing. They kill a lot of birds."

I said, "Yup! But God put 'em on this earth."

I knew he was an atheist. He didn't believe in God.

I said, "God put 'em on this earth to keep the birds down. If it wasn't for cats you wouldn't dare look up. You'd get bird shit in your eyes!"

He looked at me and said, "Well! You better keep 'em home if you don't want 'em to disappear."

I said, "You've got a nice dog over there. If you kill my cats I'll kill your dog."

Then I was afraid if something happened to his dog he'd think I did it. But we didn't have any trouble after that.

C & M Cafe built 1907. Picture taken 1908

WORKING AT THE C & M

I started working a month or two after Franklin Roosevelt got in office in January of 1933. Under Roosevelt's NRA — National Recovery Act, the C & M had to put an extra girl to work and that was me.

The C & M, named for the Chicago and Milwaukee (and St. Paul) Railroad had been in business since 1907. When I knew it the brothers Andy and Dave Ajdukovic ran it — they were Serbians. Dave tended the tobacco counter and bootlegging — and Andy, the restaurant and guiding people to tables.

Dave stopped bootlegging the minute beer became legal under Roosevelt.

Everything was served with finesse. I had to wear a little band around my head and a little white apron and a little towel over my arm. The food was good. Like the french toast. There wasn't just a little dribble of butter across each piece, there was a full square of butter. And it was made out of 2 eggs — not just dipped into the eggs to give egg coloring to it.

TWO-BIT BABY SITTER

Don was about 4 years old when I started working there. I'd take him down to the depot around 10 in the morning and buy him a 25 cent round trip ticket on the Columbian going east. He wore a cowboy hat and chaps and all the trainmen knew him. One of my sisters would be waiting at Omega. Yvonne or Betty or Olga or Agnes. They said everybody would hang out the windows to see why the train stopped and see the little pooper get off.

Then they'd take Don up to the ranch to stay with Grandma and Grandpa all day and in the evening they'd put him on the Columbian going west and I'd pick him up at the St. Maries depot.

You couldn't hire a baby sitter for two-bits!

Don Johnson ready for rail travel.

Stella in her C & M uniform except for her little apron and head band.

The Milwaukee Timetable, Oct. 30, 1930 lists the Columbian leaving St. Maries east at 9:48 A.M. and west arriving St. Maries, 6:17 P.M.

THE LAB AND THE TAVERN

We owned a female Labrador named Boots. I'd tell her to go get Rusty at the tavern. She'd get his hat and bring it home. Then she got so she'd go down without me sending her. Whenever anybody opened the door she'd go in.

Louie Widman called me up. In his heavy German accent he said, "Stella! I can't keep Boots out of here."

I'd say, "Kick her in the butt!"

"Don't do no good. She comes right back!"

I'd say, "Then call a taxi!"

So here would come Ann Bailey, the taxi driver, with Boots sittin' up front with her.

Ann said, "I tried to make her sit in back but she wouldn't go. I'm afraid of her."

Then Ann would take the 60 cents taxi pay from me and shake her head and say, "My God!"

I looked out the window one day and here come the taxi with Boots again. I hadn't told the tavern to call a taxi.

I said to Ann, "You didn't have to bring her."

Ann said, "I had to! She got in and wouldn't get out."

After awhile the boys at the tavern got Boots to liking beer. When Rusty got ready to go home the dog always went out ahead of him and jumped in the door as he opened it and slid over on the passenger side of the front seat and sat up there.

The boys used to say, "Hey Rusty! I see your dog drove you home last night!"

BIG MIKE AND BIG RED
Of the lumberjacks that used to come into the C & M I remember Big Mike Certivich. He sawed in the woods.

And this redheaded guy, they called Big Red. He always used to buy meal tickets. Well, he'd come in drunk and tip me 5 or 10 dollars. Anyway he run out of meal tickets and he'd charged a whole bunch of 'em and Legion Andy said, "No more tickets for Red till he pays."

Red came in and ordered a big T-bone steak with everything.

When he came to pay, I said, "You gotta give me the money, Red. Andy says no more credit."

He looked around and he said, "Where is the little son of a bitch?"

I said, "I don't know."

The old C & M had a long counter running along the wall back to the kitchen where there was a little window to hand the food out.

Red jumped up on that counter with his calked boots and all the people sittin' there eating and he walked right back to the little window, steppin' over their plates, "Where are you, you little wop son of a bitch?"

Then he walked back the same way, stepping over the plates. Nobody breathed.

When he got back to the cash register he jumped off and said to me, "Now what the hell are you gonna do about it?"

I said, "You gotta leave one of your shoes for security."

He reached down and took off his calked boot and threw it at me. Then he went out wearing just one calked boot and his sock.

CHINESE COOK

For awhile they had a Chinese cook at the C & M. He worked nights. He was very neat, very clean, very polite, "Yes, Ma'am". Everything had to be just so when he handled food. I liked to work with him. But people didn't want to come and eat after a Chinaman.

COYOTE TAIL

Doctor Patton, who worked with Doc Platt was a serious, no joke sort of a guy. So one time we got a coyote tail and fixed a hook on it and when Dr. Patton was sitting at the counter I hooked it on him. Then he went out and up and down the street with that coyote tail flipping on his behind. Everybody was looking at him and smiling. Everybody seemed so friendly that he showed a sense of humor after that.

THE CELEBRITY

A lot of guys wouldn't let anyone but me serve them. The girls would get mad when they left me fabulous tips that I put in my new savings account. I didn't appreciate it in those days but now I look back on it and I think, "Gee..."! But I called everybody by name and was friendly with them all.

Like when Wayne (Bugs) Harrigan came in with this stranger. Wayne was in an upper class when I went to high school. The Harrigans were always part of the elite in St. Maries — society-wise.

Bugs says, "You know this fellow, Stella?"

I said, "No. Who in the hell are you?"

He laughed and shook hands with me. "I'm Bing Crosby."

I was doubtful. I said, "Maybe you could be."

Well, next year this same fellow came in again.

I heard him ask Dave, "Is Stella still here?"

Dave said, "Over there."

He came over and put his arm around me and give me a big hug. "Remember me?"

I said, "You look like that fellow that said he was Bing Crosby."

I learned afterward that Bing Crosby's mother was a Harrigan which made Wayne a first cousin.

CREW AT THE C & M

At the C & M, Pete Jack tended bar. Mary Sullivan worked there and Homer Beg and Orie Covey washed dishes. Bill Seifert, railroad engineer on the Milwaukee, cooked nights a lot and Lloyd Ingram cooked there till he finally got his own restaurant.

LADY SNOOSE CHEWER

Mrs. Ingram had a corn cob pipe and chewed snoose. Every once in awhile she'd go spitooey! and spit the straightest stream I ever saw. She'd send me for another can of Scotch snuff, spit out what she had and shove another wad in — enough to make her cheek puff out.

Then there was old man Tobias who lived neighbors to me. His mother smoked more cigarettes than I ever saw in my life. She'd come out and yell at me every day to go to Safeway or Moseley's and get her 3 packs of Salems.

She had brown all around her lips and she lived to be pert near a hundred.

I asked her one time, "Aren't you afraid this is gonna get you down?"

She said, "Aw Hell! Cancer ain't caused by nothin' you do. It's caused by a germ — a virus. They'll find that out some day."

MOST BEAUTIFUL GIRL

Some Easterners came into the C & M one time. Legion Andy was a great greeter. He shook their hands and showed them to seats.

They told him they had heard back East that this was one of the best places in the West to eat and had the most courteous help and had one of the most beautiful girls — and that was supposed to be me.

Stella 1949 at 42

So Andy took me over and presented me to them. I had been working hard. My hair was all down. The men shook my hand and the women hugged me.

I thanked 'em. Then I went back to the kitchen and I said to the cook, "They said I'm the most beautiful girl in the world and look at me. No powder. No lipstick. My hair down. I'm sick."

The whole crew laughed about that for months.

Ivy Yarber, who worked morning shift and her folks lived in the Benewah. Ivy would laugh and say, "Stella! Some people came in. Let's put some make-up on."

I'd laugh, too and say, "To hell with 'em! I don't care if they like me or not."

ORIE COVEY SHOT
I used to tell Orie Covey if he had the sense of a hill of beans he'd get out and get a man's job instead of washing dishes in the back of the C & M. Then he went to driving taxi and chasing Joe Supak's wife.

One story was that Supak got a pistol 2 or 3 months ahead of time and lined up bottles till he got so he could shoot the necks off the bottles. Then he walked into Bill Beleau's tavern.

Orie was sitting at the bar drinking and laughing.

Supak called out, "ORIE!"

Orie lifted his glass of beer and says, "Here!"

And bang, bang, bang!

But Paul Seifert said Supak was sittin' in the backroom behind a partition.

Orie stepped up to the bar and ordered him a beer.

Supak stepped out and said, "ORIE!"

Orie looked around and Supak shot him.

Paul said Supak got two years — one suspended.

From the Gazette-Record:
Charlie Boyce testified he sold the pistol to Supak 5 days before Orie was shot.
Orie B. Covey 31, was fatally shot in the Pastime Beer Parlor, Thanksgiving Day, 1948 by 5 bullets fired by Joe Supak.
Joe Supak served two years, granted a new trial and set free.

JOB FOR RUSTY
When I was working nights Big Ole Colbjournson come into the restaurant and he said, "We need an extra man on the police force. Do you know anybody I could get?"

I motioned my head toward the counter where Rusty was leaning. I said, "There's one you can get!"

I was mad at him because he spent all his money drinking while I had to work hard to pay the bills.

Ole said, "How about it, Rusty. Do you want to?"

Rusty said, "No! I'd lose all my friends."

I said, "Your friends don't bring groceries in the house. Either you take it or I'm gonna leave you. I swear I am!"

So Ole took him in a booth and they sat there and talked and the first thing you know Rusty was on the police force.

Rusty made a good policeman.

I'll give Rusty credit for one thing. He was smart. Whatever job he took he went to the top of it quick. He got to be chief of police. But he was the nervous type and had to be on the move all the time. He lost that job over drinking and chasing around.

Then he went to work for the railroad and in no time at all he was crane engineer. But it didn't take long before he started drinking again and stepping out with the women.

I caught him several times. When I saw him I'd hold up my hand with the palm out like a cop stops traffic. That meant STOP!

One time we didn't pay the taxes on that little house we bought up on the hill. Pretty quick we got a notice from the county that in so many days they were gonna sell it for taxes. I showed it to Rusty and told him I wasn't gonna pay it. Of course, I would have paid it the last minute.

He managed to get the money — I think he borrowed it from old Bill Belleau where he spent his time drinking.

They were gonna fire him from the crane job because he was running around. So he quit.

Finally after 22 years he got mean. I had to divorce him in 1949.

I quit the C & M after 15 years and married George Bottrell. He had had a little store and beer parlor up at St. Joe.

JOB FOR SON
During World War 2, about 1945 my son Don wanted me to ask Larry Pugh if he could have a job down at the sawmill.

I said, "Remember! The thing that makes you wanted on the job is for you to be dependable. Not that you're so good but you're there every day and you do what you're supposed to do."

So I asked Larry.

Larry said, "How old is he?"

"Sixteen."

Larry said, "I hate to hire kids. One day I have a crew and the next none."

I said, "If you'll put him to work I'll see that he gets there every day."

"ALL RIGHT!" he says. "Send him down."

It went on for two weeks. Don was working night shift.

Then one day I had his dinner ready and his lunch all made as usual at a quarter to 3. No Don! Then 3 o'clock. Then 3:30. Don was supposed to be at the mill at 4 o'clock. I was mad.

I looked out the window and here he come up the hill. No hurry.

I said, "What in the God damned hell are you trying to do?"

He said, "I don't feel so good."

I said, "Then why didn't you call your boss and tell him you're sick? Go to work!"

He said, "I missed my ride."

I said, "Walk!"

So he went ahead and worked that shift.

Next day I asked, "Are you still sick?"

He said, "No! I'm better now."

I said, "Don't ever pull that again. I promised Larry Pugh that you would be there faithfully.

And Don said afterward that was the best lesson he ever had.

TOGO
The little Chinaman drove a little horse and his buggy wheels went wib-wob as they went 'round and 'round. They were all bound up with haywire. He sold vegetables like cabbage and onions and carrots.

He'd say, "You likee the strawberry?"

He picked up garbage at all the restaurants for his pigs. He saved the nice green outer leaves of lettuce for his rabbits. I think he had a few chickens, too.

The Gazette-Record reported John Togo, 96, was found dead and frozen in his shack, Jan. 29, 1950.

LUCKY INTRUDER
I've always been a hunter. I've shot maybe 5 or 6 deer. I've got a

lever action .32 Special. 4 or 5 years ago I came up on a deer — my son, Don was with me — and the deer was so close to me I got buck fever and pumped all the bullets out on the ground.

Two years ago some great big guy came to my door after dark when I'd gone to bed. I peeked out my bedroom window and I could see him trying the door. So I took my rifle and came into the kitchen and waited on the other side of the room with the gun ready.

He never knocked, just fooled with the knob.

He couldn't see me but he finally went away.

FLOATHOUSE NELL
I knew Nellie Cottingham. She'd come to my house once in awhile and visit me. She showed me pictures of her when she was a young girl. A very beautiful woman. She had a very good education. She got married and her man wouldn't work. He didn't care what she did. She needed money and she was pretty and she finally got into the business.

She said, "Stella! The day will come when people like me will be honored instead of dishonored."

KEEPING IN SHAPE
I take my car and go up Cedar Draw then hike clear to the top of the divide.

Shirley Lee that works at Safeway wanted to go with me.

I said, "O.K. But you won't be able to keep up."

All the way up the hill she come with cowboy boots and long hair flyin'.

I took a steep shortcut coming down. When we stopped at the bottom for a cigarette, I looked her over and I said, "Jesus Christ! You look like the last coming of somethin'!"

She said, "I don't know how you do it."

I said, "I do it all the time, that's how."

LOST
This same Wayne Harrigan come up a couple of years ago in 1973 when I was 66 and wanted me to go hunting with him out in Flat Creek.

So we went and I staked his boy up on a knoll and I went out and around to drive something to them. Be God danged if I didn't get lost. It was so foggy I couldn't see Baldy. I couldn't see any place. I kept walking and I was trying to find the burn because I knew if I found the burn I could find my way home. I must have walked 25 miles up there. Finally I came on a road that I knew came from the burn. Then I walked all the way to St. Maries, went home and changed my clothes and went to work for 5 hours at the Corner Grocery.

Anyway the kid made his way back down to the bottom and built a great big bonfire to lead me to it. Then he went down the road and there his dad was stuck hip high in that gumbo, tryin' to build a corduroy under his car.

The kid says, "I think Stella's lost."

Wayne says, "Right now I could care less. But if I know her, she's probably home."

About nine o'clock here they come into the grocery all mud from head to toes.

I could hardly walk. I had run downhill and it got my knees.

The kid says, "I thought you were lost."

I said, "I've spent more than one night under a tree. If you're really lost it's no use to move till daylight."

CORNER GROCERY

For years I put in late hours at the Corner Grocery owned by Bill Craner. People were willing to pay more if they didn't have the foresight to buy at the big stores during the day.

THE HOUSEWIFE

Here comes a woman in at five minutes to ten. She said, "Ready to close up?"

I said, "Yah! Just about."

"Well," she said. "I got to buy some eggs and bacon and bread. I haven't got a thing in the house to eat tomorrow."

THE COP

And Paul Sievert, the cop, he came down one night and he says, "How come the Safeway can sell a half gallon of milk for 89 cents and you charge a dollar four cents here?"

I said, "Safeway is closed right now. If you had any brains you'd go to the grocery store on the weekend. Then you wouldn't have anything to kick about."

THE SALESMAN

The General Tobacco salesman came into the store.

He said, "Remember me? I'm the guy that was in awhile back with suit and tie on. I had my boss with me and we went uptown to Ed Jewett's beer parlor and everybody was laughing.

"So I asked Ed what was so funny and he said, 'Because you bastards are all dresed up in suits!' That's why I'm dressed in jeans today and no tie."

I said, "Well, I like you a hell of a lot better like this. The last time you come in I didn't know if you was some FBI or some of that God dang Watergate Outfit up here tryin' to get some more dimes out of the people..."

THE BIG SHOT

This guy with a diamond ring as big as a walnut and a big diamond tie pin and a Lincoln Continental which he parked on the wrong side of the street in front of the grocery, he come in.

I was busy with other customers.

"How much are these peanuts?"

I said, "75 cents a pound."

He said, "They're half empty shells."

Pretty soon he said, "How much a pound did you say?"

I said, "75 cents."

He said, "They're half empty shells."

I said, "They're wormy, too."

I don't think he believed me. He bought 5 pounds.

BLACKOUT

Four years ago I had a blackout down where I work at the grocery. They took me up to the hospital in the ambulance and when I come to, Dr. Rapp was examining me.

I said, "What happened?"

He said, "You passed out, Stell."

The nurse was gonna put me to bed. I said, "I'm not sick and I'm not sleepy and I'm not gonna pay $40 a night for a lumpy old bed."

She said, "I'm gonna put you to bed anyway."

She had a'hold my arm and when she let loose to turn down the bed I said, "So long!' and I went back down to work.

Then again I had a blackout at Pat & Scott's restaurant and again I went to the hospital.

The doctor said, "I can't find anything wrong with you. Can you think of anything?"

I said, 'When I was nine I had inflammatory rheumatism. I sat by the stove for days and finally got over it. My folks didn't even call the doctor."

He said, "You're lucky to be alive. Most kids that got it, died."

I said, "You've got to find out what's wrong, Man! I drive a car. I might kill somebody."

So he sent me to Rockwood Clinic in Spokane. Doctor Castleberry.

They couldn't find anything that caused it, either.

But I want to live till I die and I don't want to live to be real old like one woman I knew. Had to have a woman put a diaper on her every night. Had to have somebody wash her face and comb her hair. I want to drop dead with my boots on.

Interviewed at St. Maries, March, 1975

During the 1910 fire, Ernie Bel and James Patterson hauled up buckets of water with ropes to put out the burning embers coming in the wind from back of the cemetery above St. Maries.

Milwaukee Sawmills at St. Joe 1908 — Courtesy Ruby El Hult

She was blowin' bad! The barge was pounding
the tug something awful!

Charley Boyce

Railroad Engineer, Tug Boatman, Gunsmith

Charles Boyce 1979

Back in Pennsylvania Dad was an engineer on the Buffalo and Susquehannah Railroad. He come out to Idaho in 1901. The rest of us came in 1902 when I was 5 years old. I was born July 28, 1897.

We lived at The Gap before it was built on pilings. The cookhouse and bunkhouse was two buildings set down into barges with the floor just a foot or so above the barge bottoms. Dad was gone somewhere on the St. Joe tug and Mother and us 3 kids was there and our cookhouse barge sprung a leak and water was coming up over the floor.

She went out and flagged down THE POWERFUL and the tug came in and started pumping the water out. It took 2 or 3 hours and I remember she built a fire in the cookstove and we had to stand on a temporary platform made of crosspieces and lumber while she fed us and the crew of THE POWERFUL.

My aunt and my grandfather Spencer on my mother's side both had homesteads on Eagle Creek. Grandfather's claim was about a half mile down from Huckleberry Peak. Good timber. One forty had over a million on it.

About 1907 we went in with a packer from St. Joe to Bruun's Halfway House on Mica Meadows and stayed there all night. I played with their kids next morning while the grown-ups were getting the horses packed. Grandfather had died a year or two before this in 1905 and I was with my grandmother.

Bruun's Halfway House had dried apples and peaches and pears and coffee and flour and bacon. I can remember canned milk back as far as 1905. There was always a controversy whether Eagle Brand milk was the best. It cost more money but a lot of people liked it to sweeten their coffee.

Dad had a homestead on Turkey Creek which runs into the North Fork of the St. Joe below Loop Creek. A small bear was hanging around the cabin so on Sunday, Dad made a trap out of poles and put a hambone in it for bait. When the bear wiggled the bait a trap door dropped down behind him. We didn't go to the trap for 2 days and the bear had already eat the poles halfway in two. Another day and he'd have got out.

THE ST. JOE IMPROVEMENT COMPANY
This is hearsay but I got it from Dad who became foreman for the St. Joe Improvement Company on both rivers, sometime before 1905. John Bolton had some kind of a deal he got out of the government that gave him the right to improve the river and then collect from anyone using the improvements. So the St. Joe Boom Co. bought this right from him and began to build wings by cribbing up timbers and filling them with rocks, on the St. Joe River which would improve the river for driving logs.

Later years when I was workin' on the railroad I used to spot some of these wings stickin' out in low water. There must have been a dozen or so.

Nobody had ever drove the Joe yet. Even Marble Creek wasn't opened up at all.

They built them little dams also on Santa Creek. Dad wasn't superintendent when they built the Flat Creek dam but he picked out all the timber and marked it to build the dam.

Then Herrick came here and refused to pay to use the improved river. He got into a lawsuit with the Boom Co. and the Boom Co. lost. So they couldn't charge anybody after that.

1910 FIRE
They were fighting the fire right back of where the old St. Maries cemetery was. I was carrying water up there barefooted.

A guy came running down the trail and he yelled, "Run, kid! Drop them buckets and run!"

Gosh! Nobody passed me getting out of there, I'll tell you. Men coming with their heads down and running wild — which you couldn't blame 'em for doin'.

BABY SITTING ENGINES

Andrew Bloom had worked with Dad back at the Boom Company and when Bloom was put in charge of the Potlatch owned Elk River Mill and logging railroad, Bloom talked Dad into moving there to run logging engine for him. They soon made Dad master mechanic.

Then a year later when I was 15 I began watching engines for them. You don't just walk off from a steam engine at night. You have to clean the fire and coal 'em up and water 'em and oil 'em and fill the sand boxes and put'em to bed.

When I was 17 I was working in a roundhouse for the Milwaukee at St. Maries with a crew, wiping down engines.

A year later in 1916 I was firing a locomotive.

In early 1918 we were all stripped off and hoppin' around down at Fort Wright while the army doctor gave us a physical for World War 1. He okeyed us all.

He was about to give us the oath when some orderly gave him a note.

He read it and said, "Boyce! Step out of line."

The Milwaukee superintendent had phoned up that with the war on they were hard up for experienced men.

Boyce in cab of locomotive about 1919.

Looking backward at Boyce's log train coming down the Maries Branch. Santa just behind last cars.

ON THE BRANCH
So I was back to firing locomotive again — this time on the Maries branch.

I used to get my brakeman's goat.

He'd say, "Charlie! Why don't you look back once in awhile. We tried to flag you down."

I'd come back with a saying of Satchel Paige of baseball fame, "I never look back. Somethin' might be gainin' on me."

The branch was sometimes awful slippery where it was shady through the timber with needles falling on the rails.

Down from Bovill, Clarkia, Fernwood and Santa we usually had 140 to 150 cars although I've hauled as many as 170. A car of logs would weigh about 60 ton and our train averaged 6 to 8,000 tons. That's a lot of weight and if she leaves the rails she'll plow up a lot of country before she stops.

I worked all through World War 1 till about 1923. Then it got to where I just worked part time. One of the reasons was that the railroad was changing to the bigger power of the Mallet — pronounced Malley — a workhorse steam freight engine and was hauling more cars to the train. That meant they needed less men.

MARRIED
Louise Cornforth had only lived in St. Maries 2 or 3 years. She came from Twin Bridges, Montana.

She was working for Dan Matthews. Dan was a small, white haired man with an ice cream parlor and noon lunch place next to where the Security Bank is now. Matthews wouldn't hire a married woman so we didn't dare let him or nobody know we were going to get married.

So in April of 1924 I used the excuse that I was going to a trap shoot in Lewiston and Louise went with me. She had $30 and I had $7. It was my lucky day. After I paid for the entry fee and birds and ammunition I came out with $41 cash.

Louise said, "Maybe you should shoot some more."

I said, "Do you think I'm crazy? I've never shot a 96 score before in my life!"

Louise had been staying with her sister in St. Maries so I took her down to her sister's that night.

At that time I couldn't hold a steady job on the railroad. I lacked seniority. The night I come back from getting married I ran into William Betts, superintendent for Wintons at Emerald Creek, on the street.

He asked me, "How would you like to be engineer on a Shay locomotive at Emerald Creek?"

I thought, "Brother! You're a married man now, you'd better get with it." So I said, "Yes!"

He said, "Be ready to leave at 4 o'clock in the morning."

There was no telephone at her sister's so I couldn't let Louise know I was goin'.

I went to my hotel and wrote her a letter I was goin' to Emerald and that I couldn't come down week-ends or anything. I knowed I was going to be up there all summer. But I said, "As soon as I get a payday I'll send my check down to you and you buy a tent and some furniture and come on up. You'll have to stay strictly away from camp. Betts don't go for having women up here."

I asked Betts if I could bring Louise up and mentioned there was already two women there. The clerk's wife and a conductor's wife. They both worked in the kitchen but they had their own private little shanties with their men.

He hemmed and hawed and finally said, "All right." But he wasn't happy about it.

RUNNING LOCOMOTIVE
Winton's had their office and warehouse where the garnet mill is now along with a shop for repairing engines and equipment. We used regular Milwaukee cars and delivered them loaded with logs right there to the Milwaukee branch line.

Where I worked was 'way up Emerald beyond Camp 9. The spur going up to a big chute landing near Camp 10 followed the bottom of a draw at a steep 9 percent grade and where we loaded was steeper yet — 10 percent. Dew and rust on them rails made it greasy. MAN! You really had to watch it.

We got paid an extra dollar a day for loading on these steep spurs. They had already lost two engines up there — runaways.

RUNAWAY TRAIN
I only lost control of two trains while I was there. One of them never got going much faster than you could walk but the other...

I said to the camp foreman, "We shouldn't go up there today. With that rail wet and rusty, that's dangerous."

He said, "You hired out to run engine, didn't you!"

So I said, "All right, if that's how you feel about it!"

Our Shay was an oil burner so we had a sand box. When an oil burner is working hard, you got to throw sand into it every 5 or 6 miles to cut the soot out of the flue. You can tell when they do that because the engine shoots black smoke out of the stack.

So I sent the brakeman up ahead with a scoop of this sand to put on the rails underneath these 4 log cars.

Besides the 4 cars of logs we had only the jammer on a car behind but it was a light load and the jammer could always hold itself and a little bit more.

The Shay had great, big hand sanders on it besides the air sander so I reached up and pulled them open and had the air sanders on. The brakeman had a peavy handle for leverage to wind the hand brakes down tight and, of course, I had the air brakes set on all the log cars.

I released the engine brakes and let the slack run out of the draw bars and set the brakes again. That was all it took. PSSSSSSSSSS! we went.

I threw her in emergency —locked all the car wheels.

I could see the smoke comin' up from the car wheels like all hell, so I knowed they were slidin'.

Pretty soon we got up speed to 15 or 18 miles an hour. I could see the old jammer boom reeling back and forth — knocking limbs off the trees as loggers say. The log cars lurching. That don't sound like much speed but it's that awful weight bearing down on you and how it can smash you.

About half a mile down the grade I went by this foreman standing there white as a sheet. He had seen the fireman and the brakeman bail off.

Then I saw the jammer man bail off. I knew he wouldn't go till things got awful bad.

I was thinking over and over, "If she don't slow down pretty quick I'd better get off, too! If she don't slow down pretty quick I'm gonna get off, too!"

Then we hit where the grade eased up and the rust was off the rails. The wheels began to take hold. If a rail is good and clean the brakes on a car can't make the wheels slide. The moment the smoke quit coming off the wheels I knowed they was turnin' and I was safe.

After that if it rained as much as two drops the foreman ordered me not to go up there.

THE ACCIDENT

The year they started to log the West Fork of Emerald I worked out of the main Camp 7. They had 60 or 70 men at Camp 7 and used to get out about 55 million a year. They had four to five hundred men altogether in all the camps. That would be a thousand feet to the man.

Outside of a few fir logs for bridge timbers, they brought out only white pine. Of course they also took the cedar poles.

Two engines would take the loaded cars clear down to the Milwaukee main line every night and bring the empties back up to Camp 7 in the morning in time for breakfast. I was waiting for Clawsen to bring the empties so I could get down to the West Fork and start loading.

Coming up with the empties one engine pulled on the front end and the other helped on the back end. This particular morning, they broke a knuckle — the rig in the coupler. The head engine run ahead maybe 6 or 8 feet before it got stopped. Clawsen and the brakey got off to put in the new knuckle. They were standing in the little space where the cars had pulled apart.

The brakeman couldn't put the pin in so Clawsen was holding the knuckle up and the brakeman was driving the pin down with the sledge.

Several men that were riding up to camp to go to work were on the front of the flatcar on the downhill side of the little gap watching them.

So Clawsen was holding this knuckle and standing directly in front of the coupling and the helper engine on the lower end pumped the air off — which he shouldn't have done and whistled "Ahead".

Rules on the railroad are that the helper never pumps the air off unless they come back and tell him.

The men below the gap said, "He's gonna shove ahead!"

Clawsen said, "He can't shove ahead. The angle cock is still open."

He was right. If the angle cock was still open the air couldn't build up and the brakes would remain set.

One of them men riding on that car — nobody ever knew who, must have already reached his foot down and closed that angle cock.

BANG! the cars come together and coupled Clawsen in between. He lived about a half hour.

PERRY'S LOG FARM
They had one other runaway while I was up there. It didn't hurt Perry Davis, the engineer and it didn't hurt the engine too bad either. (laughing) A car of logs jumped the track and slammed into a mud cut and the other cars hitting it drove them logs half way into the bank.

Everybody called it Perry Davis' Log Farm. Said Perry was trying to grow some logs there.

Louise would hear all these stories about runaways, which they had had some bad ones and then Clawsen getting killed. She wanted me to get out of there. She was afraid I'd be killed, too.

Once the snow came it was too dangerous to rail logs on the steep grades and the railroad men got laid off.

I finished that season and went to town.

SAWING BOOMSTICKS

The winter of 1925-'26, Floyd Gregory offered me a woods job cutting boomsticks for the St. Joe Boom Co. on Mica Creek. They paid around $4 a day.

I needed the money all right but I said, "I can't file crosscut saws worth a whoop and I ain't in good shape to saw."

Shay locomotive on Blackwell line at Crystal Creek.

A big, rawboned young guy come over — this was on the street in St. Maries.

He said, "I heard you talkin'. I'm a sawyer and I can file and I need work."

There's nothing much worse for a good man on one end of a crosscut than to have a tired man lagging on the other end.

I said, "I've been settin' on my can all summer in a Shay. I'd be ridin' the saw."

He said, "Listen! I can drag you all over the woods. I need the money."

So we climbed the train to Calder and hiked into Mica Creek.

He was just what he said, a good sawyer and a good filer and he did have to do most of the work till I got broke in and the fat off.

Dry white pine breaks pretty easy but it floats high and makes good boomsticks. This was beautiful fire-killed timber. We cut lots of trees 90 feet long with 14 inch tops and we'd get a 50 footer and a 40 footer out of each one.

Boomsticks are chained end to end to corral logs at river and lake landings. Then tugs encircle the logs with boomsticks and tie ropes or cables across to narrow them into brails so they can be towed down the river. Once the brails reach the lake the lines are removed and logs rounded into larger booms for towing to the mills in Coeur d'Alene.

In the old days when everybody's logs came down the river mixed up, the St. Joe Boom Company housed a permanent crew at the mouth of the St. Joe River to identify logs by brand and by bark mark and poke them through a sorting gap — called THE GAP — into separate booms for towing to the mills.

After two weeks at Mica Creek I said to Gregory, "Them other saw gangs are gettin' 26 boomsticks a day. Me and my partner get only 15 to 17. You can't afford to keep me here."

Gregory said, "You two are breakin' an average of less than a tree a day. Them other guys is breakin' 3 or 4. So they're costin' me a lot more money than you. I'm keepin' you."

FROM WOODS TO LAKE TOWING

About the time they were draying the boomsticks to the river, Al Campbell, Superintendent of the Boom Company come up to the woods to check on the breakage.

Campbell and Dad had worked together when they first come west. Campbell lined on the Joe tug and Dad was fireman. Both had ended up as Boom Company bosses. I hadn't seen Campbell since I was a small kid.

He said, "How about comin' down to be engineer on the Joe tug this summer?"

I said, "I never run a boat engine."

He said, "If you can run a Shay locomotive you can run a boat."

Say! At the end of the first week you couldn't have drove me away from that tug.

St. Joe Tug about 1914.

We had a cook on board. In fact, my wife, Louise worked the better part of two seasons as cook. The St. Joe tug did all the lake towing and worked day and night. We racked up long hours and made big money like 62½ cents an hour for engineer and captain and 35 to 40 cents for the fireman and lineman. And I liked the crew.

Captain Johnny Roholt and I traded off — 6 hours on, 6 hours off, steering in the pilot house. The fireman, Pohley, worked a straight 12 hour shift daytimes. The linemen, Ed Gaboury and Ernie Addington took turns 6 hours on and 6 hours off firing at night. Daytimes they took turns passing cord wood to the fireman from the 40 cord barge alongside the boat. The tug began with 15 cords in the hold so that allowed us 55 cords for each trip. The trip generally took 34 to 36 hours.

Mostly we had 6 or 8 cords left over but under adverse winds or with poor wood, 55 cords wasn't enough.

The average tow was about 8 million feet and a mile and a half long. One of them powerful boats with a 7 foot wheel (propellor) throws current a long ways so we strung out 30 boomsticks — about 1200 feet — between the stern of our boat and the logs to get away from throwing current against our tow.

FREAKY NORTH WIND

It was the day before Thanksgiving, 1926. In the evening we started down the lake with the last big tow of the season. It was cloudy. We had a little wind out of the west and at the start I was layin' over to the west side to keep away from Addington's wood works on Addington Point.

Before we got opposite Harrison the wind changed, blowin' cold out of the north. I turned and headed down the east side. The temperature musta been about 40 when we started. Now it dropped about 25 degrees to 15 or 20 above zero. That's the first time I ever saw temperature fall so fast.

The moon came out of the clouds once in awhile. Almost to Harlow Point, I looked back and glimpsed somethin' goin' across behind our tow. I thought it was old Ketchum's ferry goin' across from Harrison to pick up a car at Spokane Point.

Next thing we knew that old north wind just blowed us ashore on the west side before we could reach Gasser Point.

When daylight come, Johnny Roholt, the captain decided we'd unhook and go back to see if the tow was broke somewhere. Here was Addingon's wood saw shed and his conveyor right inside our last boom. What had happened was the west wind had swung our tow over to Addington Point in the dark, the boomsticks went right under his rafts and hauled them, anchors and all along with us.

What I had seen going across in the moonlight — that was the tail end of our tow swingin' across in the north wind to the west side of the lake with Addington's whole cordwood cutting outfit in it.

So we had to open our boomsticks and work the rafts out from among our logs and pull them back home.

Before noon Al Campbell come down in his launch and brought us a turkey all cooked up for Thanksgiving dinner on our boat.

We decided, "Well! We can't move till this storm is over!" so we tied up the logs and went back to eat turkey with the rest of the boat crews and sorters.

When we got to The Gap they told us that sudden drop in cold had caught thousands of migrating swallows and froze them to death in every building and old toilet and old shed. I went into the blacksmith shop and hundreds of poor little swallows littered the floor.

THE BIG BREAKUP

In 1927 The St. Joe ran into trouble. Fred Wilson was captain and we had a different crew.

At 6 p.m. Fred come into the pilot house to relieve me and said, "I don't like it! Smells like a snifter comin'."

I wasn't asleep more than an hour when Fred come down and kicked the wall. "Get up! We got a bad storm."

I could hear every wave slop water against the side and the hiss of the wind.

Midnight we'd just started swingin' around East Point. That's what we done every trip if we could because early in a normal evening we'd have a breeze from Harrison down to East Point. Then by the time we got the logs around East Point it would be 3 o'clock in the morning and a breeze would be coming out of Windy Bay and blowing down the main lake so we could slide along the west side of the lake till we came opposite Driftwood Point.

But this was no normal night. BOY! Just around East Point she was blowin' bad. The barge was pounding the boat something awful.

First thing we done was try to unhook from our tow and get the barge to a safe place. Boss Campbell had bought a big sisal towline cheap somewhere, a four inch line that took two men to handle. When it was wet, it was stiff and heavy like an iron bar.

Del Seagraves was laying down on the stern trying to unhook that big sisal line and Jake Jessick helpin' him. They couldn't stand up because almost every wave would bang down on the fantail. I went out to help and when I saw what we was up against I ran back and got an axe and chopped the line off.

Fred Wilson didn't like that but I yelled at him Del might have gone overboard or got smashed by a boomstick as he reached out to unhook.

I said, "That damn line is no good anyway!"

We took the barge into the shelter of Powderhorn Bay and tied it up. Then we went back out into the storm.

Shucks! The waves had drove our tow up on the beach and was stripping the chains out of the ends of the boomsticks before we could even get a'hold of it again.

We got a long string of boomsticks and tied one end on shore down close to Carlin Bay and stretched the other end out in the lake with the boat to catch the logs the storm was blowing on down the shore. White pine logs scaling 4 or 500 feet would jump right over the boomsticks with every wave.

The tug was rolling bad. The cook got seasick and vomited all over the galley. The fireman got seasick and I started firing in his place.

Fred hollered down for coffee. On The Joe we made quick coffee. Put water and coffee in the pot and turn live steam into it.

I made coffee and watched till the boat rolled the right direction and ran up the ladder on the side of the pilot house.

The Joe tug had a pilot wheel 6 feet in diameter. It was so big it stuck down into a slot in the floor and reached clear across the pilot house. We were turning on the top spokes all the time. Trying to hold that wheel against the rudder with the boat rolling, Fred had punched his elbows out both windows.

I said to him, "Cook's sick! Fireman's sick! You can't catch any logs. They're jumpin' over the boomsticks."

We cut loose and went over in Loff's Bay.

It had been daylight for at least 3 hours so I suppose some farmers along shore had seen us and phoned The Gap that we was all broke up.

Papa Campbell sent the Western down with Earl Campbell wheeling. Earl was afraid to turn broadside to the waves to come into Loff's Bay so he went right on down into Turner, turned around and come headin' into the wind. By that time a lot of them big white pine logs was rolled 25 feet up on the beach.

When the storm was over Campbell sent down the Western, the Bronc, and Ted Boyer with the Goose. As fast as they picked up the logs we towed them to the mills.

PAPA CAMPBELL HAD BALANCE
At The Gap, along in early March, when the ice went out of the Joe, Campbell said to me, "Let's you and I go up to the landing in the rowboat and take a lunch and we'll rear the riverbank."

We got there and started down and of course there was ice still froze in patches along the bank.

In next to shore was two small logs together and he said, "I'll take these out, Charlie. It's an awful bad day and you might get wet."

So he broke the ice with his pikepole, jumped out on them, his big belly sticking out, and shoved himself out and was driftin' down to the next bunch of logs. I can still see him lookin' around, enjoyin' things, pikepole on his shoulder, puffin' his old pipe, suit and vest, chain across the vest, white collar — the logs barely holdin' him up so the water almost touched the soles of his calked boots.

Dad told me that when Campbell was young he never seen anybody that had the balance he had. Anything that would float him, he could ride it.

I had a pretty good sense of balance but I was no good at rolling a log. That's where Earl Campbell and Gil Roe was good. Big and raw boned they'd roll a boomstick and hold it so you could couple the chain.

On the water I never seen anybody that could turn out more work than them two guys.

FUN WITH JAKE

Jake Jessick and me had a lot of fun workin' together. In the morning the guys would ride out with me in the boat and I'd dump them off along the bank to push the logs out. For Jake, I'd always pick a place where he couldn't get off without gettin' in the water up to his belly button.

He'd laugh and say, "You God damned son of a bitch! Only place for a mile on this river where a man can't get in ... "

And I'd tell him, "You hired out for a tough man. Let's get going, boys!"

We had one of them little tin horns on the boat. You'd blow it for a whistle on a boat that didn't have power for a whistle. You could just beep it a little bit if you wanted to.

I'd watch Jake wading along on shore and if he'd get in where it was a little too deep I'd just beep it enough so he could hear it.

Oh! He'd cuss me.

But he liked it and he liked me. And he knowed I was just kiddin' back and forth. If it was anything that really amounted to something I'd a'broke my neck to help him out and he knowed that.

THE MAN THAT LAUGHED

We was rearing the river for Lafferty one spring just below Mission Point. The high water was over the riverbanks and we had to get the logs out of the brush.

There were 5 or 6 boomsticks jacknifed back in the brush and this fellow, Wallace was standing on the boomsticks and if somebody pushed a log near enough he'd poke it on out toward the river.

The rest of us soakin' wet and wading around in ice water pickin' up logs. This Wallace just loafed on those boomsticks, leaned on his pikepole and smoked roll-your-owns.

I picked up a couple little logs and was workin' them out to where it was more open so I made a run and jumped on the two of them. With my wet clothes and boots full, they couldn't carry me. They sunk and one rolled and off I went into the buck brush up to my armpits in that ice water.

Wallace laughed. He thought it was a big joke which showed he hadn't worked around water much. After you fall in a few times yourself, it ain't funny anymore. A coupla other boys shoved me a big log and held it with their poles while I got up on it and wrung out my shirt.

About 30 minutes later it was time to quit and go home.

Johnny Howe was runnin' the Marble and he worked the boat in alongside Wallace to poke out a couple of logs. Wallace stepped on the stern of the boat.

The boat had one of them Chrysler marine motors and Johnny let it wind up to about 5,000 and pushed in the clutch and Wallace went end over end backward into the drink. Wallace come up sputterin' among the bark and chips.

Johnny went back and picked Wallace up and explained with a straight face he hadn't seen him.

When we tied up that night, Johnny grinned at me and said, "I think Wallace had that comin'. Don't you?"

LEAKY ROWBOAT
In his spare time Johnny Howe liked to build rowboats. He sold one to Mrs. Meisen up the river and anyway it leaked pretty bad. So we came along one day with the tug and Johnny throwed it on and took it on up to St. Joe. Johnny caulked it up there and brought it back to her.

We kidded him and called him Sieve Bottom Howe after that. And that just broke his heart.

OLD BULL
Later I hired a fellow they called Old Bull. I asked him if he could work on the round stuff and he said, "Yeh! Sure."

But the first morning he tried to run boomsticks to shore he fell in and I had to run the boat over to him.

Frank Jessick came running across the logs to help me rassle Old Bull back aboard.

I said, "Now you stay on the boat."

But he kept saying, "I'm a good man with a peavey. Just give me a chance."

So finally I put him ashore.

And say! Old Bull liked the hard work rolling logs off the bank with a peavey. He was husky and gave it all he had. But he sure couldn't ride the round stuff.

CHICKEN FISHING

We used to tie up the St. Joe tug at Al Reed's place below St. Joe on Saturday afternoons in summer so the crew could go fishing on Sunday. One man always stayed though, to watch the boat. This weekend Lonnie De Witt had hid out a woman friend of his who worked in a store in Coeur d'Alene, in the stern. He'd smuggled her aboard at St. Maries.

It was my turn to watch the boat so I was sitting up in the pilot house reading while the others were gone upriver. Something that sounded like a chicken flopping stopped my reading. Pretty soon I heard that chicken flopping sound again.

I stood up and looked out the back of the pilot house toward the sound.

Well, here this young woman had sneaked out of the boat to do some fishing on her own. She had climbed straight up the bank to where her eyes were even with the top and was casting a fish hook baited with worms over onto the field. When a chicken swallowed the hook she'd haul him in, flopping. He couldn't make a squawk.

She already had two chickens with their necks wrung, at her feet and was reeling in a third.

I said, "Wait a minute, here! Al Reed is a friend of ours and allows us to tie up here. There'll be hell to pay when he misses these hens."

Monday morning we made Lonnie put her off at St. Maries. If Al Campbell had got wind that one of us entertained a woman on board, he'd have skinned the whole five of us when we got back to The Gap.

Next trip to St. Joe, I told Reed about it and tried to pay him. But he laughed and said it was worth the chickens just to hear how she did it.

TROUBLE BUYING MOON

Jack Murphy was a mighty well built man — tall. When he wore a light hat and suit and overcoat he'd stand out anywhere. One time three of us went to Coeur d'Alene. We went into some joints to buy moonshine.

They took one look at Jack and wouldn't sell us a thing.

So we told Jack to stay to hell out and we went back in.

They said, "Who was that guy? He looks like a Federal Man."

The Feds were always six foot plus and 200 pounders.

We said, "He's a friend of ours from St. Maries. Runs log drive on the Joe river."

They were still suspicious but they finally sold us some.

WRECK BELOW CALDER

All during the Depression of the 1930s I couldn't hold a job railroading without being bumped by someone with more seniority.

So I formed a towing business about 1931. Earl Campbell became my partner 2 years later. We worked long hours and built up from nothing to owning 4 boats. Then about 1939 I bought out Earl.

As business began to grow at the approach of World War 2 I got rheumatism in my feet and ankles. Every hour in the dampness of the boats was misery. The only time I was free from it was when my feet was up against the hot boiler of a big Mallet locomotive.

Louise kept telling me to sell out. "We've got enough to get along," she said.

I said, "With this war coming on, there'll be plenty of money to be made towing logs."

"What good will more money be if you're not able to walk?" she said.

I took her advice and sold out to Lafferty in March of 1942. I came out with a new house and $40,000 which was damn good considering I'd made my living, too, during all the hard times. I've never been sorry I sold.

By then, World War 2 had speeded up the economy and I went firing again for the Milwaukee.

Malden was our home terminal at the time those men were scalded in that wreck below Calder. Our crew went up there to take their place.

On the railroad live steam means hot steam right out of the boiler. Steam that isn't live is just cooled down and you can walk through it and breathe it and it don't hurt you. But when that locomotive turned over, those trainmen got live steam.

From the Gazette-Record of Sept. 25, 1941
MILWAUKEE TRAIN WRECK
Sept. 20, 1941, Sat. at 3:30 p.m.
Engineer D. M. Hoffman 61, Fireman Harry Farrier and Brakeman John P. Hanrahan were scalded to death by steam when a Milwaukee extra freight struck a rockslide one mile east of Zane going east. The 80 car train was travelling about 18 miles an hour when the heavy Mallet engine left the rails in a cut. Several cars were derailed and others buckled and smashed.

The westbound passenger stopped and its pasengers were sent by bus to Spokane.

The Milwaukee's crack passenger trains were re-routed to St. Regis over the Northern Pacific Saturday although the regular route was again in use Sunday.

OIL FOR WAR

I became a Milwaukee engineer in 1943.

It's hard to stop a heavy train going down even a little four-tenths of one percent grade like going out of Malden west to the Columbia River. Normally when you go to stop you have to allow a car length or more of slack to each 100 cars because of the give in the draw bars.

We were hauling 100 car trains of oil every day to supply our war against the Japanese in the Pacific. They'd always leave them tank cars less than full on account of the expansion. Just before you'd get the train slowed down to a mile or two an hour that oil would slush ahead and drive you another 200 to 300 feet down the track.

After the war, trains got longer and longer with 4 unit diesel locomotives. One time they made us stop at Ramsdell and pick up 45 flatcars and we came into St. Maries with 242 cars. They said the flats had to go to Avery because Potlatch needed them to load logs that day.

That's an ungodly train. I didn't want to do it. You only got an inch and a quarter air pipe and it's hard to get the back end airbrakes set and released without too much delay. Especially to release the brakes. You got to pump and pump and pump to get the pressure up and there's a lot of leaks in a train that long.

Anyway the yardmaster at Avery found out we had them 242 cars and he said, "No way you're gonna bring them up here. We haven't got any two tracks up here that will hold that many cars."

I'd just like to have took them cars up there once. That would have been the doggondest mess. They would have thought it over before they hung stuff like that on trainmen again. But all they can see is the tonnage on that sheet!

CLOSE CALL

In 1961 we was coming out of Avery and a freight train was waiting at St. Maries to pass me. It was a sunny spring morning. The snow was melting. I was taking it easy down the canyon because rocks were falling along the right-of-way. During the night frost will heave rocks out and then when the sun hits the cuts, down they come. They can come singly or in slides big enough to wreck a train.

I played it careful till I got down to the bridge at St. Joe where you go over to the shady north side. Then I knowed there wouldn't be no rocks slidin' and thinking of that train waiting to pass me at St. Maries, I just poured her right on. I was steppin' through the dew. Believe Me!

I got down to Omega where I had to slow down for them two curves. Then I speeded up into St. Maries.

As I pulled into the yard the other freight rolled past me going east. Just before he got to St. Joe he run into a rock slide across the track. This slide was on the north slope where I had figured it should have been safe and I had been going 50 miles an hour over that same track 45 minutes earlier. I didn't miss gettin' it by much.

He was only going 27 or 28 and it derailed the engine and 2 or 3 cars.

GUYS IN WHITE SUITS

One of them cars had a carload of wooden boxes. Probably just one layer of them because I think each box weighed a couple hundred pounds. Some of the boxes had busted open and spilled out little cylinders about an inch and a quarter in diameter and maybe a foot long. Looked something like a piece of steel.

Guys in white suits rushed in by plane from Hanford. They checked everybody around the wreck for radio activity. Made them change all their clothes and turned them loose.

Searching for the missing cylinders they had a dozer plow off a little earth at a time. Finally about the 3rd day they found the last cylinder. The boxes were going east to the National Carbon Co. from the reactors at Hanford.

The engineer of the locomotive had tipped the engine over and it hurt him. He was a big, fat guy.

First chance I had I inquired about him, "How did Terry make out?"

They said, "Aw! You ought to see him. He glows like a neon tube."

I WAS LUCKY

I never had a bad accident. The only man I ever hurt was George McGee, a conductor. I was firing on the Maries Branch and the engine had what they called a hand cock inspirator to inject water into the boiler. To prime them you pulled a lever back and let boilin' hot water squirt out the side of the engine till it had enough velocity to open the checks into the boiler.

We were backing up into the mill siding at St. Joe. I was putting this inspirator on just as George the conductor got down on the step.

I hollered at him but he didn't hear me.

He dropped off on the ground and that boiling hot water hit him on one leg. It burned his leg pretty bad but not enough that he laid off. He went to the hospital and come back bandaged up and kept working. That was the only time anybody ever got hurt at all on any of my trains.

I was just lucky.

I opened the Boyce Sporting Goods Store in St. Maries in 1946 and kept it open till the fall of 1954. Then I moved the gunshop down in my basement apartment and continue to do a small amount of work for friends only.

Louise died in the fall of 1957. We had two sons: Clayton, born in 1929 and now involved in the space program with Aerojet Corporation and Don, born in 1934 and now working in a drugstore in Lewiston.

A LESSON

Back when I was 17, I was visiting Dad at Elk River and he mentioned some of their logging railroad practices. I had the swell head from firing for the Milwaukee and sounded off, telling how we did things better on the Milwaukee, letting him know that to me, the Elk River logging railroad and sawmill didn't amount to much.

He said, "Let me tell you something, Bucko! The Milwaukee and you wouldn't be here if it wasn't for these mills. The only reason you are here is to haul logs to these mills so they can cut lumber and you can haul that lumber away."

It was a lesson I never forgot.

After that, when I was running a Shay I knowed it wasn't for me to feel important or collect wages, it was to bring out logs for the mills. Wheeling a tug or wading waist deep in cold water pushing logs out of the brush was for the same purpose. My only reason for being there.

Boyce launch towing logs down the St. Joe River about 1935

Interviewed at St. Maries, May 1974

Clerk for the snoose trade

Lumberjack

Jim Brebner

Jim and Anna Brebner 1976

Charles Brebner, my dad, was born in Scotland and come over to Canada and then crossed into northern Michigan. Then he sent to Scotland for my mother and they were married. All of us kids, 3 boys and 5 girls were born here in the States. I was the youngest boy, born in 1895.

With a big family one kid helped the other. When I was a kid I could tell by my dad's voice if the kindling wood wasn't in. When he called upstairs my feet hit that floor in a hurry.

And the games — we played can can, battin' that can round with a stick something like hockey with goal posts. But what we mostly used to play was marbles.

In Newberry, Michigan, Dad worked on a newspaper. Then he was postmaster 9 years. In those days the postmaster had to rent his own building. He was open from 8 o'clock in the morning till 8 o'clock at night. People working in the logging camps on Lake Superior came in in wintertime by sled in the evenings to get their mail. He intended to keep the post office open only 6 days a week but when people came for mail on Sunday, he opened up for them.

OUT WEST IN 1907
In 1907 Dad moved us out to Coeur d'Alene. My older brother went to work for Stack & Gibbs. One day my brother forgot his lunch bucket. Mother told me to take it to him. We lived on Second Street and to get there I knew he went across Government Way, so I cut across over the hill and down through the timber — it was all timber then. I got mixed up and turned left — through the Fort Grounds and went to the Blackwell Mill instead.

TO BOOMING ST. MARIES, 1908
Next spring, after school was out we moved to St. Maries.

Dad had bought the Gazette newspaper. The town was booming.

I think the St. Maries Land Company was owned by the directors of the Milwaukee Railroad. The railroad was about to come in so this land company bought up the old Montana Ranch which was across from the dock and the Scott Ranch over in Meadowhurst and sub-divided them. They bought as much as 40 acres also in the west end of town and surveyed it into lots.

The old Gazette building is still standing kinda kitty-cornered from the Elks Temple and across from the Senior Citizen's building facing north.

In 1918 when one of the owners was drafted, Dad bought the Record newspaper which had a building next to where Bud's Drive In is now. He moved the shop down there and called it the Gazette-Record.

He ran the paper till the early 1930s and then sold it to Kendall. I think he sold it because he was getting up in age and the depression was on, too. He died in St. Maries in 1933 at the age of 76.

THE RED-LIGHT DISTRICT AND BIG MAUDE
Along about 1910 the red-light district was across the track from where Raleigh Hughes now lives. The Olympia saloon set off more toward the river like where Buell has his shop. Big Maude hung out at the Olympia. I don't know if she was married to Bronson or not but that's where men hired out to work for Bronson's camp at Big Creek.

JOHN SKELTON'S ORCHARD
Where all those houses are across the track, that was an orchard owned by John Skelton of the Skelton-Warren store. The old road went

around the orchard to the ferry and the ferry was practically right were the bridge is today.

We lived up on 11th and had to carry our water from 13th Street till the city brought Thorn Creek water to us.

One day I was in the blacksmith shop alongside an old Cherokee Indian by the name of Jack Reeves. Some woman went past the blacksmith shop and she had this baby with pink ribbons all through its bonnet.

Old Jack said, "Look how they doll them all up, now! When I was a kid they threw you out the back door in the morning and if you lit in the swill barrel, you could climb out yourself."

WOODCUTTING WAS FOR KIDS

After we come to St. Maries there was no more buyin' wood. We'd be sawin' away and one of us'd look at the other and we'd hang the saw up and head for the river. It took us 30 days to cut 30 ricks. But we had SEVEN dollars and a half apiece for the 4th of July, anyway.

I only cut myself with an axe once. Frank Trummel had a homestead out between Mutch Cr. and Cherry Cr. He hired the Mutch boy and I to make fence posts and rails. The axe was one they'd brought from Ohio — an old single-bit and it was ground something like a chisel.

I always got on top of whatever I was choppin'. This axe glanced and hit me in the instep. Mrs. Trummel filled it with flour and stopped the bleeding. Old Doc Kinsolving had to pick that flour out when he bandaged me.

One other time, I was standing on a pole and scraping a little bark off and cut part of my rubber off. I fixed it with a wad of rubber called Save-A-Sole. And in a few days the axe cut a bit of that Save-A-Sole off. After that I was more careful.

START OF THE 1910 FIRE

I saw the 1910 fire when it was little. The Daggett boy and I were putting up hay down in the Big Meadow below St. Maries. Old Darknell furnished the horses and baler and we put up the hay on shares.

The fire burning in Hells Gulch would go up to the top of the ridge one day and down the next. That was on the reservation and so no attention was paid to it a'tall. Another fire was burning over in the Benewah.

Below the St. Maries mill there was an outlet from the slough with a bridge over it. It had rotted out and the day we were hauling hay home we had to go out in the slough to get around the bridge. We got stuck.

It was just like both little forest fires had talked to each other and said, "LET'S GO!"

BELL FOR FIREFIGHTERS

The bell in town started ringing to get the fire fighters out. They sent guys to backfire down by Cherry Cr. They didn't get down there in time to do anything.

The Daggett kid and I got out of the mud and put the hay in their barn. That night we were standing up there in front of where the Catholic church is now and you could take a watch from your pocket and read it from the light of the fire.

Stickney had just logged Section 19 up in Carroll Heights back of town. Smith's mill was gone and there were still brushpiles. When the fire hit that section — you've heard the roar of a chimney burnout — that's just what it sounded like.

The house the Daggetts lived in was the one that Herb Wunderlich had lived in. My dad lived just across the street, cornerwise. It looked like the fire would burn the whole town. Daggett didn't have no insurance. We hooked up one of these old teams and wagon and hauled Daggett's stuff and some of our bedding down to the river.

The Daggett kid and I came back from the river and slept in the barn where we'd be close to the action.

HIGH WIND CARRIED FIRE
Looking down in the morning the wind was just like a big whirlygig of smoke and burning chunks of bark — a suction up the valley.

That wind jumped the fire from back of the cemetery above town, all the way up-river to the hillside back of the Patterson place. People putting out fires from big chunks of burning bark falling out of the air onto their houses and barns up there.

But it never did burn up Daggett's barn or house or the town.

TRAVEL TO FAR PLACES — HARRISON
During my high school years at St. Maries, Boy! To get a trip to Harrison — to even get that far out of town — that was something. At first we went by boat because there was no road. Then after the Hells Gulch road went in I remember getting Charlie Boyce to take me to Harrison over the flats and down that steep road past the cemetery. He had to carry an axe because the only way you could get out of the ruts where the water had run was to chop your way out.

They were pretty smart at basketball down at Harrison. Their basketball hall was in the school basement with the ceiling only 7 feet high and the ceiling joists exposed. There was no backboard but they knew how to hit the joists and bounce the ball into the basket. They'd take us to the cleaners.

ST. JOE — FEEDING HOG
My brother Bill was bookkeeper at the St. Joe mill and when summer vacation came it was always, "Come on up and stay at my house and work at the mill."

Dad tried to get me to work at the Gazette paper but I wasn't interested. The girls all worked for Dad. But **I had to be a sawmill stiff or lumberjack.**

After you crossed the bridge over the river going into St. Joe, another road went up over the hill and come back down to the St. Joe River further up. On that hill was a big logging camp. A logging railroad run up Bond Cr. Down below town was a log chute bringing logs in from the high country on that side. St. Joe was just a big logging camp serving the Kroll mills. Kroll had a little railroad tie mill and the big lumber mill.

We worked 11 hours a night so the men would get Saturday night off and have a big time in St. Joe. I worked in the big sawmill, feeding hog. Shoving slabs and edgings down into it was hard and monotonous. The big wheel with teeth on it was spinning fast to tear wood into chips and if you made the mistake of leaning over the throat it could throw back a knot or chunk and bust your head open. Once in awhile it would let out a screech and throw back a slab maybe 10 feet long and dent the rafters overhead.

BOSSED BY WHISTLES
Mill whistles shook the air yelling at you when to wake up, when to head for the mill, when to start work, when to quit work.

This particular morning it seemed like quittin' time would never come. A whistle blew and I thought it was quittin' time. Down out of the mill I went. When I got over by the little mill I looked back and nobody else was comin'. Then I knew I must have heard an early "Get to the mill" whistle.

Above the saw whining and steam puffing sounds of the rest of the mill I could hear the hateful roar of the hog running without wood in its teeth. The boss would miss the growl and screech of it eating wood. He'd be up there to chew me out.

The warm sun felt good in my face. I didn't go back.

CLERK FOR THE SNOOSE TRADE
I was sleeping at my brother's house and eating at the boarding house. Just a little ways from the boarding house had been a company store and they sold it to some guy. The big trade then in the morning was the snoose trade. After I ate breakfast, I sauntered past the store.

The fellow who did the clerkin' and delivered groceries every afternoon was Louie Braden. He said the fellow that owned the store was going back to Mayo Brothers for an operation, leavin' him to run the store. Asked me if I wanted a job clerkin'.

I said, "Sure!"

UNDERMINED BY BEER NIPS
The store bought little bottles of beer called Beer Nips for a fellow

named English, and kept them in a big ice box at the store. When English wanted some Beer Nips, they delivered them to his house along with his groceries.

Louie and I used to whack off a big slice of cheese and eat crackers and drink some of this beer. I got so I couldn't even eat my meals hardly, I was so full of crackers, cheese and Beer Nips.

Where I slept in my brother's house, the upstairs wasn't finished. There was no railing coming up the stairs or any railing around the upstairs entrance.

I had a nightmare, probably from all the beer and cheese, and I was walkin' around upstairs and I thought I was lookin' for a lantern for somebody. I fell down the stairs and darned near busted the outside door down.

ESCAPE FROM BEER NIPS TO HAYING
Along about hayin' time along come Harry Miller lookin' for hay hands. $2 a day and board. I don't remember what they paid at the store but it couldn't have been much or this wouldn't have sounded so good to me.

And I thought, "Well, I'll get away from here and nightmares, too."

I found you well earned your $2 a day. The bales weighed 100 to 150 pounds. Miller had rented the Rochat place. He hired 7 men to start with.

It started to rain. He let everybody else go but told me to stay. He put me with an old team of horses mowin' hay in the rain. I thought he was crazy. But it was timothy — everything was timothy those days for loggin' horses.

"A GOOD EASY JOB!"
When the sun come out, he said, "You've worked hard hayin' here. I'll give you a good easy job, you stay for the baling."

Him and Scott had bought this baler from the Montandans. They brought it and a little old steam engine in on a barge along with a water tank.

That year, Milwaukee Land Co. had built a flume on Rochat Cr. Jerry McCarthy was kind of a cop here in St. Maries. He was man catcher for Miller. Some of these 'jacks, he'd get 'em on the boat and send 'em up there and the boat would stop and let them off and they'd come and stand and watch that baler for awhile with their pack sacks on their backs and I suppose most of them would head over to Rochat Cr. None of 'em ever stopped.

So I was supposed to be a roustabout and cut wire for the baler. Well, that lasted a few days and then they had me pilin' bales. A fellow named Frank Matthews had a hauling outfit in St. Maries, he was a'weighin' bales as each one came out of the baler and put a wooden tag on it with the weight written in pencil. It tumbled off the scales onto a low wheelbarrow and wheeled a ways. Then from there on up the stack you juggled 'em. If Miller saw a 125 pound bale, he'd grab the wrench and screw down the baler. That was too light.

We handled hay about 10 hours a day.

Those days all the hay went through a sweat and was cured — not like now. And everything was stacked. But there was no spoilage to it. You could pick up hay out of the stack and it would smell nice and sweet. Miller's place and Rochats together baled out an even hundrd tons.

SKIDDING HOUSELOGS WITH PACK MULES

The spring of 1912 I went out for the Forest Service at Roundtop. Ashley Roach was ranger. I was part of a trail crew that set out to build the first cabin at Roundtop. While others sawed the logs I skidded 'em in with a team of pack mules and still others rolled the logs up for the walls.

Old Round Top Ranger Station built 1912

Cordemarsh from Fernwood was a carpenter who could split out a piece of cedar and take an old plane and make just as nice a casing as you'd want. But some official over in Missoula got the idea that we should whipsaw lumber for flooring and for shakes.

About the time Cordemarsh and a guy named Abbot finished putting in the floor they were sent over to Jug Camp to be smokechasers.

WHIPSAWING RAN INTO WORK

That left a kid named McMillan from St. Maries and me to do the whipsawing. We went out in the woods, sawed down some yellow spruce. I always wanted to learn how to use a broadaxe so I hewed it into a 14 by 16 inch cant. They had taken the pack mules back to Avery so we skidded the cants in with peaveys by hand. Threw down skids and drug 'em in.

Our mill was a frame on the sidehill that we could roll the cants up on. It had to be absolutely level. Then we measured the ends off and took a level straight edge and marked them up and down so we'd have points to work from in cutting our boards. Then we snapped chalklines from end to end. We charred some old alder to make a black line. We'd zip that over the line and snap it.

Then one man got on top with the saw and the other man pulled the saw from underneath and you started. The saw was stiff — a lot like an ice saw. It took us all day to cut off that first board. From that we learned that if you got over 6 or 7 inches thick, it was too wide to work the saw good. So we spent another day sawing the cant in two in the middle. Then we laid one cant flat and started sawing off narrower boards. That was faster but still too slow so we run around the woods and got white pine windfalls that were wet and nice and soft and would cut like cheese. So we whipsawed enough lumber and put the roof on the cabin.

The following spring, Cordemarsh and I went to run telephone lines from Roundtop to Fishhook Peak to join up with the Association Telephone that they had into St. Joe.

The knots had fell out of some of those boards I'd put on the Roundtop cabin roof so the roof was a kind of a disaster.

So after Cordemarsh and I got through stringing telephone lines and cleaning trails we went over by the Fishhook cabin where there was some good cedar and split up a bunch of shakes. When the pack string come in, we got them packed up to the cabin so we could double shake the roof and cover the knotholes.

THE JUG CABIN WAS BEAUTIFUL

The Jug Cabin beyond Monumental Butte was a beautiful cabin. It set up on rocks and was hewed out of those old twisty trees up there. Had one of those little three-cornered cupboards in the corner. And an upstairs for storing tools and stuff. When the Forest Service burned that down, it was a crime!

PULLING LUMBER ON THE GREEN CHAIN

When I graduated from high school in the spring of 1913 I went down to the St. Maries mill. Kroll owned it at that time. Jack Henriksen had the lumber piling and green chain gypoing.

Jack put me pullin' on the green chain. They had a lot of guys on the green chain. I was pullin' heavy shop and across from me was a great big old Norwegian pullin' little old one by sixes. I wore light shoes. Pullin' those heavy planks I just about had to crawl home that night.

I got to thinkin' "If I'm gonna be a horse, I'm goin' up where they use horses."

NIGHT TRIP TO FALCON

My brother Alex Brebner was ranger at Falcon above Avery. He scaled logs for the Forest Service that Bogle was logging. My mother give me some blankets and stuff and I packed up my packsack.

I caught the passenger train through St. Maries at 11 something at night and got off at Falcon. There was a loggin' railroad switchback down to the North Fork and Bogle's Spur. I got to the camp in time for breakfast.

My first job was swampin' so they could put a skidway along a chute. In those days all those foreigners that had been building the railroad, they all took to the woods and 99 per cent of the labor up there was Czecks and Polocks.

Finally in come a carload or two of horses and they started skiddin'. They paid $60 a month and board for a guy driving team or single horse. Common labor paid two-six-bits ($2.75) a 10 hour day but they took out six-bits (75 cents) for board.

SHOTGUN BUNKS
An old style, eastern bunkhouse — shotgun bunks, (you climb in feet first from the end). 3 tiers high. Just a board runway at the end of the bunks where you climbed out. The middle of the floor was only dirt.

My bunk was up high, not too easy to get into. I wasn't in it long enough to find out if the bunkhouse was lousy. I took my blankets and slept out in the hay shed.

A SKINNER AT $60 A MONTH
I got a job jiggin' on the chute with one horse and got my sixty a month and board. We were loggin' burnt stuff, heavy to white pine. They had a lot of snow in there and the timber was checked so it wasn't too dirty a job.

They used chutes to bring the timber to the logging railroad. The logs run live a ways down over the hill and then they trailed 'em into a dry landing. (In hot, dry weather, burned timber can be dirty to handle and the air full of charcoal dust. "Live" logs slid in chutes down off the steep hillsides. Where chutes levelled off, the logs were pulled or trailed by teams into a bunching spot or landing. "Dry" landing refers to one on the ground as opposed to landing in a pond or creek. Ed.)

Bogle's went kerflewie (broke) there. Oscar Hopkins finished the job.

As you go up the North Fork above Avery, past the mouth of Loop Creek you can still see where the old logging railroad used to run — the headlogs where it crossed the creek.

FAST CHUTE BELOW FISHHOOK
My brothers logged with Oscar Hopkins afterwards. Their chute came down the sidehill into the Joe just below the mouth of Fishhook. The timber came from some nice country on a bench above. The chute was real steep and the gooseneck shavings piled up several feet high on each side of the chute. Even then, some of the logs would hit the river so fast they'd make it clear over to the railroad track. (Used to slow logs down were gooseneck spikes laid over with their heads stuck up in the bottom of the chute. They cut off shavings the full length of the logs. Ed.)

W.S.C. FORESTRY NOT PRACTICAL

I went to Washington State College in 1915 and '16 to take a degree in forestry. But I'd worked in the woods and the junk they taught was so far out for someone that was practical that I just couldn't go it. They didn't teach the things you needed to know. So I quit and went back to the woods.

HITTING THE PALOUSE HARVEST

In those days the logging was done in winter so there was nothing to do in the summertime. It wasn't till fall they'd start buildin' chutes or cuttin' dray roads or skiddin' and deckin'. So us locals would maybe go out in the Palouse country on harvest and after that was over with, go for the Canada harvest.

CANADA GRABBED FOR THE DRAFT

In late summer of 1916 when I went up there, Canada was getting into World War 1. You couldn't get off the step of the train before they were grabbin' at you.

The recruiting officers got $10 for every man he signed up.

We were stayin' at a hotel and there was a fellow with gray whiskers. A recruiting officer was after him.

The fellow said, "I'm too old."

"Oh!" he said. "Shave those whiskers off. We'll take you."

Fellow was playing the bagpipes and I went down the street to listen.

A recruiting fellow started tryin' to talk me into joining the army.

I said, "No! If the United States was into it I'd be joining the U. S. Army but I'm not going to join the Canadian Army."

He said, "If you've got cold feet we've got some warm German sox that will fix that."

My partner grabbed me and said, "You come on! Let's get out of here."

I found out afterwards they pick an argument with you and stir up a fight. Then they take you to the hoosegow. The judge would give you a choice of so many months in jail or join the army.

LONG LIVED MICA FLUME

I think the flume that lasted the longest in this country was Mica Cr. It was built in 1916. They first built a road into the upper end of Mica Meadows and set up a sawmill to build the flume. Then they hauled a little narrow gauge railroad in from Calder. For a long time you could see marks on the trees where they'd hooked cable around them to block and line the Shay locomotive in over the steep road built for it.

The first logs that came out of there in 1917 had the Rose Lake Lumber Co. stamp on them, logged by O'Neil & Irvine. They had bought ten claims and paid $10,000 each or a total of $100,000. Some of those claims today would be worth more than $100,000. But the homesteaders thought it was wonderful to get that price. $10,000 was a fortune then.

Must've been 25 to 30 million feet a year taken off that creek for years and years.

In '17 they had a man catcher name of Steve Klugg in St. Maries and he sent me to Mica Cr. Cruel Jimmy Holmes was walking boss. They put me to firing the little narrow gauge locomotive. $2.75 a day minus 75 cents for board. 10 hours a day. 6 days a week but you had to pay board on Sunday. The track was built right down in the creek so when you needed water all you had to do was take the hose out and siphon water into the boiler.

FIRING LOCOMOTIVE THEN DONKEY
They had logs all skidded and decked, ready to load. Then the fellow that was engineer on this little locomotive had some relative in Coeur d'Alene that he'd promised the job of firing so the Push gave me a job firing the donkey instead. I was supposed to go up early in the morning and steam it up. They used the donkey to pull the empty log cars up the track for loading. The little Shay didn't have the power. But it could pull 'em down all right after they were loaded and up to Camp 3 to unload in the dam.

BRUUN'S HALFWAY HOUSE
Bruun had had a Halfway House in upper Mica Meadows for homesteaders going from St. Joe into Marble Cr. and that's right where the camp was.

One rainy day when I wasn't workin' I was layin' in the bunk and I picked up some old magazine and here were advertisements in it for automobiles that had just a handle instead of a steering wheel.

OATMEAL SLIM — POKER DAVE
The lumberjacks called Kennedy, the camp boss, Old Oatmeal Slim.

Then there was a skinner called Poker Dave. When he was workin' you'd hear never a word out of him. But at night in the bunkhouse he was a different guy. He told about back in Virginia he'd been pulling a trail of logs across a draw and the team would pull so hard they'd raise the logs in the air and a fellow could walk right in under it.

Another time he told about big catfish back in Virginia. A guy planted some spuds on the riverbank and this catfish come right out and eat the whole spud patch.

WOBBLY STRIKE FOR 8 HOURS AND BATHHOUSE
I was only there a short time and the I.W.W. declared a strike for an 8 hour day with the same pay and a bathhouse.

The boss granted the 8 hours but the river was at flood stage and he'd have a boiler for the bathhouse as soon as he could have it freighted in.

I know the capitalists went to extremes and worked the heck out of us. Had to sleep in old hay and on the ground, carry our own beddin' and all that old stuff.

THEY FED GOOD

I thought they fed pretty good for the six-bits. 'Course I was a kid and I eat pretty good anyway. They had a box with shelves in it and when we'd go up the hill in the morning to work we'd carry some pastry, tea and coffee. And then for lunch the bull cook brought a big box with hot meat and gravy, maybe beans and different vegetables in gallon cans. Alex McDonald and I was swampin'. It was our job to come in early and build the fire. We'd get the water boilin' for tea and coffee and there was always pastry. The more pastry you could jam into the 'jacks, the cheaper you could feed 'em. Meat and ham and protein products was the highest priced stuff.

It went along for over two weeks when a bunch of I.W.W delegates camped down at Calder rolled in and closed down the camp.

The war brought the gypo business. After that almost everything was contract piecework.

Then I went to the army.

MARRIED

My wife and I were married in 1920. We lived out and had our own camp off and on.

Anna Brebner

Graduate in the first class

of St. Maries High School

Jim and I went to school at the same time in the old Lincoln Building on 3rd St. up above College. But we didn't marry till after he went to Washington State College and to the service in World War I.

I was born in 1895, same year as Jim. My folks came to Coeur d'Alene in 1907. My father, John Angus McMillan built houses. We lived there 4 years. Then my mother and father came to St. Maries to take over the boarding house for Herrick. At one time Dad had a furniture store where the Western Auto is and another time they had a candy and ice cream store where the Handy Corner used to be.

I graduated in the first class to graduate from the St. Maries High School. In 1975 the Gazette-Record had a picture of the basketball team: my sister, Mrs. Gregory, Mrs. Elmer Smith, Mrs. Cecil Sanford, myself and Mrs. Sanford's sister.

My folks went to Davenport for a few years. My father died there. My mother came back here and bought the Kootenai Inn. The only time I did any working out was when I kept Mother's books for her at the Kootenai Inn. I had gone to the Blair Business College in Spokane after attending the Academy in Coeur d'Alene.

JIM BREBNER CONTINUES

I FOUND WOMEN WORK HARD
I found out the hard way now much work a woman does. One time when one of the girls was born and my wife was in the old St. Maries Hospital, I'd made arrangements with a woman to come and stay at the house. Anyway, the woman didn't show up. O'Neil had that flume in Bond Cr. and Ira Fleming and I had a gypo job on a chute that fed the flume. We were makin' pretty good money.

Between cookin' and washin' I couldn't get away from home long enough to get anybody. In those days a woman stayed in the hospital about 12 days where now they kick 'em out the next day. Yes sir! I found a woman sure has to work. And in those days of the old wood stove, they had to heat their own water for washing, bake great big batches of bread, put up all those lunches for the kids goin' to school.

Finally my sister showed up and I was able to escape back to the loggin' job.

TOUR OF MARBLE
Along about 1924 Oscar Brown and I was on Emerald Cr. yarding logs into a basin and from there a donkey took the logs down a little draw. This was for the Wintons.

The donkey crew had blew up and brought our work to a halt.

Oscar said, "Let's take a little trip."

So we went up to Clarkia and took the trail that went over into the Marble. At the top of the ridge you looked down into Marble Cr. and all you could see was a big solid green of timber. Look at it now! It doesn't look like that anymore.

We went down to Camp 3 just above the mouth of Bussel Cr. I had worked for Everett & Kelso on Cranberry Cr. just above there, back in the days when you packed your own bedding. I was swamping (**using an axe to clear a trail for a team and trimming limbs off the logs. ED.**) In those days the teamster just drove the horses. Had what they called a chainer who put the chain on the log and handled the riggin'.

I said to Oscar, "Let's see what's happened to old Cranberry Cr."

Here was a gully, 10 or 12 feet deep. Everett & Kelso had built a big dam up toward the head of the creek and was sluicing logs down. Later that same year I heard about the several million foot jam that hung up there at the mouth of Cranberry Cr. on the main Marble because of the big boulders that washed down Cranberry Cr.

FREE MEALS AND BED
Oscar and I visited every camp on our way up Marble. Those days you always ate free if you came in at mealtime and if it was evening the cook showed you to a bunk. The last camp we went to — Steve Cooligan was runnin' it. Way up to the head of Marble. But the interesting thing, we could have had a job at every one of these camps.

Then we drifted back down Marble Cr. taking our time. I don't know how many days we were gone but we never bought a meal and we toured the country. Then we went back to Emerald.

TRADING LOGS FOR GROCERIES
When the Depression came along mixed logs (red fir and tamarack) was sellin' for $10 a thousand (board feet) and yellow pine around $13. Only you couldn't sell any.

So we went to Russell & Pugh at Springston and they said they'd take some logs but we'd have to take it out in trade from the Company store.

We had this land up the Maries River. I had the horses and this other fellow lived up near the Swope place. And then Charlie Boyce was to get his share for towing them to Springston with his launch.

So I got a couple or three more men. It was steep and mostly a hand loggin' chance. I told these fellows we'd put the logs in a brail and take them to Springston and trade them for groceries.

We had a lot of fun. We'd walk up to a tree, "Well! Here's a sack of sugar!"

"Here's a ham! Here's a sack of horse oats! Here's 10 gallons of gas!"

All the guys was jokin' puttin' that in.

THE STOREKEEPER SAYS, "NO!"
So Charley Boyce went off downriver with the logs and all our grocery orders. But the storekeeper wouldn't honor the orders because they didn't have Russell's signature on them.

So I went to Springston and hunted up Walt Russell and had him sign all the orders. When he found out we'd already been turned down once by the storekeeper he turned around and put all the sacks and boxes and cans of groceries on the tugboat Springston and brought them all to St. Maries.

FOOD CACHE IN THE BASEMENT

So down in our basement we had cases of everything. Hams and bacons. Oats for the horses. Cases of canned stuff. Sacks of rice and beans. Only thing we couldn't get — the boys and I spent a couple of hours trying to get a tire on a car we had. The tire we'd got from Russell & Pugh was just a little bit too small. So a tire was the only thing we didn't get.

THE LITTLE, BIG TEAM

I had a little team. They weren't very big but they were big in the collar (hard pullers). Weighed a little better than 1500 apiece. They weren't what you call fast but I always used them. If I knew they needed a block and line to move a heavy log, they got a block and line.

One time up on this skid trail. Steep as the dickens and dusty. Logs run just as much in dust as they would in good old slick. I was goin' down that hill with the trail behind me and the logs started runnin' free in the dust and the tongs unhooked. Those horses knew it. They took off with the rocks a'rollin' behind 'em and the logs a'danglin'.

They didn't lose their heads and run too far ahead. When they reached level ground and the logs stopped, they stopped, too. All I had to do was reach over and grab the tongs and hook on again.

SOME SKINNERS ABUSE HORSES

I've seen a lot of would-be skinners abuse horses. Howlin' Jimmy Jacobson had some of the best horses you ever seen. But I wouldn't trust Jimmy with a horse. He knew how to handle 'em all right but Oh Man! Up on Emerald Cr. he had a team of percherons that he had paid $800 for . He'd bought 'em at the Spokane Fair. Boy! They were as nice and supple a team as you ever seen. But old Jimmy would see a log up on the sidehill. Up he'd go. Get to a windfall, he'd jump 'em over the windfall. Oh, he was rough on horses.

REAL HAPPINESS

The best part of my life was when we bought that place down where Doc Thurston now lives. The kids helped me pay for it. We had four boys and three girls. John was my youngest boy but we had a girl that was younger. We lost one boy. All of us worked together milkin' cows, raisin' beef. In the morning the kids helped me milk and do chores without being asked. At night if they played basketball, I did their chores. But if I was away on a job the chores got done probably better than if I had been there.

Kids would come out from town to visit. My kids had horses to ride. Cultivatin' and stuff was fun for town kids and they loved to help.

There was only one day I never expected the kids to work and that was on Sunday. That was their day.

I give my kids pigs and calves. Just one time I ran into a little problem. I was over in Ephrata running patrol for building that air-base. It was one of those summers when it rained a little at night, just enough to keep the weeds growin'. I come home and the garden was full of weeds.

The wife said the kids wouldn't go out there to pull weeds because the ground was slimy as the dickens.

I said to the kids, "You pull weeds for the pigs and I'll give you a pig apiece."

From then on, they loaded a washtub on a wagon and Boy! Did they pull weeds and keep those pigs filled up with weeds!

When I took the pigs to Spokane I paid the kids what their pigs sold for, right to the penny. They turned around and bought their clothes for school.

That really was the best part of my life, workin' there with the kids.

St. Joe Pool Hall & Commercial Hotel 1913 about the time Jim Brebner worked at St. Joe. Courtesy — Mrs. Dave Nelson.

Interviewed 10-30-75

Roy Brickle

Fired A Runaway Log Train

Roy Brickle 1975

Rode Flume

I been sittin' in this damn chair for six months. I get out of breath just going' to the bathroom. I've got emphysema and my wife has asthma. I never go no place because I don't like to ride in a car.

I was born in 1895 in Fond du Lac, Wisc. I drove logs in Shola, Pennsylvania and on the Big Moose River in New York and in Wisconsin on the Menominee.

DANCING IN THE CAMPS
Back east in the camps, you stayed all winter. Saturday night, a dance. Men would tie a red whatcha-call-it on their shirt or tie it around their arms and they were the girls and the others were the men. Square dances with fiddles and everything.

SONGS ON THE WISCONSIN DRIVES
Manishee, Michigan, we used to sing all the time, and in Wisconsin — the songs about the Big Spotted Steers and the Little Brown Bulls. The one about the lumberjack that lost his girl in town. The Jam on Jerry's Rock. Oh God! There was a lot of them old ones. They'd sing 'em in the camps and on the drives when they was workin'.

> "They say there's just one river, Jack
>   there's just one river more.
> And that's the River Jordon
>   And she's on the Golden Shore.
> They say there is no rear to sack.
>   The banks are high and dry.
> We'll stand upon her rocky shore and
>   Watch the logs go by."

SONGS CAME TO St. MARIES AND St. JOE

I came out here in 1913 and 60 years ago when the lumberjacks come from Michigan and Wisconsin and lower Canada, (it was the spike-pickers — railroad workers — that come from Missouri) they used to sing 'em in some of the camps and in the saloons in the Maries and St. Joe but they was never as strong for it as they was back East.

THE SINGERS

The Green River Kid used to sing 'em back there and out here, too. He got hit on the head and robbed in Seattle. Killed him. Jimmy Wright used to sing all them songs out here. He had a good voice. He's dead now.

And Smokey La Fan made that song, "They're all gone down but me and I'm left to watch the Camp", 65 years ago and he sang it out here. His last name meant "fountain".

LITTLE JOHNNY B'DORR

Johnny B'Dorr. He couldn't read or write but he could sing. We went to Spokane one time on the 4th of July. Settin' in the restaurant. Hasher fetched him some soup and he was eatin' that soup — hotter'n fire — and the sweat drippin' ' off the end of his nose into the soup.

He says, "Faith an' by Jesus! I think I'm gainin' on 'er!"

If he was drivin' a car, "Whoa! Whoa!" If he wanted to stop, "Whoa! Whoa!" I was in Johnny's car one time, me and Black Paul, Tom Mann, George Jenereau. He ran off the bank on the way to St. Joe. I was sittin' in the back seat and tore the coat right off me.

Johnny used to be here all the time. Went to Klamath Falls and broke his leg. Got back to Spokane some way. They put him in the poor farm and he died there. Little Johnny B'Dorr.

BIG MAUDE

Along about 1910, Bronson that Bronson Meadows was named after, he had a camp up Big Creek and if you wanted to go to work up there you had to go down to the Olympia and get a ticket from Maude. The Olympia Bar was right across the railroad from O'Dwyers — Safeway now. A big slough over there at that time. Big Maude had cribs there — it wasn't a hotel. Bronson was her husband.

Just past where the end of the road is now in Big Creek, is a rock cliff and there used to be a hole dynamited through there so they could take packstrings to the camps. But Man Oh Man! Loggin' that fire blacked timber. Talk about dust. Horses all black. Men and horses choked up.

Jim Roddy lost an eye at Camp 7 up toward Bronson Meadows on the hillside. He had 10-12 men working for him there, moving camp. He had a metal box with some loose blasting caps in it and he didn't want to fool with carrying the caps. Instead of leaving the job to one of the men, he done it himself. That's where he made his mistake. If you're a boss you're not supposed to do that.

He swung his hand back over his shoulder to throw the box away and the jar set them off. The explosion knocked one eye clean out. They took one piece of copper out of the ball of his other eye. After that he could see just a little bit, like looking through a little hole and he could only tell daylight from dark.

Herrick logging train at Big Creek 1911 with log loading jammer.

BIG CREEK TRAIN WRECK

When the train ran away, Jimmy Moses was running engine. I fired for him on Alder Creek later and he told me about it. This was after the 1910 fire and they were logging off every bit of white pine they could save. They took nothing less than a 12 inch top. The track was laid as fast and as cheap as possible and meant to be used only one season. Next year, the flood might come and maybe wipe it all out.

The engine was pushing two carloads of ties and one carload of steel rails ahead of it to build more track. Thirty or more Dagoes and Bohunks(**Italians & Bohemians**)riding on the cars. They were travelling up the creek and went over a high point. When they started down the other side, the track had laid there all winter and got rusty. Grass growed over the rails made it greasy.

Jimmy Moses set the brakes but the train started sliding. He locked the locomotive wheels with the steam jam. The wheels started spittin' sparks, and that means she's sliding and it don't take no time till she's gone.

Jimmy Moses was giving the danger, "Toot! Toot! Toot!"

Johnny Lee was brakeman and he yelled at the men to jump off but they were scared and hung right to her. Then Johnny jumped overboard. He got scratched up but that's all.

Moses tooted as long as he could then he jumped off. He only got scratched.

The reason the engineer jumps — My God! Everything in there where he's settin' is steam pipes and if the engine dumps over, the pipes will break and scald him to death.

The train slid all the way to the bottom of the hill. Along the way the men on the cars jumped off and a bunch of 'em got killed and hurt. The cars jumped the track but the engine stayed on.

John Dennis says Bill Trezette told him that the cars did not jump the track and he rode the train through till it stopped on the flat.

It spilled the ties and the rails off. They never moved that stuff out of there. I think it's there yet. It was on the left branch where Robinson's cabin was. The railroad went over the hill to Camp 8 to get timber out of a basin.

KILLED IN WRECK OF LOG TRAIN WHEN TRAIN GOT AWAY FROM ENGINEER
Carlo Jusick, 35, Italian, Relatives, none, Effects-none.
Tony Gerboy, 30, Slavonian,Relatives-none, Effects-none.
T. H. Tripas, 32, Slavonian, Relatives-none, Effects-none.
S. Petroff, 32, Slavonian, Relatives-none, Effects-none.
R. Carrillo, 37, Italian, Relatives-none, Effects-none.

St. Maries Gazette Oct. 6, 1911 — The wrecking of a log train at Big Cr. last Sunday caused the death of 5 men and the wounding of a number of others. The men killed were riding on flat cars, to which they stuck after being notified by the brakeman to get off. The accident was the result of the train getting beyond control of the crew in charge. When the smash came through the cars jumping the track, the mix up was something awful. And it is a wonder that any of the men escaped with their lives. Dr. Platt of this city was carried to the scene by special train to attend the wounded men. All the men killed were foreigners and unknown in this section of the country.

BIG FLOOD OF 1913
A big flood in the winter and spring of 1913 washed out the railroad and that's when Herrick quit there and went up Marble Creek instead. Otherwise they might have logged there another year or so.

The Benton boys used to make whiskey up there for 10 years, anyhow, at the mouth of Cabin Creek. Near their cabin was a big jam with ties and rails in it where the flood piled up remains of the old railroad. Some junk outfit went in there and took the rails out.

ST. MARIES FUNERAL
When old Dillman died — he was head of the woods work up at Emerald Creek — they took him to the cemetery in St. Maries in a horse drawn hearse — no cars then — and people following in horse

and buggies. They started to go up the hill there and the hearse door opened up and old Dillman slid out into the middle of the road. Stopped the whole works. They had to load him back in.

Gene Shaney run camp for Dillman for years at Emerald Creek. Old Dillman left him a house, the old Idaho poolhall across from the O'Gara restaurant and about $40,000.

Shaney couldn't even write his own name. He got drunk and went to Spokane and he'd tear a check out of the book and say, "Make out a check for $10."

They'd make it out for $100 and he'd mark his X on it. Boy! They took him. Two of the girls got most of it. They run a hotel in Spokane.

The girls knew he was a good logger and afterwards they staked him to a team of horses and put him on his feet on a job in Canada. Then they followed him up there. They own the whole damned town up there now.

MARIES RIVER DRIVES
The drives in the Maries River near Clarkia (everybody pronounced it "Clarky") didn't amount to much. The early drives maybe beginning around 1908 was from Emerald Creek down and mostly before 1913 when I came. There was a Dam 6 up by Emerald for splashing the logs. In one of those drives a boat full of rivermen hit a sheer rock and capsized just above the loops. They lost 2 or 3 men drowned. But Doobie and St. Peter both came through there lots of times. Both small men.

McGoldrick took the last big drive down the Maries River and had a big jam at Lotus around 1923.

CLARKY
I run the Idaho Hotel in Clarky 1924. The Gynors run Shorty Wade's place after he died about 1930. Clarky was good during the drives on the Marble and after the end of that in about 1928 it was never no good. You'd pass up that son of a bitchin' town and go to Fernwood.

FERNWOOD WIDE OPEN
Fernwood was the best town in Idaho. If you wanted to drink, you could drink and if you wanted a game of cards with a 5 dollar stack or a hundred dollar stack, there was always somebody would match you. Plenty of women, too.

THE BIG SPENDERS
I helped lots of them guys spend their homesteads. Gold Tooth Griffith he come down to Santa with $10,000 from sellin' his homestead. He was rich. Here come from Spokane, Gold Tooth's wife and daughter. Never knew he was married or anything — nobody knew it. She left him 50 bucks and took off and was never seen afterwards.

And the blacksmith, that old Jack Mc Caffery. He got $10,000 or better. The biggest and nicest homestead on Emerald Creek. He come down to Santa and bought the joint and the woman that owned it. Ordered barrels of beer.

He said, "Drink all you want. The women too. All free."

He went through it in a month and a half.

NORTH FORK OF THE C D'A AND SKIDOO JOHNNY
Dollar went from the Marble up the North Fork of the Coeur d'Alene in 1916. I worked for Skidoo Johnny at Camp 7 above Pritchard about 8 miles. It was about a mile up the draw behind the Mink Ranch on the right side of the river. Nothin' but a trail up there. Along come Kennedy with a big mule. He had two bales of hay and two sacks of oats on one side and a big camp range on the other. He was packing it into Camp 7. Mulligan Hank was the cook. Most all the cooks I knew had nicknames: Pork Chop Whitey, T-Bone Slim and Wisconsin-Jim McKisick.

Skidoo Johnny was gypoin' for Dollar. Slim guy. Crazy! Nuts to get logs. He wasn't educated.

ROLLWAYS BUSTED LOOSE
They skidded logs into big rollways at the top of the hill. Gonna send 'em down the log chute. The way they blocked them rollways, stuck logs endways into holes in the ground in front. The ground got soft in the spring and the logs tipped over and the whole thing come down. A million feet scattered all over hell. Had to be skidded to the bottom of the hill and into the river.

DRIVE DOWN THE NORTH FORK OF THE C D'A
First time I ever got over $2.50 a day was on the log drive that spring. Paid $12 to $14. Long hours. Dollar had Camp 8 up Big Creek above the Blue Slide. The logs from Camp 7 and Camp 8 come together. Hell of a big drive.

Tommy Holland and Billy Pearson was there. Old Chief and Little Chief, too. Lots of Indians come out from Michigan and Wisconsin with lumbermen like Herrick. Lots of tribes back there on the St. Croix River. Chippeway, Flambeau. Indians mostly like water work — log drives. Wouldn't saw or drive team.

To start with in the morning. Had to jump into that cold water clear to your chest and wade across. Workin' on the other side of the North Fork. When the bull cook brought the grub down the trail at noon — had to wade back. Eat. Wade back in that cold water, maybe hang onto the horse's hames in the deep places. At night, wade back again and walk up the trail to camp.

Further downriver had a wannigan.

He said, "Put your packsacks in here. Keep 'em dry."

Down by Enaville the God damn wannigan hit a sweeper (a tree tipped down over the water) and turned over. Lost everything in the river. Packsacks, stove, grub — everything. But nobody drowned.

ROLLED BARRELS ACROSS THE RIVER
In the 1920s I built chute for Roddy & Schwab on the south side of the St. Joe River across from Zane. Zane was a siding about a mile and a half above the steel railroad bridge above Falls Creek. We used to get gasoline in barrels at Zane and roll the barrels into the St. Joe River and roll them across by hand to the Roddy & Schwab landing. We had a lot of trail chute up on top but where it came down to the river one chute was so fast we had to use a lot of goosenecks to slow down the logs and even so, it broke up all kinds of timber.

CHUTE BUILDER LOSES DIAMOND
I think Louie Coty built chute in that draw behind Walt Scott's place above St. Joe. The two Gynors were chute builders and worked with him. Gynor is a French name and is pronounced "Gon-yore". I know Oiva Gynor had a diamond ring, a big one, and it slid off his finger when he took off his gloves and he lost it somewhere up there when he was building chute. He never did find that ring. It was worth a lot of money. I think all them guys was about the same age — Chute Smith, Sloughfoot Murphy and Frenchman Louie Coty.

George Yenner built chute, too. I worked with Yenner above St. Joe and on the Maries branch. He built chute on Hugus and Mica.

DE BRAY'S CROSSING
At the mouth of Hugus Creek, Ed and Bill De Bray had a cable and basket for crossing the river. They lived on a piece of ground on the Hugus side owned by McGoldrick. The travel upriver was by train and the people had to have crossings to get to their land and jobs on the south side of the river.

PETE HAD AN AWFUL TEMPER
First time I knew Pete Madison he was flunkeyin' on a drive in Wisconsin and I was drivin'. Then they took 59 of us guys to Pennsylvania for two years. Then I come out here and ran into Pete in a Roddy & Schwab camp at Alder Creek. Pete got a brother but GOD! Them two guys never would meet without a fight.

Pete had an awful temper. One time he set a plate on top of the coffee pot and the flunkey said something to him.

Pete jumped up and went to the door and put on his hat. He always put on his hat when he got mad. He invited the flunkey outside and when the flunkey come out he nailed him.

Roddy parted 'em. Then he canned the flunkey.

FIRING ENGINE ON ALDER CREEK
I was firin' engine for Jimmy Moses at the Alder Creek Camp. Big

timber. Everything came out by rail to St. Maries. On Skunk Creek, a little branch of Alder, one day the engine was puffin' along and all of a sudden it started rocking back and forth and the thing just tipped over. We crawled out of it. Nobody got hurt. But while she had her feet in the air, Jimmy Moses examined the wheels and he see the tires was wore thin.

NEW SHOES FOR THE LOCOMOTIVE
Jack Vinsky had been a blacksmith for years so the boss told him to get new ones.

So Jack didn't ask nobody. And we didn't know he had no experience with tires for the Shay locomotives. He heated them up and shrunk 'em on. Took 3 or 4 days.

Jimmy Moses and me steamed her up. Jimmy throwed on the power. ZZZZZZZ! She never moved. ZZZZZZ! Never moved a bit. Stood there with the wheels turning but goin' nowhere.

"My God!" Jimmy says. "Jack Vinsky! You put case-hardened tires on this locomotive."

Jack says, "Sure! What's wrong with that?"

"You can see what's wrong," Jimmy says. "You got to have soft steel tires or they can't get a'hold of the hard rail."

So Jack Vinsky had to take 'em all off. Load 'em on a speeder car. Take 'em down to the junction. Load 'em in a car there and send 'em to Seattle.

Got another set of tires, soft ones, and put 'em on.

Then the first thing we done. Too big a load of cars coming down the hill from Camp 2. Almost got away so we slid the engine and wore the soft tires flat. Had to replace 'em again.

OVERLAND DUTCH
Overland Dutch cooked for Roddy & Schwab and for Ankor. He wouldn't be in camp a week till he had moonshine mash working behind the stove. He worked on the Marble and was a wonderful cook. Everything on the table in the way of cookies and rolls, cakes and pies. Later I saw him selling Sal Hepatica on the street in Seattle. They called him Overland because when he got ready to travel south he put on a yellow raincoat and started out. Took nothin' else. Just climbed a freight and away he went.

RIDING BENEWAH FLUME
It was always fun to ride the Benewah flume when you was headed for town. Saturday night we'd get in Tyler's pond where Tyler's homestead was and the pond is there yet, and ride 3 miles. The first time I did it, son of a bitch! I didn't know you could ride into the pond at the dam.

We was going fast. 15 miles an hour or better.

About 300 feet above the dam, Bill Lindquist says, "Jump! Jump!"

He jumped but he knew where to land.

I jumped over the side of the flume and hit on the sidehill. My feet almost went right through the bottoms of my shoes and I went rolling and got all skinned up.

Flume riding you don't want to carry a stick or anything with you because if you get off balance you'll touch the stick to the side of the flume and it'll spin you right around. When your log hits the pond it makes a wave and that checks your log but still your log will get out of the way of the next log coming from behind. From the road you can still see the old dam 2 ½ miles below.

RUN AWAY TRAIN
I was on Beaver Creek below Santa firin' when a loaded train ran away. It was night and goin' down that 2 mile grade, the sparks started spittin' out the engine wheels.

Pinky Brady, the engineer, steam jammed her and locked the locomotive wheels. This was before air brakes come out. With that damn Shay engine, once you steam jammed it you couldn't cut it loose.

The cars banged, rattledy banged, swaying. Dark! You couldn't see anything. All you could do was shut your eyes and jump. I don't know whether Pinky jumped ahead of me or after. As he jumped, a log rolled off one of the cars and killed him.

But the engine stopped the train down on the level and not a car left the track. If he'd stayed he'd have been all right.

Same thing happened on the railroad on Sheep Creek. It's a mile and a half above Santa. Blackwell train ran away. Where the engine and tender come together there's a metal apron. The engineer Jim Wilcox got his foot caught there and got hurt.

DRAY HAUL AT SANTA
1922 and '23 was about the last of the winter dray hauls. Roddy was sleigh and dray hauling stuff to a railroad landing a mile above Santa and loading it on cars for Herrick's St. Maries mill.

Dray hauling, you didn't want to have it too God damn steep or you'd have to rough lock 'em — throw a chain around the runners to hold 'em back. Drays had only one set of runners and one bunk — 7 or 8 feet wide.

They rolled the first layer of logs on, then threw a loose wrapper chain around it and fantailed the ass end out on the ground with their peaveys. Then they'd roll a coupla logs on to keep the wrapper tight and roll on two more tiers.

Some of the farmers used a stiff A frame dray and took only 3 or 4 logs. But the regular dray had a swinging bunk and the outside logs set out good and held on by corner bind chains and a good load 3 tiers high.

You can't set the logs too far ahead or the logs won't spread out behind. You can't lay the whole tail end on the ground or your horses can't start it. The more level the ground the further ahead you set your logs to let the dray runners carry the load — the steeper the ground, the further back and spread out.

WEEDLE KILLING
I worked with Frank Strand at Santa. He was sawin' for Roddy and I was skiddin' on the dray haul about the year before he got in trouble over that Weedle girl.

The Weedle homestead was above Renfro's, and Strand's homestead was above Weedle's. Weedle's boy and girl had to come by the camps on the logging railroad down Renfro Creek to go to school at Santa.

The girl was only about 15 years old. Strand was in his early forties. She wasn't stuck on Strand.

Weedle told Strand to stay away from the girl and Strand shot him. The posse surrounded a house where Strand was hiding at Gold Center. Deputy Sheriff King shot him.

FARMER JOBS
I didn't work in Falls Creek or Fitzgerald. Those were farmer jobs. All the locals worked there. Dan and Wally, the Whitcomb brothers built the Falls Creek flume. They built that log house there at Walt Scott's place, too.

O'Neil went broke at Mica Creek. Him and Paddy Keenan went to Canada and went broke up there and come back. Then O'Neil got a job on Bond Creek at St. Joe for Ohio Match and he made her there. Hendrickson was the guy that built the Bond Creek flume for him.

Bert Kizer always had a few horses. Last time I worked with Bert was when he was skiddin' for O'Neil at Bond Creek.

Gazette-Record, Jan. 1, 1931 — Ohio Match has shut its camps at Bond Creek down for the winter. Next summer it plans another 3½ miles of flume and another set of camps.

ARGUMENT OVER RELIGION
Garveson Creek, a branch of Bond Cr. heads on Pettis Peak. They just happened to name the creek after Garveson. Garveson was walking boss for Ohio Match under Bailey. Old Garveson used to go

into his shack in Camp 3, which was 6 miles up from the St. Joe River, and read his bible.

Ohio Match Bond Creek Camp 3. 1933.

Old Quigley and Garveson had been friends for years back East in Wisconsin when Quigley blacksmithed for Garveson. Quigley stayed at what they called the Quigley Feeder Dam 2 miles below Camp 3 and he used to have to hobble up to Camp 3 to get his chuck on Sunday. He'd visit Garveson and get into a hell of an argument over religion.

Out in the yard of the camp, Quigley got mad at Garveson and he says, "Oh! Go on back in and read your bible."

Garveson says, "That would do you good, too."

Noel Farrell and Dave Nichols heading up the Bond Cr. flume 1934.

Quigley was all doubled up with rheumatism. "Oh!" he says, "I'm too god damned old to brown nose now!"

RIDING BOND CR. FLUME
Camp 6 was just above Camp 3. I'd phone Quigley at his feeder dam 2 miles down and tell him to turn his water into the flume. I'd turn my water on and wait maybe 10 minutes before I'd start to roll the logs in. When a log dropped into the flume a big fantail went up as the water hit it. The flume was only 48 inches across the top here but at the lower end it was 6 feet wide.

The flume made a quicker way home on Saturday nights. 4 miles in 8 minutes. Lee Carpenter and I put our stuff in

our packsacks and put 'em on. There was a running board at the top of the flume and you run 3 or 4 steps and jump on the log as she goes or it would take your feet right out from under you. Flip you.

Before you got down that hill you was travelling with a lot of speed.

It was so steep along by Camp 1, the logs would outrun the water. Camp 1 was about a mile and a quarter from the Joe river. Below it the flume levelled off. We'd jump off when we came to the road bridge and walk in to St. Joe. One time Lee's little dog fell in the flume and he went all the way down the flume and dumped into the St. Joe River and swam out to the bank and came back to camp.

Lee Carpenter 1951

The flume jammed and piled logs against Camp 1 cookhouse at Bond Creek 1935.

Roy Brickle standing in a jammed Bond Creek flume 1933.

DOUGHNUTS ON A STICK

RUTH — I used to walk up the footboard of the flume past the cookhouse of Camp 1. The cook, Speed Bannister, would reach out the window with a long stick he used to take doughnuts out of the deep fryer and hand us some.

Gazette-Record April 28, 1932 — The Ohio Match flume at Bond Creek was damaged in places by dynamite thought to have been dropped in with lighted fuse and floated down till it went off. Some dissatisfaction has been expressed because local people were not put to work when Ohio opened for the season. The flume was repaired with a much larger crew including some residents of St. Joe.

JAKE POAGE

The way Jake Poage lost his leg was at Camp 6 at Emerald Creek and they was on the hill and they had these 3 cars and the engine and the jammer on and the engine couldn't hold 'em and they started goin' down the hill. So Jake jumped off with the cable from the jammer and fastened the tongs on a big windfall. He couldn't get out of the way quick enough and the cable came tight and jerked the windfall against a stump with Jake's leg caught between. But he held the train. Ira Horne was brakeman there and this was before Boyce worked on Emerald in '24.

Charley White had the biggest ranch on Emerald one time. He was a top cook with the reflectors for the Forest Service. He could turn out the finest biscuit and pie and cakes out in the woods or along the trail.

Bill Roddy's wife taught school in Emerald in 1908. She was Viola Martin — mother of Don and Ron Martin.

Jake Pogue and me was in a joint together in St. Joe. Kickbush had a Table Supply up the street a half block but he rented us the old store building for a bootlegging joint.

I ran a regular store in St. Joe 20 years from 1945 to 1965.

Kickbush store at St. Joe with hand crank gas pump 1928. Charley Ross, Glenn Dittman, Marie Pray (later McWhorter), Mrs. Emma Kickbush, August Kickbush, dog, unknown kids and Ed Mottern.

BURNING THE RIVER

Neff and his curly haired boy worked on the log drives and lived at Calder. John Neff told me one time he was out in the middle of the river on a gravel bar with water all around him building a little fire to fry some trout.

A young fellow from the Coeur d'Alene Fire Protective Association came along and he hollered out at him from shore, "Mr. Neff! It's fire season. You can't build a fire there."

Neff looked up and says, "I been 40 years on this river and by Jesus! I never set 'er a'fire yet."

Jimmy "the Whiskers" Whitaker hung around our joint. He was a pretty good guy to know. He'd go all the way up to Camp 3 on Bond Creek and steal hams and bacons. Anything! Say! He'd steal a carload of sugar a grain at a time.

THE LIVE ONE
Clint Belmont, tug boatman from Coeur d'Alene said he was drinkin' at Nellie's floathouse. Headed for shore on the floating walk.

Nellie and Josie didn't want him to get away. Depression times. 1930. He still had money on him. One on each side helpin' him walk — pushed him in the river.

They pulled him out of the river. Then they got him back in the house buyin' drinks. Stuck his pants in the oven to dry. They all got drunk and the pants burnt up.

Jimmy "The Whiskers" Whitaker and Dave Nichols, packer at St. Joe 1933.

Early in the morning Clint was in that alley behind where the First Security Bank is.

"Hey!" he says, trying to flag somebody to bring him a pair of pants.

LOUIE USED A HOOK
Louie Catoure that lived down in a floathouse was French-Canadian out of Wisconsin. Lost one hand. Had a steel hook instead. He didn't gamble but when he got drunk he got mean. Cops was afraid of him. The leather stub he screwed the hook into was heavy like a club. Let you have it over the head. But the hook was the worst. He'd tear your clothes off.

When the cops got him down, first thing they did, they unscrewed that hook.

SANTA BEDROOM
In the second floor of the Hendershot Hotel in Santa they had a small room over the kitchen where Mrs. Hendershot and the kids slept. The rest of the upstairs was one big room for the guests. In those days everybody carried blankets. Hendershots had spread out three or four bales of hay on the floor and you paid four bits (50 cents) a night to unroll your blankets there.

THE BEAR AT CAT'S SPUR

Cat's Spur was named after a homesteader named Katz. This Ed Kleinard got tackled by a bear and Shorty Wade, his partner swung his peavy like a club and hit it with the steel end. Killed it.

The two of 'em run a saloon at Clarky. This Ed Kleinard was a fightin' son of a bitch. No matter how big they was he tied into 'em. His feet was the worst. He was liable to hit you any place with his feet — alongside the head or in the guts. I seen some God damned big men that hadn't learned that. He was an old man but he still didn't back up from any of 'em.

ONE ARMED TOM HAY

I think one armed Tom Hay come up from Oregon. Logged some. Wherever there was a game, he gambled. Played at Dutch Jake's in Spokane. Dutch was good, too, but Tom Hay won everything in the place and the joint and Dutch Jake's woman along with it. She was the belle of the house. Hay married her. Come up to St. Maries.

Along about 1914 there was lots of poker in uptown St. Maries. Jake Poage was dealin' cards in the White Pine saloon where the Economy is now.

About 1915 Tom Hay reached in and stole a pot at Billy Sparrow's joint. That's where Florence Gaskill's cafe — Pat & Scott's is now. Guy named Freeman had a cigar makin' place next door.

Big Jack Gillis, he was in the poker game and his brother Curly Jack. French Canadians. Them French Canadians come across the Great Lakes and into Wisconsin. Went up them rivers to a good trappin' spot, got a Menominee or Chippeway woman and trapped. Worked in the woods. The ones out of Canada was part Shano Indian. Some of 'em come out to Idaho.

It was Big Jack Gillis that see one armed Tom Hay steal the pot. Big Jack was alongside that state coyote trapper, Barnhart. Barnhart had a hatchet slung in his belt.

Big Jack grabs the hatchet.

He says, "You do that again, you one winged son of a bitch and I'll cut your other arm off!"

Later, a red headed fella from California come bummin' around. I don't think he could even gamble. Good lookin'. Younger. Old lady Hay run off with him.

Ruth Brickle

"Why don't you buy a bossy?"

I was born in Michigan in 1907 and my folks moved out to St. Joe when I was 2. My dad, Dan Bottrell hauled mail and freight from the depot and from St. Joe over to the Ferrell post office and down to the Kroll sawmill.

Ruth Nichols Brickle 1975

SCHOOL AT FERRELL AND ST. JOE

Right next to the old Ferrell post office on the docks about 1912, there was an undertaking place. It had gone out of business and they had left a bunch of coffins in the back end. Us kids used to scare ourselves by going back there where it was kinda dark among those coffins.

I went to school in Ferrell quite a few years, then they made the kids go over to St. Joe. Russell Merriman had the post office in 1929 and I went to school with his two boys. Jim died of lung cancer and Lloyd, the other one, was having some kind of an argument with the woman that ran the tavern. She poked a shotgun across the bar and threatened to shoot him. He pulled the muzzle up against his middle and said, "You wouldn't dare."

And she pulled the trigger. I don't think she had all her wits about her.

Bert Kizer used to sing those old lumberjack songs from Michigan and Wisconsin to us kids. He didn't play an instrument at the same time. He just sang.

SCOTT PEDDLED MILK

Frank Scott, the old man, had a little one horse wagon, kinda boxed in and he had the milk in 5 or 10 gallon cans. Along in 1918 and '19 I can remember Mother giving us our kettle for milk and we'd go out and catch him and he'd measure out with a quart measure. He delivered milk for years like that around St. Joe. At that time his house was over on the river bank down closer to Ferrell than where the Walt Scott house is today. It burned down.

LOVER OF HORSES
Noel Farrell was crazy about good horses. If he saw one he liked he couldn't rest till he owned it. One time a man brought a trained Tennessee Walker into the country. He put a price of $300 on it when good horses sold for $50. It wasn't long till Noel had it in his corral.

ONE ARMED POOL PLAYER
Duke Harris was one armed. They say he used to gamble down at Glidden's place in the Maries and he was up around St. Joe when the saloons and everything were there. Funny part of it, he was a good pool player with that one arm and he belonged to the St. Joe baseball team.

Roy: He was a damn crooked gambler.

Ruth: He was crooked in other ways, too. He'd sell you anything. He collected 50 bucks from me for a down payment on a building alongside the St. Joe store that we were gonna buy. He didn't even own it.

I didn't know it till the old postmaster, Merriman, that lived right across from the building came over and asked me to pay the rent.

THE OLD HOUSE
That old house of Mrs. Mahl set there in St. Joe for years after she moved away. The whole town went in and out of it.

We used to say, "Do you think the floor will fall in?"

Then one day a car drove up to the store. This young woman got out. She went into the store and asked Roy where Mrs. Mahl used to live.

Roy come outside and pointed next door. "Right there."

There was a man and a coupla kids in the car. She got the man and a hammer out of the car and the two of them went under the house. The old lady Mahl must have told her right where to go. They took a box out from between the floor joists, come back out and got in the car and went out of St. Joe.

Nobody ever did know what was in that box.

JIMMY "THE WHISKERS" WHINGDING
The old bugger would drink a little all the time but Boy! When Jimmy "The Whiskers" Whitaker went on a drunk, he went on a drunk!

One time up there in St. Joe, he started out on a toot and I don't know how much money he had stashed away in those big old bills — before the government made all our bills so much smaller. He kept bringing them out — I don't know if he spent it all but I never saw any big bills from him again.

LUMBERJACKS CHANGED NAMES

One thing I remember about lumberjacks. They often changed their first and last names completely. One lumberjack, Homer Clark, who died in the St. Maries hospital, nobody knew his right name till he died: Frank Waters.

He'd worked in Roddy's camp. Roddy said, "Who the hell is that? I never heard of no Frank Waters."

CUT HIS THROAT

And when some of 'em got to drinking you never knew what they'd do. Tom Yote cut his throat late one night out in the middle of the road but he didn't do a good job of it. At St. Joe. He laid on the porch of the cafe and beer hall that Red Hult was running, next to the bank building and hollered all night out there. If I'd known what it was I'd have been scared to death.

In the morning he still hadn't bled to death. They took him to the doctor and had him sewed up and he lived.

SPERRY GARDEN

Old man Sperry worked his hillside garden with a great big hoe 2 feet wide. Everything he done was done by hand. It was too steep for anything else.

SPERRY GARDEN AT ST. JOE 1937
2½ acres of sub-irrigated hillside, its berries and fruit were featured on the finest Milwaukee dining cars. Dirt steps ran up the center with grapes on each side. Right and left front — black-caps with strawberries behind. Pear trees upper left.
Photo by Leo's Studio. Courtesy — Ann Rocco.

He liked little kids. He used to carry hard candy with no wrapper in his dirty pocket.

My mother used to tell us, "Now you kids take the candy and thank Mr. Sperry but take it and wash it before you put it in your mouth."

When I was a kid we used to go up to his house. He had no floor — just dirt. The place looked like a packrat's nest. We didn't stick around very long.

About once a year he'd come out in clean clothes, then he'd wear those till about the next spring.

He used to pack his berries over to the train and to St. Joe in 5 gallon cans.

ROY — You know what made him come West and be a hermit? He shot his wife. He was going out hunting with a shotgun and she hollered at him out the window. So, just for the hell of it, he turned around and shot at her. He thought the shotgun wouldn't shoot that far but the shot hit her and killed her. He didn't tell me this but somebody else told me about it.

RUTH — He was such a good hearted old man. If you gave him whole wheat bread or huckleberries, he'd give you everything in the place. And he'd work till he was tired and then go to sleep up there at the top between 2 trees so he wouldn't accidently roll down the hill.

Sometimes a big squash would leave his garden and roll down into the road and bust. You could take it home. Nothing the matter with it.

I think that poor old Sperry meant to step in front of that train.

ROY — No! He was walking from St. Joe down across the slough and when he stepped right on that track, he didn't hear the train. He couldn't hear a thing.

RUTH — Well! They were going to put him on welfare. And he didn't go for that very strong.

TOM HAY
When Tom Hay was old he got an infection in his foot. My sister, May, was going by that house he built up on Third in St. Maries. He hollered for her to come in and help him. He had to change the bandages and he couldn't do it with one hand.

She went in every day for awhile and fixed it for him.

I think that's probably what killed him. Maybe gangrene set in.

MOOCHING GRUB
Paddy Hart celebrated too long in St. Maries — went broke. He went up to the door of a house and asked the woman for something to eat.

While she was gone making up a sandwich, her little 5 year old girl came to the door and she says to Paddy, "Do you like milk?"

Paddy says, "You bet I do!"

She said, "Why don't you buy a bossy?"

Paddy said, "Listen, little girl! I couldn't even buy the ding for the cow bell."

FLOATHOUSE JOSIE

Roy: Floathouse Josie and a sister come originally from Germany to Butte, Montana. Hell of a good lookin' sister and bigger than Jo was. The sister and a husband came one time for a visit. Her and the husband played Hawaiian music in classy places in the east. The sister was not in the business.

Jo came to St. Maries in 1921. She had married Cody who used to tend bar in Durkins place in Spokane. She didn't marry Dick Gaskill till '26 or '27.

FLOATHOUSE NELL

Ruth: We used to see Nellie walking down the highway with her little packsack either going out prospecting or coming in. We'd pick her up and give her a ride.

Nellie liked to go into the restaurant and order a little bowl of soup. My sister, May, was in the restaurant when some school girls were sitting close watching Nell and giggling and whispering to one another.

Finally one of them got courage enough to turn around and say, "How's business, Nell?"

Nell stopped and then went on eating. Finally she finished the soup and turned toward them and said, "Business was pretty good before you chippies got to running around town!"

That shut 'em up.

CHEATED OUT OF BIRTHDAYS

I was born on the 1st of Jan., 1907. New Years Day. So I never got to celebrate my birthday. My brother, George was born on Christmas day. He hid in a haystack when he was a kid because it all came together and he never had a birthday. And my sister, May was born on the 19th of March. If she'd been born 2 days earlier she'd have been born on St. Patricks Day.

Interviewed 4-15-75 at St. Maries, Idaho

That mule throwed me so fast and so high!

Marble Creek Jerry

Flunkey

Jerry Broderick 1979 at 77.

My father was Lute Conroy, a hardrock miner who worked everywhere from Nova Scotia to all over the United States. Before I was born, Dad was in this mine shaft and there was a bunch of men goin' down, maybe 5 or 6, and the cable broke and they were all killed except him. There was a fire, too, and the rescuers got Dad out but from the smoke, miner's TB settled in.

Dad and Mother moved out to Ritzville, Washington looking for a homestead. There was a big rancher with a thousand acres. In the middle of that thousand acre ranch was a vacant 160 acres that nobody had ever filed on. Dad got wind of it somehow.

When Dad come through the field with a one horse wagon the rancher run out and yelled at him, "What are you doin' on my place?"

Dad pulled out his paper from the land office. "I filed homestead on this hundred and sixty."

It just happened that the creek run right straight through this 160 and that was the rancher's water supply for his cattle.

The rancher looked at the paper.

He said, "Let's go over to the house and talk about it."

So the rancher helped Dad build a little house and hired him and my mother to work for him.

I was born on that homestead July 5, 1902 out from Ritzville.

Dad was a sick man during the time he was on the homestead. He died in 1905.

Mother sold the homestead to the big rancher but the money was soon spent and she had to go out practical nursing. In those days people didn't have hospitals to go to. There was no such thing as a registered nurse. Doctors came to the homes to see people and if anyone needed nursing they got a practical nurse that lived in with the family. The nurse didn't get much more than her board.

Us kids had to stay with anybody what would have us. My Uncle Joe Butler took my 2 brothers. Grandma and Grandpa Taylor weren't really my grandma and grandpa but they were related some way through marriage and took me to live with them in Spokane.

When I was six I went to school out by Minnehaha and got all the kid's diseases one after another: German measles, red measles, mumps, whooping cough, chicken pox... Then when I was pert near seven I went to school at Hawthorne, right across from where the Deaconess Hospital is now.

Then my mother took up a homestead at Lamona, Washington about 10 miles from Odessa on the Great Northern Railroad. She took me down there to live with her. Lamona was a post office, a butcher shop, a drygoods store and what-not, all under one roof.

I was in the 7th grade when I had to quit school and go to work in ranch kitchens. I'd get 50 cents a day and my board. When I got big enough I worked as a dishwasher in Spokane. My first job waiting table, I got a dollar and a quarter a day.

Then between World War 1 and World War 2 I worked in Dempsey's restaurant for $1.50 a day. That was on Front Street which was a short street till it later turned into Trent — now it's Spokane Falls Boulevard. Also I worked at Soper's Tavern in Spokane and that's where quite a bunch of Wobblies hung out. That was the only union that helped the wages as a whole at that time. They fought for the bindlestiff. (**Bindlestiff was a tramp worker who carried his blankets and belongings on his back.**)

In the spring of 1923 I had signed up to work on a ranch at $30 a month. So the night before, I was out celebrating and slept in late the next morning. My train didn't leave till noon.

Ruby Thornburg come up to my room and woke me up. She was part Indian and bootlegged later.

She says, "What's a flunkey?"

I had to think that over.

She says, "The woman at the employment office said they got jobs for flunkeys."

I said, "Did you ask her?"

Ruby says, "It's got something to do with serving food family style. What the hell is family style? It pays $60 a month."

That was double the pay I'd get on my ranch job. I jumped out of bed and up we go to the employment office.

So we said, "What's a flunkey?"

"It's a camp in the woods with long tables. You wait tables."

So Ruby paid a dollar and a half to the agency for the job and I went out and borrowed $5 from my stepfather and away we went.

When we got to St. Maries they said our train couldn't go up the branch line because the logging train coming down was off the track and we couldn't get by. So there we sat.

I said, "I'm getting hungry. Let's go eat."

Ruby said, "I only got 55 cents left and I still got to buy fare from St. Maries to Clarky."

I says, "Don't worry about that. I borrowed $5."

It was eleven o'clock at night when we got on the passenger coach of the empty logging train and started. When I got off there at Clarky at midnight — now I'm not exactly a coward — I'm not afraid of horses or cattle but when I saw a hundred whiskery guys leaning against the station with those old tin pants — legs chopped off short — If somebody had said BOO! we'd have jumped back on the train.

Tin pants were of tightly woven tan canvas and worn outside other pants to protect them from the wet. Sometimes river drivers coated them to the knees with paraffin. Even without the paraffin they were almost as stiff as stovepipe. Loggers chopped them off just below the knees to cut friction on the kneecaps and to make it easier to step upward from creek bottom onto logs. Worn with a jacket of the same material a lumberjack could stay dry in casual rains. They did not sweat a man as would airtight rubber wear but they were noisy both from the zip zip of the legs rubbing together and the swishing as they plowed through the undergrowth.

About that time one of these whiskery ones put a hand on my shoulder. "You girls want to go over to the ranch to work?"

"Ranch?" I says.

"Rutledge Ranch!" he says. "It's the headquarters for the camps and the log trains."

I said, "We're goin' to flunkey — wherever that is."

He said, "Just follow me and you'll get there. But don't talk to me. I've got an awful hangover."

We left our suitcases in the station and single filed after him down the railroad track. Pretty soon it was a trestle and us walkin' on ties in the midnight pitch dark. We couldn't see where to put our feet and had to trust to God the next tie would be there. Pretty soon you could make out white down below us and the water was roaring underneath. If I had saw what I was gonna walk over I'd have backed out but now we was too far to turn back.

When we got among the big dark buildings of Rutledge Ranch he roused out the bookkeeper — Art somebody — to find us a place to sleep. This Art started leadin' us upstairs somewhere and I wondered what we was gettin' into. It was a bedroom over the cookhouse.

In the morning the gong woke us up. We went down into the cookhouse and ate oatmeal and ham and eggs and toast and pancakes and powerful coffee.

The bookkeeper said, "You climb on one of them empty flatcars and head for camp. I'll send over to the depot for your suitcases and send them after you."

We rode the flatcar through the woods till it stopped at the Halfway Warehouse. A brakeman came along and said, "You can get off now. This is as far as we go."

Shovelling snow to clear the warehouse tracks. 1923.

We stood around in the mud in our low shoes watching Stonebreaker load up his packstring. We was wearin' knickers that was baggy and like pants the golfers now wear.

I said, "Where we goin' from here?"

He said, "Camp is 6 hours away over that ridge."

I could see us sloppin' along in the mud for miles after that packstring.

I said, "Do we get horses to ride or do we get on this flatcar and go back to town?"

"Can you ride a horse?"

I said, "Ever since I was a kid I played with horses instead of doll buggies. My friend Ruby can ride. She was raised on the Flathead reservation."

There was a dozen loaded horses ahead of us. We rode at the tail end through a foot of mud. Then higher up the hill into two feet of snow. It was spring and water running everywhere. My horse grunted and stopped to lay down and roll. I kicked him hard in the belly with my toe and kept him on his feet.

RAILROAD CAMP

Camp 23 was a railroad camp with supplies, bunkhouses, cookhouse and everything in boxcars. The 6 of us girl flunkeys had a car of our own with double decker bunks for a bedroom.

First thing we heard was the joke going around camp. Somebody had asked Gaffney, the superintendent, how come he was hiring girl flunkeys and he was supposed to have said, "The lumberjacks in Marble Creek are getting too stove-up. We're bringing in the girls to marry off to these old men so we can get a new crop of lumberjacks."

One day, Gaffney went barreling through camp on his old black horse, Duke. His speed showed something was wrong. The bookkeeper told us that a mother and daughter flunkeyin' up at Camp 3 was makin' money on the side and he was going up to fire them. Anyway, the mother and daughter came out next day.

Our suitcases didn't come so for two weeks we wore knickers. Then we put on our white waitress uniforms and felt like real flunkeys.

But after work we'd change to overalls and boots and walk around the woods.

One day I said to Bob Corby, the cook, "Why can't we wear overalls in the cookhouse?"

He said, "I don't give a damn what you wear so long as they're clean."

FLUNKEY WORK

The cookhouse boxcar had the big wood range in the center with tables for 46 lumberjacks at each end of the car. We got up at 6 o'clock in the morning and went to work at 7 to set the breakfast on the table: sourdough hotcakes, ham and bacon and eggs, mush, toast , canned fruit...

On the back of the cookstove a great big can always steamed full of coffee. Men could come in and stand around odd times drinking coffee and eating leftover doughnuts or cake or pie along with it.

Bob Corby noticed that sometimes the lumberjacks didn't clean up the flat cakes so he sent out for different food colorings and some aluminum doodads for decorating cakes. He put them out with pink, green and yellow fluted trims and flowers and leaves.... Boy! Did they clean up the cakes after that! The walking boss noticed it right away and said to the cooks in the other camps, why didn't they make good looking cakes like Bob Corby.

I remember once a coupla guys came in and sat down at a table and just set there.

Finally one of them said, "We'd kinda like to be served."

I had to grin because that showed they'd never been in a logging camp before.

I said, "Between meals it's a stand up and serve yourself. Here! I'll show you."

After we cleared the breakfast table and washed the knives and forks we reset the table for dinner and set sliced bread on. Then we peeled vegetables.

ONIONS BY THE SACK

One day a week the cook served fried onions for dinner. It took a whole sack. I liked to chop vegetables at high speed and the other girls didn't like that job so I said, "If you girls will do the clean-up, I'll slice the onions today."

I was slicing away for all I was worth and a lumberjack stuck his head inside the side door close to me and asked, "You comin' up in the woods today?"

I almost cut my index finger off.

The head cook, Sourdough Bob Corby put a splinter on each side and bandaged it up.

He said, "From now on that door is to be kept closed. We don't want any more accidents."

After we finished the vegetables we could go to our rooms for maybe 25 minutes. Then came preparation for serving dinner at noon.

—136—

At one o'clock we were supposed to get out of the dining room and didn't come back till 4 p.m. to set up the kitchen for supper.

If the guys ate supper fast and we worked hard at cleaning up we could get out of the dining room by 5:30. That gave us time to visit flunkeys at the other camps or maybe their girls would walk up to see us.

DONKEYS ATE WOOD
I heard the men talk about donkeys and thought they meant animals. I climbed up on a pile of four foot cordwood alongside the railroad track one day. Here come Pete Johnson who somebody told me was a donkey puncher.

I said, "Where's the barn where they keep the donkeys and what do they feed 'em?"

Pete laughed. "They're big machines. You're sittin' on a pile of their feed."

ANOTHER SOURDOUGH BOB
We heard there was another Sourdough Bob over on the Orofino branch but our Sourdough Bob was from Texas. He was a good guy to work for. And Oh My Gosh! Did he make good bread, big buns and delicious pancakes out of sourdough.

There was second cook and a woman dishwasher, too.

THE FISH POND
Right next to the track the creek had made a little round pond. The men would go fishing up the creek and the cook would fry up their fish for them when they came back. But the fish that was too little to eat they'd throw in this pond. Pretty soon we had a lot of them. The cook would stand on the steps of the cook car and throw breadcrumbs or hamburger to them. Then us flunkeys went out in the woods and got clumps of ferns and planted all around the edge of the pond.

When the men came in from work the fish would hide under the ferns but other times when they saw just us around they'd come out and swim around.

BEAR AT THE INCLINE
Jerry Titus was donkey man at the top of the Incline. His 12 year old boy Jim, was laying in the bunk reading a story about a grizzly called Silvertip. It was hot in the tent and they had rolled up the sides to let the air through.

Jim was reading about the bear pouncing on something and he heard a little noise. He raised his eyes up over the book and here was a black bear right in front of him.

He could have rolled off the bunk and right out the side of the tent but he let out a yell and panicked! He tried to jump through the canvas roof.

The bear was as scared as him. It undertook to get out through the canvas at the back end. In the ruckus the tent collapsed on 'em.

Jim didn't want no more experiences like that. He wanted go to back to town.

THE INNOCENT MULE

In one of them Stonebreaker packstrings they had a beautiful mule — if you call a mule pretty. Nice long ears and tapered nose and big innocent eyes. He was real dark bay in color. He was so small they used him to pack the mail because that wouldn't be heavy. Instead of tying his halter rope to the next mule ahead they just tied it back to his own saddle and let him roam along behind.

At all the camps the flunkeys and cooks fed him candy or sugar cookies or cake. If the main trail and the other mules went above the cookhouse, he'd take off on a side trail and go down there to get his treats. A regular pet.

This time they come into Camp 23 they had already been to the other camps so there wasn't hardly any mail left on the little mule. While the rest of the pack train was at the barn unloading bales of hay, the pet mule was standin' between two logs close to the cookhouse while the girls fed him sugar cookies.

So I just thought, "Well! He'll pack mail. He'll pack me."

I stepped up on the nearest log and took hold of the packsaddle and swung on him.

I was never throwed so fast and so high!

Lucky for me I lit between the two logs. If I'd lit crossways of one of them logs I'd have broke my back. But I hit so hard it almost laid me out.

The packer came out of the cookhouse in time to help set me on my feet.

He said, "That mule ain't broke to ride."

As if I hadn't just found it out!

THE SHIVAREE!

The stuff on TV and in books ain't true stories so I always wanted to write a book about logging camps. But I can't spell.

The true stuff is like this camp boss, Devlin Hicks. He come in from Virginia and new to the job and he had a little musn't-touch-it mustache and a curled Van Dyke beard with a corkscrew on the end. He thought he was SOME STUFF!

He took one of the girl flunkeys into town overnight and come back next day. Us girls got together and thought it would be fun to shivaree 'em. We let the lumberjacks know, too. After dark we gathered around the office and started beating tin cans and pans and trays. The men took it up and started tootin' the locomotive whistle and hollerin' his name.

Poor Devlin Hicks! He come boilin' out of the office so doggone mad he coulda killed us.

He could see it was us girls that started it. He hotfooted over to the cookhouse and said to our boss, Sourdough Bob, "You shouldn't have let the girls do that!"

Bob said, "They did it on their own time."

Devlin Hicks said, "You're their boss. You should've stopped 'em. You're fired!"

I think the girl flunkey did it because she had hopes of landing him for a husband. But she pushed herself a little too much.

The Higher-ups heard about it and Devlin got fired a week later. But Devlin had asked for it. He should have known a boss never fools with a flunkey.

Next morning, Sourdough Bob and his wife packed their suitcases up the road toward Clarkia. He no more than got to town when he got word to come to Camp 6 as head cook.

All us girls had quit at the same time and went to town. In a few days we got word that Sourdough Bob wanted us at Camp 6 for flunkeys. When we got there the whole camp was still laughing about the shivaree at Camp 23 and how Devlin had got himself fired.

Sourdough Bob Corby and wife leaving Camp 23 — fired. Fall 1923

CAMP 6

Camp 6 was log buildings. Like the rest of the camps it was cutting burnt timber from the 1922 fire. Just before the snow came they were cleaning up the slash. The fire got out of hand and the whole hillside at one side of the camp was burning.

We worked all hours to keep coffee and sandwiches ready for when any firefighter could dash in and grab a bite.

As the fire moved closer the whole crew was fighting to save the buildings. The boss pulled a few men off the fire to load supplies, beds and everything onto wagons. They hooked the horses to the wagons ready to go.

CATS AND DOGS
We had an old cat with kittens and got her in a box and loaded her along with our clothes on a wagon. The dogs underfoot was barking and rushing around. There was lots of food for them at camp and somebody was always bringing another dog in.

The fire got so close you had to turn your face away from the heat. We knew it would be only minutes before we'd be making a run for it.

Then all of a sudden the wind changed and blew the other way. We didn't have to move out.

Crew and a Camp 6 bunkhouse. 1923

SLEIGH HAUL
Camp 6 had 300 men and 40 teams getting ready for winter sleigh hauling. They were widening the road down Bear Creek and making another road for the sleighs to return so the empties wouldn't be in the way of the loaded ones. They were building a big V plow so they could keep the road open all winter. The logs would be hauled to the Camp 18 Dam and be splashed on down Bussel Creek into the Marble in the 1924 spring floods.

Poking logs to enter the sluice at Camp 18 Dam. Spring '24.

BACKWOODS ENTERTAINMENT
We were 18 or 20 miles from town and had to make our own entertainment. Radios had been invented but only rich people could buy one.

Gazette-Record, Dec. 27, 1923 — On December 6th, banker Carl Kraemer invited friends to listen by radio to an address by President Coolidge. Every word was distinctly heard and even the handclapping of the galleries. What would our grandfathers say to this!

Camp 18 Splash Dam on Bussell Creek below the mouth of Bear Creek, 1966. Courtesy — Jack Johnston

One of the girls got hold of some canned juice and yeast and made wine behind the kitchen range.

I went for a walk up an abandoned skid trail. A snag had fell across it. I dropped to my knees and was crawling under it when I looked a little bear right in the face.

I was scared! Not of the little bear but of the mother bear. She wouldn't be far away and she could come charging with fire in her eyes.

When I turned to scramble away, the suspenders of my dashboard overalls hooked up on a limb of the snag. I reefed this way and that and couldn't get loose.

In my mind I could see that mother bear coming at me with her mouth open. I gave it all I had and broke those suspenders. Then I ran down that skid trail like a deer, holding my pants up with both hands.

I'm tellin' you that was the last time I ever crawled under a windfall.

GARBAGE DELIVERY

Every morning I drove the sleigh for the bullcook to haul the garbage out. All of us girl flunkeys hollered and made a big time of it.

The walking boss, Tommy Stevens, had a fine chestnut sorrel named Bud that he let me ride up the skid trails and down to Camp 18. Camp 18 had a small crew, maybe 25 or 30, and I liked to visit their two flunkeys.

Molly Austad, Jerry, Mrs. Corby and Bob Corby sleighing out the garbage at Camp 6.

Jerry on the sleigh haul road. April, 1924.

When the snow got deep and they were pulling the V plow with 15 teams it was fun to climb a horse in the middle of the string and help handle the reins.

Other times I'd go watch the big donkeys pick up the sleighs and turn them around and then load them with logs.

SCOTTY

There was a quiet bookkeeper in camp named Scotty. We could always kid with most of the men but could never get a smile out of Scotty. Somebody said he had been in the Boer War and been caught prisoner.

We were talking of taking snowballs and washing Scotty's face.

Sourdough Bob said, "Wait a minute. I think that's one little red faced guy you better not fool with."

But I couldn't get it out of my mind. Standing in the door of the cookhouse one day I tossed a handfull of loose snow at Scotty as he went past. Later, I was passing his office and he gave me a wad of snow full force in the face and he wasn't smiling.

So we kinda let go the idea of washing his face.

THE PRIZE FIGHTER
About six months after that we got a relief cook. Jack had been a prize fighter but had got injured and went blind in one eye.

He looked at us in overalls and he says, "I thought they had girl flunkeys here."

We said, "We are girl flunkeys!"

He said, "I never did see girls wear pants before. If you're gonna be boys you can go outside and ask for man jobs. If you work for me you'll wear dresses!"

It would be a long walk back to town so we talked it over and went back to white dresses.

Jack always wore whites and one of them little chef's hats. When he thought nobody was watchin ' he'd practice dancing around and punching past the sink where the dippers and pots hung. But I'll say this for him, he sure knew how to cook.

When the men had gone out to the jobs I'd change to overalls to do the cleaning up and settin' up tables for the next meal. I don't know if Jack liked it but he.didn't say nothing.

OTHER JOBS
Sometimes they closed the Marble camps awhile in winter or I got tired of the place and went to work outside, like at Yakima on a ranch.

In 1925 at the age of 23 I had a baby girl, nicknamed Dempsey — Micky Mildred Collins. She grew up tall and graceful.

About 1928 men quit staying in the camps and commenced driving cars to work so there wasn't any more need for girl flunkeys. I came back to Spokane and worked as food jockey, beer jockey, anything I could get.

Later years, till a hit and run car put me on a cane, I worked as cleaning lady at the Deaconess Hospital.

Interviewed April, 1977 at Spokane, Washington.

Dave Brown

Fire Fighter

Radio Man

I was born October of 1908 in Tennessee. In 1929 I was working in a Philadelphia shipyard as a marine electrician. I had a vacation coming so in April I went out to Los Angeles to see my grandmother. I was so sick of Philadelphia and the traffic and the shipyard

Dave Brown 1979

work that I started looking around for a job in Los Angeles. It was the time of the stock market crash and brokers jumping out windows. The Depression was in full swing. There were no jobs.

RIDING FREIGHTS
Then I got word that there was no job waiting for me in Philadelphia, either. I rode a freight train to San Francisco, found a few months work on boats doing electrical work. Then that folded up. I hopped another freight train and tried Seattle. The only thing I could find there was handling bales of hay for the Carnation Farms. At that time they were hand milking 7 or 800 cows. Handling bales was too hard for me. I was a little guy.

LONG LINE OF MEN ON TRENT
Again I hopped a freight and went to Spokane. No work there either. Down on Trent I ran into a long line of men. I asked them what they were doin' and they said they were hiring out as firefighters.

So I got in line. I had a suit on. When I got to the window the guy looked at my suit and then he leaned forward so he could see my feet.

"We can't hire a man with oxfords," he said.

I wandered off to one side.

BORROWED CALKED BOOTS
An old lumberjack sitting there says, "What's the matter, kid?"

"I can't get on because I haven't got the right kind of shoes."

He took his calked boots off. "Here! Put these on and roll your pants up. Take off that suit coat."

I got into the middle of the line this time. Some of 'em didn't like it too well — but it was a long line. I got up to the window again.

The guy says, "Haven't I seen you before?"

"No!" I says. "You haven't seen me before."

He frowned and then leaned ahead and checked my feet. The boots did it. He hired me.

FIREFIGHTING AT MOON PASS
They shipped us to Moon Peak summit. That was the September, 1929, Slate Creek fire that started in Big Cr. and came over the hill into Slate. That's where I met Charley Scribner, ranger of ward Peak District.

After the Slate Cr. fire wound up there was another fire in November on the hill at Avery. I fought till that was over and went to work on the railroad section at Ethelton.

DUTCH TRAPPED AND BOOTLEGGED
At Hoyt Flats just below Ethelton, Dutch Brown was trappin' and makin' moonshine. There was no road up Slate Creek at that time but he had a trail to what he claimed was his cobalt mine. The trail led to his still — that was his cobalt mine.

Anyhow he used to bootleg whisky and old Joe Prune, the section foreman, would take it to Avery on the speeder. I was just a peon — a section hand pounding spikes and tamping track and I'd help haul these guys to Avery when they were drunk.

This Dutch Brown had picked up women in Spokane. So this winter of 1929 he thought he'd have a cook in his cabin. He brought this woman up from Spokane.

THE WOMAN HAD A BOYFRIEND
Well, this woman had a boyfriend in Spokane she had run away from. One day this boy friend got on the train and rode to Avery and then hiked down 6 miles to Hoyt Flat.

The cabin had a little lean-to porch. The boyfriend got within 15-20 feet and started shooting through the door of the cabin.

NO BACK DOOR ESCAPE

Dutch Brown and the woman had no back door for an escape. Dutch shot back through the door and by accident shot half the fella's leg off.

He was bleeding to death out there but Dutch and the woman wouldn't go out till they were sure he was dead. Then they reported to the deputy sheriff Macaby at Avery.

So the deputy came down and hauled this guy into the cabin — it was just a little, one room 12 by 12 cabin — and and laid him in the middle of the floor.

WATCHING THE BODY

Macaby says, "I got to deputize somebody to stay with the body till I get the coroner."

Everybody on the section was superstitious and Italian except me. They backed off.

"Well, kid,"Macaby says. (I was 20 years old.) "You're it! You gotta stay with this fella."

They all took off on the speeder — took the woman and Dutch over to Wallace — and left me completely alone. It was gettin' toward dark. The only light I had in the cabin was 2 or 3 candles. This guy was layin' on the floor with a sheet over him.

I laid down on the bed in the corner and tried to get some sleep. I couldn't sleep. Then after while I heard a little noise.

THE SHEET WIGGLED

I looked over the edge of the bed and the sheet was wiggling. I thought this guy was comin' to life. I was petrified. I couldn't move a muscle.

After while I kinda calmed down a little bit and I got up my nerve and picked up that sheet and here were some cats eatin' on that guy's leg. That was what made the sheet move.

After that I didn't sleep a wink. That was the longest night in my life.

The deputy and coroner didn't come back till mid-morning. They took this dead boy friend to Avery on the speeder and shipped him away.

The coroner's jury exonerated Dutch Brown because he shot in self defense.

Reported in the Gazette-Record 12-22-29 — At Hoyt's Flats, near Ethelton, Mr. and Mrs. Erwin Ploetzke were roused from bed at 10 a.m. Sunday morning by her ex-husband, Franklin, who demanded entrance and then began walking around shooting holes in the house.

He emptied 10 shots from an automatic.

Ploetzke had an 8 MM rifle and he finally fired once in return and had the luck to hit Franklin in the foot. Franklin bled to death while Ploetzke went to Ethelton to phone a doctor.

Ploetzke was judged to have fired in self defense.

Dave Brown with one of the donkeys he used to pack supplies to his tent lookout.

JOB FOR A LONER

In the spring of 1930, Scribner wrote and asked me if I wanted to be a lookout on Bird Cr., now called Bluebird Point.

I liked being a lookout. I'm kind of a loner anyhow. At that time we had 86 lookouts on the St. Joe. Last year (1977) we had only Huckleberry, Middle Sister, Dunn Peak, Crystal Peak and Conrad Peak. St. Joe Baldy isn't our lookout anymore. It's maintained by the State. We didn't have a lookout on Mallard, one of our oldest. It hasn't been manned for years. The same with Surveyors and Snow Peak. We can't get anybody to walk up Snow Peak anymore or get their own water. We had to bring the last ones water and wood by helicopter.

WADING THE JOE

We had an early fire in about 1931 on the south side of the Joe river. Dan Zobec and I were trying to cross from Nugget Cr. but it was May and high water. We kept moving further up the river falling trees, hoping to use one for a foot log across but it was so deep and the high water so fast that each time it carried the tree away.

We finally got up to St. Joe Quartz where we had a telephone line crossing to Thor Mountain. We were able to get one end of the wire down so we'd have enough slack. So we hung onto this wire and were wading waist deep in the icy river. We got almost across and there was a little falls about 6 feet tall.

OH! FOR WINGS

Dan looked at the falls ahead and at the other bank and said, "If only we had wings like the angels!"

From there on the water would wash over our heads, then we'd get a breath of air and it would happen again. We were numb from head to foot and wringing wet when we got across and had to empty water out of our packsacks. We started a fire and dried out.

RIDING THE CABLE
We were gone on this fire 2 or 3 days. When we come back they'd got a cable across the river at Nugget and rigged a bosun's chair out of insulators so we could ride across.

I got across all right.

HYPNOTIZED BY FAST WATER
Dan was next. When he got out in the middle of the river where the wire sagged him close to the water he looked down. When you look at running water, pretty soon you're hypnotized. You're goin' upstream and the water's standing still. You get dizzy.

Dan wrapped both arms around the wire and froze.

We hollered and hollered before we could get him to look up instead of down. Then we were able to get him the rest of the way across.

THE STIFF DRINK
When Dan and Galloway were building the Spring Creek cabins, I was coming down the river and I always stopped to see them because I'd worked with 'em.

Dan said, "Do you want a little drink?"

A bootlegger at Marble Cr., Frank Breslar, made a powerful moonshine that looked like water.

Dan was always very hospitable and I didn't want to hurt his feelings. "Yeh! I'll take a little drink."

He hauled out a big coffee cup and filled it to the brim.

I took a drink and I thought I was gonna die. It was so raw I couldn't get my breath.

RADIO REPLACED TELEPHONE BUT —
When the Coeur d'Alene Fire Protective Association folded up in 1932 and the Forest Service established the Calder District, they didn't have more than a few beat-up telephone lines, so they brought in radios. We had a radio station in St.Maries, another at Calder and Herb Uttley operated one on St. Joe Baldy. Then in addition we had 3 or 4 portable sets that could only send in code. Trying to get groceries through code from untrained men was a hassle. Besides the radios were in a sad state of disrepair.

Fitting, the supervisor, got so disgusted because we couldn't get satisfactory service for our radios from Missoula that he made me communications man.

Then we got all radio phone sets. But the Forest Service had only one frequency, and on a high point, you'd call Huckleberry Lookout and maybe get an answer from a Huckleberry Lookout in California, Oregon or Montana.

When a storm was coming up — maybe 24 hours ahead of the storm, you couldn't hear anything on the radio. So we had to put telephone lines to Baldy and Cemetery Ridge and Elsie Peak and Lemonade and all over.

Original Ranger Station at Calder 1934
Dave Brown, Ernie Bentley, packer; Charley Scribner, ranger; and Lawrence Glover. The mules were housed at one end, the middle was warehouse and the other end was office. It was so close to the railroad track that all night long either the mules were screaming or the rumbling, whistling trains kept you awake.

CEMETERY RIDGE PLANE WRECK

When Joe Livermore and Haid's airplane disappeared, Dec. 18, 1936, I got an SPS radio unit from Missoula to help in the search. Brand new and lighter, it weighed only fifty pounds with the batteries loaded on my back.

EDITOR:
JOE LIVERMORE AND ARTHUR HAID ADMIRED

When the Northwest Airlines mail plane flew into a night snowstorm on Dec. 18, 1936, it meant a lot more to people than it would today. Planes were few and flying was a daring adventure. Pilot Joe Livermore of Spokane and co-pilot Arthur A. Haid were known by sight and reputation to thousands of people on the dark earth beneath them.

The Lockheed Electra twin-engined transport left Missoula at 12:35 a.m. Destination — Felts Field, Spokane. The first troubling indication that they were off course came when at 2 a.m. they started circling a great bowl of light in the sky where Potlatch sheds at Elk River were burning and their radio began asking Spokane the name of the town below them.

PLANE CIRCLED THE FIRE
For an hour they circled and gathered ice on their wings while the airline radio operators in Spokane frantically phoned towns in every direction.

At 3 a.m. the word, "You are circling Elk River, Idaho. Proceed west till you strike the Spokane-Pasco radio beam."

They left just as the people of Elk River were lining up cars on the main street to headlight a landing strip.

ALARMING PHONE CALLS AND NEWS FLASHES
The word that Livermore and Haid were lost already spread by the frantic phone calls flashed to home radio receivers over the whole area. Radios were a new development and people commonly sat into the wee hours listening to dance bands, beginning with those in the eastern time zone and then as the lights went out in the east, tuned to bands further west till finally the last dance music faded out on the west coast and the Hoot Owl and then the Early Bird programs took over. The news brought people outdoors in small towns and farms and woods clearings to anxiously scan the blizzardy sky and listen for the drone of Livermore's plane.

LISTENING FOR THE LOST PLANE
Buford O'Keefe of Bovill reported that he actually sighted the plane directly overhead going southeast at 3 a.m.

At 3:19 Livermore reported he'd found the beam and would report again at 3:24. At 3:24 he reported his reception was clouded with snow static and he had 1 hour of fuel left.

That was the last contact.

Next morning, high winds and low clouds hampered the search but 2 army planes and 4 Northwest Airlines planes took to the air along with famous veteran flyer, Nick Mamer.

CONFUSING REPORTS — SEARCH PARTIES
Confusing reports came in of people having heard planes around Bayview and Rockford. Parties of Forest Service people and CCC boys spread out from Bovill and Clarkia, scouring the mountains.

Livermore had a wife, Lorna, and a 10 year old daughter.

Lorna said, "Joe is the best pilot in the world and would have made a safe landing."

Arthur Haid's wife was in the hospital in Seattle with an 8 day old daughter. She was not told of her husband's disappearance.

CUNNINGHAM REPORTS TO THE NEWS
Fred Cunningham, former game warden, came showshoeing out to Kellogg from his cabin near the head of Big Creek to report that he had heard a plane in the blizzard.

NEWS REPORT

At 9:30 a.m., Dec. 21, Lieutenant Byron S. Cooper and Sergeant A. G. Hylent of the 116th Observation Squadron reported sighting the wreckage of the plane strewn along Cemetery Ridge at the head of Big Creek.

Charley Scribner, Calder ranger, had been waiting at Felts Field for the rain and snow to let up and says, "I was in Cooper's plane and Sergeant Hylent was in the plane of Lieutenant Claire Hartnett. We were flying about a quarter of a mile apart to keep an eye on one another as we combed the territory. I was along because I knew that area. I had to pull Cooper out of the clouds a few times when there was a mountain in the middle that he didn't know about. He took a lot of chances.

"When we came in the night of the 20th., Hartnett said to us, "That last sweep I just got a glimpse of something over the edge of the clouds that didn't look right."

"So the next morning Dec. 21st., Hartnett went right straight back to the spot and we followed him in. There was the wrecked plane strung along the hillside just below the top of the ridge. A little higher and he wouldn't have struck it. The location was near the southeast corner of Section 23, Township 47 North, Range 3 East in the head of Early Creek.

"And another thing — plain as day there was a set of snowshoe tracks going straight along the top of the ridge and right down to the wrecked plane. I've always thought they were made by Fred Cunningham. They used to have a snowshoe contest in Kellogg going up Kellogg Peak. For 3 years straight, Cunningham beat 'em all. He was tough.

"The wreck was not on Cemetery Ridge as reported by the papers but 2 miles north of it. Origin of the name Cemetery Ridge — Coming up to the west end of this ridge from down in Early Creek is an old homesteader trail now numbered by the Forest Service as Trail 44. After the 1910 fire the bodies of the firefighters who died in Early Creek were brought up this trail and buried on the north slope of Cemetery Ridge about the center of Section 34. They were taken to St. Maries and re-buried there 2 years later".

As reported by the newspapers — Fred and Jay Cunningham, Gerald and John Brennan of Kellogg reported reaching the wreckage at 6:45 a.m. on Dec. 26th about 300 feet from the top of the ridge and 600 feet from where they had camped for the night.

SPOKESMAN-REVIEW Dec. 28, 1936 — The rescue party, with its tragic load, led by Deputy Sheriff Alvin Sherwood of Kellogg, Idaho, left Early Creek ridge, scene of the air disaster, shortly after 2 p.m. Sunday on the first leg of an arduous march on skis and snowshoes over more than 10 miles of forest trails, following the Early Creek and Pine Creek drainages to a roadway on East Pine Creek, where a motor party will pick up the weary rescue group and proceed via Kingston to Kellogg.

It was learned that the Thornhill Funeral Home had been ordered to send a hearse to Kingston, Idaho, and as far up as possible on the Forest Service road up Pine Creek to meet the toboggan party sometime this morning.

Late last night, however, conflicting information was received here that the bodies were to be brought out by Big Creek and Calder, Idaho and not by the Kellogg route.

Shortly afterward acting on a tip, newspapermen found out that the division superintendent of the Milwaukee Railroad had ordered the crack Olympain train to stop at Herrick to drop off two caskets.

ACCOUNT OF THE ST. JOE SEARCH PARTY AS TOLD BY DAVE BROWN, WITH PICTURES BY NEIL FULLERTON

The minute he heard about the lost plane on December 18th, Fitting, the supervisor of the St. Joe National Forest began rounding up a search party. Dean Harrington was the party chief. He was our fire control staff man at the time.

On the 21st., when the army plane with Calder ranger, Charley Scribner aboard, reported the location of the wreckage, we set out with a ground party to the Big Creek cabin on the East Fork of Big Creek.

It was storming constantly. By the time we made it to the site of the wreck a day or so later, with our radio and shovels, everything was completely covered with two feet of fresh snow.

Even with compass and maps we couldn't be sure we were anywhere close to the wreck. We spread out and searched the ground. Then by sheer luck, Elmer Marks found a hand sticking up out of the snow. We wouldn't have found the plane if Marks hadn't found the hand.

I set up a radio station under a canvas shelter alongside the wreck itself. I talked to Fort Wright through our base at the Big Creek cabin. We had installed a couple of army radio operators there from Fort Wright. They was transmitting on their own army frequency in code.

We came 7 miles back to the Big Creek cabin every night. I think there was 18 of us in that little about 10 by 12 cabin, including the 4 men of the ski party that came up from Spokane because Joe Livermore, the lost pilot, was a member of their club.

Henry Phoeneff was our bull cook. He worked for the Forest Service and trapped and lived in a cabin near Pocono. Where Moe's mill later located, there was a railroad section named Phoeneff after him.

We had one of those Kimmell stoves in the middle of the Big Creek cabin. It's a tin box without a bottom and it has to set on dirt. We had surrounded that little section of floor with four logs holding some dirt and the stove set on the dirt. During the night apparently some duff in the dirt caught fire and started burning those logs. The cabin filled with smoke. 18 people were sleeping in the bunks, under the bunks, over the bunks and all around this fire on the floor. When somebody yelled "FIRE!" there was a mad dash over people to get out that cabin door.

We finally put the fire out but it sure disrupted some tired people.

Christmas Eve everybody was kind of tired and thirsty. We'd already been up there 2 or 3 hard days.

A CASE OF XMAS CHEER
Fullerton and Elmer Marks and some others gave me me money and I showshoed out. The Northwest Airlines representative who had come to Calder added $25 to the pot and I drove to St. Maries and got a case of Christmas cheer. I came back and left the car at Herrick and took the case back to the Big Creek cabin that night.

I don't think we went out Christmas day. Settin' around this cabin we'd open a bottle and hand it around. The skiers would just take a smell but Fullerton and Dean Harrington and Elmer Marks and Marsh Ells and Walt Botts...they used up two of those bottles before it made the circle.

We drank up that whole case in the next 2 or 3 days. Drinking it mostly as a pickup after we got in tired at night.

We never saw those guys from Shoshone County. Cunningham was getting all the publicity and we were doin' all the work.

We had an old lumberjack in our party. Soon as he found out that we found the plane, he beat it right out to Herrick where the newspaper guys were, to get his name in the paper. The Forest Service canned him.

ERRONEOUS NEW REPORT
SPOKESMAN-REVIEW 12-28-36
Kellogg, Idaho, Dec. 27 — Somewhere out on the storm-torn blizzard-blown peaks southwest of Kellogg tonight a small band of brawny men are battling the elements in the long and sorrowful trek back to civilization with the bodies of Joe Livermore and Arthur Haid, pilots of the ill-fated Northwest airliner that crashed in the fog and dark Dec. 18. They started from the scene about 3 p.m. and with luck will make Fred Cunningham's cabin, the halfway mark tonight.

ENCOUNTER FEARFUL GOING
Deep snow, windfalls, buck brush, steep slopes and the heavy storm will hamper them, and the progress will be slow and wearing, particularly so in that many of the group are inexperienced mushers and

are now beating back over a trail they had but recently, dog-tired travelled.

Fred Cunningham, his brother Jay, and brothers Jerry and John Brennan, who found the plane, left Kellogg at 3 o'clock this morning and mushed straight through to the scene of the wreck. They hardly paused before taking up the long trek home, increasingly difficult because of the heavily laden toboggan bearing the bodies....

The cabin of Billy Wendt, miner, marks "this end of the trail", and it is near his cabin the party's cars were left behind. This afternoon Wendt, who knows the mountains well, took one look at the gathering storm and said:

"It's already snowed five inches here. It will be far worse up there. I wouldn't estimate when they'll get in.

"Cunningham, fortunately, is an uncanny woodsman and knows the trail like a book. They might never get in otherwise."

SPOKESMAN-REVIEW Dec. 28, 1936
This deadly day brought the only touch of humor. The Fort Wright radio picked up a message from Mike Potinsky, radio operator at the Big Creek cabin calling a commissary order to the CC spike camp at Calder, "Send up a couple pairs of wool sox for me — also send up an alarm clock for the cook".

Postal Inspector R. C. Sheldon said a Christmas package containing rosaries had broken open at the wreck and the cross of one was found lying on the torn uniform of Pilot Livermore not far from the collar of his shirt. His broken wristwatch had been shattered at 3:23 a.m.

Dave Brown continues:
The ski troop from Spokane really did work good. They brought a kind of stretcher on skiis. We didn't have anything like that.

We had to dig out the bodies and do a lot of shoveling around there to find the plane. Livermore and Haid were thrown clear with the seats still fastened to them. In fact, they were frozen into a sitting position which made a problem to load them onto the sled.

HARD TRIP OUT
We had about 800 pounds of mail and bodies on that ski stretcher sled. I didn't get in on the pulling because I was packing the others' snowshoes and my radio equipment.

Walt Bott and Marsh Ells digging out the wrecked plane.

They couldn't pull it wearing snowshoes. Like sled dogs pullin' each man had to pull on a rope and wallow that load up to the trail on top of the east end of Cemetery Ridge, then west along Cemetery Ridge 2½ miles to the head of Donaldson Cr. where Trail 44 comes from down in Early Creek. Then they labored south on Trail 44 down Donaldson Creek another 2½ miles to the East Fork cabin.

Marsh Ells, Dean Harrington, Noel Farrell and sled with the bodies of Joe Livermore and A. A. Haid.

Noel Farrell had mules waiting there. He packed the bodies and mail to Herrick at the mouth of Big Creek, Dec. 28th.

A CC Truck waited with coffins. The bodies were frozen in a sitting position. There wasn't room in the coffins. We even had quite a time putting them in the rough boxes. Two or three of us had to get on top and hold the lid down so we could nail it.

The bodies and mail were taken to Calder and loaded at 6:30 p.m. on the baggage car of the Olympian, Livermore for Spokane and Haid for Seattle.

NOTE: I believe the plane wreckage remains are in the northeast corner of Section 23 at the very head of Early Creek.

Neil Fullerton was in the rescue party and took the pictures.
Courtesy — Homer Hartman

THE LOST CC BOY

The way it got started, the CC boys would be talking about the big cities just over the mountains and this young fellow was deluded into thinking he could find them. So he started up the Eagle Creek trail that goes past Quarles Peak and the State Line divide to see the cities of Montana.

When he failed to come back that night the main force of searchers hit the Eagle country from the river. Another fellow, Roy Perkins and I took the train up to Adair and then snowshoed up to Quarles Peak to see if he had gone through there. There was 6 to 10 feet of snow so without snowshoes he couldn't possibly have waded through and there

Dec. 28, 1936 at the Big Creek cabin after bringing in the mail and the bodies from Cemetery Ridge. Marsh Ells, George Irwin, Walt Bott, Elmer Marks, Fay Chenoweth, Henry Phoeneff, Dean Harrington, Arndt Ofstarndt, Dave Brown, Noel Farrell, Paul Gillingham and John Ring. (Neil Fullerton not shown).

was no sign of a track. Another 50 searchers camped on Craddock Ridge and could find no tracks either.

The ranger, Jerry Handel insisted, to close the case, that the boy had gotten over into Montana.

He said, "You guys just missed his tracks."

The searchers coming up from the river did find bits of clothing hanging on the bushes up Eagle Creek where he had probably panicked in the dark and started running.

The next year the blister rust boys found his bones at the bottom of a cliff.

A LOT OF LITTLE FIRES

Along about 1940 we had a fire back of Mud Lake beyond Mallard Peak. It turned into a lot of little smokechaser fires that had us goin' day and night. John Dennis must have been 60 years old then. He was one of a dozen of us sent back there with our smokechaser packs and grub. By Golly! He just about wore us younger men out. That fella had more stamina!

Hilding, was a long legged ranger that would go to fires on the run, eating a sandwich. He had a short legged little assistant.

ED HANSON CARTOONED

Ed Hanson had a gift for cartooning. He got a big piece of cardboard paper and drew a picture of Hilding flying down the trail with his smokechaser pack, eating a sandwich and his short legged little assistant behind him eating a sandwich, too.

I saved that picture for 30 years. When Hilding retired they had a party for him in Coeur d'Alene. I sent that picture to him, framed.

THE SANDERS FIRE ALMOST GOT ME

What made the fire at Sanders so bad was 100 degree temperatures during the last of August and the first of September when everything was already exceptionally dry. It was about 1944, when most of our experienced Forest Service people had gone to World War 2.

Instead we had army officers, navy officers, air force officers, M.P.s and German internees, policemen and Japanese internees and Mexicans from the blisterrust camps — 1100 firefighters and only a hundred or so of our own supervisory personnel.

We'd build fireline and the fire would jump over it till around 3500 acres were burning.

We had four big camps. The fire come down the hill and burned one camp up.

I had both radios and telephones to maintain. A telephone line came from East Dennis down across the mountain to West Dennis. There were fissures running up the mountainside that we had burned and then there were some unburned ones. In one of these fissures the fire had burned the telephone line in two. I spliced the wire and was going across the steep mountainside checking the wire through unburnt timber ground. The smoke got terrific. I couldn't see anything.

HEARD IT COMING

Then I heard this big hissing and crackling coming up the mountain. I knew I had to get out of there. I threw down my shovel, climbin' outfit and packsack and took off running. I ran till I thought my heart was gonna come right out of my throat.

I just broke out into a burned area that was still smoldering and hot when that sucker came roaring up through the trees behind me.

I was full of smoke. I just managed to get over to a stump and lay over it till I could catch my breath.

We never did get the best of that fire. The rains finally came and put it out.

I'm still in charge of radios after 45 years.

Nellie Cottingham knew I was radio man for the Forest Service. She used to call me to fix the radio at her floathouse.

I know she had a prospect up Street Creek and another out around Freezeout. One morning I was heading out of town and here she was walking up the road with a big packsack on her back. I stopped and picked her up. When we reached Street Creek she told me to stop. After I started up, I looked in the rearview mirror and there was Nellie with that heavy packsack going right up the steep roadbank, like going to a fire.

Interviewed at St. Maries, Idaho, Oct. 1979

Wallace Daniels

Whinner, rear and stomp!

Wallace Daniels 1979

I'm Scotch, Dutch and a little English. Born 1895 on the North Carolina-Tennesee border. I'd been working in the Cranberry Iron Mine till I went into World War 1. After I got a load of gas I knew my health wouldn't stand mine work anymore. My buddy in the service was Don Tatum. He told me to come with him to Idaho. He lived out by Indian Springs.

In 1919, Wagner, Jim Tatum's father-in-law took me over to Willow Creek that runs into Cave Lake near Medimont.

He said, "There are 3 claims in Willow Creek that have been let go. Why don't you pick out the four forties with the most timber and file homestead on it.

So I did. I took the best cabin, too. I got patent (title) on it in 14 months by commuting, living on it every day for that period of time. Had to pay a dollar and a quarter an acre that was supposed to go to the Coeur d'Alene Indians.

I got acquainted with Edna Christiansen at Powerline schoolhouse dances. She graduated from Plummer high School, attended Lewiston Normal and was teaching 10 pupils in all 8 grades. She taught there 1923, '24, '27 and '28. We were married at Coeur d'Alene in 1928 so we've been married 51 years.

I got tangled up in a fight at the Powerline schoolhouse one night. I was so drunk I could hardly stand up and one of the McManns that used to live up Evans Creek really clobbered me. He wasn't near as big as I was but he was quite a scrapper. Me bein' drunk he thought he'd whittle me down to his size.

Jim Tatum said to him, "I'll do Wallace's fightin'! He's too drunk to fight."

Jim didn't any more than get his mouth open when McMann knocked him about 15 feet.

The next Saturday night there was a dance over at the Indian Springs schoolhouse and that bunch from around Medimont went to all them dances, too.

When I came in the door I saw this McMann on the stage where fiddlers like Newell played. I hung my overcoat up and put my rubbers in the cloakroom.

McMann come runnin' down stickin' out his hand. "I wouldn't of hit you for anything in the world if I'd known you was drunk."

I said, "I'll tell you one thing, fella. If a man can't knock me down, drunk as I was that night, he's got no business tryin' to knock me down when I'm sober."

Them rough Maitlands, Fred and Leonard, they was always good friends of mine, too. That doggone George Maitland don't drink a drop any more. Just as nice a guy as you'd ever talk to.

I worked for Russell & Pugh hauling logs from the Kelly place out to the chute above the Meikle place and shot them into the lake. Saavy Procopio had his first team, on that job. I don't think he was over 18.

I drove Ted and Dick that belonged to Russell & Pugh. There was an old bachelor there, Jim Comer. He drove Babe and Trixie, a team of mares. Balkiest team I ever saw.

Later, down at the head of Black Lake, Jim was skiddin' around the hill and he got stuck.

I said to Jim, "If you'll take them buntin' devils off of there I'll give the log a pull."

So I made him unhook and I pulled the log around the hill.

It made Jim mad. He always growled at anyone that had to give him a pull. He was an old man then, a little childish.

Sandie Bailey and Clem McKinney was logging for Rutledge the summer of '23, on the east side of Bussel Creek about 3 miles up from the Marble. They had a crew from around Harrison: Russell Reynolds, Cal Bailey and me and Otto Cathcart and Don Tatum. I always went to bed with the chickens and got up early so I fed all the horses.

There had been a big burn in 1921 and we were logging black stuff. The bark was already slipping. They had to get it out before the bugs got it. Sometimes if you worked hard and got up a big sweat, you got a little black but all in all it was a nice job.

Mrs. Cobbet was cook and Marble Creek Jerry Conroy was a young woman hashing there. Quick as they was through with the dishes, Mrs. Cobbet and

Bussel Creek job 1923. Skinners come with teams from the barn: Otto Cathcart, Russell Reynolds, Wallace Daniels, Don Tatum and Cal Baillie.

Marble Creek Jerry would come down to the barn with a bowl of sugar. You know how crazy them damned horses are for sugar! We had to forbid them coming down till we was through currying them horses. Quick as they heard the women's feet, you couldn't do anything with 'em. Whinner, rear and stomp.

Our log chute was better'n a mile up a little creek above camp. Marble Creek Jerry would walk up there with her calked boots on and ride on the front logs we was trailin' on the chute. Sometimes the logs would outrun the team and you'd have to skip the tongs and let 'em go.

That didn't scare Jerry none. Before they got up dangerous speed she'd take a flying leap off into the mud.

I was workin' with Clem McKinney. Clem was pretty damn catty on his feet. Could ride most any log. He was always diggin' me about bein' awkward.

Jerry come along one day on the opposite side of where we skidded logs into the chute. Pretty high off the ground the chute was on that side.

Clem saw her comin' and he says, "Let me help you across, Jerry. Wallace is so awkward he'd fall over his own feet."

He jumped into the chute to offer her a hand to jump across. These logs had a lot of loose bark and Clem had a piece stuck on his calks. Down he want, flat on his back.

God damn comical! I'd like to have had a picture of that. And if Clem had admitted it he could have screamed when he hit hard on his back. It almost paralyzed him for a minute. But he was too much Irish to say anything with that girl standing right there.

Our mile long chute ran from the dam on the level for a ways up this little creek and then it climbed a steep stretch. I was coming up the chute one day driving my team. I was next to the outside of a curve of the chute, between it and a cliff. This curve was a place where a lot of logs jumped the chute.

I heard somebody screaming 'way up above at the top of the chute, "**Look out below!**" and realized a log had got away from them. There was no time to get the team away. Only one chance for me.

I jumped into the chute and flattened myself against the inside of the curve.

I could hear the hiss of the log and the bumping sound. Here come a big red fir going like hell. I shut my eyes so I wouldn't see the team get it in the chest.

It roared past, riding the high side of the chute but didn't quite fly out. Where the chute straightened further down it rolled back in and was gone from sight.

When I went down to check it, that log had gone so fast it made it across the level place where we generlly had to trail with the team and into the dam.

We got a $2 a day bonus if we stayed till the job was done. They furnished the horses and paid us skinners $4.50 a day.

Rutledge paid us 2 extra hours also to flume our logs and theirs out of the dam in the evening. We put in 83 days on that job from June till we pulled out.

1925 I went to work early in the spring for Everett & Kelso on the Cranberry Creek job. I was driving team there, too. I had a double bit axe stuck in a log behind me and when I went to roll a log in front of me I stepped back into the axe. It cut a slash through my calked boot above my left ankle. I hadn't worked more than an hour.

Kelso took me on a horse and we rode out to Clarkia and I took the train down to the doctor at St. Maries. By the time my ankle healed, their job was finished.

Later, during the Depression I worked for the Forest Service building roads and leading a crew at a CC camp.

There was a tragedy down at the Hoyt Flat CC camp. The camp had about 100 men and was made up entirely of World War 1 veterans — the only one in the whole area. During the 1933 flood Ed Burns, the foreman was using a double ended swiftwater boat, 20 feet long and 5 feet wide in the middle, on a cable across the river.

Coming home from work, too many of the men piled into it in a hurry to get back across to the camp at Hoyt Flats because they'd got word that several buddies they knew over in Montana were coming in on Passenger train 15 coming west.

The boat capsized and two of them drowned.
From that time on they used a raft.

**Ed Burns and CC World War 1 veterans crossing the Joe
to Hoyt Flat in the 1933 flood.**

CCC Camp 187 at Tin Can Flats 1937

Wallace Daniels right and his good, hard working CC crew from New York.

Wallace Daniels and Dick Stokes on road maintenance east of Avery. 1935

After I retired I lost an eye from infection following a cataract operation, November, 1973. Six months later I lost my sight in the other eye so I've been completely blind since that time.

Interviewed at St. Maries, Nov. 1979.

Art Darrar...Packer

That mule would

pull out your shirttail

with his teeth

Born 1905 Art Darrar at 35

Dad homesteaded in Elk Basin about 16 miles over toward Elk River from Clarky. I was borned in Clarky.

After I growed up and married, I built a house between Trout Creek and Calder. Les, my brother, has a house above my log house. Walt, another brother spelled his name different--Darry— but found out he was wrong when he had to get his Social Security card.

FIRE OF '18 STARTED HEAVY LOGGING IN MARBLE
Before the fire, just a few were logging there. In 1917 Dad had a camp on the right side of Daviggeo Creek. He shovelled snow in July to build a chute there. A half mile from Dad's camp Lavigne had a camp on the left hand side of Marble going up. He had a running chute down to the Marble.

Lavigne was part Indian. Horse skiddin' outfit. The fire caught his camp. All they saved was the hogs that Lavigne kept to eat the leftovers from the cookhouse. When the hogs saw the fire coming they jumped in the toilet.

Pete Nelson lost his camp, too. Other camps up toward Hobo burned up. On the right side going up was a donkey camp. Them donkeys tore the country up just about as bad as a fire.

After the fire, no trails. Timber layin' everywhere. A man didn't know where he was. They was logging with fire still in the logs. Horses all black, the men, too. A fright!

The timber outfits benefited from that fire. People with burned homesteads didn't have any choice about selling.

PACKING AT AGE 14
At Marble Station in 1919 Saugstad had a post office, a store, a hotel and restaurant in the little draw on the north side of the track. The Rutledge was going strong in Marble Creek. They had a big warehouse right by the railroad station. They transported their stuff across the Joe to the south side in a couple of big boats with cable and trolley arrangement. Then the packers loaded up.

I packed for Noel Farrell. He packed for Dick Talbot who contracted packing for the Rutledge camps. You'd get up at 3 o'clock in the morning to get started at daylight. Didn't get no sleep. Go out and saddle them damn broncs.

That was quite a sight to see 30 head of big, stout mules start up Marble Creek in the early morning with packs on 'em. We was packin' 14½ miles up to below Eagle Creek. A good day's round of 29 miles. 300 pounds to the animal. We'd make 2 trips and lay over the third day to let the pack stock rest up.

Lumberjacks walked a long ways into the camps in them days.

BREAKING SADDLE STOCK
I had several good riding horses. We used to go in for heavy ones because that was harder'n packin' on account of a saddle horse had to carry a load both ways. I had some awful mean sons of bitches, too. Some we bought so green you had to drag 'em out of the railroad car, throw 'em to put on a halter, put 'em in stocks to shoe 'em. Tie up a foot to get the saddle on.

For a time we packed from Camp 11, a distance of 10 or 12 miles up the hillside to camp 19. If anything upset on the trail you just had to dump it and leave it right there.

Once I packed a 500 pound tent up there on a mule. Had the men roll it up as tight as they could. The men helped me get it on — and that wasn't no easy job! The tent went clean acrost the mule and took pert near the length of him. Then I roped him in it. There was a wide trail from Daviggeo up to Camp 19. I kept goin' 4 hours without a stop till we got there.

CHIPMUNK — THE MULE
I had one kind of brown mule name of Chipmunk. I don't think he'd go over 900 pounds, but he was hard to handle. Puttin' a pack on him you had to put him between poles, tie up a leg. He'd buck, kick, rear and snort. I shod him in front and he'd hold his foot right up to you. But he was watchin' you all the time.

You couldn't even tie him in the barn — he'd break away. So you had to let him foller at the tail end of the packstring. He could carry his 300 pounds and he'd move along careful and eating the whole way.

When the packstring reached camp he'd push right up to the head end to be unloaded ahead of the rest. If you didn't unload him he'd pull your shirttail out with his teeth.

PACKING ON FITZGERALD CREEK
O'Neil put that flume in Fitzgerald. They cut the trees out of the way and skidded a little sawmill in pieces three miles right up that steep creek bottom. I didn't see it but that's what they told me. The mill cut lumber to build the camp and the flume to the river.

I was drivin' team there in about 1922. The way I got started packing, Runaway Shay come into camp one day and took the packstring all over the woodpile. They called him Runaway Shay because he was always runnin' away. He'd leave a team right in the woods and he was gone.

When Jones, the walking boss, looked at them mules all tangled up and packs spilled, he got his tail in the air. He yelled to Runaway Shay, "Tie them horses to that pole and leave 'em there. You're finished!"

Then Jones says to me, "Do you think you could handle them mules?"

I said, "I ought to be able to."

THEIVIN'
We packed out of the town of St. Joe to Fitzgerald. You didn't dare pack part of the way. If you left the stuff somebody'd steal it. So I packed a little hay and oats all the way to the camp and put my brother, Bert, in a tent at Zane Siding to guard the groceries and just packed halfway at a time.

One morning I left Zane and started up that steep hillside to camp. I had 15 mules tied nose to tail. I shouldn't a'done that. Goin' around a switchback this little blind mule jerked the whole string off the edge of the trail. They rolled clear down to the bottom of the canyon.

The kid helpin' me got excited.

I said, "We'll just sit down and have a smoke, let 'em fight it out. If we go down there now we'll get our brains kicked out."

They finally quieted down. I slid down the hill. They was wound up in a hell of a tangle. But we was lucky. Only one of the mules got a hip hurt.

Later, about 1927 when Russell and Pugh took over Fitzgerald, I packed a big circular saw, 5 foot 8 inches, up there for Walt Russell so that sawmill could cut lumber to extend the flume up the creek another half mile. That saw was something to pack! But I had a mule that didn't give a damn what you put on him so long as he didn't get knocked off the trail.

I set the saw pert near straight up and put a bale of hay on the other side to balance it. Then I roped and re-roped mattresses around the teeth of the saw.

Wooden kegs of nails, you'd have to put a loop around the bottom end and a loop around the top end and notch 'em in so they wouldn't slip.

One time in early spring they wanted me to pack some oats in.

I said, "How much snow?"

The boss said the camp watcher had shovelled out the trail.

He didn't!

Right below camp I hit 5 feet of snow. I was riding a big mare and she jumped up and down breaking that trail in. I'd take ones from behind and let them break a short ways to give her a rest. When we wallered into camp the mare was all in.

CHUTE BUILDING
In the fall of 1929 I worked with that old chute builder, Louie Coty. He had Ed Edwards, Lloyd Gaskill, Russian Alec Luchuck, Johnny Freeman and me helpin' him. Our chute went to the right from the upper dam a half mile above camp. Then we built another that went straight up the canyon from the upper dam and then to the right. We dug the ties in solid and set the curves solid — a dandy chute.

We was supposed to have more chute building but we had made too much money. $10 a day apiece. Wages was about $4 a day at that time. That worried Russell & Pugh. They laid us off.

Then Len McCrea, the foreman, hired a bunch of kids that didn't even own calked shoes. They put in a pole chute. Left them ties sticking out. First God damn logs that come down jumped the chute and hit them ties stickin' out and knocked the chute all to pieces. Just wasted work.

In the early 1930s the lower half mile of steep flume running to the river filled up with logs and broke down. That ended loggin' in Fitzgerald.

IT'S THE SMALL LOGS THAT GET YOU.

I got hurt 23 years ago, August 1949 in Trout Creek. When you got a big log or one out of shape you watch it and stay out of the way. But the little logs fool you. They shit out quick and don't make a sound. The log that got me had only a 6 inch top.

We was loadin' all small logs. I was alongside the truck. This little log was settin' on the face of the load.

I said, "Looks like them God damn logs is gonna shit out."

I started past the truck to get a peavy offa the jammer to hold 'em. No more'n said that when **WHAM!** The load shit out and this log come down offa the truck and hit me. Knocked me down a little slope. Musta hit me first on the shoulder but there wasn't no mark there.

I went out for a little bit.

When I come to, the guy says, "What's the matter?"

I said, "I feel like I'm bleedin' around the waist."

It had hit me from the waist down and snapped 3 vertebraes out. They had to put 'em back in. It didn't break the main nerve in my spine. It mashed it.

I said to the doctor, "What's the chances of me walkin' again? I want the truth of it."

He said, "We'll have to wait and see."

I went to a hospital in Portland and they put a lot of bedsores on me. I come home and couldn't get the bedsore on my right leg healed up. It wouldn't heal!

Finally one toe dropped off. Two years ago they had to take my legs off at the hips. So I ain't had 'em off very long.

It's so easy to get hurt in the woods.

Interviewed at the Valley Vista Nursing Home. St. Maries. 1972

Cable Bridge across the Joe at Marble Cr. '34
Courtesy — Ruth Osier

Walt Darry

Logger & River Driver

Walt Darry, 77, in 1975

My grandad, Charley Durphas was the first one to come out from Wisconsin in 1900. He worked as locator for people from the East. He used to get $50 for locating someone on a homestead.

I was born in Boyd, Wisconsin, July 15, 1898. In 1902 Dad followed Grandad and we came into St. Maries on the boat. (Probably The Spokane which was built 1901.)

We had to stay overnight at a hotel down by the boat dock at the bottom of 1st. Street. Somebody had a bear on a chain down there on that board walk. My mother kept comin' and dragging me away. I wanted to play with that bear.

PACKED HOMESTEADERS
Grandad had rented the Hatton ranch — that white house between Fernwood and Clarky behind the meadow on the north side of the highway — and we moved out there. Dad and Grandad picked people off the stage at Fernwood and brought them to the ranch. Then with riding horses and 6 packhorses they packed them and their supplies out to homestead locations and helped them build cabins. Charged them for the use of the horses but not much for the work. Dad's outfit packed the Flewsies out to homesteads, too and Flewsie Creek was named after them.

A lot of excitement for us kids. I can remember Grandad packing me back into the hills in a packsack when I was 4 and homesteaders coming back to tell their experiences. Us kids would take it all in — especially the bear and cougar stories.

STAGELINE EMIDA TO TENSED
We moved to Emida, 1907, when Dad bought the livery barn there. It was a big one that stood right on the corner where you make the turn to go to Charley Creek. It was big enough that he rented half of it for people to store wagons loaded with wheat or hay overnight.

Dad ran stage and mail from Emida to the Mission at Tensed and to the Maries. He used to buy as much as a hundred ton of hay off the natural grass meadows around Emida.

SANTA 1909
Then in 1909 we moved to Santa and started a livery barn there. The railroad was building through Santa with lots of hand work and grading with horses and fresnos. Santa was a busy place with men blowing money at Hendershott's and O'Donnell's saloons.

The post office used to be down by Hendershotts. Hughes ran it. We freighted, too, for Walker's store. I think he came in about 1912.

We freighted from Santa to St. Maries over Beaver Hill. The road never came near Mashburns like it does today. The old fellow, Nate Devitt that built that big house with all the evergreen trees around it where the road forks one way to Santa and the other to Emida, in order for him to go to St. Maries, he had to come back to Santa and then up over Beaver Hill.

SLEIGHS TO WAGONS
In the spring the Halfway House to St. Maries was used sometimes for stages that would come from Santa by sleighs and then go on to St. Maries with wagons. Bert Renfro sent many a gold shipment through to St. Maries from Tyson Creek.

SCHOOL TO LOGGING
The first school I could get. We had to leave Santa and walk about a mile and a half to a log building on the right hand side of the Sanders Road. When Dad and Frank Buell worked on the Santa Creek drive I went down with my brother, Les, from the schoolhouse and started walking logs in the dam. I fell in and when Ray Cruthers pulled me out by the hair I was unconscious and damn near drowned.

I finished 8th grade about 1912 and went to work skiddin' cedar poles for Plug Kerry. I was s'posed to get $30 a month.

When I went to settle with him, he said, "I don't owe you nothin'!"

The old man and us had worked all summer and he beat the old man out, too. We had a big lawsuit in Coeur d'Alene. Only time Kerry had to pay. We beat him.

1910 FIRE
The old road from St. Maries to Emida went up Thorn Creek to the flats then swung back to the Maries river and crossed the Flat Creek dam. After you crossed the dam you went up on the hill and stayed back from the river and didn't come near Santa Creek till you reached the Johns Creek road.

During the 1910 fire they was afraid the fire would take the town of St. Maries and sweep east through the flats and up toward Santa. Homesteaders from the flats was bunched to make a run over the Flat

Creek dam and head for the open meadows around Emida. Same thing at Santa. We had teams and wagons all loaded with homesteaders belongings, ready for a run for those same open meadows. We was waitin' for Joe Dubarry to phone us from the Flat Creek dam. But the fire didn't come our direction.

THE MARIES RIVER LOOPS

The loops start at Rover Tunnel and go down to John Creek. Louie Larson was taking the drive, pert near the last year they drove the Maries.

Louie Larson come along one day after I'd rolled off a log into a deep hole and was crawlin' out on the bank. He says, "What are you doin' today, Walt?"

I said, (laughing), "I'm pilotin' the boat through some of these deep holes."

Jack Keenan and Dick Wilson, just the two of 'em was gonna run our wannigan boat with our cooking stuff, clothes and beds, through the loops.

I was sackin' (rearing logs) and I had a good watch and didn't want to get it wet so I gave it to Jack to keep for me.

The boat went past, goin' like a bat outa hell. When they saw it headin' straight into the rock cliff, Jack, he got scared and jumped out. Dick Wilson jumped, too, but he made it. The boat was all smashed to pieces.

They found Jack's body just above John Creek.

JUMPING CLAIMS

There was a lot of crap going on in Marble in the early days. You had to build a cabin and put in a garden spot and live on that homestead 6 months out of the year. If you was gone working over 6 months these claim jumpers would come in and jump your claim. The government would kick you off and the claim jumper would sell your homestead to the big outfit.

THE MARBLE DRIVE

Sandbar Stewart handled the drive on Marble before Jim Grindl. Tommy Stevens took it out one year, too.

There was 120 million on that drive in 1917, all told — Rutledge and Herrick logs.

All that lawsuit trouble between Herrick and Rutledge over chargin' Herrick a dollar a thousand for driving Herrick's logs. Herrick got smart in 1918 and hired Lee Mashburn and five of us to follow behind Rutledge's crew.

We'd set there sometimes for days till Rutledge got their logs off of a bar and then what Herrick logs they left we'd roll 'em off into the water and the flood would carry 'em on ahead of the Rutledge logs. Then Rutledge would have to roll 'em off next time to get at their own logs.

Herrick paid $5 a day. Rutledge paid $4. About 10 hours. We didn't work no ten hours, though — we put in maybe 6 hours. We had a rag (tent) camp moving along with us moved by Dick Talbot's packstring.

Talbot was a rough one. Rough on stock and rough on himself. He never took less than 350 pounds to the animal. And that was an 18 mile pack each way, Marble Station to Hobo. He went up and back in one day.

This drive that Lee Mashburn run for Herrick come all the way from Hobo Creek to the Sorting Gap at the mouth of the St. Joe River.

SLOW WORK AT SCOTT'S SLOUGH
But some of it was slow and hard. Beginning on my 20th birthday, the 15th day of July, 1918, we was 30 days just cleaning out the logs that had piled all over in the brush in Scott's slough at St. Joe. Couldn't use horses. Just heavy hand work. We dug a trench and took the logs one at a time and drug 'em out through the muck to the river.

HURT KNEE AND BOOTLEGGING
In 1920 I was working for John Ankor and my peavy slipped when I was rolling a log and I busted the cartilage in my left knee. It never did get completely over it. A doctor wanted to operate but I've known people that had operations like that and ended up with stiff knees. I wouldn't take a chance.

As long as I had to limp around I thought I'd pick up money bootlegging. It wasn't easy to peddle the rotgut from around St. Joe so I bought good whiskey for $10 a gallon at Saltese.

I'd stick maybe 3 gallons in a packsack and climb into the cab of the freight locomotive. I was friends to the engineer. When the train got to that crossing by the river bridge at St. Joe he'd whistle a bunch of short toots like there was cows on the track and slow down almost to a stop so I could get off.

MOONSHINE DANCES AT FERRELL
Then I'd take the whiskey over to the cabin I rented with Big George Selkirk in town and we'd bottle it in pints. There was a good floor in the old schoolhouse over in Ferrell and we'd put on a dance. I'd play the most of the music with a mouth organ and George would be busy selling lumberjacks whiskey for $5 a pint. You don't need much in the way of music if you got moonshine. There was a sheepherder name of Jack Haugen that tended a flock of sheep up toward Falls Creek and he'd come down and kick up his heels, too.

PEDDLED PINTS AT THE MARIES
Maybe next day I'd fill my packsack with pints and start walkin' down the track to St. Maries. I'd stay with my mother a few days at her bar, restaurant and rooming house down in Oldtown just across the

Walt Darry's mother's joint in St. Maries 1920

road toward the river from the Mountain View Hotel. She had divorced my dad about 1915 and married Walt Miller.

I hid bottles all around that end of Oldtown. This sheepherder, Jack Haugen come down from St. Joe and hit me up to buy a bottle. I took him up to where I had one bottle cached.

COMES THE SHERIFF
A couple days later Sheriff Steele come down with a warrant for my arrest for selling whiskey. The judge set my bail at $500. I let the county support me and stayed in jail, besides the jail was full of my friends from Santa, Fernwood, Clarkia, Calder and one from St. Joe. The sheriff had made a big round-up. We got to comparin' notes. All of us had sold a bottle to this damn sheepherder.

THE TRIAL
Mine was the first trial 13 days later. I had Mike Doohan for my lawyer and a jury trial. I told the other boys in jail, "You watch! I'm gonna plead Not Guilty. If I get free you can do the same thing and all go free."

The lawyer weeded out the jury so it was mostly people from around St. Joe that knew me well and also knew this stool pigeon sheepherder.

The stoolpigeon got up and testified how he bought the whiskey from me and went down and turned it over to the sheriff and signed an affidavit that he bought it from me.

The prosecutor shoved the bottle in my face. "What is this in here? Ain't it whiskey?"

I said, "How the hell do I know? It could be water. I never saw that bottle before."

I swore to God I hadn't sold the sheepherder any whiskey — that it was all a made-up story.

None of the people on the jury had ever bought whiskey from me and they didn't like that stoolpigeon. The trial only took about half a day. They turned me loose.

The rest of 'em in jail all pleaded guilty. No wonder they got sentenced and fined.

The lawyer charged me $50 and I donated him a gallon of whiskey out of good feeling.

The only way I can figure that I got free was that I was a bigger liar than the rest of 'em.

HAULING BOOTLEG SUPPLIES
I later got a 1926 Model T Ford. It was a coupe and I cut it down to haul corn and sugar for the bootleggers around St. Joe and up the river. I used to haul for Kreuger over in Ferrell to make home brew and supplied Harry Burns and Dad Peters up by Marble Creek and a pile of other bootleggers up and down the river.

Jake Pogue was running a restaurant where old Kickbush's store had been at St. Joe. That was after his leg was cut off. He was at St. Joe a long time peddling whiskey on the side when the drives was on.

To go by road into St. Joe them days you didn't run that loop away around into Bond Creek but cut straight across toward town on a wooden trestle from the river.

KILLING OF BLONDEY COLE
I was witness at Chet Ward's trial after he killed Blondey Cole. I was settin' on the bench in front of the Skelton & Warren building when Cole come out. He got in the car and collapsed up by Babbitt's barn. Then Chet Ward headed for the tall timber.

After Ward went to the pen, Jake Pogue went to Clarkia and took over Ward's joint.

Blondey Cole was shot Aug. 4, 1929. Ward was convicted May 8, 1930.

LOGGING AT HOBO
I put in 1922 and 1923 for Andy Everett & Charlie Kelso. They logged Ole O'Dean's homestead for Fred Herrick. Some of O'Dean's homestead came down Cranberry but some of it lay over the ridge and came out on the Hobo side.

We built some roll dams in Hobo so the logs coming out of the chutes would hit water instead of the rocky creek bottom and split. We didn't have to roll the logs out of the dams. When the flood come it rolled 'em over.

Loading logs at Cats Spur 1935. That's me on top. Tom Cash on the right handled the cheat stick (scale rule), Tom Schoenwahl and William Patterson loaded and my partner Ed Williams run the hoister.

LOADING LOGS AT CATS SPUR

For seven years from about 1932 to 1939 me and Ed Williams was in together on a jammer loading cars above Clarky for Roddy & Schwab. Bill Currie unloaded the logging trucks as they come in. Then he quit. Then Earl Pagel unloaded but a log came off the top of a load and killed him. So then my brother, Bert took over. Tom Schoenwahl and William Patterson hooked. Tom Cash was scaler. Ed Williams was hoister and I top-loaded.

NOT DARRY BUT DARRAR

My dad was French Canadian. He couldn't read or write and someway on the trip west to Idaho his name got changed to Darry. Later years some relatives wrote to him and my mother and said the name was really Darrar. So my mother went to court and had the names of the kids changed. All but me. I said, "I've used the name Darry so many years that I want it kept that way."

Interviewed at St. Maries, April 21, 1975

Bill Degen

Hobo & Woods Worker

Dreamed of Rozella

Bill Degen 1979

I was born the first day of fall in the small town of Loyal, Wisconsin, September 22, 1907. Like the rest of Wisconsin the sawmilling had gone out around Loyal and the woods cleared into the fields for dairy farming. Wild violets grew profusely through the pastures. Beautiful!

All of Wisconsin was once forested with the finest white pine. That's where Weyerhaeuser got his start. There's a little town yet in the northern part named Weyerhaeuser. Humbird Lumber Company got their start there, too and there's a little town by that name right west of my home town.

Those big lumber families started intermarrying. That was one way to keep the money in the family. Used to be a little monthly magazine called The Family Tree put out by Weyerhaeuser. Inside the cover was a facsimile of a tree with all the family branches coming out to show who was WHO in the dynasty. It was circulated in all their camps. The motive was to promote loyalty amongst the employees. God save the king! you know.

GROWING UP WITH ARITHMETIC

I had 4 older sisters. I was the only boy. Long before I entered the first grade I could recite the multiplication tables up to and including the 13s. Dad thought the school would require the 13s and wrote them down for me. So when I went to 1st grade I could do 3rd grade arithmetic.

Then later when I was in the 3rd grade the 5th grade class was at the blackboard. A lot of those boys were 15, 16 years old and couldn't add a simple problem. It wasn't their fault. They had to stay home and work instead of coming to school.

The teacher used me to shame them. "Why there's a little third grader in the back of the room can add it! Willie! Come up here."

I had been sitting back there adding it as fast as she wrote it so I showed off and marched up there to write the answer. I liked arithmetic so well, for fun I'd glance at a long column of figures on the board, turn my face away and retain the numbers in my mind and add them up.

BUILDING A FARM

None of us liked town. I remember how glad the whole family was when Dad bought an 80 acre farm. I was only nine but I pitched in with the rest to clear the ground. We saved milk money to get dynamite so we could blast out white pine stumps you couldn't have put in this room. Mammoth great stumps 6 feet across and roots that reached out 20 feet or more. We blasted 'em apart, split 'em and pulled the roots out one by one. So many stumps we set 'em on edge for solid fences.

Dad sold that place, machinery, cattle and all for what seemed like a fortune — $14,000 cash — at the end of World War 1 in 1918.

THE BEER DRINKERS FARM

A year later Dad paid cash for a new 121 acre place in a rundown condition but in a beautiful location. A river loaded with fish cut across one corner.

The fences were broke down, the cattle thin because half the time the people didn't feed them. The pasture land was let go to hell and the soil eroded with no tame grass growing any more — just going back to brush. Dad checked with the cheese factory and Emil told him those people hadn't been hauling over 2 cans of milk a day at the most.

Again our whole family went to work to rebuild a farm: Dad, Mother and the 5 of us kids. I was 12 years old.

The people that had been farming the place had spent their time drinking beer. It took me and my sister, Margaret a whole week to gather up the empty beer kegs from all around the house and even out in the fields. Kegs from pony size — 4 gallon — to barrel size. Oak kegs with iron bands around 'em. When we stacked them up in the yard the heap was as high as the peak of the house.

We lived there about 2 years and built up the place till it produced 600 pounds of milk a day.

Then my mother got sick.

Dad didn't think things through. He should have kept the place and hired a woman to do Mother's work. He could well afford it by then.

Instead, he held a big auction and sold everything — farm, cattle machinery and all and moved back to town. He took Mother to Mayo's Clinic. She was operated on for cancer of the breast but she failed real fast after that and died.

DAD WAS BARN BUILDER

Then at the time I started high school Dad went into contracting the building of dairy barns. Dad had only gone through the third grade but he knew how to use the square and do carpenter work. He was six foot three and all man. He'd take a team and skid in big logs maybe 2 feet in diameter in winter when the ground was frozen. The country was all level there.

Then he'd put them on a rollway, snap a chalkline on them for a guide and score them first with an axe to the depth he wanted, then hew them into square timbers with a broadaxe. He framed and cut all the pieces according to plan and fastened them using wooden dowels and mortising, in sections on the ground.

Then he'd hire maybe 20 husky men and have a raising bee, all done by hand. First they'd raise a wall section just high enough to get 15 foot pikepoles underneath.

The builder, in this case Dad, would be the director. He'd say "HEAVE!" and they'd get ready. When he said, "HO" they'd shove up on the pikepoles. Sometimes it would take about a week to get the sides up. Then the rafters and roof went on a piece at a time. One barn was 40 feet wide and 120 feet long, set up on a concrete wall. That was his biggest.

MORE MATH

My second year of high school a new teacher named Riskine introduced a commercial arithmetic course. Three of us sophomore boys: Wilson Spry, Millard Jenks and myself entered it. The rest of the class was seniors.

The teacher noticed that the 3 of us youngest could keep up with him and it irked him.

One day he said, "Some people in this class think they're pretty sharp." He looked right straight at us boys. "I'm going to start writing numbers in a long string and move across the blackboard. It will be addition, subtraction, division, multiplication — everything. As I write you'll only have a fraction of a second to see the numbers because my left hand will hold an eraser. When I erase the last number I'll write an equals sign and I want the answer."

The instant he finished writing our hands went up — and ours were the only hands. We gave him the correct answer.

He looked disappointed and wrote down some more difficult problems. We still gave him the correct answers. Of course there were no fractions — just whole numbers. But I thought it was the most fun I'd had in a long time.

From that time on Mr. Riskine treated us with respect.

ROZELLA

About the time I graduated from high school I fell in love. Her name was Rozella Cronin. Her parents called her Dolly when she was a baby and that name stuck with her. I was about the only one outside her family that knew her real name. Oh Boy! She was beautiful. She had long hair that came clear down to her waist, you know. It was in ringlets — natural ringlets. Brunette. Brown eyes.

One evening she confided to me that when she was a little baby she had straight hair. She got some disease — probably typhoid fever — lost all her hair and after the doctor saved her, her hair came back in ringlets.

I dreamed of getting married, buying a home for her.

DEPRESSION

Along came that terrible Depression. It tore apart families. Whole communities went bankrupt. My dad was already sick and not able to work any longer but he had savings enough for his old age. Then the bank closed its doors and the nickels and dimes he and others had worked hard for and saved was wiped out.

I tried working in the printing office for the weekly in my home town but it paid so little I had to quit. Then I worked for a construction outfit hauling sand and gravel for forty-two and a half cents an hour. That doesn't sound like much but that was fair wages then. But a year went by and I never had an entire settlement on my wages.

I had to sue them to get my pay. That didn't end the job. They wanted me back and then again, they couldn't pay.

I left town to work at short jobs in Michigan and Minnesota. Sawmills were all gone but a few portable mills were picking up the leavings. They done custom sawing for people, then moved somewhere else. I took odd jobs. I worked for the county surveyor a few weeks. If I brought home a few extra dollars it went for Dad's medical bills.

It was early in the fall. Rozella and I had gone together 9 years. She was just a farm girl and couldn't find work, either. Her people were poor, too.

I went over to tell her I was at the end of my rope. I couldn't find work anywhere.

She says, "What are you gonna do now? Will you run your car over a bluff into the river and kill yourself like Pierce Metcalf did?" Pierce was a young guy we both knew.

I could tell she was discouraged and all done with me.

I mustered up some brave talk. I said, "Hell No! I'm gonna start to live now." I didn't tell her I'd sold my car for $65 and intended to leave the country.

We parted without words. I felt like going on a big drunk but I went home to Dad's house and visited with him a few days.

Four years before this in the summer of 1932, 10,000 hungry World War 1 veterans had made their bonus march on Washington and General McArthur under Republican President Herbert Hoover took the army and burned out their tin can shacks and run them out of Anacostia Flats with bayonets and tear gas.

MAYBE WORK OUT WEST
I drifted down to the tavern asking about jobs and some said you could find work out West. Henry Davis was talking about driving his car out to Montana. His brother-in-law was going to finance the trip. The brother-in-law was one of those World War 1 vets that had got run out of Washington, D. C. But under Democratic President Franklin Roosevelt, the government had kicked through with bonus money to him.
I said, "Henry! I'd be willing to pay my way to ride West with you."

Henry said, "No, Billy! I've known you ever since you were a little kid. This is gonna be on me. You just come with us and do part of the driving."

So off we went. Henry and his wife and brother-in-law stopped at their relatives in Montana. Montana had no jobs so I started hitchhiking on the freights to Idaho, Washington and Oregon.

Everyone was out of work and riding the freights. When I commenced to meet lumberjacks in the hobo jungles I felt more at home.

I ended up in Yakima. I knew some folks there from my home town that had sent word they'd help me find work.

I hunted up the address but their house shades was all pulled.

I stayed around town 3 or 4 days and came out again and again but they never came home. I couldn't stay around any longer. I had only $20 left.

I finally found a job shocking wheat for a dollar a day and room and board out of Ellensburg. It ended in 2 weeks but I was $11 richer.

I gathered with the migratory workers up town in Ellensburg every day in hopes a rancher might come along and hire me for a day or two. One day a guy told me a job was offered to him at Deer Lodge, Montana, feeding cattle for the winter. It paid around $30-$40 a month and room and board. He said he wasn't going to take it. I could have it.

BUMMING THE FREIGHT
It sounded like a fortune to me. I climbed a Milwaukee freight headed east for Deer Lodge. If there was no job in Deer Lodge I was

going to try to make it back home where I could at least starve among friends.

I was in a boxcar with 65 people. Must have been two or three-hundred people on that train. A lot of women and even little kids. They stayed in a group with their men and each other. It was getting cold. All we had to cover us was newspapers and from the swaying of the train and the vibration they kept sliding off.

Whenever the steam engine stopped to take on water or coal we'd get out and trot up and down to get warm. All of us stayed right close to the train so when the whistle blew we could pile in.

The further east we went the colder it got. It was pitch dark. I didn't know where the hell we was. Some of the guys said we was headed toward Minneapolis and I knew we'd have to go through Deer Lodge.

THE REEFER

I picked up with a guy that seemed a pretty decent sort. He had done a lot of bumming and was more savvy than I was.

I said, "I've got to find some warmer place."

He says, "I saw a reefer two cars back. If it's loaded it'll be locked but if it's empty we'll have a chance."

The first time the freight stopped, I followed him back and climbed up on top of a refrigerator car. The roof hatch at the end of the car didn't have a seal. We opened it and slid down into the empty ice compartment. A heavy mesh screen separated it from the main part where fruit could be carried.

That was my first experience riding in a reefer. I've often thought since that was a damn dangerous thing to do. If an inspector had come along he would close that hatch again and latch it shut. We could have been stuck in there to suffocate or freeze to death in that insulated car and nobody could hear us yell.

But we was out of the bitter wind and the air was absolutely still so our body heat gathered around us. As the train rolled and the hours passed we dozed a little.

After what seemed like a day the freight stopped. We got to wondering why it didn't move.

I says, "Maybe we've been set out on a siding. Let's crawl out. If it's daylight we can see where we are."

From the top of the car it was pitch dark like the inside of a cow. We felt down the ladder to the ground. The wind was cold like a knife.

"Holy God!" my partner said. "We must be in the arctic."

My teeth was chattering. When we pulled out of Ellensburg I was dressed in light summer clothes. I was wearing a pair of coveralls over them to keep them clean and respectable for a job. Damn good thing I had the coveralls. I'd have froze for sure.

We started walking alongside the freight.

A little light showed up ahead.

I said, "Maybe that's a barn or chicken coop or pigpen or haystack. We can crawl in and get warm."

WAITING ROOM

The light turned out to be from in front of a railroad station. We walked around the building looking for a door. Went into the waiting room. There was at least a hundred from our train. People hunched up on the floor. Coats buttoned up tight sittin' on benches. Shiverin'. Women and kids, too.

I walked over to one of the steam radiators. The damn thing was ice cold. I tried them all — even the one in the men's toilet. All cold.

I walked up to the ticket window and says to the station agent, "How much longer before the freight pulls out?"

He looked at his watch. "Well, it's eleven o'clock now. It'll pull out about two in the morning."

I says, "Have any of these radiators got any heat?"

"No!" he says. "No heat. And we got orders not to build a fire in that stove, either. All of you listen to me! When that freight whistles, all you guys wake each other up. And by God! I want all of you on that freight."

I was dead for sleep. I curled around the radiator. I figured they might accidently give some heat and warm me up.

Next thing I woke up and it was broad daylight and I was the only one in the waiting room. I hadn't done anything wrong but I felt kinda cheap. No doubt they'd tried to wake me but couldn't. I'd missed my ride and maybe missed out on that job at Deer Lodge.

I walked up to the ticket window. There was a different agent there. "Is there a town near here?"

"Yeh!" he says. "Up the hill."

"How far?"

"Couple of blocks."

I went into the washroom and tried to wash my hands and face with stiff fingers and cold water. Mopped off with paper towels. That helped wake me up.

HUNGRY

I says to the agent, "Hey! Is there a restaurant anywhere?"

"Yeh! About a block."

All I had was $17 and I was starvin'. And cold. I hadn't eaten the day before — or maybe it was two days — who the hell knew?

I walked into this restaurant. There was just the cook and hasher.

I wrapped myself around a stack of hotcakes, bacon and eggs and lots of scalding hot coffee. Then I ordered another breakfast just like it.

I looked out the window at the mountains across the valley all white with fresh snow. This was only the second day of August, 1936.

I said to the hasher, "What's the name of this town.?"

"St. Maries," she says.

"Montana?"

She laughed. "No! Idaho."

I paid the sixty-five cents for each of the breakfasts and walked up the street till I heard a lot of loud talk and noise coming from a tavern.

Old Blake & Hayworth Tavern, now Holsteins Bar & Museum run by Ed Jewett, 1975. Logging relics include: wood fan carved by civil engineer Warren Wood, 14 foot wood chain complete with round and grab hooks carved by Alie Mason, ewe wood spoon whittled by Pete Johnson, homemade skip for driving trail dogs made by Bill Robinson, lamp & curling iron used by Annie Olson at her joint in Clarkia, a level donated by Ed Ramey, bird cage by Whittlin' Jack, cut nails from the old Mountain View Hotel and a typewriter from the old Glen Miller Shingle Mill.
Ed Jewett at right.

FRIENDLY TAVERN

That was Blake & Hayworth's place where Ed Jewett is now. Two men behind the bar: a little short old man — that was Blake, and a tall, slim fellow, that was Hayworth.

I pushed through men to the stove. My front was warm when I faced it but every time I thought of that snow across the valley my back got the shivers.

I said to Blake, "All I got on underneath these coveralls is BVDs, wore-out overalls and a thin summer work shirt. Where can I buy some heavy underwear?"

Blake says, "It's Sunday so the stores are closed. But I know the manager of Penny's. I'll phone him for you and he'll come down."

Man! When I changed into that pair of six dollar, one-hundred per cent wool, heavy Black Bear underwear in the back room and come out by the stove I began to warm up. I commenced to like St. Maries right then.

Some lumberjacks started telling me about logging camps only a mile or two out of town and if "You can't find anything else, you can always cut wood."

WORKING FOR MIDNIGHT

Next day I was cutting 4 foot cordwood for Midnight Gibney at a dollar and six bits a cord, split and piled. The job was a mile east of the Halfway House at the head of Flat Creek. Me and my partner holed up in an empty shack that used to be the dining room for the old McGoldrick camp. Midnight arranged for us to get credit for groceries at Ernie McLaughlin's.

Midnight Gibney lived the life of an aristocrat. All he done was drive that truck — that's the nearest he came to manual labor. His name came from his work at night stealing cordwood from other people. Most of the business houses at that time heated with wood. I think buckskin tamarack brought $15 a cord. It wasn't hard to cut but it was hard to keep your crosscut saw sharp, especially when you hit them knots.

Midnight loaded up truckload after truckload of our wood but he never offered to pay us. One day we caught him. Me and my partner pressured him for a payday.

He didn't give us any money but he reestablished our credit at the store.

We stayed there that winter of '36-'37. The snow piled up six foot on the level — came right to the top of the door. We couldn't work so we laid in the shack. We had stocked up on food and had a couple of big tamarack wood trees skidded next to the house.

At that time the Eagles had their lodge on the third story of that building right across the street from where the Security Bank is now. The ground floor was forestry headquarters. I wasn't an Eagle but a friend of mine invited me to the dances so I could listen to the music even though I didn't dance, and buy a thick sandwich with coffee — all for a dollar and a quarter.

DAD DIED
When I left home in Wisconsin, my sisters — three of them had married and still lived around Loyal — didn't know that Dad had diabetes bad. After I got settled in St. Maries I contacted them. Dad had already died and been buried weeks before.

OFF TO THE WOODS
In the spring I hired out to the Forest Service survey crew laying out a road in the Fishhook Basin country. It was all big, beautiful white pine and spruce. You had to look up and find a hole at night to see the stars. Now it's been raped and skinned and made a regular desert.

Our rag camp was at Breezy Point which was the end of the road coming up from the river. Sam Frazier from Clarky was cook. Plenty of good food.

We saw mule deer every day and lots of nights they'd play right around the tent. They'd jump high and come down on all 4 feet and make the ground echo and wake us up.

We laid out a road to Fishhook springs. The surveyor was George Erwin. Including the civil engineer there was 5 of us. I'd had a little experience back in Wisconsin working with the county surveyor so George picked me to do the chaining (measuring) and using the abney level which determines the grade.

CATCHING A FOOLHEN
There was all kinds of small game like grouse and foolhens. I had never seen a foolhen. Buck Alcorn was cuttin' right-of-way. In the evening after we was done workin' we'd always sit and visit awhile. Buck told me a foolhen was so dumb you could pick it up on a stick. I thought he was jokin' me.

By 9 o'clock we was in bed.

We was comin' back to camp after work and I happened to be walking ahead in the trail. Here set a foolhen right on the upper side of the trail on a little windfall.

Well, I found a nice little stick. I tapped it two or three times on that windfall. Next thing I knew he stepped onto the end of it. I was real careful not to jar it and I raised him to my shoulder. And you know, he was still on my shoulder when I got to camp!

I didn't want the rest of 'em to bother him so I tossed him in the air and he flew off.

Once in awhile we'd see a moose. And bear. Bobcats. Probably the first time most of them had ever seen a man. Long as you didn't make any fast move they'd stay put.

On Sunday Jim Titus and Harry Madison and I went trout fishing down off the hill to the Little North Fork and in Fish Lake.

From Fishhook spring we started surveying over to Marble Mountain. At that time they just had a table for the map board on the highest point and a tent for the lookout man.

That's where Clare Cory was lookout for the Coeur d'Alene Protective Ass'n back in 1927.

The packer says to him when he unloaded the supplies, "Say! You haven't got any lightning protection here. I'll tell them when I get back to the station.

Before the packer came back on the next trip there was a storm and Cory didn't report in by phone. He had been killed right there August 27th. at his mapboard by a bolt of lightning.

BOSS WAS ROUGH

Rastus Smith was our camp boss. A real nice guy to work for. He never came out to look down our collar.

But George, the civil engineer, boss of the survey crew, was kind of rough. George had given me a pad and a pencil to write down the footage between stations.

He said, "In the evening you turn that in to me so I can put it on the map at the tent."

Well damn it! It isn't as though it was all open country. Some places was jungle and no matter how thick the brush is, you burrow right into it. So each time I'd write down the footage I'd have to fool around, hunt up a good pocket to put that pad and pencil away. Then, when I walked ahead to pioneer out a course, I'd have to wrap the chain up. I got tired of diggin' this pad and pencil out and puttin' it back in my pocket.

George was a hell of a good engineer. He savvied his work all right. But if anybody made a slight mistake George bawled the daylights out of him in front of the crew

We had surveyed 4 miles toward Marble Mountain.

George came at me cussin' like a blue streak, pullin' his hair with one hand and his hind end with the other.

"What the hell are you doin'?"

I was stunned. I said, "I've been doin' my job the way you told me. Chaining, taking the grades on the abney and blazing and marking the center stakes."

I've been watchin' you! You didn't write down the footage on the last two stations."

"Oh yes, I did!" I says.

He says, "Let's see that pad!"

Well, for about three days the pad had only totals. It never showed the individual figures and where I'd added it.

I said, "There's too much messin' around diggin' that pad out, puttin' it back, diggin' it out, puttin' it back. Oftentimes we only go 66 feet or maybe only 30 at a time. I add the numbers in my head — write down the totals later."

"Oh! Jesus Christ!" he says. I thought he was gonna bust his suspenders and go straight up.

"How long you been doin' this!" he yells.

I said, "I'll bet you a five dollar bill that if we chain this over again —"

He said, "I've worked with a lot of men. There isn't a man livin' could remember all those numbers and add them in their head and get it right."

The rest of the crew stood there listening. Billy Byrd was in our crew. He was an old time timber cruiser.

I thought, "Oh Jesus Christ! Am I gonna lose this job?"

Billy Byrd tapped George on the shoulder.

"Settle down, George. I happen to know Degen pretty well. If that man tells you he's sure he's right," he says, "don't dispute his word."

George Erwin looked at Billy Byrd and he says, "What in hell do you know about it! You couldn't add 2 and 2 and get the right answer. Come on! We have to chain all over again from Fishhook spring."

It was getting pretty late in the afternoon when that happened. We went back and started and late next day we got back to that last stake again. George had kept track.

I had, too. Writin' it all down on my pad just in case he made a mistake. If he was off just one number — one foot — I'd have him.

I compared notes with him. We had the same numbers.

He hadn't read the last center stake.

I says, "George. How about it? Gonna call me on that bet?"

He commenced to scratch his head.

He went to read the center stake. Then he added up his total on the pad. He looked at me. He looked at Byrd. He looked at the whole God damn crew.

"I'll be a son of a bitch!" he says. "You added those numbers as you went along, all of them, in your head. And remembered the total."

It made a big impression on the whole crew but it wasn't anything really earth shaking. Most everybody has a gift of some kind. Mine happened to be mathematics.

The organ Nellie played at her floathouse for the lumberjacks to sing. Now owned by Ruth Osier.

FLOATHOUSE NELLIE

Being a single man my social life around St. Maries kind of centered around the taverns and Floathouse Nell. I never played around with Nellie, you know. But me and some friends would go down and buy a few shots from her in the evenings after the beer parlors closed.

She could really play the violin. She had an organ in the floathouse and she'd play for a bunch of us to sing. I'd suggest a tune and we'd buy a little of her whiskey to coax her.

We sang tunes like Old Black Hawk, Red Wing, Colorado and Silver Threads Among The Gold.

NELLIE WAS GENEROUS

She fed a lot of us lumberjacks home cooked meals at her floathouse. You bet! And if she'd meet us up town she'd timber up at the bar. Free drinks for everybody.

She was quite a diplomat when she had a whole gang of rough men in her house. She'd nip trouble in the bud.

And Nellie was kind hearted. Whenever I was all done gettin' drunk — broke flatter'n hell and headin' back to hunt work, I'd be feelin' pretty rough, you know. Closer I walked to Nellie's place the more I'd think, "I wish to Christ I had a pint to settle my nerves and to wake up on the first few mornings."

I'd stop in and put the lug on Nellie for a pint. It might not be the best but it was better'n none.

She'd ask me where I was gonna go, if I had a job waitin' for me.

I'd tell her I was gonna make the rounds — hit up the camps till I got a job sawing or swamping.

She'd say, "Well, I know when you get done you'll stop back again."

I'd say, "I won't forget you."

Then I'd put this pint in my packsack, you know. Way down in the bottom in case somebody would reach in the top lookin' for whiskey.

Nellie showed me a picture of herself when she was young before she got the worse for wear. She had been a beautiful woman.

One time years after Nellie was dead I was hunting elk up a draw not far from town. All by myself. I run into a stake drove into the ground and here I found a location notice in a tin can with her name on it. Nellie Cottingham.

The Atlas Tug owned in 1925 by the St. Joe Boom Co., coming downriver through St. Maries with a tow of logs. Along the right shore a string of floathouses occupied by Nellie, Josie, Molly, Giggles and friends. Picture taken from the Red Collar dock.

Josie was another well known woman on floathouse row.

After Josie left the business and her boathouse — just up the St. Maries River there right close to where the old wagon bridge crossed — one afternoon I went there to get me a coupla drinks. They had the door open, you know, and music goin' in there...and Swede George, short, sawed off guy was in there dancing with this beautiful young girl. This was maybe 1939.

I walked in the screendoor. I bought a drink for the three of us. I set there a little while, you know, but all this time they kept a'dancin'...this young girl and Swede George. He was quite a cut-up when he got a few drinks...course they'd probably already had their fun.

I ordered another drink just for myself. I was gettin' down to the last of the Mohicans — broke. They was still dancin' after I got the second drink drank, didn't seem to get friendly with me anyway so I got up and I walked out.

But this girl she called me back. And she bought me a drink. I was sittin' there and she was sittin' in her chair across from me and Swede was there yet but he was gettin' heavy eyed. So I talked a little bit, you know. I asked her if she was a native of St. Maries.

"No,"she says. "I'm from clear back east."

I says, "So am I."

"Oh?" she says. Didn't ask me where.

So I asked her what state she came from.

She says, "I'm from Black River Falls, Wisconsin."

I told her, "I've been there lots of times."

She says, "You son of a gun! Are you really from Wisconsin?"

I said, "You know where the town of Loyal is?"

"Hell yes!" she says.

And she started gettin' talkative.

So of course I pumped her a bit, you know.

"Well," she says. "I'll have to tell you about my first sexual experience. He was a tall, good lookin' red head. He could keep you laughing. When he smiled it gave me goose bumps."

I said, "That sounds like a guy I went to high school with."

She says, "I don't think you'd know him."

I says, "Do you mind if I take a guess?"

"Go ahead," she says.

I says, "Did he have a small mole on the left side of his chin? Was his name Barry Zornes?"

A sad look come over her face and she clammed shut.

Probably Zornes had promised to marry her like he did some others. And she loved him and he threw her off. Maybe she lost faith in herself. Lost her self respect. Yet she was a real pretty girl and pleasant. She could have had almost any decent man she wanted.

Happenings like that made me think of Rozella, you know. She was 3 years younger than I was. I'm 72 now. That would make her 69. Years after I left Wisconsin I heard she finally married a cheesemaker — a man a lot older than her. Out here in Idaho I ran into women different times that appealed to me but I just couldn't forget Rozella. I'd circle the bait like a fox — and stay away.

Interviewed at St. Maries, Idaho Oct., 1979

Elk Prairie Station 1950

Left-Wash Applegate says, "Dick Talbot got $70 a ton for packing stuff from Marble Station into Everett & Kelso's Camp on Cranberry Cr. 3½ cents a pound. He'd make one round trip a day for two days and then lay off on the third for the horses and mules to rest."

Mamie Dittman

Crossed the Atlantic in a sailing ship

Mamie Dittman at 91 October 1979

I was born in Lux, Russia of German parents in 1888. When that part of Russia was taken over by the Poles in 1901 my parents left for America.

I was three years old when we crossed the Atlantic on a big sailing ship.

During the six weeks passage the ship carpenters were building a stairway from the top deck to the one below and everyone had orders to keep the children away.

Somehow I managed to fall all the way down from the top to the bottom deck. It left a knot which I still carry on the top of my head. After the fall I was unconscious so many hours that everyone thought I was dying and my parents told me years later they were seriously discussing burial at sea when I came to.

We landed in New York and my dad got a job driving one of these old fashioned busses drawn by horses. We thought they were such pretty horses! We'd get into these buses and I remember on my brother's side the windows were green and on my side they were red.

Six months later we moved to Wisconsin where my dad's father and mother lived. Dad bought a little piece of ground in the German settlement. There were seven of us in the family. I learned at home to speak, read and write German and at public school I learned English. I was there until I was 19.

My sister, Millie, had married a railroad man and lived in Spokane. Then when the Milwaukee railroad was using thousands of men building down the St. Joe River, my brother-in-law thought Ferrell would be a good place to set in. So he left his railroad job and he and my sister took over the Riverside Hotel in Ferrell and wrote me that I could come live with them and wait tables. My brother-in-law also bought a team and wagon and drayed supplies from the boats to the business houses there.

COTTONWOODS ARCHED OVER THE JOE

When I came up the river on the steamer Idaho in 1907 the river was so narrow in places that the cottonwoods touched across it and the boat would go through the arches. All along the banks were big white pine. And the cedars at Reed's draw! The most beautiful cedars — some 5 and 6 feet through.

July 4, 1908 at Ferrell showing The Flyer on the right and a little of the Bonita's stern wheel housing on the left.

Now, when you look at the river spread all over the meadows and the big white pines and cedars gone — so different.

About 5 boats landed at Ferrell every day, unloading, always a bunch of men — sometimes a few women. Everyone talked homesteading.

The railroad built a station at St. Joe in 1908. Harry Sawyer was lawman at both Ferrell and St. Joe. I knew him real well. He wasn't married. He never mentioned his background. I never knew him to drink. But he made people toe the mark and was pleasant about it. He couldn't have been more than 45. Those red light districts were all around but they kept their place pretty well. People said Harry Sawyer could be tough if he needed to be. I don't know that he had any shooting scrapes.

Harry Sawyer made a point of walking home with me past the bars and joints whether it was day or night.

I had never waited table before but I got so I could remember orders — 8 at each of two tables. By and by they put in another table and that made 24 orders. We didn't write orders down in pads like they do now. I got so I could remember most all the orders in one trip.

One fellow said, "I'm going to watch. She'll get mixed up!"

But I didn't. Of course, they didn't have many kinds of dishes on the menu.

WOMEN HUNGRY MEN
Everyone wanted to date me. I'd go to the kitchen and ask the cook about each fellow.

She'd say, "Don't go with him! Wait for Henry Dittman. He's in the East visiting his folks but he'll be back."

DATING
About six months later, Henry Dittman came back. Henry was born in Chicago in 1884 and moved to Wisconsin. A friend told him about Idaho.

Henry and I started dating. There wasn't much to do on a date in Ferrell but you didn't expect much of anything then. We'd go boat riding or take a gun and go hunting, or walk to the Hanging Garden.

Henry told me that when he came from the East he stopped in the big Milwaukee Railroad station in Chicago and here on the wall was a big, lighted picture — THE HANGING GARDEN OF IDAHO.

Some fellow was looking at it and Henry said, "That's where I'm headed for."

The fellow said, "You're kidding!"

Henry said, "That's the truth. That's my home."

THE HANGING GARDEN

Right alongside Sperry's garden on the upriver side, Mrs. Bill Ferrell had a blackberry patch. They could fill their buckets and slide them down the steep hillside on a wire into a little cabin. You know! She made a thousand dollars off of those blackberries in one month.

Sperry never irrigated. He just hoed around the plants a little bit every day. A wonderful garden. Strawberries! Oh Boy! He had pears and prunes and apples. He had two long rows of grapes on each side of the stairway that went up from the road. Then raspberries and black-caps, watermelon, muskmelon..."

They claim in the early days Sperry was a druggist in the East somewhere and he had had a love affair and it didn't turn out. So he came West and started that garden.

TYING THE KNOT

In 1908, about a year after Henry came back, we went on the steamer Flyer to Coeur d'Alene and into Spokane on the Electric. Frank Theriault and my sister, Pauline, came with us to be best man and bridesmaid. In the af-ternoon we were married in a little Lutheran church up on Sprague Avenue by Rev. Kusse. He was German.

Mamie and Henry Dittman's wedding picture 1908

After the wedding we had our pictures taken and in the evening we took in a show — not a movie. It was a dog show and one of the best I've ever seen. They used live dogs and their feature act was one where the dogs performed a wedding ceremony.

Two dogs, dressed like a bride and groom came walking out on the stage on their hind legs. Behind them two smaller dogs dressed like little boys walked on their hind legs holding up the bride's train in their teeth. The preacher was a solemn looking dog in a suit wearing spectacles.

Pauline and Frank Theriault were married a year or so later.

SPERRY BROUGHT VEGETABLES

We lived in Ferrell and Sperry would come from his garden over to our house in the evening with vegetables he hadn't sold. And he'd often drop by and have lunch with us. He was always generous to us. I don't think he was hard of hearing at that time.

I know he was grouchy. But no wonder. He batched and they say he ate enough indigestible baloney to reach around the world.

After we moved upriver to Zane, Sperry sent us a nice, big box filled with all kinds of fruits and vegetables and big writing on the box, "FROM THE HANGING GARDEN".

I'm sure Sperry was quite deaf when the train hit him. Some people think he did it purposely. He always kept a train schedule and carried a watch. But his health hadn't been good for a long time. It might have been that baloney!

SCARED STRONG
Our home at Ferrell was right next to the big Elkhorn Drug store. The store was burning. I was sure our house would go, too. I had a heavy trunk filled with things. In the excitement I carried it out of our house and put it over the fence by myself. You know! It took 2 men to carry that trunk back?

PACKING FOR HOMESTEADERS
Henry had filed on a homestead up Big Creek and he done a lot of packing for other homesteaders using Jack Drummond as a helper. He charged $500 to locate homesteaders on their ground, survey it and

Henry Dittman leaving his barn at Ferrell

Ole O'Dean, Frank Theriault, Jack Finney, Tom Cuddington

build their cabin. Walt Hess and Will Kennedy homesteaded right near where we did. To go upriver they forded the Joe just below where the St. Joe bridge sets now. There was a shallow bar there at the time. Water came up to the horses' bellies.

I rode along sometimes when Henry packed homesteaders to Marble Creek. Henry and Frank Theriault, who had the barn at Ferrell and about 50 horses, were packing together for awhile. Then Henry bought Frank out.

Henry and Frank were laughing and telling about how back in 1904 Bill Theriault, Harold Theriault's father, was helping some homesteaders drive a few dozen logs down Marble Creek to build a cabin and Bill fell in. He was always smoking a short stemmed briar pipe. The creek was high and Bill wasn't a swimmer. As the current carried him down the creek the homesteaders ran as fast as they could along the bank but they couldn't keep up with him. When they finally caught up, Bill had crawled out and was sitting on a rock still smoking that pipe. He must have held his head high like a scared dog.

THE IRON MASK
Henry packed supplies to a few odd mines like the one up Falls Creek, the Iron Mask. I went along when he packed the diamond drill

to pack homesteaders into their claims. 1908

Henry Dittman, helper Frank Drummond, Will Kennedy and Walt Hess.

in. They had maybe 5 or 6 men working there and little cars on rails to bring the rock out.

We walked into that tunnel, kept a'goin' and My Gosh! I don't like to be in those dark places with only candles to light my way.

When we got to the end of the tunnel the boss put the drill in place and he says to me, "Now you're gonna run that the first thing.!"

So I went over and took a'hold of it.

He snapped it on. Boy! It shook me and shook me.

I stayed with it about 3 minutes then I told somebody else to take it.

I've forgotten what mineral they were looking for but in places along the tunnel it looked pretty good and again it wouldn't. I was glad to get out of there.

They stayed with it another year or so then quit. Now there's hardly nothing left and the brush has grown over so you can't see where the buildings were.

The Day boys from Wallace had a prospect up another branch of Falls Creek, now named Day Creek after them. Had 2 or 3 men working there. They didn't find any mineral, either.

NOT PREPARED FOR TWINS

When the twins were born the paper carried an item: **Twins were born to Mr. and Mrs. Henry Dittman. The father is still living.**

Henry had to go to St. Maries and buy more baby clothes.

A judge and his wife lived right across the road from us in Ferrell and she was always willing to take care of the twins when I'd go away somewhere. Then, of course, I'd take care of her little boy when they'd go.

I corresponded regularly with my mother in German but I only set out to visit her and my dad in Wisconsin, once. On the train to Spokane it kept me so busy following the twins around I was all in. I turned around and took the first train back to St. Maries.

Then the next time I got ready to go, Corrine, my daughter, came down with the flu and she was real sick that night and I thought, "Gee Whiz! I can't leave in the morning with her sick like this."

Then Mother died and Dad did, too so there was no reason to go.

1910 FIRE BURNED OUT CABIN

Just a few feet away from our homestead cabin up a side canyon on Big Creek the water came over a rock ledge and dropped in a 12 foot falls. It sounded so much like it was raining real hard that when I stayed there it kinda bothered my sleep at night.

The day of the big wind when all the fires ran out of control the firefighters thought they could save themselves by getting under this waterfall.

One fellow — he was 18 — said to the rest, "If you fellows follow me I'll take you out."

They said, "You're crazy! Nobody can make it out of here."

He put on Henry's high topped boots he found in the cabin and Henry's big hat and ran for his life. And he made it! But he burnt one foot so bad he was in the St. Joe hospital about 6 weeks.

Back at the cabin as the fire came closer the falls began to dry up and then the water turned hot and the cabin caught fire and burned right beside the firefighters. They were found laying all around the ashes of the cabin. 13 of them,

The young fellow that made it out alive came to our house at Ferrell and said to Henry, "Can I keep these boots and the hat?"

The hat had holes burned through it and the boot leather cooked stiff and black.

Henry said, "Keep 'em for souvenirs."

LOCATION OF THE DITTMAN HOMESTEAD
St. Maries, Idaho
15 January 1976
Dear Bert:
   We own the NE¼ of the SE¼, Section 35, Township 47 North, Range 2 East in Shoshone County.
   As far as we know this is a portion of the Henry Dittman homestead.
Very truly yours,
(signed) Carl M. Buell

Editor —
   This places the homestead in a branch of Big Creek now named Dead Man Gulch and about 1¼ miles airline southeast of Lemonade Peak. Mamie Dittman's account places it roughly in the same area: "You remember how far the Herrick railroad went up Big Creek after the 1910 fire? It went about 6 miles to where our trail took off to the northwest from right where the railroad stopped. Pierce Creek was as far as the railroad went. It turned the corner and went up Pierce Creek a ways." (The railroad later went much farther up the main Big Creek to the Middle Fork.)

OTHER FIREFIGHTERS WHO LOST
   Harold Theriault remembers that on the same day the firefighters around the Dittman cabin lost their lives, Henry and Ed Basett mounted saddle horses and rode from Avery to warn the firefighters at Setzer Creek.

They left a note with Grogan, the cook, at the fire camp alongside Setzer Creek, telling the crew the fire was running wild and to come out right away. The two men then rode back to Avery.

When the crew came in to eat and read the note, only the foreman, Jim Sheehy and young Doc Theriault hit the trail for Avery. The rest decided it would be safer to take refuge in a natural clearing on the hogback between Storm Creek and Beaver Creek. Their unidentifiable burned bodies were found in the clearing — all their watches had stopped at the same time.

The only identifiable body was that of Grogan, the cook. He had died in the waterhole beside the camp.

Mamie Dittman continues:
BACKFIRING AT ST. JOE
One night when the fire was moving in from the southeast toward St. Joe they backfired that hill and all that big timber by the St. Joe bridge to save the town of St. Joe. The fire came close around the town but didn't come down into it.

After 1910 there was one fire after another. I got so I could feel when there was going to be another one. I've always been so afraid of fire.

LOGGING THE BURN
The year after the fire, 1911, while I stayed at Ferrell, Henry logged burned timber on Big Creek for Herrick. Before the fire I'd take the twins and go up to the homestead and stay perhaps a month at a time. It was so pretty with 4 million feet of big white pine trees on that 160 acres.

Now everything was mutilated and black.

Herrick took the best of it as fast as they could get to it. And he didn't pay much — everybody had to sell for whatever they could get.

In 1915 when our twin boy and girl were 6 years old we lived upriver near where Walt Scott lives now. Our neighbors, the Hoopers had twins, too — a boy and girl. They lived in Shoshone County and we lived in Kootenai. They give us a teacher up there just for 4 little kids in the first grade. The teacher was Elda Wright who used to live in St. Maries.

HONEY JONES
He homesteaded the meadow just below Falls Creek in about 1907 and raised bees and sold honey. We could never find where he came from or anything because he never talked about himself. His beard reached down to his ankles so he often braided it and coiled it up inside his shirt. He built seats and tables in secluded nooks around the falls and made trails to them so people could go sit there and commune with nature. He protected the deer.

Honey Jones in a dug-out by the Falls about 1918. Courtesy — Annie Eckman

Honey Jones Home about 1918. Courtesy — Annie Eckman

He charged a dollar for families coming in boats or by team to picnic and camp in his meadow.

When we lived up by Scotts, we saw Honey Jones often. He took a great liking to Henry and I. He gave us honey.

He said, "Build yourself a little shack on my ground."

But he let the snakes run right through his house. I hate snakes and couldn't stand for anything like that. Anyhow, by this time we had 4 children. Children get mischievous and we didn't think it would work out — him being a bachelor that had lived alone so long.

A funny thing happened. A fellow about 20 came along and Honey Jones took a great liking to him and kept him around.

Henry happened in to visit.

The kid was sittin' there talkin'.

Henry got Jones to one side, "Better watch that kid!"

Jones said, "Oh! I think he's all right."

Henry said, "Look at his eyes, kind of blurred-like."

Jones says, "I never noticed that. I'll watch him."

A couple days later that kid drew a knife on him. He must have been a mental case.

Lucky thing a neighbor happened in right then. They took the knife away from the kid and phoned the sheriff.

HONEY JONES LIVED TO BE 91

Annie Eckman says, I do know that Honey Jones was of Scottish descent and he lived with the Indians somewhere around this area before he settled at the mouth of Falls Creek.

He was an educated man with a good command of language. He had the most fabulous books. A whole set of Arabian Nights, Dante's Inferno, a lot of those old classics.

I wasn't afraid of Honey Jones. I was a little kid and could get by with practically anything. He didn't want people to mess with his bees nor pick flowers and then throw 'em down because he had so many things planted.

He didn't believe in banks. He used to hide money on the place. He lost about $9,000 hidden in the rafters of the house that burned. So in the next house he kept his money in gold coins.

He used to give me a $5 gold piece each Christmas and one on my birthday. Mom said he used to get the coins out when she was up there visiting and let me sit on the floor and play with them. My son has one of those $5 gold pieces that I gave him.

At 91 Honey Jones became sick with dropsy. His legs swelled up. Dad and Mother lived in Ferrell at the time and they went up every day to take care of the place and to bandage his legs.

He knew he hadn't long to live. He asked my dad to make a plain board box for him to be buried in.

Honey Jones Funeral 1927
2nd from left, Zola George; Frank Scott facing beyond the center of the coffin; Nat Sherrd, in coveralls; Jack DeLys in sweater; beside him, Annie DeLys Eckman, age 10; behind Annie, Jack Booth; beside Annie, her mother, Margaret (Maggie) DeLys; Doctor Brown with white hair and goatee; Sandy Norry facing left beside Brown; Mrs. Reed, 2nd from right.

Courtesy — Annie Eckman

When he got real bad my folks stayed up there day and night. Mom said the night he died he wasn't conscious but she and Dad were sitting there talking, maybe about getting him a casket, and he reached up and thumped the wall. Mom thought he could have been trying to tell them something.

A lot of people thought he had quite a bit of money when he passed away but he didn't.

He willed his place to my parents Jack and Maggie DeLys. I inherited it from my mother.

My folks moved to Sandpoint and lugged his books up there and gave the Sandpoint Library any of them that they wanted. The rest were at the Brown Place and I don't know what happened to them.

The grave now is practically in my son's front yard.

Editor: Jones had given orders that no preacher should officiate at his burial. They hauled Jones on a flatbed truck down the meadow and then up the old tote road and carried him along the hillside to a spot he had earlier chosen for his grave that overlooks his homesite and the river he loved. Frank Scott acted as speaker. They placed a concrete block, ground level, at his head, inscribed THOMAS JONES 1836-1927.

If you walk 195 paces toward St. Maries from the Falls Creek bridge you can look up the hillside about 200 feet toward Honey Jones' grave. His old smokehouse stands hidden in the brush between the meadow field where his house stood and the river.

About 1920 when I stopped with my dad to buy honey from Honey Jones there was a sign on his gate — handwritten — "I. W. W.s Welcome — Preachers Keep Out!" Dad told me Jones called himself an atheist.

Mamie Dittman continues:
FLU EPIDEMIC OF '19
When we read how another and worse flu epidemic was moving in, Henry built a log cabin on his logging job a mile up Trout Creek and moved me and the 5 children away from people.

Nearby was a cool, natural cave with water dripping from the ceiling, a good cellar for storing eggs and corned meat and vegetables.

When snow came the kids harnessed their collie dog to a little sled and it pulled them around on the skid trails. They had lots of fun.

Jack was only 4 years old. He started across a footlog with snow on it and fell into the creek. He was floating on his back downstream with the toes of his boots sticking out when Dave, who was 9, ran after him and hauled him out.

Everything was fine till we ran out of supplies and Henry had to go to town. He must have brought back the flu bug. Henry didn't get the flu but three of us got awfully sick.

One night I was so weak and feverish that I thought I was over the bridge. I asked Henry to make me a cup of peppermint tea.

Then I could feel life coming back.

Lucky, none of us died. The Theriaults lost 2 boys: Fred and Eddie.

LIFE AT ZANE
We moved to Zane to be closer to the camps so Henry could come home weekends.

Zane was a railroad siding with one of these little depots — just a phone booth, about a mile and a half above the mouth of Fitzgerald and a half mile below Trout Creek. They changed the name Zane to Trout Cr. now.

Henry bought land on a knoll above Zane and built a log house. He built a real good cellar so we had a place to store our own cream and milk and butter. Henry drilled two wells but they both run full of quick sand so we had to pack our water in buckets from a spring just below us. Sometimes we filled a barrel on a stone boat and pulled it up with the team. I took my washing down there one time but that didn't work so good. No place to heat the water and I had to lug the wet clothes back up to hang them out on the line.

We had nine kids — 6 girls and 3 boys.

One reason our family got along well, we lived out and the kids had no one to play with but one another. And each one had their own jobs to do. Dorothy usually helped with the cooking. Hazel washed dishes and cleaned the house. Corrine and Ruth and Olive liked to work outside. They helped with milking the 3 cows and feeding the pigs and chickens. The boys packed wood and helped with outside chores.

Henry was a wonderful family man. He left it to me to punish the kids. Like if Helen and Olive were quarreling I'd give them a licking and send them to separate bedrooms. After two or three hours they'd get so tired of being alone in the bedrooms they'd end by cleaning them up.

And of course, when Henry spoke they knew "Pop was the power" and obeyed.

TYPHOID FEVER
When I was pregnant with Olive in 1923 I went down to Ramsdell to visit my sister Millie who had owned the Riverside Hotel at Ferrell. Her husband was unloading logs off the flatcars there so they could be towed by steamboats to the mills in Harrison and Coeur d'Alene.

Those days it was common to use water out of the river. Back home in Zane I came down with typhoid fever and stayed right down in bed for seven weeks.

Henry got hold of Doc Platt and he came and stayed at the house 3 days. Henry always saw to it that I had a good doctor for sickness and when I had my babies. Lots of times I had a good nurse, too.

SCHOOLING
By this time we had 4 kids of school age. The district paid to build a board school right beside our cabin. With the children of the Greens and McWhorters there were 11 pupils. The teacher boarded with us.

TAUGHT PIANO
I've played piano since I was 10 years old. My brother taught me the chords. At Zane the Buell girls came down from Calder to take piano lessons and I taught all of my own kids to play. The boys didn't keep it up long, though. They were afraid they'd be called "sissy".

John Neff worked on the drive for years. He boarded with us. Weekends he'd go up to his home below Herrick. 1931.

COOKING FOR DRIVE
Then about 1924 Henry lived at home and worked on Jack Murphy's drive. Between the girls and I we done all the cooking for 9 to 12 drivers for about 4 years. They ate breakfast and supper at our house and carried lunches for noon and slept in the bunkhouse next door.

They were a nice bunch of men.

Sometimes I'd run out of meat or something and Murphy would say, "Well, I'm going down to the Maries. Come down with me and I'll bring you back."

FERRYING LUMBERJACKS
Henry and I were good swimmers. Living along the river we taught the older ones and they taught the younger to swim.

Ruth and Dave and Jack would watch lumberjacks as they got off the train at Zane and walked up the track. They were headed for John Ankor's logging camp across the river. The kids charged them a quarter apiece to pole them across the river in our double-ended swiftwater boat. When the water was high they charged 50 cents. When it was extra high and the current would carry the little kids a long way down the river before they got across, the lumberjacks were so happy to get across they often gave them a dollar.

The kids put the money into a can to go for groceries.

RUTH SAVED A LUMBERJACK
It was in the wintertime when Ruth who was then 16, happened to step outside and heard somebody hollering HELP! down at the river. There was a long pikepole standing by the house. She grabbed it and ran down.

Here was a man broke through the ice with his arms across the hole.

Ruth broke the ice to free a cedar log and she poled it out to him, breaking the ice as she went. Then she pulled him up on the log and brought him back in.

She took him up to the house and give him a change of dry clothes.

When he left he said, "I'll never forget you!"

Later, the cook and the storekeeper at St. Joe, Mr. Kickbush, tried to get Ruth the Carnegie Medal of Honor but couldn't because there were no other witnesses besides her immediate family.

According to the Gazette-Record 12-12-29, the man Ruth Dittman rescued was employed as cook at a camp near Calder. His name was Skelly. Ruth says he was cook at the camp on Hugus.

TOTE ROAD
For years we used that old Milwaukee Tote road. We didn't realize how really narrow it was till somebody tried to run a dual wheeled logging truck over it and found that the outside dual wheel had to hang out in the air.

Henry used to tell about Bill Pray driving his first car down a steep pitch on the tote road and it got to going too fast and he was hollering, "Whoa! Whoa!".

SCHOOL AT CALDER
Dorothy left home after the 8th grade and worked for her board and room and went to high school one year on the coast and three years in St. Maries. Then she attended teachers college in Lewiston. She taught school in Calder, then Herrick, Marble Creek and 4 years in Avery. 10 years altogether.

Dave went to work in Alaska at age 17.

Ruth and Jack tried high school in St. Maries and didn't like it so they went to work in the camps. Ruth flunkeyed. Jack logged.

There was a 19 year spread between the oldest and the youngest so they were always strung out going to school. The year Olive went into the 1st grade in Calder, Corrine was in the 8th grade and Hazel and Helen were in between. They had saddle horses to ride to school so

Henry sent up hay and the horses stayed in the livery stable. Other times the children walked to school. If the snow was deep Henry took them in the sleigh. The school district allowed $10 a month for transportation. Then 2 winters Ruth cooked and took care of the younger ones in cabins at Calder.

Then when Hazel, Helen and Olive went to school at St. Joe, Dorothy took care of them one time and Ruth cooked and took care of them another.

About 1934 we decided that instead of sending one or two to grade school in one place and one or two to high school in another, we'd move them and me to St. Maries. So Henry built a log house in the trees not far from Doc Sullivan's. The bus came along and picked the children up in the morning and brought them home at night. It worked beautifully.

HENRY INJURED
One time I was mighty thankful that some of our girls learned to get on the end of a crosscut saw or split shakes or drive tractor in the hay field.

In about 1940 Olive was helping Henry skid out some cedar poles up Bond Creek.

They had separated the team. Henry would hook a pole to Olive's horse, then he'd hook one to his own and they'd be ready to go. This one time Henry's horse took off before Henry was ready. The pole rolled and smashed his leg against a stump. The leg was badly broken and only Olive was there to help.

Olive helped Henry astride one of the horses and took him up to the road and helped him into the pickup. Then she unharnessed the horses and haltered them to a tree.

Henry had never allowed the girls to drive so she had never run any kind of car but she had run that tractor in the hayfield. She drove Henry down out of Bond Creek and to the hospital in St. Maries.

Henry was laid up for a long time after that. He died of a heart attack in 1961 at age 77.

Dave stayed in Alaska with a good job. Corrine and Hazel both graduated from St. Maries high school. Corrine married Neal Pierce. Hazel married Stub Moe.

Helen and Olive both worked their way through the University of Idaho. Helen, now Helen Bierne, became Commissioner of Health under the governor of Alaska. Olive became a high school teacher in St, Maries and married Jack Farrell and lives near Calder.

Bob lives near Stub Moe in a log house Henry helped him build. Bob has his own logging outfit. Jack logged for years with his own outfit and has retired. Dave became a log house builder and general carpenter at Fairbanks, Alaska until his recent death.

One tragedy: Ruth lost her husband, Roy Osier. He was on a crew driving logs on the St. Maries River during spring highwater. He was on a log that started to turn. He fell and hit his head on another log and was knocked out. Before they could get to him he went under and was gone among the logs.

Gazette-Record 6-2-49 — Roy Osier, 36, drowned at the Lotus log landing.

I live with my daughter Ruth in her home that used to be the Red Rooster Dine & Dance place.

I gave music lessons till 3 years ago when the ends of my fingers began to feel numb.

I wrote and published 3 songs, **Maple Tree Hill, On The Shadowy St. Joe** and one in which I tried to express what I feel for my children.

NOW OUR LITTLE BROOD HAS FLOWN

Verse:
Years pass away so rapidly.
    Why can't they tarry awhile?
It only seems just yesterday
    Since we walked down the aisle.
Chorus:
Now our little brood has flown
    And I am at home, alone:
Watching, wond'ring, waiting
    For their safe return.
May the good Lord guide their way
    As he did in bygone day
With health and love and
    Hope along the way.

Interviewed at St. Maries, April 25, 1974.

Howard Ebert

Lena Ebert

Taught last school at Tyson

Fernwood was wild

Panned gold for fun

Howard & Lena Ebert both 85, 1980

I was born in Cleveland, Ohio 1895 and came to Coeur d'Alene with my folks in 1911 when I was 16. Dad didn't homestead. He stayed here till 1914 and went back to Ohio again.

I had been working for Blackwell in Coeur d'Alene. They built a mill in Fernwood in 1912. When it started operating in 1913 they sent a bunch of us up here to work in it. I stayed with a couple other fellows down along the river in a tent.

FERNWOOD WAS WILD

I've seen as high as 300 lumberjacks on the street on a Saturday night. Three big saloons and they would be crowded. An awful lot of big camps on Renfro, Tyson, Crystal and the Big Blackwell camp across the river. Cox and Bean Belly Thornton logging, too.

Nick Miller, across the river, helped build the railroad up here in about 1908. My brother-in-law Mike Tunney had a restaurant over at Taft, Montana when they were putting the Taft tunnel through for the Milwaukee. He told about the snow goin' off in the spring and the dead bodies they'd find. Men knocked in the head for a dollar.

The Crawford mill was gone from Fernwood when I come in 1913 but I saw a few slabs lying around and a pile of sawdust. Down at the end of the street in the hole was the **Halfway House** for the stagecoach that came from Tekoa.

Crawford sawmill before '13
Fernwood

DRAYLINE TO DEPOT

1918, Old Stube Walkup and Poker Bill had a livery stable across the street. Poker Bill's real name was William Cowles. He always wore big whiskers and drove the freight wagon for old Stube Walkup with mail and freight up from the depot.

Poker Bill got that name not from playin' cards but from being on the log drive. The logs was gonna hang up and somebody hollered, "Poker 'er, Bill! Poke 'er!" meaning poke the logs out into the current with his pikepole.

Spring Drive at Fernwood 1920

SANDBAR STEWART

Sandbar Stewart was foreman of the drive. They named him that because all the fellows wanted to stop in town but he made 'em camp on a sandbar up the river so they couldn't come in and get drunk. Many millions of feet of logs got dumped in the river between St. Maries and Clarky and they had drives that brought in still more from Santa Creek and Emerald.

In 1916 my brother-in-law had a job cookin' for Carey & Harper in the Marble. I went in and helped him. At that time Carey & Harper had 3 camps. The one where I worked was on Eagle Creek with Steve Fite as foreman. Frank Harper, son of the logger, was bookkeeper for the camps. I had gone to business college with Frank in Coeur d'Alene.

IWW

It wasn't till after the Wobbly strike of 1917 when the Wobblies burnt their bedding and wouldn't work unless the companies furnished bedding that they got steel bunks. There was a big Wobbly camp down by the river across from Fernwood during the strike. Governor Alexander came up from Boise and made a speech to them and tried to get 'em to behave, I guess. After awhile a stockade was built in St. Maries and the sheriff put an awful bunch of them in it. Paul Hulp was quite a notorious Wobbly and oldtimer here that was put in the stockade.

FRANK STRAND

I knew him well. I sawed with Frank Strand in the woods in the fall of 1922. In a way he was a nice fella but it seemed to me he was always looking for trouble. He was a bachelor and dark like he might have some Indian or Mexican in him. When I was sawing with him he had two guns. I think one was a .38 and the other a little .22 pistol.

One time I said, "Frank! Why in hell do you carry that big gun?"

He said, "Can't tell when you'll get snotty."

I said, "When I get snotty I'm comin' at you with an axe."

"I believe you would."

I was tired of him cryin' about something all the time. After awhile I quit sawing with him. Then he couldn't get a partner to saw with.

The next summer, a day or two before he shot old Weedle, I was talking to him in the store. He had some moonshine in his packsack. Old Stube Walkup was kind of deputy sheriff and Strand was passin' remarks about old Stube and old Stube was sittin' at the end of the counter taking it all in.

I tried to get Strand to hush up.

I didn't know Weedle but the trouble between Strand and Weedle was over Weedle's daughter. I think she was just a teenager and Strand must have been 40 or 45 years old.

Frank was goin' back to his homestead one Sunday morning. Weedle's place was right alongside the road.

Weedle said to him, "You ain't so smart this Sunday as you was last Sunday."

Frank out with the gun. They said there was two bullet holes in Weedle's heart and you could have covered both of 'em with a dollar.

TAUGHT LAST SCHOOL AT TYSON
Mrs. Howard Ebert

I was born Lena Hedrick, 1895 at Hatton, Washington near Ritzville. My folks built a home on their homestead land. I attended school in Spokane and took my normal training at Cheney. Then I taught grade school at Harrington, Washington.

Tyson pupils 1919: Vaughn girl, Ruth Hoyle, Edna Seaman, Wayne Seaman, Howard Seaman, Marion Seaman, Vaughn boy.

I came to Tyson in 1919 to teach school. By then it wasn't much of a town. The gold rush was pretty well over but I did get to pan some gold. Just for fun. Most of the trading had gone over to Santa and Fernwood. Next year the pupils attended school at Santa where it was more convenient for their families.

I boarded with Mike Tunney and his wife and Howard Ebert was staying there too because Mrs. Tunney was his sister. That was my last year of teaching. We were married in 1920. We had 5 children: Howard, Charles, Elaine, nicknamed Janey who married Grover Blevins, Arline Johnson — her husband died, and Ronnie our youngest son. In May 1980 we'll celebrate our 60th Wedding Anniversary.

Howard continues:
HYDRALIC SYSTEM GOLD MINING
One of the Tysons and Bert Renfro discovered gold at Tyson. There was 3 or 4 Tysons in it. I think then some eastern concern bought 'em out. The outfit had been operating a few years before I came to Fernwood in 1913. The eastern concern put the pipeline in from way up Olson Creek. It cost a lot of money to put in at least 5 miles of pipe down across the valley and up the other side over the mountain and down 2 or 3 miles of flume to the reservoir. Then it was piped again from the reservoir down in a ten inch pipe and cut to 3 inches to wash off the overburden. That took a lot of force. They could knock a cow down at 300 feet with it.

Then they'd wash the gravel off the bedrock through sluice boxes and let it dry overnight and in the morning sweep the sluice boxes and gather up the gold.

POCKETS BULGING WITH NUGGETS
This is just hearsay but Monty Shevlin, he was timber cruiser, he tellin' about some fellow in there at the breakfast table before they went out to sweep the gold. He eat an awful short breakfast and

jumped up and went out. W en Monty and them got through eatin' they come over to the diggins and there he was. This fella had overalls on and he had his pockets just bulgin' with nuggets he'd picked up.

He said to Monty, "Don't say anything. I'll give you some of it." He reached in his pocket and give Monty a few nuggets.

Monty carried them around a week or two. Got down to St. Maries and took them into the bank and he had better'n ten dollars worth of nuggets.

So the rumor was that the outfit got quite a bit of gold but most of it was hijacked by the employees.

I was logging with my brother-in-law Mike Tunney over at Tyson in 1919 and staying at him and my sister's house when Lena Hedrick was teachin' school there. She came and boarded with us (laughs) and I been boardin' her ever since.

END OF THE MILL
At the mill I worked in the engine room quite a bit and then on trimmer and tail sawing. At the time the mill shut down in 1928 after being shut down part time earlier and leased to Jerry O'Neil to manufacture a couple million feet of match plank he logged from Willow Creek, I was scaling in the woods for Billy Dunlap, Blackwell buyer. Bill was a nice fellow, sensible, honest and fair.

Since that time I worked in the woods but mostly on county and state roads, running patrol.

Interviewed Jan. 1980.

Blackwell donkey near Emida 1918 — Courtesy Mary Fleming

Carrie Ells

MOTHER

Carrie and George Ells 1975

Maries River Driver

George Ells

Charlie Creek was wild

I was born in Emida on the ranch Nov. 13, 1904. We didn't have no doctors. We didn't have no law. We didn't have nothin'. The county seat was Rathdrum and you couldn't get a sheriff over here in less than 2 days on a saddle horse.

I can remember riding with Dad and Grandad in a little light wagon to St. Maries and then on past Plummer and to Coeur d'Alene to prove up on a homestead. Three miles down Santa Creek we turned left and climbed the hill right over Peterson Mt. and come out at Flat Creek dam, 7 miles downriver from Santa. Crossed the dam to the road from Santa, joining it toward St. Maries from the Halfway House. Then down Thorn Creek to the Maries. You can still drive a pickup in dry weather from Emida to where the Flat Creek dam was.

Going from St. Maries to Santa the wagon road dipped down into Soldier Creek and come out and then went down Beaver Creek Hill. Near the top of Beaver Cr. Hill one time a team ran away and drove the wagon tongue into a tree and broke it off. A few years ago Oscar Blake cut the section of tree out with the tongue still stuck in it and sent it to Boise.

LOST HORSES
In 1910 when I was 6 years old we lived at Cherry Creek in that old house where the tavern was. Dad was hauling logs with 4 horses and wagon for Heuett's little tie sawmill there. One night Dad turned the horses loose. The railroad right-of-way was supposed to be fenced but the train killed three. Tore the hip off our 17 hand high bay horse.

Dad wouldn't shoot her because if he killed her the railroad wouldn't pay him. He fought the railroad somethin' desperate to get 'em to come and put that mare out of her misery. They finally did and paid him.

DRIVE ON CHARLIE CREEK

There was 12 million feet decked along Charlie Creek one spring. I believe it was Spot McDonald logging McGoldrick's timber. Charlie Creek is not too deep but it's awful swift. When they opened the big dam 5 miles up Charlie the water roared down and carried logs all over the fields. It was wild enough that lumberjacks lost a lot of peaveys. Pretty near every time I'd go fishin' when I was a kid I'd see a peavey handle sticking up in the bottom of one of them deep holes.

The drivers skidded the logs out of the fields and worked them on down into Santa Creek and the next splash dam. This dam was below the concrete highway bridge just 4 miles down Santa Creek from Emida, and washed the logs down into the St. Maries River.

Dad was in bed with rheumatism when they come and wanted him to go on that drive. I can remember him telling them that he wasn't able to do a thing, that he sure wished he could go down and help them, that we needed the money bad.

In the morning he said, "I guess I'll just get up and go to work!" He musta worked only 2 days in that cold water and the rheumatism never bothered him again for years.

LOUIE LARSON — MARIES RIVER DRIVE BOSS

When the drive started, Louie Larson hired every man that come along until he had more than enough men. Then some morning he'd throw the bunkhouse door open and as they filed out he'd say, "You go get your time. And you. And you, too."

Experienced men said if you looked up he'd fire you. If you paid no attention to him he'd say nothin'. But what he done really, he just sorted them out in his mind ahead of time and knew the ones he wanted to keep.

As the drive worked downriver, Louie used car camps on the Milwaukee Railroad and set them out on siding. Old Lady Hendershotts at Santa was the first place we'd camp. Boy! She was the best cook in the world. Her hotel fed family style at the great long table that was packed full of everything you might want to eat.

One of those Larsons used to amaze me. On the drive he wore them heavy wool pants. When they get wet they're heavier than tons. I don't know how he kept them on. I wore just heavy wool underwear.

One time I was out holding a log in the river with my peavey so it wouldn't roll onto the guy that was picking the face of a jam loose. When it came loose my log rolled underwater and I had to let go and jump to save myself and it drowned my peavey. Larson had just got through firing a man for losing his peavey. But he didn't say a word to me.

TALK SWEDE
Aaron Danielson, he's dead now, came here from the old country and he couldn't talk hardly a word of English. He met Larson on the road and fell in alongside him jabbering at him in broken English that he wanted a job.

Larson stopped and looked him up and down and grinned. He said, "Talk Swede! Then I can understand you. I'm a Swede."

RIDING THE LOOPS
Very few men could boat through the loops of the Maries River. Paddy Keenan and a couple more of them drownded trying it. Al Dubey and St. Peter, both Frenchmen, could do it.

What makes the loops is a big ridge running out into the river. The railroad tunnel goes through that ridge at its narrowest spot. Where the river loops around the end of the ridge there's a stretch with a solid mass of waves 4 feet high. You never see logs pass through there because they're clear under water.

I watched Dubey and St. Peter. They had a bateau 42 feet long that came to a point. When they hit that rough water the front end tipped up in the air with one man and then it plunged and all you could see was the stern tipped up with the other man. When the boat hit the water each man paddled for all he was worth.

FUNNY FEELING — WARNING
I was back on Granddad's quarter section clearing out a place to deck some cedar poles. No wind or nothin'. I had a funny feeling and looked up. Here come a big limb 6 or 8 inches around, right square at my head. It must have been just hangin' in a tree and took that time to fall. I had time to more or less tumble over and it missed me.

Another time I was gettin' ready to go to work and some guy come to the house to sell me life insurance and I wouldn't even talk to him. At the time I was skidding some of them monstrous big cedars over on Harvard Mountain. Gordon Traicoff was sawing cedar there and rode with me to the job.

When I stopped at Traicoff's house there was the salesman and he had sold Traicoff some insurance. As Traicoff grabbed his lunch bucket and climbed into the car he says, "Now! I suppose I got to get killed to collect."

It gave me a funny feeling. I said, "I wish you hadn't said that."

A day or so later Traicoff was sawing and a tree come down and killed him.

But maybe the closest I ever come to gettin' killed, I was hunting back of the hill with Mark Derry, walking side by side down an old road and a bullet whizzed right between us.

I said, "Mark! We'd better take cover."

We dived into the brush and I said, "There you go! If you wasn't wearing that red coat he'd never seen us. If I was you I'd throw that coat down right here. I wouldn't wear it another inch."

GUY PULLED KNIFE

At St. Joe in Red Hult's joint I saw an old guy get wild and pull a knife. Red chased him 3 times around the room and made a grab and had the knife. Nobody hurt nor nothing. But who else has got nerve enough to try grabbing a knife?

GUS HAD WOODEN LEG

Gus Danielson was a carpenter around Emida. He had an artificial leg that extended up his thigh, and a knee that would bend when he walked and he wore a shoe on that foot same as any man would. He looked so natural that people often forgot.

One day Gus was sittin' on the counter in Alan English's and Ollie Dawson's store. A lumberjack that knew him came along and gave Gus a hard whack on that leg. It pretty near broke his hand.

Gus just sat there and grinned at him. Gus said there was advantages to having a wooden leg. He'd drive a nail in it and hang a saw there while he did carpenter work on the roof.

CARRIE ELLS

I lived all my life in Emida but I can say I was out of here once, anyway. My mother went to stay with her parents in Farmington, Washington in 1914 for me to be born.

My dad's name was Tom Laws. He drove logs in this country for years. Dad and Mother had a restaurant and hotel from 1911 to about 1925 in the old building still setting here.

Seems like I've lived most of my life in that big, old hotel. I moved back in to help my mother when she was sick so we were there when she died of diabetes, Christmas of 1943. Then following that, I was sick with the flu for a couple of weeks before Karen, my sixth baby was born April Fools Day, 1944. When I brought the new baby home the other five were all sick. My oldest girl was upstairs in bed and I brought her downstairs into the hotel living room and put her in bed with two of the younger ones.

Dr. Platt came. He said, "I don't know what's wrong with this girl. Send her back upstairs. Don't keep her with these two."

Phoebe was running a high fever one night. In her delirium she was grabbing hold of the sides of her crib and crying, "Kitty's going to scratch me! Kitty's going to scratch me!"

Two of the kids had broken out with scarlet fever when Dr. Platt examined Edward. He was awfully sick. Dr. Platt shook his head and said, "I don't know what the devil's the matter with him!" Then he looked in Edward's throat again and there he had the measles.

So here I was trying to keep them all in separate rooms all over that big building so they wouldn't be spreading sickness to one another.

Afterwards Dr. Platt figured Edward must have had measles and scarlet fever at the same time because, though he hadn't broken out from the scarlet fever, the skin peeled off his heel in big chunks.

It turned out that three kids had scarlet fever and all five had measles. I was nursing the baby and since I was immune she was and didn't get either sickness.

Hotel & Cafe opened by Mr. & Mrs. Tom Laws 1911 Emida

The diseases were contagious so neither my husband, George, nor I was allowed to enter a public place. George could go to work and I'd go over to the store and post office, run by Lillian English at the time, and she'd come to the door. I'd tell her what groceries we wanted and she'd bring them out to me. And she'd make my phone calls to the doctor.

We couldn't get any help and it was awful hard to keep up with the washing and cooking and house keeping and the buying besides tending the sick.

Finally, George's nephew, Dick Carmen came up a day and completely swept out that whole big building and did up all the washing.

The kids were sick all through April and May. Then as if that wasn't enough, later in the summer they all got chicken pox — which wasn't quite so bad as before and I came down with a mild case of pneumonia. Altogether I had 11 babies with only one born dead.

Interviewed at Emida 1975

Rancher

Doris Farrell

I was mad. I dumped out all their milk

Doris Farrell 77. 1979

I was born Doris Latham in December of 1902 in Grand Valley, Colorado. My folks came to Ferrell, Idaho when I was six years old and homesteaded 80 acres up the draw from where I live now. Kind of a bench on the right hand side of the draw as you go up where he built the house. Still some fruit trees there.

I went to first grade in the church at Ferrell in 1908. Afterwards they built the schoolhouse. I went to school with Mable Ahr, Kathleen Reed and my sister, Ida, about 1913.

When the 1910 fire came close my dad buried our canned fruit and stuff in the yard. I was eight years old. The fire came close but didn't burn the place.

Later, my dad traded the homestead off for two houses in Ferrell. Dad done carpenter work. He worked on the big boarding house and most all those houses in St. Joe. I think, old Bill Ferrell and his wife always run the St. Joe Hotel in Ferrell quite a ways downriver from the Riverside Hotel.

When I was 13 in 1915, Dad did some carpenter work in Calder and I worked for Mrs. Frank Buell taking care of her children. I also went up to Marble Station and took care of Dick Talbot's kid. A year or so after that we moved to Calder and Dad took over the store. My mother

Jake Williams, packer at Buell home at Calder. Doris Latham holding baby Dorothy Buell. 1915

Calder store run by Doris Latham Farrell's father.

cooked and had a restaurant in one part of the store. The present store building is altogether different. The old one was either torn down or burned.

Both my sister and I worked in the restaurant. Used to be a lot of logging camps in Mica Creek and those other places and I hated to see them guys pile off that passenger train and come into the restaurant — maybe 60 of 'em — and we'd have to get dinner for 'em.

Ferrell post office about 1912. L. Mrs. Putnam and daughter, Bythella, then Annie Smith Latham, Doris Farrell's mother.

Doris Latham and Noel Farrell married Nov. 3, 1918

Noel Farrell crossing the river at Calder 1919.

Noel Farrell was working for Ross Howard's sheep outfit and he came in and out of the store. That's how I met him. He was born in New Meadows, Idaho in 1895 and seven years older than me. I was almost 17. We were married Nov. 3, 1918. Noel wasn't related to the Ferrell that platted the town. His name was spelled different. Farrell.

Dad traded off the store for a ranch just below Calder. That's where my son, Jack lived for years. Noel and I bought the ranch from my dad.

We lived on the ranch and Noel packed for the logging outfit up Mica Creek. There wasn't any bridge at Calder then and he always had to ford the river. Our little Australian Shepherd dog, Keno, rode across behind his saddle. Later he packed up Bond Creek for Ohio Match, to Fitzgerald for Russell and Pugh and Falls Creek for Ohio.

Noel also packed to forest fires several different years. He had several strings.

Noel Farrell about 1925   Noel skidding logs at Calder.

Noel packing during flood of 1933-'34 at Ferrell.

We lived in Coeur d'Alene in 1929 and Noel packed into the Winton camps on the Little North Fork of the Coeur d'Alene.

Back at St. Joe again, in 1934 we bought the old Wittenburg place where I live now.

In 1936, Noel was doing some freighting by wagon for Ohio Match. To get to their Bond Creek camp he had to go through a place Jenkins owned in Sly Meadows. Ohio Match was supposed to have a right-of-way so Noel didn't expect any trouble.

Lafe Jenkins and his two boys stopped Noel and the wagon over in Ferrell and told him he couldn't go through their place at Sly Meadows.

Noel told them he was goin' anyway.

The three of them beat him up.

It was summer and no school and our 8 year old boy, Jack, wanted to ride with Noel that day but Jack was late getting up. I got him dressed and we hurried to catch up.

When I caught up with Noel I didn't hardly know him. His face was tore up and bloody. He wouldn't say a thing about how it happened. He stopped over in St. Joe at a house where we knew somebody and washed up. Then he and Jack went ahead and made the trip.

Those Jenkins were funny people. Right after that they waved and hollered at us like nothing ever happened. I didn't want to have any more to do with 'em because you'd never know when they were going to jump on you again.

Noel didn't hold any grudge at all.

The Jenkins were milkin' cows and brought milk over for some kind of trade they'd worked up with Noel.

I was still mad at 'em for beating up Noel. I dumped out all their milk and told them to stay away.

Noel coming off St. Joe trestle during high water.

Lymen Sperry in his garden about 1918.

LYMEN SPERRY

In his cabin Sperry had an old bed springs on the dirt floor and hay thrown on top of it and he curled up in some dirty bedding. A kerosene lantern for light. A wood block for a table.

His cabin was only a short distance from our house up the draw above the sheep shed.

I picked a lot of berries for Mr. Sperry. He paid me 10 cents a gallon.

He worked for us every summer. In the early morning he'd come down near the house and shout, "Up for the hay!" He was ready to go to work in the hayfield.

Every spring he washed up in the creek and put on new shirt and overalls.

Every spare hour he worked digging and blasting his tunnel deeper into the hill in search of gold till he had gone over 700 feet. Then he decided he was prospecting the wrong place and framed another entrance with cedar timbers and began driving another tunnel only 50 feet from his first one.

He told Noel one time, "I'm not crazy. I know I won't find any gold but it gives me something to look forward to."

THE TOTE ROAD

One time Noel was hauling a load of cattle down the old tote road from Calder. He got to that steep hill just west of Fitzgerald Creek before you pass the steel bridge. The truck started rearing up in front. That's how steep the hill was. The truck could have turned and dived 200 feet straight down onto the Milwaukee track. Noel put our boy, Marvin, on one front fender and our boy, Jack, on the other fender and that furnished enough weight to hold the truck down so he could climb that hill.

Birthday party for Mrs. Emma Ross 1958.
Mrs. Wunderlich, Helen Scott Wunderlich, Emma Ross, Harry Miller, Esther Dittman, Jane Meisen (profile); unknown, Mrs. Harry Miller, leaning forward; Mrs. Annie Latham, boy, Jimmy Meisen.

Noel died in 1961. My son, Marvin, never married so he lives with me on the old place. We grow a big garden and chickens and I put up fruit and vegetables for the winter. My son, Jack, puts up hay in summer and feeds his cattle here all winter so I see him often.

Some of my relatives think I should have a nice mobile home because it would be more convenient. But I've been here a long time and I like this old house and I'm comfortable in it. I'd never want to leave it.

Interviewed 1979 at her ranch at the mouth of Wittenburg Draw near St. Joe.

Perry Fleming

HARD WORK & HELL RAISING AT FERRELL

as told to Ruby El Hult

Perry Fleming, boy Roy Howard, Geo. Kemmell, Dave Nelson, Ira Fleming 1907

I was born 1881 and come west from Maryland by train.

In 1907 Ferrell was head of navigation on the St. Joe River for all the steamboats from Coeur d'Alene. The Milwaukee Railroad was building west over the Bitterroot Mountains and down the St. Joe Valley. She was a wide-open town if ever there was one. Mostly just red light district. Every nationality on the face of the earth was there. Very little law, though.

TIMBER EVERYWHERE

At Ferrell the timber came right down to the meadows. The Milwaukee Land Company had already laid out St. Joe City on the hillside above Bond Creek. They was going to build a big sawmill, too. Both the townsite and the millsite needed to be cleared. The A. L Flewelling Lbr. Co was doing the job; that was just another name for the Milwaukee Land Co., if you ask me. Al Holmes was the boss. He was desperate for men. Even had two or three mancatchers in Spokane — employment agencies grabbing men off the street.

MORE HOURS — MORE PAY

I hired out for $3 for a 10 hour day, swamping brush and shrubs at the townsite with an ax. Pretty soon I found I could go back after supper and work as long as I wanted to. Turn in my time when the timekeeper came around. I was young and a working fool.

Pretty soon I got changed over to the chute crew on Bond Creek at $4 a day. Then the money panic of 1907 came on. Every Monday the walking boss came around and cut wages 25 cents a day. When he cut the chute crew's wages, we all quit.

I got back to Ferrell May 1, 1908.

GROUND CHUTE

By that time they'd built a little logging railroad about 3 miles up Bond Creek to the head of the meadows and brought in a shay engine. That fall a little, old fellow named Banta took a job of logging off a hilllside up there.

The crew was Minnesota sleigh haulers. I'd never been on a sleigh haul job but I did know ground chutes. So when the frost came I picked out a uniform sized log each evening and broke a track down the hill with it.

By late fall I had a good icy chute. The ground was froze; there was two or three inches of snow on top. About 2:30 the afternoon we finished skidding I rolled three or four logs into the chute — put the peavy to the first one and it went down that chute like greased lightning.

We had from 300,000 to 400,000 feet of logs in there, and we began rolling them in from both skidways and pushing them down. In two days we had all those logs to the foot of the hill and in a week had them all decked at the railroad.

PARTNER IN RESTAURANT

That winter a young fellow named Clint Haniwalt came out one morning to swamp for me. He was about 22, in a fine suit, no overcoat or gloves. It was snowing, very cold. At noon I took him to the wanigan and got him rubber boots, wool socks, long underwear, wool pants, a jacket and some gloves. After that we were good friends. A few nights later we went to Ferrell to take in the sights. Clint had run a roadhouse in Arizona and as soon as he'd looked the place over he said there was big opportunity in Ferrell. Earlier, Murphy and McFarland had built an addition to the saloon, started a restaurant. A fellow from Spokane run it and to draw trade he hired a good-looking hasher. But he fell for her himself and when somebody else beat his time he went on a big drunk, blew the works and skipped. The restaurant was closed. Clint said if I had $1,000 not in use we could make a stake.

ELIMINATING COMPETITION

I'd been working lots of shifts, had saved enough money. Clint talked to Ed Murphy and we made a deal to open the restaurant. Billy Williams had a grease joint on the wharf — a three-hole oil stove where he cooked hamburgers, hot cakes, bacon and eggs. We bought him out for $100 and closed the place. For $125 we bought Ike Timberlake's soup wagon and run the wagon off the dock into the river. We spent $100 for dishes, cooking gear and a couple of mirrors — and were in business. Our place was named the Shamrock and was the first decent eating place in Ferrell. Haniwalt and I each worked a 12 hour shift.

BIG MAUD
Ferrell was nothing but saloons, gambling joints and dancehall girls — a real free-for-all. I had around 250 fancy women gettin' their meals in my place. There was Big Maud: She'd been raised over in the Palouse country. Her rear was so broad that when she sat at the bar she took up two stools. Later she went to Spokane, corralled all the sporting houses and managed them. There was Maud the Mule, a big redheaded, freckle-faced dame who hung out at Mattson's Saloon. She later had her own house in Avery.

LUMBERJACK JO
She grew up in Republic, Washington. She was around 35 or 38, a swell-looking gal about 190 pounds, with beautiful black hair down to her knees — but she was without exception the most vulgar talking woman I ever knew.

THE LAW
Ferrell was in Kootenai County then, and there was a deputy sheriff, Harry Sawyer, who was part Indian, who came around now and then but not often because the county was so big it ran clear over to Montana. There was no lock-up on the river. If Sawyer arrested anybody he had to take them to Coeur d'Alene.

One morning when Sawyer was in town Jo was drunk and met him along the dock. She sung out loud and clear, "Look at that Indian son-of-a-bitch," and then went around town telling everybody how smart she was.

Sawyer looked her up later in the day and said, "I'll be around to see you take the 7 o'clock boat tomorring morning."

When I came on shift early in the morning Jo was sitting in the place bawling. "I can't find my good for nothing pimp."

"What do you need him for?"

"That Indian is going to take me to Coeur d'Alene and throw me in jail. If I had some money I could leave town."

"Where could you go?"

"I'd go up to Avery."

The Milwaukee was just running work trains, no passenger trains yet. I gave her $10 and she took the early morning train upriver. A fellow named Billy Ahern went to Avery on the same train fishing told me about it. Another jane called Fighting Mag was on the same train in the caboose. She and Lumberjack Jo sat side by side and started to see who could talk the dirtiest.

When the conductor came collecting fare he knocked their heads together and said, "One more peep out of you and I'll wait till we get to the steel bridge and throw you both in the river."

In Avery they got so drunk they were laid out in a barn — in one of the horse stalls.

Jo came back only after she heard Sawyer'd left town. She stayed then till they voted whiskey out.

MAY
A pretty girl named May hit town and got on in the Murphy and McFarland saloon hustling drinks. the first night she was working big Ed DuBray came up behind her, twisted her arm. I guess he meant it playful but he broke her collar bone. Dick Browning was running a little rooming place and May stayed there and I helped take care of her and fed her out of the Shamrock. A shingle weaver came along. He married May and they went to Newport, Washington, where he became the superintendent of a shingle mill. After two years he sent me a check for $150 for what I'd done for May.

IVY AND GEORGIE
Both flewsies were such drunks they never had any money. They used to eat on the tab at the Shamrock for a week but after that if they didn't pay up I cut 'em off. One time when they were broke and no credit, Ivy brought over a set of furs and hocked them. They were worth a thousand dollars and had been given her by one of the boom bosses.

Georgie came into the Shamrock drunk and I ordered her out. I turned around and started for the kitchen, and she picked up this salt cellar and bounced it off the back of my head. I turned around and came back and picked her up by an arm and a leg, carried her out on the dock and tossed her in the river. She could swim like a fish but every time she came back to the dock I would step on her fingers.

Ivy was yelling, "Don't drown her! Don't drown her! I'll come get her."

Ivy found a rowboat and rescued her friend and after that Georgie stayed clear of me.

ROLLING THE LADS
There were four janes in Ferrell rolled four Swede rock workers. A guy named Hoy and I helped them celebrate. We bought all the champagne in Ferrell and St. Joe City — spent $3500 between Friday night and Tuesday morning.

I run the Shamrock for ten months, then local option put liquor out. Everything went flat. I made a lot of money at the Shamrock but spent it. Not quite as fast as the four janes, but almost. I walked away broke, just put a sign on the door: "Take all you need but not more than you need."

Interviewed 1969 at St. Maries

Harry Glidden

Friend of Lumberjacks

Bird Lover   Gambler

AS TOLD BY HERB GLIDDEN

Harry & Inez Glidden 1964

My dad, Harry Glidden was born in Rochester, New York in 1880. He came west to Spokane in 1902 and worked as a carpenter or at any other job that came along. He had learned to play poker back in New York and he played poker wherever he could. There was no law against playing poker in them days.

CLAIM JUMPERS

He came through St. Maries and was staying in the hotel at Santa and playing cards when the blow-up over claim jumpers took place in Marble Creek. (**Boulette was shot Aug. 21, 1904.**)

Dad told me one of the claim jumpers got away with his suspenders shot right off'n him. He came running cross country to Santa, cryin' and hollerin' for help.

Mr. McKinney, Inez McKinney Glidden Gertrude McKinney Fleming. Front row — Lulu and Mrs. McKinney

—229—

I used to set in a swing and listen by the hour to Frank Theriault and my dad talk about Marble Creek and the claim jumpers. Frank Theriault packed Boulette out to Marble Station and packed another body in later that had laid out all winter. (**Tyler wasn't found until much later but was assumed he had been killed the same day as Boulette.**)

Annex Building St. Maries 1910. Fannie Dunn ran upstairs rooms. Vang's Clothing store in near corner and Harry Glidden's Pool&Cards entrance overhang right front.

Dad had a joint: cards, pool, tobacco — but no beer, between the railroad tracks and the river on 1st Street. Dad never took a drink and never smoked and he didn't go much with people that drank a lot. Right where Murphy built that apartments, that's where the poolhall was.

I've got a little memorandum book where Dad listed names of people he loaned money to that was never paid back to him. (Some names from a page dated 1917 with amounts from $2 to $10 noted after them: French Shorty, Frank Do, Jim Brooks, Jim Lind, Ginpole Harry, Whisky Johnny, French Tom...)

Dad had a lot of friends among the lumberjacks. The time of the Wobbly trouble in 1917 those lumberjacks were encamped on a vacant lot right up 1st Street past Bud's Burger which used to be the old bank building.

Where the Midway Restaurant is now was a building with drugstore downstairs and Doc Platt's offices upstasirs. The vigilantes got up on the roof and was gonna shoot the Wobs down in that vacant lot.

Son Herb Glidden holding pistol his father carried.

Dad went down and told the Wobs, "You guys better get outa here before somebody gets killed.

The vigilantes got wind that Dad went and told the Wobs. One of 'em, Ham Recordine let it be known around town that he carried two derringers and was gonna shoot Dad.

When they met face to face on the street, Ham threatened and threatened Dad.

Dad had a long barrelled .32 centerfire Colt single action revolver in his overcoat pocket. He said, "Well! Just get 'em out. Don't stand there talkin' about it."

But nothing happened.

PLAYED POKER AT CLARKIA

Dad played at Clarkia when the Marble was rolling in 1918. He was great friends to Frank Tom and played in his place in 1928 and he played at the Gynor joint — the old Kleinard & Wade place, too.

He'd take your money playin' cards but he'd never beat you out of nothin' and he made sure he always kept his word. In a poker game he'd tell you, "Now! You're on your own. We're playin' cards for dough."

AN ELEGANT COOK

Dad was a really good cook. He could put out a dish like a New England boiled dinner — a big dish for several people. And hotcakes! He sent back east for pure buckwheat flour and maple sugar in gallon cans in case lots. The freight from Vermont cost more than the syrup. Dad went to work for the Forest Service once as cook but he got fed up with them right off the bat and quit. He liked fine cooking not just dealing out common grub.

Dad quit work altogether shortly after I was born in 1929. Later he told me he lost better than $50,000 in the market crash of that year.

LOVED TAXIDERMY

Carl Aikley was a nationally known taxidermist. He was cousin to Dad and taught him how to use excelsior and string at a bench in the basement to mount birds and animals. Dad loved birds and studied them constantly. He sold his collection of mounted birds to a game warden named Wooster. Wooster sold the collection to the College of the Pacific and they were — maybe still are — on display at Stockton, California. The curator of the De Young Museum in San Francisco said, "I'm a taxidermist myself and have inspected many collections and this one rates tops."

Carl Aikley wanted to take Dad to Africa with him but Dad wouldn't go.

POLED THE SWIFTWATER
After I was born in 1929 we camped all summer long. Dad poled a boat up the swiftwater to Honey Jones place. Stayed there a few days and then worked on up beyond Mica Cr.

Dad was pickin' huckleberries up the hillside near Mica Creek and some guy steps out of the brush and says, "What are you doing here?"

Dad says, "Pickin' huckleberries or rocks or whatever."

The guy says, "You haven't got any business here."

Dad suspected he had got too close to somebody's still. Dad and Mother went back to their camp and the moonshiners pulled down the river soon after that.

TICKET SELLER — NO SALES
Year after year Profitt sat in that ticket office at the St. Maries Red Collar Line dock ready to sell tickets and no passenger boats to use 'em on. Lafferty paid him to stay there and do nothing. Something to do with Lafferty holding the franchise for towing logs down the St. Joe River to Coeur d'Alene.

The Gazette-Record reported Elija J. Profitt died April 6, 1950. Lafferty was maintaining a franchise as a common carrier held earlier by the Red Collar Line Steamship Co. It offered the advantage that rail rates for lumber cut from the logs his tugs towed to Coeur d'Alene could be figured from the river landing point to the ultimate destination with Lafferty being paid a high short haul rate for his part of the transportation.

COMING OF THE CHAIN SAW
It was hot summer there at Trout Creek and here come one of them clouds and **Whang!** the lightning hit a big white fir that hadn't been cut. And took off. **Whooo!** Right up the ridge burning in the tops of the trees.

That was about 1952 and the first year I remember chain saws being used in the woods. John Ankor's job. There was still a filin' shack at the camp and a man to file crosscut saws.

Happy Van Luven was swampin' there. Leonard Carpenter and Mitch's brother Pete was there. We run up the ridge and moved the jammer before the fire got it.

RUSSIAN ALEC HURT
I was second truck in line at Moe's Trout Creek landing when Russian Alec got hurt. Alec was unloading truck. This log was 16 feet long and about 14 inches in diameter. He looked up and **BAM!** It hit him right in the head.

THE ALMOST FIGHT

When Dad was old he got into an awful chewin' match with Ham Recordine about the Wobbly business back in 1917.

Ham come back to town from Carolina for a visit.

Dad was settin' on a bench in front of the phone office and along come Ham.

Dad had a cane and Russian Alec was there and he thought Dad was gonna hit Ham with his cane. Alec sat down on him.

Dad said, "I wasn't gonna hit him with the cane, the old son of a bitch! I was gonna get up off the bench and hit him with my fist."

Both of 'em about 85 years old and gonna fight. Can you imagine that!

LOVED HONEY JONES PLACE

Dad and Mother loved that Honey Jones place. Most every year we camped there at least once. That's where I scattered their ashes. Right there in the meadow by the mouth of Falls Creek.

Interviewed 1975 at St. Maries

Fred Herrick camp at Big Creek 1911.

James M. & Josie Griffin

Packer

Homesteaders

A mule can eat you!

I was born in Nebraska City, Jan. 14, 1890. When I was 6 or 7 years old my parents made the trip to Idaho in a covered wagon. We came to Clarkia because our friends, the Scotts had homesteaded there.

My father, Sherman Griffin took a homestead where the road starts up Emerald Creek.

James M. and Josie Griffin

My uncle, Merrill Roberts, homesteaded where Clarkia is and offered tracts for sale. My mother died when I was young and Aunt Mandy Roberts took care of us kids at her home for awhile.

CLARKIA'S 4 POST OFFICES

About 1900, the post office was just a little store about 1¼ miles up Emerald Creek but Clarkia people cut across to it on the Cedar Creek road from the campground at the bridge over the Maries River between Fernwood and Clarkia.

The second Clarkia post office was at Metropolitan Siding where the trailer houses are now.

The third was 'way up at the end of the meadow above Clarkia where Brown lived. Then the fourth occupied part of the store in Clarkia where it's now at.

RAILROAD BURNED

I was skidding logs with my own team for Herrick in Big Creek before and after the 1910 fire. After the fire it was an awful sight. The rails kinked from the heat and lifted track, burned ties and all straight up in the air.

Herrick rebuilt the railroad and logged the burned stuff.

Frank Roberts, James M. Griffin and Harvey Scott. Scott went to the service in 1917 and never returned. Finally, the army returned his civilian clothes.

Coupla fellows come up to saw. Herrick asked them if they knew how to cut trees.

They said, "Yes."

Herrick said, "Be sure to yell the direction the tree is about to fall."

So they cut this big tree meaning to fall it up the hill, so they yelled, "**Timber! Up the hill!**"

They didn't know much about falling timber and when it went the other way instead, they yelled, "**Look out below. Tree comin'!**"

It smashed right across the top of a loader run by a donkey. The loading crew took after 'em and run 'em out of the woods.

1913, I homesteaded just 4 miles from Clarkia and a mile below Gold Center.

SHOT HORSE'S JAW OFF

Along about 1915 I was workin' for Harry Brown at the upper end of the meadows above Clarkia. Brown and McPeak had bad feeling over a poker game a couple years before.

Brown told McPeak, "If you try to go through my place I'll shoot you!"

The Forest Service trail went through there. McPeak came riding along and told Brown he was going through.

Brown pulled up his rifle and fired. The shot blew the horse's jaw off.

Ira McPeak rode back to Clarkia, got a gun and rode up to Brown's house and yelled for him to come out. But Brown stayed in the house.

Later years they patched up their feud. McPeak married Brown's daughter, Sylvia. They had two children, Kenneth and Alta, and lived on the old place with Brown.

In 1917, I packed for the Forest Service from Avery up Kelly Creek, past Bear Skull, Trim Tree Hill, through Bathtub and Twin Lakes to the ranger station at Elk Prairie. Later, I packed the survey outfit that laid out the road through there.

Then I packed supplies into Rutledge Camps on Marble Creek and a sawmill into Camp 2 on Bussel Creek where they cut lumber for the flume. I packed nails for building the flume, too.

1918, they unloaded donkeys from the railroad and we put 'em together at Clarkia. We put out a block to skid them across the Maries river. The water came up over our feet when we rode across with the donkeys on their big skids. Then we fired them up on the other side for the trip over the ridge into the Marble.

Packer, James M. Griffin standing. Ranger using mule for a back rest. Pole Mt. Lookout cabin 1917.

BAD LANGUAGE

Mrs. James M. Griffin: I came along where they was working on them donkeys and the language my husband was using! I told him I was going to take him home and wash out his mouth with soap.

Griffin packstring crossing the cable bridge over Marble near Camp 4, 1918.

I was born Josie Helen Scott, Nov. 11, 1887. My father, David Scott, homesteaded where the Clarkia Ranger Station is. I was 14 when we come to Clarkia.

Folks had some lean pickings them times, I'll tell you! My cousin, Frank Roberts worked everywhere for farmers and in harvests. He was 18 when he took my dad's pigs down to Farmington in 1904 to trade them for a cow. Dad gave him a list of groceries we neeeded for the winter and Frank packed 'em back to us on the cow

After I married James M. Griffin I lived on that homestead up near Gold Center all alone and then later with little kids while their papa was away packing all week long at Big Creek and around Avery and over in Marble Creek.

CHICKEN RAID
Sometimes it was scary. This one night I heard something. Pretty soon two or three of our chickens started squawking.

I picked up my .30 .30 rifle and started for the door.

Then I stopped. "That's no animal. That's somebody doing that. They're shaking the chickens to make a racket so I'll come out." So I didn't go out.

But the next day I knocked the chinking out next to the door so if they come back to raid our chickens again I could shoot without opening the door.

HAVING BABIES ALONE
When I knew that Harry was gonna be born, I told my oldest boy, "You go get your papa just as quick as you can get him. Tell him I'm sick."

So David got on our fast little saddle horse and run him 4 miles to Clarkia and 2 more miles to the school section where my husband was hauling gravel onto the state road.

If only David had stopped at Dirty Dutch's place, Dirty Dutch had an Overland car and would have drove lickety split after Papa.

My baby was starting to be born. I told my son, Lester to go get Mrs. Maher at Flewsie Creek.

Her son-in-law come with her. Mrs. Maher said she was scared to deliver or take care of a baby newborn.

I told her to ask the son-in-law to run get Mrs. Jake Martin up Gold Creek a mile and a half away.

But before Mrs. Martin could come I said to Mrs. Maher, "Get me some hot water and string and something to cut the cord. The baby is turning purple and I can't let it go any longer."

So I took care of it myself. Twice we had to take care of babies by ourselves.

GOOD NEIGHBORS
Dirty Dutch Seitzer was a good hearted bachelor that would do most anything for you. He donated an acre of his homestead ground for the Gold Center schoolhouse. After the schoolhouse was abandoned in late years, Savvy Procopio 'dozed or burnt it up when he was logging there.

Dirty Dutch was German and he couldn't hardly speak English. He had got out of Germany so he wouldn't have to serve in the Kaiser's army. I learned him to read and write a little. I have wrote lots of letters for him and he got so we could make him understand what we were saying.

They was brothers — Johnny Dutch and Ben Dutch. Johnny Dutch never homesteaded — he just lived with Ben Dutch. They was both strangers to soap.

Dirty Ben Dutch rode one time with my son, Lester and his wife, Mary, when they was hauling a load of garbage from the CC camp at Foolhen Hill to Dirty Dutch's place, to feed his pigs and chickens. Dirty Dutch stood in the back of the pick-up and poked down into the garbage with his fingers and took something out and ate it.

THE STRAND KILLING
Frank Strand was a bachelor and he bootlegged and moonshined down around Santa. The other man, Weedle, had a wife and a boy about 15 and a girl about 17. And the story was that Weedle told Strand to stay away from that girl "or I'm going to shoot you."

Strand's homestead was further back up Renfro Creek and he had to use the road to go through Weedle's place to get to town.

Well, that night the boy and girl went up to visit Strand again.

Next morning, Weedle's wife heard something and she opened the door. There was Strand on his horse. Weedle was splitting wood in the yard. Strand shot him with a .45 automatic.

Strand knew a posse would be after him. He headed in the dark of night for the Martins' place at Gold Center. They was friends of his.

FUGITIVE IN THE MANGER
We had a little barn below our house close to the road. When I went into the barn to milk the cow that night, the cow was nervous and wouldn't eat and I suspicioned that Strand was hiding in the manger.

I wasn't scared. I got the stool and went ahead and milked the cow.

I said to my boy, David, "Now, Son. If Frank Strand would come, he wouldn't harm us. We always been good friends. He's the one that gave Bessie, our little bird dog, to us."

But when I got back to the house and got the door shut, I got the shakes. I put out the kerosene lamp and sat there with the .30 .30 rifle pointed at the door but Frank didn't come.

Frank Strand got to York Martin's house and the posse hid out in the trees around the cabin all night. When it was light enough to see, Frank came out. One fellow shot him and Strand turned and went back in that house.

The posse didn't know how bad he was hurt so they waited all day long. Almost dark, one fellow said, "I'll open the door. I'll call out and if he don't answer I'll go right in."

Strand had been shot plumb through and so first he got two pillows and cinched one in front and one in back to stop the blood. Then he climbed on the table and opened the trap door to the attic. Up there he'd be able to shoot through the cracks and pick off the fellows outside.

That was as far as he could make it. He fell off the table and when that man opened the door Strand laid dead on the floor.

The posse loaded him in a buggy and brought him down the road to show him off at everybody's homestead. Then they tied him to a board and stood him up against the Clarkia depot and took pictures of him before they shipped him off to the coroner.

Son, Lester Griffin, now 66, goes on with the Griffin story:

I was 10 years old when it happened. The story I heard then and over the years is that Frank Strand and the Martins had been moonshining together. So when the posse got after him, Strand headed for York Martin's place and told York to go to Clarkia and round up more ammunition for his Luger pistol and his rifle. He told York he was gonna hold York's wife and young kid to make sure York didn't bring the posse back.

But as soon as York left, Strand went down and hid in our manger and watched out the cracks. York came back alone but he had tipped off the sheriff.

Then Strand followed York Martin back home and told him to send the wife and kid down to Jake Martin's place — only a quarter of a mile below. Jake was York's dad. And they better not squawk or he'd shoot York. All of this is on York's say so.

Just at gray daylight, Strand left York in bed and went out the front door and down to Gold Creek, 150 feet away to cross the footlog to the White Rock Springs Trail. Probably he figured on going back to Montana where he come from.

When Strand left the house, York Martin run stark naked out the back door to get to the protection of the posse.

The footlog was a tree that had fell into the creek from the farther bank and the roots tipped up. One man with a shotgun was hiding behind the roots. He got so excited he didn't take good aim. Some of the shot did hit Strand in the face, though.

At the same time, the man — I promised not to name him — with Mama's borrowed .30 .30, on the hillside behind Strand, opened the fireworks. The rest of the posse was scattered around the hillside hiding behind stumps.

Strand had a rifle in one hand and the Luger in the other. When he got hit, he throwed the pistol and it went in the creek. The Martin kids found it a week or so later. Strand turned and run back into the house.

All day long, the posse, they'd fire a few shots into the board house. They didn't get any return fire but they kept pop shooting all afternoon.

About 4 o'clock they sent a buggy to Clarkia after gasoline. They was gonna throw it on the blind side of the house and burn him out.

Frank Strand Is Shot to Death on Gold Creek Homestead.

Spokesman-Review
June 19, 1923

ST. MARIES, Idaho, June 18.— Frank Strand, alleged slayer of E. Wedel, a farmer near Santa, was shot and mortally wounded early today in a gun battle with a posse of seven men headed by James McDonald, a state officer. The battle, which took place on the homestead of York Martin on Gold creek, seven miles east of Clarkia, started at 3:30 this morning and terminated an hour later. Strand had boasted he would not be taken alive. After being mortally wounded by a rifle ball which passed through his body, a rifle shot through the fleshy part of his left arm, one in the right thigh and another in the left leg, Strand managed to reach the Martin cabin, 50 yards away, where he was found dead on the kitchen floor.

Officers Notified.

Strand appeared at the Martin cabin early Sunday morning and had breakfast, after which he took his rifle and two revolvers and went into the timber, telling Martin that he would return at night. Shortly after he left Martin motored to Clarkia, notified Officer McDonald and returned home. The officer organized a posse, went to the Martin place and in the evening formed a cordon around the cabin, awaiting developments. Strand and Martin slept together that night, got up early and had breakfast, after which Strand left the cabin by the front door. Martin went out the back door and joined the posse in the battle which immediately ensued. Strand succeeded in getting into the thick underbrush along Gold creek, from where he replied with 12 or 15 shots to the 25 or 30 that were fired by the posse. Before he crawled from ambush to the cabin he shouted not to shoot any more and that he would surrender. McDonald told him to come out with his hands up and that he would not be shot. Strand's answer was several shots from his Luger. No further shots were fired by the posse.

Killed Five Men.

Strand told Martin he had killed five men several years before in a gun fight in Texas.. He also told Martin that the posse under Sheriff C. G. Gregg came very near getting him in the battle last Monday afternoon at his homestead on Renfro creek. Several shots pierced his pack sack close to him. Strand's body was brought here tonight.

Strand shot and killed Wedell in the latter's dooryard at his ranch near Santo on June 3, witnesses said. He fired three bullets from a rifle into Wedell's body in the presence of Mrs. Wedell and their three small children, according to reports. The killing, it was said, was the result of a long-standing controversy over a line fence between Strand's and Wedell's land.

That's when this Federal Revenue officer, Ross said, "Nobody is gonna burn anybody alive!" and walked over and kicked the door open.

After Strand was killed and the house all bloodied up, nobody wanted to live there anymore. Mama bought the writing desk and the dresser.

THE WITCH

Used to be a woman named Chugweltz lived up Eagle Creek. She'd put on the God damndest witches clothes and parade around and mumble to herself and then she'd rub secret stuff on your seed warts to make them disappear.

Her boy looked at Strand's body down at the depot and then afterwards saw his own reflection in the drugstore window uptown. The mother believed that anybody that looked into a mirror after somebody was dead, till after they was buried, would be the next one to die.

For a week she howled and cavorted and throwed magic stuff into a bonfire to save the kid's life.

KILLING OF BLONDIE

The first joint on your right as you enter Clarkia — now the Wagon Wheel — had belonged to Ed Kleinard and Shorty Wade, but by 1929 they had retired to the woods to make moonshine and it belonged to Ginpole O'Brien.

The little bitty building beside it belonged in 1929 to Chet Ward who had a poolhall, confectionery and bootlegging business on the side.

About August lst. 1930, Ward claimed that Blondie Cole had stole his wife — or the one he was living with anyhow, and took her and their pet bulldog to St. Maries.

So on Sunday, August 4th, Ward drove down to First Street and the St. Joe River at St. Maries to do something about it. Blondie Cole had bought the old Skelton & Warn building for a rooming house. Ward climbed the stairs to the second story and in front of two roomers — Stephen Lott and John Christianson, shot Blondie with a .32 automatic. Then he wheeled for Clarkia.

Blondie Cole managed to get down the stairs to his car, drove about a block as far as the Oddfellows building, set the brake and passed out. 40 minutes later he died in the St. Maries hospital from a bullet in his lung.

Ward's new 8 cylinder Studebaker car speeded through Fernwood. Twenty minutes later, Sheriff O'Rourke and Deputy Ira Horne and their 8 cylinder Studebaker burned through Fernwood after him.

Skelton & Warren Bldg.

JOY RIDING AIRPLANE

That same day, a barnstorming airplane was taking people for rides out of Bechtel's field just above Clarkia. But first, the pilot, Virgil Adair, him and Ginpole O'Brien had been buddies in World War 1, went down to celebrate at Ginpole's joint, on homebrew and moonshine.

Then up the two of 'em came to Bechtel's field for an old buddy joyride. Virgil was a World War 1 ace and famous for acrobatics.

They say that a woman at Lewiston complained to Virgil during her airplane ride that she had expected it to be more exciting and Virg loop the looped her twice under the Lewiston-Clarkston bridge.

Virgil revved into the air, flew Ginpole upside down over the joint so close to the ground that he clipped the telephone wires on top of the section house right across the road.

Virgil didn't know he'd cut the wires and done Chet Ward a favor. With the telephone wires cut, the Law couldn't get word to the deputy at Clarkia to stop Ward.

Me and Bert and Albert and Tuffy Robins and Clark Gardener was waitin' up there in the field for a ride. Dad Propst was with us. Dad had a full set of gold teeth. When he grinned it looked like a sunrise. He was an awful nice old man. He had a straw hat on his bald head and here we stood all in a crossways line and Dad Propst grinning away with that plane zooming in. The plane come so low one wheel knocked Dad Propst's hat off.

If we'd had any sense, us kids wouldn't have still wanted a plane ride. But the owner, Porter was standing right there and we rushed over and paid him four-bits apiece. Soon as the plane came to a stop and Ginpole climbed out, the five of us kids jumped ahead of everybody else and all of us got our feet into the cockpit seat intended for only one passenger. The only way we could stay in was by hanging onto each other. Me and Bert Robins was almost man grown. I was already 17.

Then Virgil run her up by the little sawmill on the point at the head of the field. He turned her around and gunned her. She got up speed and bounded into the air 25 or 30 feet but we was too much weight and back she dropped onto the ground. Then back up we went and down again. Then up.....

I yelled, "Next time we get close to the ground you kids let go of me!"

She hit and I jumped and went end over end. Bert bailed out with me.

When we stopped rolling we could see that lightening the load had helped because the plane bounced along a hundred yards and started climbing into the air. There was a ginpole right beside the railroad track where they loaded logs and the pilot didn't have enough elevation to clear it — maybe he didn't even see it. The propellor shattered head on against the ginpole. The plane skidded around the ginpole and dived on her nose in the mud and 3 of them kids come boiling out not hurt.

Me and Bert Robins run over to Porter yelling, "We want our money back!"

Porter says, "Get outa here! Look what you done to my airplane."

Bull O'Keefe was a big lumberjack we knew from Bovill. He grabbed Porter by the collar and the seat of the pants and turned him upside down and shook him till all his money fell out on the ground.

While we dropped on our prayer bones grabbing for money, O'Keefe kicked Porter in the butt and hollers. "G'wan! **You coulda killed them kids!** If you come back here again, I'll break your damn neck."

WARD ON THE RUN
While this was happening, Chet Ward streaked into Clarkia just ahead of the sheriff. He run into his joint and cleaned out the cash register and back into the car.

In those days the main road was the Samson B Trail and it went through Clarkia and up past the schoolhouse and back across the meadow to where the oiled highway runs now.

At the corner in Clarkia, Papa and a bunch of men was settin' on the front steps of the store that later belonged to Frank Tom. When they seen the airplane nose dive off there a mile away they jumped up in fear some of us kids had got killed.

Right then here come Chet Ward in that big Studebaker around the corner on two wheels. They naturally figured he had seen the plane go down and was rushin' to the wreck. Out they ran into the middle of the street waving their arms to get a ride.

When Chet waved a pistol out the open window in their faces and left them choking in a cloud of dust, they thought he must be crazy.

Then the sheriff and deputy rolled up and told them about the killing and they was hot on Ward's trail. So they told the Law that the day before, this Ward had made a run from Clarkia to Lewiston and bragged all over town there wasn't a car in the country could go as fast as he went.

Ira Horne said, "We got the same kind of car. I don't know if we got as much guts as Ward has but we'll try to catch him!"

And away they tore for Lewiston.

TRAILING THE FUGITIVE
When the sheriff didn't find any trace of Ward at Lewiston he come back two days later with federal prohibition agent, Julius Johnson. Nosin' around up Cat Creek they found Ward's car covered with fresh

cut brush and found Kleinard and Shorty Wade and R. S. Phillips steaming up a still close by. They arrested the three of 'em for illicit manufacturing whiskey and for aiding and abetting the escape of a fugitive.

Three days later, Ward ran out of eats and turned himself in to Lou Smith at Santa and he, too, ended up in the St. Maries jail.

The Gazette-Record reports Ward's trial: At his first trial Ward got a hung jury. At his second trial, May 8, 1930, he was convicted of first degree murder and sentenced to life in the Idaho pen.

RETRIAL GRANTED
July 16, 1931 — Bill Keeton was defense attorney — Ward claimed Cole had pulled a gun first and he, Ward shot in self defense. The two roomers who had earlier testified they saw the shooting, had disappeared. Ward was acquitted.

A body, thought to be one of the roomers was found some weeks later.

Dec. 10, 1931, Ward and his wife were arrested under the Mann Act for transporting Montie Bright from Spokane to the Cozy Corner Cafe in Clarkia for purposes of prostitution. Ward was sentenced to 4 years in McNeil Island federal penitentiary and his wife drew 8 months in the Kootenai County jail.

A MULE CAN EAT YOU!
Mama's dad said, "One thing about a mule. If he lives to be a hundred years old, he'll remember to kick you once."

I don't know if that's true but I know if a mule gets mad enough it will try to eat you alive.

In the fall when Dad turned his pack mules into the meadow at Clarkia he let me and Lou Gardner use a couple for elk hunting. The two we picked hadn't their manes roached or nothin' so I thought, "I'll run them into the barn and make them look respectable."

I throwed a rope onto one mule and got him to stand in the stall while I reached over and roached him.

The other mule was watchin' the whole procedure. So I threwed a rope on it. When the rope tightened, she made for me.

I run up the ladder through the hay hole into the hay mow.

She crawled after me till her head was stickin' above the hole.

I said, "Good enough for you!" So I twisted the rope around an upright pole up there and tied her head up and while her head was upstairs I went down another hole and started roachin' her mane.

Pretty quick, like a cat she braced all 4 feet against the ceiling and the old lariat broke. She hit the floor on her back. She scrambled up and took after me.

As I went through the barn door I slammed it hard as I could and hit her right in the face.

A HORSE TRADER

You've heard of Clarence Phillips — notorious bootlegger and horse trader from away back — well, just as I went through the door, Phillips was outside.

He says, "What in thee hell is the matter?"

I said "There's a mule in there."

He says, "You got thee mule in there? Let's see it!"

"No!" I says. "Just leave it alone. There's two of 'em in there. I'll open the door on the back side of the barn and let 'em out."

He says, "I'll trade you a horse for thee mule."

I said, "What have you got?"

He says, "How about old Whitey — that horse that Jim Cox had?"

I says, "Bring me old Whitey and I'll give you 2 mules."

He went and brought the white horse down.

I took hold of the door and I says, "Get your loop ready because I'm not goin' in."

Well! He just looked at me like he felt sorry for my ignorance and opened the door. When that mule made for him he hauled off and hit that mule alongside the head with his hat. The mule stopped and batted his eyes.

Then Phillips put a rope around the mule's neck and says, "Come on!" and led thee mule right out of there.

LOST PLANE

We was wintering out on Moscow Mountain that night in Dec. 1936 when the sawmill in Elk River burned. We could see the light in the sky. Zeke Turner later told me about the lost mail plane circling around over the big light.

Zeke told me they rushed around lining up a bunch of cars to throw light in the main street so the plane could land. But it didn't wait and swung off to the north and crashed on Cemetery Ridge.

WHISKY IN THE BEAN CAN

About 6½ miles up Merry Creek where Mann Creek comes in is where Camp 35 was. At Camp 35 they averaged a man a day hurtin' him and killed one a month.

I was a cat driver but this day the boss come to me and he says, "I got a place that nobody else will clean up. I want you to go in there settin' choker for Davidson.

I knew Davidson had been off for a week drunk. I said, "I'll go one day with him, that's all. And I'll take my two old choker setters with me." They was good men but neither one of 'em could hear.

Davidson was feelin' ugly all morning. He had whisky in his lunch pail and no lunch. That only made him worse.

Along in the afternoon there was a big log run endo against a stump.

I said to my two old fellows, "Get the hell out of the road up on the hill. I'll hook this one."

I hooked onto the log toward the middle so when Davidson pulled it, it would walk end over end. I said, "Now take that up with the winch and set it over behind the drag."

Davidson spit out, "I'll show you God damn sissyfied cat drivers how a man takes logs out!"

I said, "You go ahead and kill your own God damned self if you want to!"

I took around the cat on the run. Here was one of these old fellows with his back to me lookin' up the hill at the other one, motioning at him. He hadn't even heard me warn them.

The log was tipping endo and I knew it was gonna hit him and I let a scream out of me that he couldn't hear. I made a dive and hit him right at the ankles.

It knocked him over just enough that the log coming down grazed him from head to waist. But it smashed in an angle on top of me.

They took me to the St. Maries hospital that night.

The next day, they brought the old fellow in. He was rumdum. He was in the hospital 2 or 3 days and then he just got up and walked out. Quite a while later they found a body in the St. Joe River and they figured he had just walked into the water.

The knowledge that a work mate has sacrificed his health or his life in saving you can burden the one saved with an unbearable sense of guilt which may lead a man to take his own life. — Ed.

Mary Griffin, Lester's wife: When Lester was in the hospital it was World War 2 and everything was rationed. And we had no paycheck to live on.

This woman, Mrs. Charley Barden come to our house in Clarkia. She said, "I don't think you and the children are eatin' very good."

We didn't have no refrigeration. When I'd buy a hunk of meat with my ration stamps she'd help me make a stew and keep it in fruit fars in a cool place. She'd hold the baby, clean the house and sit and listen to me worry about Lester. She was about the kindest woman ever lived.

Then Oral Avery come to me and said,"Mary! Anything you want you come to the store and get it. If something happens to Lester and I don't get paid, fine and dandy."

That Oral Avery was a wonderful man.

Lester: The accident in November of 1942 ended my working days. After I got well enough to get around, we moved to Deary to be near my folks. Five of us formed a volunteer ambulance at Deary. If there's an accident I can't lift nothing but I can give first aid. We charge enough to keep the ambulance going. We don't make nothin' for ourselves.

FRANK TOM

A bunch of us that didn't drink used to hang around Paul Larson's garage or Avery's store or Frank Tom's place.

When loggers would come in to Frank Tom's, sicker'n hell after a drunk, he'd let 'em have a packsack or calked boots or whatever they needed. Frank Tom never had a price marked on a box or nothin'. He never overcharged anybody in his life but I found out he sometimes undercharged.

One time I bought a pair of Forester shoes — this was when I was still workin.

I was standin' there by the door with them under my arm. Lambert Ellingsen came in and he says, "Hey! I want a pair of shoes like Griffin's got. You got size 9?" Lambert had a big house and a big car and he wasn't a bad guy but his wife went around with her nose stuck in the air.

Frank says, "Yah! I got size 9."

Lambert says, "How much are they?"

Frank says, "To you they're 18 bucks."

I thought I must have misunderstood Frank. As soon as Lambert walked out with his new shoes I said, "How much did you say these shoes are, Frank?"

He says, "Like I told you. To you they're 11 bucks."

I said, "But you told Lambert 18."

Frank said, "But your old lady don't fart through silk like Lambert's wife."

I went up from Deary through Clarkia, November 1949, hunting. I stopped in to visit Frank Tom.

Frank says, "Les, this is probably the last time you'll ever see me."

I said, "Oh? I don't think so."

He said, "Yeh. I've got cancer right here in the throat and it's going to get me." Soon after that he died.

FLOATHOUSE NELL

About 1954 I was driving freight truck with supplies from Bovill to Camp 44 on Fishhook Creek south of Avery. I'd go up loaded by way of the Joe river. Coming back I cut across to come out at Clarkia.

Going along the side of Crater Peak, here on the right hand side of the road was a couple of old lumberjacks building a board shack.

Course I stopped to see what was going on. Inside the shack was Floathouse Nell hammering away. This was the time of the uranium craze and people roaming the woods with Geiger counters.

Nellie said, "I need a headquarters shack! I've struck uranium down the side of Crater Peak."

After that I stopped for coffee and BS almost every trip. Nellie loved to talk about her uranium find. She thought she would be rich.

Tour 1 with Lester Griffin

Set your speedometer at zero as you turn off the oiled highway into Clarkia. Where **Virgil Adair** flew the airplane upside down and clipped the telephone wires in 1929 was just to the left of the railroad crossing. The **Depot** where they leaned Strand's body in 1923, stood between the two tracks on your right.

The first building on your right — named the **Wagon Wheel** now, was a bootlegging and women dump for 20 years under **Ed Kleinard and Shorty Wade**. All us kids sold Ed and Shorty whatever mink, weasel and other hides we trapped because they paid us cash.

In 1929 the place was owned by **Ginpole O'Brien**.

Next, right up against it was the poolhall of **Chet Ward** in 1929. Later it became a family style restaurant under **Ann Olson**. She was really

Ginpole O'Brien's Joint '29 Pic '79

Chet Ward's Joint '29 Pic '79

Italian with a Swede husband. Ann was a rough talker and sold moonshine but her and Elmer run a respectable place.

Nobody had a bigger heart than Ann Olson. Lumberjacks left their money with her and if they came back drunk and asked for it she'd tell them there wasn't any. But as soon as they came back sober and ready to go back to the job she'd pull out her little book and count out their $800 or whatever it was.

"That way," she said, "these damn joints don't beat 'em out of all they earn!"

Just before you cross the little river bridge was the **Idaho Hotel** on your left — girls and saloon. On the right was **old Lady Appleton's** gals and saloon.

Merrill Roberts home at Clarkia 1902 with a clay lined fireplace and chimney of wood and mud construction. Griffin children: Harriet, Eunice, James M. and Alfred.

Mary's Cafe & Tavern '80

Clarkia Mercantile '79

On your left just after you cross the bridge stood the old log building that was **Oral Avery's** first store. He ran it 7 years till 1924. **Andrew Caverni's Cafe & Poolroom** stood on the right. Also on the right, further on is **Mary's Cafe** which stands on the site of **Charley (Peg) Henry's Barber Shop.**

Straight ahead beyond the corner was where **Frank Tom's** store was. On your left in the field, stood a white house called **Robert's Meadow Hotel.** Behind and northwest of the hotel stood **Merrill Robert's log house** with the fireplace constructed of boards and mud and clay lined chimney.

You turn right and pass the present grocery store and post office which **Oral and Genevieve Avery** owned for 36 years to 1960. On the left, behind the jackpines stood the **Elk Hotel** — the nice hotel — run for years by the **Schuberts.** When they sold out it became a dive.

So far you have been travelling on the old **Samson B Trail** on the way from St. Maries to Lewiston and Boise.

Gazette-Record 6-12-24 — The **Samson B Trail** from Boise to the Canadian line through St. Maries is marked by an orange stripe or band with a black B in the center, all paid for by a music dealer in Boise named Sampson, for the purpose of guiding tourists into Idaho. Sampson plans 6,000 miles of such trails.

Turn left at the schoolhouse leaving the **Samson B Trail** for the road to Gold Center. Turn right again after crossing the little bridge over the Maries River.

At about 3 miles you pass a draw with a tiny creek on the left where **Anthony's house** stood. The homesteader trail went up this draw past **Josie Gunderson's cabin** and then over past **Bert Minike's** and back to the bottom and on upriver. It wandered up and down because one homesteader went to his place and the next one went to his.

3.2 miles from the railroad crossing is **Dick Titley's place** on the lower side of the road.

3.6 — the draw that held **Dick Titley's prospect.** Dick took me and Mary and the kids to look at it. We took samples with a little pick axe like prospectors use.

Dick said, "Mary! I want you to send them in to be assayed so nobody'll know they came from my mine. They're scheming to buy me out for next to nothing."

4.3 — Right up the hill from here was **Bert Minike's homestead cabin.** He owned a big team of draft horses. When 2 or 3 days passed and the horses came down by themselves to drink, Papa and somebody else got suspicious and went up to see if Minike was all right.

Bert must have opened the barn door and went to let the team out. One horse kicked him right in the face. When I was a kid we'd go up to look at the place on the dirt floor where Bert had laid and rolled his head back and forth. He was dead when they found him.

The Maher cabin was up Flewsie Creek about a quarter of a mile.

4.5 is Dirty Dutch's homestead. His house set on the upper side of where the road now runs and was next to Two Bit Creek.

4.65 is where the shack stands in which the schoolteacher lived, on the right about 40 feet from the road. The Gold Center schoolhouse was just to the right of the road.

Gold Center School girls 1919. Margaret and Marie Maher; Alma, Edith and Lenore Rogers; Annie and Myrtle Martin.

Gold Center School boys 1919. Ike Rogers, Jim and Floyd Martin; Bud Maher, John Rogers, David and Lester Griffin.

Griffin Homestead Cabin built 1913. Lester holds his mother's .30 .30 Winchester Carbine with which a posse member shot Frank Strand 1923.

4.8 Our old homestead log house still sets about 150 feet above the road. We packed our water from the creek except for 3 months of the year when it came out of a depression lower down where a few spearmint plants still grow. The old trail ran along the sidehill past our cabin. Up there to the right of the house where the jackpines and other little trees grow now was our garden ground.

The barn where Mama was milking the cow when Frank Strand was hiding in the manger was here below the house and up the bottom about 50 feet. Right across the St. Maries River where the trees have all been butchered, was the most beautiful little creek and when Mama made lemonade the water was so cold it would make your teeth chatter.

For a great many years the road didn't go beyond Gold Center. The Indians that came to pick huckleberries up on Grandmother Mt. and White Rock used to leave their buggies at our place where Mama could keep an eye on them, rather than taking them to the end of the road.

We got so we knew a lot of the Indians from Lapwai and Tensed.

In 1918 an Indian girl — 'course we was always watchin' from our house, left the bunch and walked across the footlog over the river and laid down behind some willows. Pretty quick a young Indian man come up to the house and said, "We won't be able to move right away. One of our women is having a baby."

Afterwards she carried the little baby to the creek, washed it, and they took off for the mountains.

5.6 GOLD CENTER
This is far as the road went. Fishermen from Moscow come up here to catch trout 14 inches long just as fast as they could pull 'em in.

The Chinamen digging for gold had their flume right along the creek on the right hand side of where the road runs. That was probably before 1910. We came in 1913 and the workings were still here. The Chinamen used a hand driven dredge with small buckets and turned with a long double crank operated by 2 men on each end to scoop gravel from the creek bottom and run it through their sluice boxes.

5.7 Cross the bridge and take the left fork for White Rock Springs.

Bucket and chain from hand dredge used by Chinese at Gold Center before 1910.

Remains of cabin built at Gold Center by Chinese before 1910 and used by Dan Smith for a homestead cabin after 1913. 1974 photo.

5.8 You can look diagonally cross the canyon at an almost bare hillside. At the top it almost levels off. It was the site of the Gold Creek cabin the Chinamen built. Beyond it were around 20 tent frames where other Chinamen lived.

Dan Smith came in 1914. Not realizing the Chinamen cabin was on ground he was homesteading he started building a cabin over across the Maries river. He chopped his left index finger off. He come down to Mama to get it bandaged. His finger that wasn't there itched a great deal afterwards and he said it must be from the ants that were near where he buried it and they must be chewing on it. He went up and dug up the finger and re-buried it.

When Dan realized the empty Chinamen cabin was on his own ground he moved into it and then up the hill a ways he dug a prospect hole and got out a lot of rose colored quartz. He thought if he dug deep enough he'd hit a vein of galena coming through from Kellogg. He named it the Mable Ellen Mine after my sister.

You take a left fork that goes down into Gold Center Creek. 150 feet ahead is a washout where the bridge used to be. Park your car.

A half mile up this old road, Gramp Creek comes in from the left. Here is what's left of the board house Jake Martin lived in when he homesteaded here and raised hay and whiskey in this bottom that is now eroded and worthless.

Jake Martin homestead cabin, 1974 after 60 years.

This road was used during the '20s by Runaway Chase and Toter Bill freighting big wagon loads of supplies with 4 horse teams to the Halfway House at the foot of Grandmother Mountain. Then packstrings picked up the loads and carried them on over the ridge and into the Carey & Harper camps on Delaney and the mouth of Freezeout Creek. Hauling freight was a summertime chance only. Us kids used to make the roundtrip to the Halfway House with Toter Bill. But Runaway Chase didn't cater to us kids at all.

In those days Gramp Creek was called Eagle Creek. Gold Creek was the name of the main St. Maries River and St. Maries River was the name of what is now Gold Creek.

Another quarter mile, the bottom road reaches a snowsled bowl piled up by bulldozers and abandoned now for the one on the highway at Bechtels. On the bare hillside on your left is where the man that borrowed Mama's .30 .30 stood to shoot Frank Strand in the back. The York Martin house stood about 50 feet out from the little spruce tree on the right of the road and then about 45 degrees toward you another 75 feet out in the bottom.

Directly across the creek to your right is an opening in the trees where the trail went to White Rock Springs. Frank Strand was trying to reach that trail when he was shot walking over the footlog.

Footlog crossing 1923 Gold Center Cr. to the WhiteRock Springs Trail. 1974 photo

Lester Griffin standing on the site of the York Martin cabin above Gold Center where Strand was shot in 1923. 1974

Tour 2 with Lester Griffin

Return to where the road forks into Clarkia. Set your speedometer at zero and head up the oiled highway toward Bovill.

1.7 The Bechtel place. Over near the railroad track on your left is where the airplane shook off us kids and then dived on its nose.

2.8 Mazie's log cabin stood on the right beside almost dried up Mazie Creek just before you come to the little road that turns off to the right up the draw. Mazie bootlegged and free lanced around the Clarkia joints. She still lived here in 1933 or '34. All them old de-horns, the ones that wouldn't hang out with the more respectable men, they'd come up to Mazie's place to buy the stuff.

2.9 The highway curves right but it was along the Swede John fence running straight away that Chet Ward, making his getaway after killing Blondie Cole drove off a quarter mile in the lane that was Cat's Spur and then ran his car a half mile up Cat Creek on the right and covered it with brush.

Milwaukee log train at dusk passing the highway crossing between Clarkia and Fernwood. Jan. 1980

Interviewed at Clarkston, Washington and Deary, Idaho, 1973.

Josie Gunderson
Lone Homesteader

I hollered and nobody answered

Josie Gunderson 1972

I was born on a dryland farm in South Dakota of Norwegian parents Dec. 13, 1885. I went to grade school there. Later, I lived with my brother on a homestead in Canada. That gave me the idea of homesteading.

So in 1915 I went on the train to Coeur d'Alene and put my name into the drawing for homesteads. I was 30 years old. All I had was $100 to my name.

I went to work at St. Maries part time at housework and at the laundry. Then came a card that told me they had drawed my number.

At the land office they had told me there was homesteads around Clarkia so I went there and looked around and asked people. About all there was at Clarkia was a log store and a building for supplies.

I took a homestead northeast of Clarkia and about a half mile west of Anthony's. I hired the neighbors to build me a cabin.

Josie's homestead cabin.

While the neighbors were building I wandered off in the woods. I wanted to see my land. Pretty soon I got completely turned around and didn't know where I was. I couldn't hear their hammers and axes any more. I went one way and then the other. I couldn't find my cabin.

I hollered and nobody answered.

Then it was getting dusk. I remembered that the neighbors had instructed me if I ever got lost to walk downhill. So I went downhill.

It was pitch dark when I got into a brushy bottom and I couldn't tell any more which way was downhill. Then I could hear water running. I got through the brush to it. I stooped over and put my hand into the little creek to feel which way it was going. I followed it down to where it ran into the Maries river and from there I could see a house light.

I still didn't have the slightest idea what direction was home so I went there and asked. The neighbor told me I had come out on Merry Creek. He guided me home with a coal oil lantern.

This same neighbor, later loaned me a shotgun so I could shoot grouse. I didn't shoot many. One morning I opened the door and a big bob cat was on my porch looking at me. One second he was there and the next he was gone.

I liked living on the homestead by myself and seeing the animals and the birds. But I could only stay there summers because I had to go out and work for a living.

Rutledge Ranch, logging railroad headquarters at Clarkia 1922.

In 1918 I was working as flunkey at the Beanery in Burke when the Armistice for World War 1 was signed. the railroad engineer ran up and down the track through the Tiger Boarding House tooting the whistle. (**The canyon there is so narrow the railroad, the road and the creek all ran through the Tiger Boarding House.**)

Then I worked different times at Clarkia at the Headquarters cookhouse. It was a place with warehouses, horse barns and a bunkhouse for the logging railroad people but it didn't have many people like they had in the logging camps.

I heard them talking there about how a carload of logs broke loose on the Incline and a crew was working on the track and it jumped over them. They were so scared they quit.

I sold my homestead to the Rutledge Timber Co. in 1940 and went to Seattle to work awhile.

Interviewed at the Silverton Nursing Home, 1972.

Josie at 57, 1942

Myrtle Isaacson

Bribed to keep my big mouth shut

Stephen and Myrtle Isaacson 1960

My maiden name, Benscoter, comes from a Pennslyvania Dutch name, Van Benscoten. I was born on a farm at Kendrick, Idaho, Feb. 1, 1903.

Dad said he had too much relations around Kendrick and sold out. We wcre one of the first families to move into Bovill in 1910. They were building the Milwaukee railroad through there and on into Elk River. Dad started freighting with team and wagon and worked in the woods.

During my elementary schooldays in Bovill I made life miserable for the young women of 16 and 17 like Nellie Galloway and Annetta Kellom. They weren't supposed to be going with fellas. I was 10 years old and I made them bribe me to keep my big mouth shut. Annetta married Harris Bellows. His mother was a Benscoter, a sister to my dad.

Blackwell Mill at Fernwood 1913   Courtesy of Chattie Inman

Right after World War 1 in 1919 we moved from Bovill to Clarkia. I worked for Cavernis. They had a bar and dining room and pool tables on the right as you enter Clarkia across from where Oral Avery had his first store. Caverni was Italian. She was Spanish. They had a good floor. They'd push the pool tables out and have dances.

Stephen Isaacson played drums at the dances and was an exciting out-of-towner from Fernwood. He was a real good Waltzer. With the right person he'd squeeze a little. Of course my sister, 3 years older, and I was both young and foolish and always had a good time. And Stephen, 7 years older, a man of the world. Fernwood had a movie house and Stephen ran the movie projector there and owned a meat market.

A. M. Sinrud store, on left Isaacson's Meat Market 1924 Fernwood

After a year at Cavernis I waited table in the dining room of the Elk Hotel for the Schuberts. When the train went up the line if it whistled 4 times that meant they'd be stopping at noon for dinner.

Clarkia was a good town when the Rutledge Timber Co. was there and built all them buildings. I quit the Elk Hotel and went to flunkeyin' at the Rutledge Ranch. That was the logging railroad headquarters a short distance from town, with big barns to winter logging teams. Josie Gunderson worked there at the time and I got acquainted with Marble Creek Jerry as she went in or came out from flunkeying in some of the camps over the hill. Max Turpin was washing dishes. Mrs. Douglas was cook and she used to get awful mad at her son Floyd and I because we swiped her sweet chocolate.

When I was working I always helped my folks out with money. Dad had worked on a loader and that's dangerous. He got a broken leg and it never was set right.

When the snow got deep and shut down camps in the Marble they'd hire Sourdough Bob Corby to cook at Rutledge Ranch for the winter.

DANCES AND CELEBRATIONS
Stephen and I went together off and on. I had other fellas and he had other girls — just young folks and didn't know any better. Stephen didn't drink much although he got awfully drunk sometimes when he'd go out with his men friends. We went to dances at the Gold Center schoolhouse where Genevieve Avery's father, Mr. Maher used to call the square dances. There were big celebrations on the 4th of July in

both Clarkia and Fernwood and we could circulate from one town to the other to take in all the excitement.

MARRIAGE AND CHILDREN
After a couple of years we got married. Stephen was born in '22; Elaine that married George Hays in Bovill was born in '24 and Patricia born in '26 married Elmer Tillotson. Our last baby was Donald in 1929.

In about 1928 the meat business got so poor that Stephen went cooking in camps again. He had cooked in camps before I met him. I run the meat market about a year till I got tired of running it alone. Then we sold it to Guy Lowry.

While I stayed at home with the kids Stephen kept on cooking like at the CC camp at Clarkia and the one up East Emerald.

LOOKING AGAIN FOR A JOB
After the kids were all raised I started looking for a flunkey job. Potlatch wouldn't hire a cook's wife in the same camp as the cook. They offered me a job at Camp 40 but I refused. I wanted to work in the same camp as Stephen. Finally, in 1946 Potlatch gave in and I flunkeyed at Camp 36 where Stephen was.

In 1951 Stephen went in partnership with our son Steve in a grocery store and meat market in Fernwood. About 1959 my husband had a stroke following surgery for hardening of the arteries. Young Steven had to take over the store altogether then. My husband died September 28, 1968. I've continued to live in Fernwood ever since.

Young Steve Isaacson, now 58, says, "Dad's name was Stephen Paul Isaacson so his initials were S.P.I. They called him SPIT. My name is Stephen Harris Isaacson so my initials are S.H.I. A fellow, C. A. Dahl came into the store one day and I used his initials and called him CAD. He came back with my nickname. I should have quit while I was ahead.

Steve Isaacson, Fernwood postmaster 1980

Interviewed January 1980 at Fernwood, Idaho

Everybody likes his Swedish accent

Arvid Johnson

When I was about 18 years old eight of us went to a dance which was about a Swedish mile from where we lived at what they called a station. We didn't get in a fight about women. But 70 or 80 of the men there tried to chase

Arvid Johnson 81, 1980

us home and we went outside in the yard to settle it. We was outnumbered 10 to 1. I had two in front of me and one come behind. He swing around. He had a pair of brass knuckles and he hit me alongside the mouth and the blood spurted out of me.

All eight of us got beat up. A deputy there said we started it. We couldn't find 4 witnesses to make him out a liar. My chum got 10 days in jail. Others got more and some less. I got three months suspended sentence.

My grandfather said, "You better go to the United States to live with your mother and stepfather. Sweden ain't big enough for you.

I said, "Then give me the money."

So he drawed a thousand dollars from the bank and he send me over here.

ALMOST A MINER

I lived at Mother's house in Butte. I work on surface but I belong to union there. We had to belong or get canned.

One day I got rustling card. That is a card from union gives me right to ask Company for job underground.

My mom found out about it and she said, "I hear you get rustling card."

"Yah!" I said. "I did."

She said, "Promise me one ting."

I said, "What da hell is dat?"

"That you never go in the mines," she said. "Because I can't get along out here without you."

"O.K."I said, and I never did.

CASCADE TUNNEL JOB
I work in Cascade tunnel, too. Great Northern. It was a tough one. Seven and eight-tenths miles long.

The big man, the Walker, he come and he vanted to know if go down underground.

I say, "The big tunnel?"

"No! I want you work in shaft on east end."

"Yah!" I said. "I can do dat."

But there was a whole shift quit. Three or four of them guys friends of mine.

Them said, "Don't go in dere."

"Why?" I said.

Said, "Already 279 men killed this place. There goin' to be another cave-in any minute!"

Them said, "That's the reason we is quittin'." Said, "Where did you come from?"

I said, "Spokane."

Dem said, "Go right back to Spokane again."

So I do dat.

HIDING MOON
I come in 1923 to Fernwood. There was about hundred lumberyacks here every day. Them used to hide yugs in the ground. Them took a posthole digger and dug a hole right down and put in the yug and put a little sod on top. I bet there is 10, 15 yugs that nobody found. Right between the railroad and the old saloon there.

BLOWED A WAD
This Sven Jackson took contract from Potlatch to pull the logs in the river and he anchored the donkey out in the river and he pulled pretty near 4 million feet in one pull. He made hundred and nine dollars a day for 39 days. Them was money, 50, 60 years ago.

Him told me he went to Spokane with $15,000. "I blowed it in," he said, "and went $600 in the hole besides. And on top of that when I come back to loggin' camp a steel sliver hit my eye and I lose my eye. That's hard to take!" he said to me.

THE WOBBLIES
I'm an old logger. I was goin' to yoin the Wobblies in 1925. But then it splitted up. The Wobblies was good union. Them get lots of things for workin' man and done away with packin' bedroll along. Them got rid of bedbugs, too.

1926 I work in Emerald Creek and for Ripley down on Chet Henning's place — there where the clear-cut is.

THE INCLINE
Some of them guys look up at that steep Incline and all that snow and turn right back and go home. (Laughs) The track was shovelled. We walked the track straight up the mountain. Oh Boy! I get more tired when I went down the other side.

One day after I am old a guy come to my home. Started talkin' about workin' in Marble Creek and his dad he run the donkey on top of the Incline there."

"Yesus Crist!" I says. "I must have seen your dad then, because I stopped up there and talked to the guy that run that donkey."

AN OLD HOBO
I work in Marble one season. I work all over. but when the Depression come I can't get a yob no place.

I did a lot of hoboing for 14 months under President Hoover. I walk the highways. I ride the freights. Here in Fernwood they tell me Henry Nordingham was a hobo.

"That's all B. S.," I said. "He had a sleepin' bag all the time. I took a yumper over my head and crawled into the brush to sleep!"

You want to see my hobo watch. I got it hided in here. I paid $60 for it but I been offered a hundred and twenty-five.

GOLD STRIKE
One time I was in Tyson Creek poachin' and I get tired and set down to eat a sandwich. There was a schoolma'am tree there. (A tree that has branched into two trunks or legs.) I started lookin' at them rocks, you know, and Boy! OH BOY! They look like good. I knock some of the rocks to pieces and look them over. I started lookin' at the ground and I could see the vein of gold quartz about 50 feet right on top of the ground.

My Goodness! I been there five times after and I had Jim with me and the bushes growed up so you couldn't crawl through again.

I cannot find it, that gold!

COULD LICK CASSIUS CLAY
You know something? I got a chum in Chicago could lick Cassius Clay in 15 seconds. He hit with the hand first and then with the head and then with the feet. Talk about vindmill.!

He is old sailor. Born in Oslo, Norvay. Henry Amundson is his name.

I said, "Vas you any related to Roald Amundson, the great artic explorer?"

"By Yesus!" he said. "It could happen."

Henry could lick anybody.

Fernwood is my home. I never wanted to go back to Sweden. I like the United States. I tell you something. You could go all over the world, to Russia or any country and don't find it so good.

I got nine-hundred and forty-nine hills of potatoes in my garden!

Interviewed June 17, 1976 at Fernwood, Idaho

Guy F. Russell homestead cabin near Fernwood 1903

Pete Johnson

the magnificent ride

River Driver

Wobbly

Pete Johnson at 86. 1975

I was born March 22, 1889 in Ostersund, Sweden. My mother and stepfather came to Canada in 1902 when I was 13, attracted by homesteading advertisements. When we got to Winnipeg it was 45 below zero.

We came from a modern city with electric lights and every thing. And my God! We came where they had kerosene light, outside toilets, no sewer and a city pump on the corner to pump water. We felt like going right back to Sweden.

The old man went pickin' ice out of the Canadian Pacific Railroad switches for $2 a ten hour day. I don't know if that was the going wage at the time but whatever they offered you took it. There was no union nor nothing.

I worked for $5 a month for a farmer from Sweden and he beat me out of my wages — my own countryman!.

PEDDLED PAPERS

At 16 I was peddling a Swedish language newspaper in Winnipeg. There was a saloon there called The Scandinavian. About that time — 1905 — the union between Sweden and Norway was dissolving and there was more civil war going on between the Norwegians and Swedes at The Scandinavian than there was in the old countries.

Those Winnipeg newspaper boys had a tight union of their own for selling on certain corners the Free Press and The Telegram. I didn't know about that.

They didn't know my paper was Swedish and no competition to them and they ganged up and kicked hell out of me. I couldn't speak English to explain.

My youngest brother was going to school. I started going to school, too. I had had 6 years of school in the old country. I always have been a bookworm so I was steeped in geography and history of foreign countries.

The teacher put me in the first grade and sat me down to build with alphabet blocks. She came along to teach me my ABCs. I picked up the alphabet book and read the letters to her. I made four grades in one week and then quit. I couldn't figure any use in going to school there. In a year's time I picked up the street language.

In 1906 when World War I started, Canada wasn't especially pro-British but Lord Beaverbrook who was a big publisher in England bought a string of newspapers in Canada and spread the propaganda of Germans running around with babies on their bayonets; maids with their breasts cut off.

I'll never forget the spring of 1916 when they were recruiting the Scandinavian Battalion called The Vikings Of Canada. We Scandinavians didn't enlist fast enough so they went up to Prince Albert. Them big, black Sioux Indians joined The Vikings. After that Custer massacre those Sioux had come across the line from the United States. Made us the darkest Vikings you ever saw. What a tough bunch!

VOLUNTEER ARMY

The Canadians refused to pass the draft but they got a half million man army by volunteer out of a population of 10 million people. And over in France they clapped the

Pete Johnson in Canadian Army uniform 1919.

Canadians on the back and said, "You are all brave boys!" and put them in the front line trenches.

The English had poor leadership in General Haig. The Germans blew the Canadians out of the trenches and left nothing but rubble. I was lucky to be assigned back of the lines bringing up supplies.

SHELL SHOCK
Young Tom Radcliffe was buried in a dugout under shelling and he was dug out. When he come home you wouldn't know him. He'd stand and tremble and break out in a sweat. His whole system shattered.

At the front we got news that the war fever cooled in Canada after the trains of wounded and cripples come back in the latter part of 1916.

And a friend wrote me that Canada had a British play "The Better Hole" right from the front lines. They done some shootin' on the stage to make it more real. One fellow in the audience was shell shocked and he got up and hit the man in front of him on the top of the head. He was shakin' all over.

CONTACT WITH THE WOBS
I first ran into the Wobblies in early 1916 before I went into the army, when they organized a construction job of the Canadian Northern into Prince Rupert.

When I came back in 1919 after 3 years in the Canadian army they pulled a strike up there and tied up everything solid.

A delegate named Lyle laid out the beliefs of the Industrial Workers of the World to me and I began to see the light.

FIRST LOG DRIVE
I came down into the U.S. in 1919. My first job was on the drive on Bussel Creek, breakin' down decks under a boss named Fred Ross. We were attempting to flume from a little dam at Camp 1 and the pond would run out of water in 10 minutes and leave the big white pine logs stuck in the flume.

Then they tried to send down double length logs. That was worse. Then they let the flume stand idle on the bank and drove the logs down the creek. The logs hung up down below so they built another dam at Camp 18 about 2 miles above the mouth of Bussel and then were able to splash them out of the mouth of Bussel and into the Camp 11 dam and the last dam they built was a big one at Camp 7 to splash logs all the way to the Joe.

WOBBLY REMEMBERATIONS
Wherever lumberjacks gathered in bunkhouses or in Clarkia hotels or in the dives of Oldtown St. Maries they still talked about the big strikes of 1917. I don't remember all the demands but in addition to the 8 hour day at the same pay they wanted shower baths and bedding

furnished to get rid of the lice and bedbugs, better food and the doing away with them damn tin dishes.

Coming into Clarky in the spring of '19 right where the road crosses the railroad track by Shorty Wade's joint was the warehouse with one of the old 1917 signs still nailed on it, WE, THE UNDERSIGNED, WILL NOT KNOWINGLY HIRE ANY MEMBER OF THE I.W.W. Signed: Potlatch, Winton and all the rest.

HERRICK BLACKLISTED
Herrick was the first one to grant the 8 hour day in the fall of 1917 and the rest of the lumber association blacklisted him.

JOB ACTION
When the Wobs ran out of funds they transferred the strike back to the job — like at Steve Cooligan's camp for the Milwaukee Land Co. on Emerald Creek.

They all went to work for Cooligan. They instructed the loading crew at the steam jammer to blow the whistle at the end of 8 hours and they all marched to camp.

The cook was Wobbly too. He stuck a ONE BIG UNION banner right across inside the cookhbouse dining room.

Steve Colligan came and told 'em, "This is a 9 hour camp."

They didn't argue but worked only 8 hours again on the second day.

He fired the whole shebang.

They left and another gang hired in and pulled the same thing.

The Milwaukee caved in on the hours and pay but they didn't have the bedding.

The Wobs gave them time to get it.

PICKET CAMP AT FERNWOOD
In late summer of 1917 the Wobs established a picket camp down the river at Fernwood against the Rutledge camp on nearby Crystal Creek and against Blackwells on the Hump.

Here come the Law in all its majesty and penned them up in the St. Maries bullpen.

St. Maries Record Aug. 14, 1917 — A stockade is being built at the fairgrounds across the river. Eleven I.W.W.s are in the county jail and another eleven temporarily sent to Moscow. Bunks are being placed in the exhibition building, barbed wire fence around it. Moscow's Mess Sergeant has been borrowed to oversee the construction.

St. Maries Record Oct. 12, 1917 — Prosecutor Allen A. Holsclaw writes Boise asking Gov. Alexander to influence the U.S. Government to take over the 38 men in the stockade. 16 are aliens and he feels the county shouldn't have to bear an expense which belongs to the entire country. The soldiers are to leave Saturday and all the expense will again fall on the sheriff's office.

St. Maries Record Dec. 4, 1917 — The remaining charges against I.W.W. Secretary Guiney of selling I.W.W. literature are dismissed and he is set free. The remaining stockade prisoners are set free.

They fed 'em free for 3 months and turned 'em loose because it hit the county's pocketbook nerve. Harry Anderson — he had a restaurant in Old Town and had cooked in logging camps — the day the Wobs were let out of the bullpen he served them a big turkey dinner.

And the funny part of it was that Rutledge, the Wobs discovered later on, had warehouses full of bunks and bedding and mattresses but they were holding off for President Wilson to proclaim the 8 hour day so they could give credit for it and the bedding to the War Department sponsored 4L company union that was to be formed March 1918. The 4L was supposed to wipe out the Wobbly movement.

THE TIMEKEEPER AND THE 4L
The 4L stood for Loyal Legion of Loggers and Lumbermen. It included the little bosses in its leadership so they could control and report what went on at meetings. I was in Camp 2 on Bussel Creek. The timekeeper and scaler, Lemuel Nordman called a meeting.

He says, "We've got to discuss putting in more hours on the flume."

One guy jumped up and said, "I make the motion we cut the day to 6 hours."

Somebody else seconded him and called for a vote. Everybody voted in favor.

Nordman says, "Why! You're all a bunch of Wobblies!" and walked out.

Camp 2 was up the draw on the Marble side of the Incline. They had a short flume down from it that they never used. Mind you there wasn't enough water for a flume but they were crazy about flumes at the time. They stuck a flume up every draw.

WOBBLY HANGOUTS IN SPOKANE
Two of us got tired of the woods and headed for Spokane and the bright lights.

In Spokane we had a fellow with a good voice. He used to sing at meetings and get togethers in the Wobbly Hall. It was a big second story hall in the middle of the block on Main between Washington and Bernard.

We used to leave there 40 or 50 strong to go to the Wobbly Corner on the Northeast corner of Main and Stevens — where Whites Shoe Shop is — and listen to soapbox speakers. This was the center of the area prowled by lumberjacks. Diagonally across the street on the Southwest corner of Main and Stevens the Hallelujah Boys performed — the Salvation Army.

MOTHER BILKIS

Going north from the Wobbly Corner the Volunteers of America was about the middle of the block and just beyond it on the sidewalk was where Mother Bilkus preached.

We got a great kick out of her. She'd point at the Volunteers building and say, "That son of a bitch he's sleepin' with her!"she'd say. "God bless the Wobblies!"

She told about a lumberjack that had no money for a room. She took him home. "In the middle of the night," she says, "he got rambunctious. I had to put the run on him! God bless the Wobblies!"

I was up in Calgary on the harvest and damned if Mother Bilkus didn't show up there. "God bless the Wobblies!" She wasn't afraid to speak up.

CY'S CORNER

Just north of Mother Bilkus' beat was Cy's corner at Stevens and Trent. Cy kept any paper or magazine that would sell. He didn't care if it was Wobbly or Girlie or Republican or Norwegian or Russian. He sold 'em all. That's where I bought the Industrial Worker.

GLOWING JOBS

Just around Cy's Corner on Trent and next to it Huk had a shark employment agency. He used to write up all his jobs as top-notch: "BRAND NEW CAMP", "ALL WINTER WORK" and "SEE BOSS INSIDE". During the time of a quickie strike in 1919 we formed a semicircle in front of his door. Not a man could get in.

Huk come and stood in the door lookin' at us. Pretty soon he come out with an eraser and wiped off all those A-1, dandy jobs. Then he wrote: "Wanted! 50 Wobblies To Keep Men From Goin' To Work!"

Huk had a sense of humor all right but he was always in trouble with the labor commission for misrepresenting jobs. We paid a $2 fee for getting a job and there was the rumor that the boss got $1 of it. Some bosses played the racket pretty heavy. They'd can a bunch every few days and send to the agency for more.

East of Huk's on Trent was the O.K. Cafe and the Dempsey Hotel. They used to say that some of the cheap chuck served at the O.K. came from leftovers of banquets at the Davenport Hotel — like steaks that could be washed off and served.

And when Jack Dempsey was boxing champ of the world and came into the Union Station they said he spotted the Dempsey Hotel across the street and said, "See! They've already named a hotel after me."

BOOZE CACHE

The Northern Hotel run by Blondey Cole was in the second story over Cy's Corner with a separate entrance from Trent. Blondey had a bar downstairs that served bootleg and an ingenious hiding place for booze that the dry squad never found.

To go upstairs to the Northern Hotel you entered a narrow door off the bar and climbed some steps. The wall on both sides of the steps was covered with flowery paper. Blondey Cole was a good carpenter and he showed me a thin crack along the wall paper. He shoved a narrow knife blade in the crack and tripped a door that opened to shelves loaded with pints.

Blondey was too cagey to keep more than one pint of moonshine at the bar. When he took a new pint out of his cache he could look down the stairs at the door which had glass on the upper half and see the back of the barkeeper standing there. That meant the coast was clear.

But if the bartender had looked down the block and spotted Hockeydahl of the Dry Squad coming their way, he stayed away from the door. That signalled, "The Law! Hide the hooch!"

Somehow Hockeydahl got wise to their signal system. One time he hid around the corner till he saw Blondey hand the bartender the pint. Then Hockeydahl whizzed to the street door and in three strides to the bar and reached a long arm over and grabbed.

The bartender brought the bottle down hard on the sink and smashed it and the booze ran down the drain. "Ah Ha!" he says. "You missed!"

TRAPDOOR DELIVERY

At another joint up Main the barkeeper stepped out over a trapdoor in the floor, rapped twice and up lifted the trapdoor with a hand holding a bottle.

Hockeydahl got wise to that one, too. One day he roamed in and when he reached the spot, he all of a sudden put out his arm to fend off the barkeep and rapped twice on the trap door. Up came the hand with the booze. Hockeydahl caught the hand by the wrist and lifted the guy out, booze and all, and slapped the bracelets on him.

CENTRALIA 1919

Two of us grabbed an armload of boxcars and went apple knockin' at Wenatchee. We landed back in Spokane the day of the shooting at Centralia. There was a lynch mood in Spokane. Legionaires running around. They raided and smashed up the Wobbly hall.

Finally, a fella came in on the freight from Centralia and told us the facts about 4 Legionaires shot that day and about the Legion busting into the jail and castrating and hanging the Wobbly veteran Wesley Everest from the railroad bridge that night.

SHOLLY ROOKS

After that crazy Centralia, we used to meet in a bootleg joint down on Trent called The Pines. Charley Brooks, the guy that ran it, had worked on the Marble. He was a Finn. The other Finlanders called him Sholly Rooks.

He rolled his Rs. He says to me, "You want a rrrrrink?"

He went to the backroom and fetched a flat pint of moonshine. "Satan save us! " he says. "You take a big rrrrrink! "

I worked with quite a number of Finns, like Big Matt Oya, the hook tender. He used a Finn for wood buck down on the donkey. That was hard work. A donkey used from 2 to 4 cords of wood a day. He never went much for having his own countrymen in his crew because he figured it would show favoritism. He might have another Finn on the riggin'. That was all.

Our second Wob Hall was small and on the ground floor between Trent and Main across from the Wallace Hotel.

CHICAGO TRIALS AND SABOTAGE CHARGE

In 1919 our papers carried the full story of the sabotage trials in Chicago when the lawyer George Vandiveer fought the cases for the Wobblies. Often he didn't get paid.

Anyway, the Panhandle Lumber Co. brought a damaged saw from their sawmill at Ione, Washington to prove they had sawed into a spike in one of the logs. They claimed it was sabotage by the Wobblies.

Vandiveer says, "Did you see a Wobbly drive that spike?"

Nobody could testify to it.

"Where's the man that sawed into it?"

They had nobody.

"Then what is that saw doing here," he says, "if you don't know who drove the spike and who sawed into it? Isn't it a fact," he says, "that you were out of logs and so you were sawin' boomsticks? And you know there's crosspieces nailed onto boomsticks and you brought one up into the mill with a spike in it and that's what you sawed into."

He made a fool out of that manager of the Panhandle.

I'll tell you something. I wore out two red cards and in all that time I never heard a man that ever advocated anything like that. Of course, God knows, you could hire some of these stools and prostitutes to do something like that to blame on the Wobblies and the Hoosiers would all believe it.

Look what happened in the Palouse country. A little rock would get in the thrasher with the grain and make a spark and set off a dust explosion. Blow up the rig! And they'd blame the Wobblies. Claim we threw matches.

I went out to overhaul an engine for a fellow at St. John.

He said, "You're not one of them I.W.W.s, are you?"

"No! No!" I says. But when you stop to think of it. It was a fright — the ignorance.

LUMBERJACK SINGING

About 1920 I stayed overnight at Magee's sleigh haul camp over in the Minolusa Valley near Plummer. In them days that whole flat was standing timber. Nights in the bunkhouse they had regular song fests. There was a little fellow that could just make those old Scottish hornpipes and jigs run out of a fiddle. Some of the lumberjack songs were adapted to the tunes of hornpipes.

About the only other place I heard that kind of singing was at Camp 3 on the Marble. They chanted the songs, generally no instrument with 'em. I had heard some of these same songs in Canada sung by the French-Canadians. Oldtimers from Michigan and Wisconsin brought them to Idaho.

The Wobblies built some of their songs on old tunes. One that we sang was set to the hymn Sweet Bye and Bye. Joe Hill wrote the words. Here are a couple of verses:

THE PREACHER AND THE SLAVE
Long haired preachers come out every night.
    Try to tell you what's wrong and what's right.
But when asked how 'bout something to eat
    They will answer with voices so sweet:

CHORUS:
You will eat, bye and bye,
    In that glorious land above the sky.
Work and pray! Live on hay!
    You'll get pie in the sky when you die.

2nd Verse:

And the Starvation Army they play
    And they sing and they clap and they pray,
Till they get all your coin on the drum,
    Then they tell you when you're on the bum:

Chorus:
You will eat, bye and bye,
    In that glorious land above the sky.
Work and pray! Live on hay!
    You'll get pie in the sky when you die.

(All together, shouted) **IT'S A LIE!**

THE SHORT PRAYER

Like most Wobblies I didn't have much use for religion or preachers. Most always seemed to be on the side of the boss. But I never made fun of any man's religion.

I remember this ex-Salvation Army man that got a job at Harrington's Camp at Cat's Spur near Clarky. At the table he happened to get a seat between Jake Harrington's brothers, Vince and Warren. Vince used to pile up his plate with both hands till nothing more would go on it.

While Vince was loading his plate, the Salvation Army man bowed his head and unloaded a prayer. When the poor devil looked up, the food had passed him by and was all at the other end of the table. Then, by the time he got some passed back to him the other men had already left the table and the cook and flunkeys were scowling at him.

I said to him out on the job, "You'd better get wise! You'll starve to death if you don't pitch in."

I noticed after a few days that he just bobbed his head like "Amen!" and reached for the grub.

JAKE HARRINGTON MEETS JIM MADDEN

The Harringtons were a fighting clan, you know. Warren wasn't much over average size but Jake and Vince, they were big men. The Harringtons all came from Buckingham, Ontario. They dated back to the Royalists that left the American Colonies during the revolution and settled along with the rest of the red coats in Canada. English-Irish mixture.

The legendary I.W.W. Jim Madden came into camp bringing a load of books and papers and looking for work. He ate supper and stayed overnight.

After breakfast, next morning, Jake Harrington offered Madden a strip.

Under the gypo system a man would be offered a marked strip of timber to saw or skid at so much per thousand board feet.

Madden said quietly, "I don't believe I'll take it — not at that price."

This was in front of the bunkhouse. Men with tools and men and teams were heading out to work.

Jake raised his voice so everybody within 200 yards could hear. "By God! Then you're gonna pay for your supper and breakfast or I'll take it out of your hide."

Madden polished off Jake with a couple of swift ones, dusted off his hands and said, "That was the easiest breakfast I ever paid for."

LUMBERJACKS LOYAL TO OLDTOWN
Lumberjacks used to come in off the Maries Branch passenger train 50-60 men at a time. They'd get off at the Y in Oldtown and spend their money in places like Harry Anderson's restaurant on First Street not too far from where Minerva now has her restaurant-tavern, or Anna O'Gara's Cafe, or Harry Glidden's Card Room, or the Annex Rooms, or the Anderson's Mountain View Hotel, or the Midway Restaurant, or Oliver Neilson's clothing store, or Vanderveer's Cafe, or the Lumbermens Hotel or the Parker Hotel.

Many of the restaurants would give a broke lumberjack a meal and in the hotels the rooms weren't always cash on the line for a man that was broke.

After the 1917 arrests and the bullpen, the lumberjacks spent the time between trains with their friends down in Oldtown. Then instead of going through the uptown they'd walk down the railroad track to the depot and take a train back up the Branch or into Spokane.

SHORT STAKERS AND CAMP INSPECTORS
Fellows that worked for only a short time in the camps were called Short Stakers. A lot of 'em used to follow the Great Northern out of Whitefish, Montana down to Newport on regular beats. They'd drop into camp in time for supper and eat and sleep and take off next morning before the Push could pressure them to go to work.

I worked at Humbird's Camp 4 out of Priest River one winter. Fellow by the name of Samuelson was cooking at Camp 4 and I happened to be in the kitchen getting a cup of coffee.

Looked up the road, "Ho! Ho!" says he. "Here comes my Saturday night crew."

Here come 10 Finlanders. There was no extra bunks so they slept in the washhouse. Monday morning they took off to the next camp and Saturday afternoon they'd be back around again.

They called these tourists Camp Inspectors.

WOBS
Items from the Gazette-Record:
11-18-19 — 3 Wobs arrested in St. Maries and held in county jail, unable to raise bail of $2500, each.

11-18-19 — After Centralia incident the 40,000 members of the 4L vow to work with the American Legion to rid the Northwest of radicals.

12-09-19 — Portland — 2 arrested men sign pledge of allegiance and denounce I. W. W. and are released from jail.

12-19-19 — Federal Immigration Department pledges to deport I. W.W. alien members captured in Idaho.

2-17-20 — 7 Wobs arrested in Wenatchee.

2-27-20 — 18 members of I. W. W. on trial at Sandpoint.

12-13-23 — Edward Krier on trial for being I. W. W.... Convicted

QUICKIE STRIKE ON THE MARBLE
I was working at Camp 22 in 1922 when the men on the Marble Creek drive pulled a strike demanding $6 for an 8 hour day. I don't know how many million feet of burned timber was in the creek but it was the biggest drive to come out of the Marble.

All of us in camp pulled out in sympathy, just left the cookhouse crew and barn boss in camp and headed for the Spokane skidroad....or anywhere. There was no need to put pickets out. A man worth his salt in the woods wouldn't go in to scab anyway.

Jim Grindl used to boss the drive regular for Rutledge. Jim was kind of a half breed. He used to work the Barnabys and Hardys and Tom King — all big, dark men — maybe quarter breed Menominee Indians from Wisconsin. I've read in books where the French Canadians wore sashes but I think somebody dreamed it. They did wear stocking caps and wore shoepacks — that's a cross between a moccasin and stitchdowns — a pliable boot of oiled leather with a heavy sole.

To break the strike the Rutledge shipped in a bunch from Chicago: taxi drivers, bums off the skidroad, petty gangsters and a few dashboard overalled stubble jumpers off the farms. They had never seen a log in their days. Didn't know which end of a peavy to use.

Jim Grindl took one look at 'em and refused to put 'em on. He knew they'd all drown.

Down on the Spokane skidroad we heard by the grapevine what was goin' on. When the strike demands were met, we all drifted back into camp.

WOOD 'EM UP LIKED TO FIRE MEN
Leland Denny came into camp one Monday morning pretty sick from drinkin'. Layin' in the bunk.

Wood 'em Up George, about all the outfit he had was some horses, he was decking alongside the chute on Hobo Creek.

He came into the bunkhouse and saw Denny. "This is no place to lay around and sober up. Get into your car and go to town."

Denny rolled out and headed for the door.

"Wait a minute!" Wood 'em Up says. "You got a pretty big car haven't you? I'll give you some company."

He went out and fired four more to make up a carload.

Wood 'em Up liked to fire men. Any excuse would do. He would come upon a man working in the woods and say, "Hey, Jack! Is your axe sharp?"

If the man said, "Yes! You crazy old fool. You think I'd work with a dull axe?"

Then Wood 'em Up beamed and went on.

But if the man looked at his axe blade, Wood 'em Up would grunt, "You're fired!"

One day Wood 'em Up stopped down by the skidway and saw a man flattening a skid, "Is your axe sharp?"

The fellow glanced at the axe.

Wood 'em Up growled, "You're fired!"

Then he glanced across the skidway and saw the man's partner squatted down behind a stump with some paper in his hand and he yelled, "And you're fired, too."

The only time I had anything to do with Wood 'em Up he used to come charging down to Camp 5 on a big, black stallion and then back up the trail to his camp at the upper end of the chute.

One time he tied up the stallion and come over to our donkey. "Well!" he says, shouting to be heard above the steam. "It's beginning to look like fall. The boys will be storming into the brush for the winter."

He figured he'd be sitting pretty then, he could start hiring and firing them.

He had a rag outfit — tent camp — on Hobo and when he finished that job he pulled out. I don't know where he went.

THE BOHUNK KING, THE OX AND THE KAISER

The Bohunk King run the camp. He was Russian, I guess. A fierce lookin' man with a big mustache on him. He come from back in Wisconsin along with Jim Grindl and Wood 'em Up and the Kaiser and the Ox. The Kaiser and the Ox were a pair of big, hulking brothers. The Kaiser had a handlebar mustache with corkscrew ends. The Ox moved slow and talked slow and had shoulders 2 axe handles wide.

When the big logging horses were loaded into railroad cars back in Wisconsin the shoes were taken off so they wouldn't injure themselves or another horse, as they shifted footing in the boxcars on the curves.

Some Wisconsin lumberjacks was tellin' a joke that they also took the shoes off the Blue Ox and the Kaiser in Green Bay, Wisconsin and put 'em in a boxcar and didn't open up to let 'em out till they got to Coeur d'Alene.

In later years the Ox broke his leg and it healed in the shape of a bow. He limped around bull cookin' at the old hospital in St. Maries for years.

STRAND KILLING AT CLARKIA

I worked with Frank Strand at Sandpoint. A damn nice fellow. He was telling me the trouble he was having with his neighbor. Frank had to go through Weedle's place to get to town. "He thinks I'm monkeying with his daughter. I haven't the least idea of doing that," he says.

The girl is the one that told the truth later on.

What I heard was that Weedle was coming at Frank with the axe.

Frank said, "Don't come any closer or I'll shoot you."

Frank shot in self defense. Then he must have panicked. He was in the clear and if he had turned himself in he'd have been acquitted. Well, a man that lives by himself a lot of the time gets nervous about his neighbors. I could notice that when I was talkin' with him.

Then that homeguard posse gathered.

Afterward one of 'em came into Clarkia and told how Frank was stoopin' over to fill a bucket with water in the creek to pack back to the shack. Those sons of bitches shot him like an animal. Then they had a photograph of him in the window of the drugstore at Clarkia, layin' there riddled.

SUDDEN FLOOD

Of the about twenty donkeys brought into the Marble, there were only 2 big Willamette donkeys like the one remaining a mile up Cornwall Creek. Long liners — they had a mainline drum with 6,000 feet of two inch cable, a skidding drum with around 12,000 feet of three-fourths and a haulback drum with 12,000 feet of five-eighths cable.

That same donkey set on the flat right at the mouth of Cornwall Cr. in 1924 when I worked on the drive. For some reason they left a cable strung across Marble Creek. I don't know why they kept it there unless it was for a handline when they waded across.

We were working our way downstream, rolling logs off

Donkey at Cornwall Creek 1975.
Bert Russell

the bars and shallows when without any kind of warning, here come a four foot wall of water.

Somebody yelled a few seconds before it hit. We scrambled to get hold of that line. That's all that saved some of us out in the middle from being swept downstream and drowned. We found out later a driftwood jam up Homestead had let go.

THE EAGER DONKEY PUNCHER
This was on Blackwell Hump. The donkey puncher wanted to make himself look good with the boss. At the end of the shift he made sure he took out one last 2,000 foot drag instead of allowing us men at the far end who hooked up the logs, to walk to the donkey by quitting time. So we had to walk that extra half mile to camp on our own time.

One night we hooked him to a stump and whistled him to go ahead easy. Then we walked to camp on the railroad track where he couldn't see us. We could hear the donkey snortin' off there in the woods.

Finally, he figured something must be wrong so he set the brake and walked that half mile out through the woods and found we'd anchored him to a stump 3 foot through.

That cured the bootlicker.

OFF TO THE HARVEST
After the Wobblies got 100 per cent organized in the harvest in 1924 you had John Farmer right by the whiskers and the scissorbills — men ignorant of the class struggle — had no chance to scab.

Big Smokey Joe and I left a good paying job on the drive and set out to pester John Farmer. We caught a freight at the mouth of Marble and me, like a fool, had left my red card stashed with Jimmie Ryan, a bootlegger in Clarky.

WHAT? NO DUCAT?
I'd no more landed in North Dakota when it was, "Let's see your ducat." Holy Mackinaw! I.W.W. delegates right and left to see if you were lined up.

I tried to explain that I didn't want to take out a new card. My old card had dues stamps and pages of $5 Defense Stamps that showed how long I'd been a member. One book full and another card besides.

I told 'em, "I belonged to the Wobblies when some of you fellas was still in diapers!"

"Bull!" they said.

I wrote Jimmy, "For God's sake send me my card. I'll never get out of Dakota alive."

Finally my card come through the mail. I caught one of them smart delegates and I said, "Here! Take a look at this!" I says.

"Ah Ha!" he says. "You're one of them 500s. You're comin' to the harvest fields to scab on us 400s."

Number 400 was the Agricultural Union. 500 was the Lumber Workers. Some of those crusty old fellows in the 400s thought we should stay on our job and leave them alone. But Hell! Each union recognized the other's memberships. We was all Wobblies.

THE HARVEST STIFF

I was walking along the sidewalk. One of them tramp harvest stiffs called me, "Come over here!" he says. "How's chances to put the riggin' on you for a little handout?"

"Naw!" I says. "I just blew in. I haven't got any money."

He says, "You got a good pair of calked shoes. Peddle 'em!" he says.

(Laughing) The brassy devil!

THE DUTCHMAN

I was pitching bundles onto a wagon rack and hauling to the feeders.

The old Dutchman farmer says to me, "Take that team of mares."

Well, each mare had a colt. The colts would push in to suck the mares. I couldn't stop the little devils. If I was in the line of wagons, that would bring everything to a stop.

But we were a good crew. Everybody could handle horses and knew how to work. Inexperienced men would have had runaways when they tried to get the horses close to that noisy machinery.

We'd been working from CAN SEE to CAN'T SEE for $3 a day. We had a meeting and picked a committee. In the morning our committee met with the Dutchman. "We want 9 hours and $4 a day."

He'd had no experience with Wobblies — or unions of any kind for that matter.

"Well!" he says, "I'll have to go up and see Ma."

He come back — you bet he did! He had 1200 acres that needed thrashing.

"I'll go you one better," he says. "9 hours from barn back to barn and $4. But you'll have to keep it quiet. The county agent has been telling us that $3 is the going wage and if we pay more we'll get black-balled by the other farmers and by the banks."

I told him, "You'll find it pays to hire good help. We know the work and we'll keep on doing you a good job. Not like these greenhorns that don't know how to stuke and your shocks will blow down."

T-BONE SLIM

I ran into T-Bone Slim in the harvest field. He was a tall, friendly tramp lumberjack who ran a regular column and articles in the Wobbly paper, The Industrial Worker, that was read all over the country. He's the man that wrote a poem that thousands of workers memorized.

THE LUMBERJACK'S PRAYER

I'll pray dear Lord for Jesus sake.
Give us this day a T-bone steak.
Hallowed by Thy holy name
But don't forget to send the same.

Hear my humble cry, Oh Lord!
And send me down some decent board:
Brown gravy on some German fried
And sliced tomatoes on the side.

Observe me on my bended legs
I'm askin' you for ham and eggs
And of the hottest custard pies
I like, Dear Lord, the largest size.

Oh! Hear my cry Almighty Host
I quite forgot the quail on toast.
Let Thy kindly heart be stirred
And spread some oysters on that bird.

Dear Lord, we know Thy holy wish
On Friday we must have a fish.
Our flesh is weak, our spirits stale
You'd better make that fish a whale.

Oh, Hear me Lord! Remove those dogs
The sausages of powdered logs
The bull beef hash and bearded snouts
Take them to hell or thereabouts.

With alum bread and pressed beef butts
Dear Lord! You damn near ruined my guts.
Your whitewash milk and Oleorine
I wish to Christ I'd never seen.

Oh, Hear me Lord! I'm praying still
But if you won't, our union will
Put porkchops on the bill of fare
And starve no workers anywhere.

At the last when the Wobbly movement busted up, poor old T-Bone Slim went wino. Nowdays The Short Stakers and Gypos have no interest in either the songs or the poems.

THE PAY WAS CLEAR

Board was always included in your pay and there was no withholding taxes them days. We slept in haybarns or in the graineries. There wasn't much danger of fires, the Wobblies were pretty careful men. If we got one of those scatterbrains we put him in his place. If we got a hothead we cooled him down so he didn't spoil things.

FREE TRANSPORTATION

We rode freight trains everywhere. There were better'n 200 of us going up to Devils Lake.

The brakeman was good natured. He laughed and said, "Gosh Sake! Get on them cars and stay there. I can't see the engineer to give signals.

HARVEST IN CANADA

At the end of the Dakota harvest we moved up to Canada — their harvest was later.

We ran into a farmer that had been using fellows from back East that had never been around a thrashing rig or horses. He said, "I need men that know what they're doing."

I says, "We're experienced men. We just finished thrashin' in Dakota."

He says, "Well, how..."

I says, "We've upped the wages to $5. How many hours do you work?

He says, "Well, how..."

I says, "We got to know how many hours! We worked 9 hours in Dakota. And what about blankets?"

"I don't know," he says.

I says, "We threw away the blankets in 1916 and this is 1924."

So we got the blankets and the wages and the hours.

After the first day we had a meeting with him. I says, "You've got a bum cook. We can't work on that kind of chuck."

"What can I do? She's the only cook I could get."

"We got a cook right with us. Mulligan Slim."

"GREAT!" he says. "Bring him in."

He was not a farmer, himself, as it turned out. His brother was sick and he had come out to take care of the place. He had the main agency for General Motors in Ottawa, mind you!

And say! We got to talkin'. We told him we were organized in the Wobblies.

"Yeh!" he says. "I've heard about them. If I ever hire men again it's gonna be Wobblies." He was a hell of a swell fellow.

We worked like clockwork for him and wound up his fields in no time.

THE MOUTHY RAILROADER
There was a whole bunch of us in a boxcar leaving Moose Jaw and headed for Rose Town in the wheat belt.

One of these homeguard railroaders poked his nose in the car door and said, "What business have you fellas got to ride around free like this? I've a mind to call the mounted police and have you all arrested."

Some big Russian went to the boxcar door and looked down at him. "Go shove your head down the outhouse hole! And the mounted police with you."

The railroader backed up a safe distance and shut up.

We worked in Canada right up till the snowdrifts.

RED PASSPORT
The treatment from railroaders was different when we got back to the states. A couple of us got on a freight in CleElum. We climbed into the only open car we could find, a gondola. We knew it would be cold.

Somebody hollered, "Hey! What are you fellas?"

"Lumberjacks!" I says.

He come up — a brakeman. He says, "We're pickin' up a stockman's car that's goin' through to Montana. Come on! Ride in comfort."

It was a coach hooked onto the stock train. We no more than sat down when he come packin' kindling and lighted the stove.

Pretty soon the conductor come in and he says, "What are you fellas ridin' on?"

I hauled out my ducat but the young fellow with me didn't have a red card.

The conductor gave him a lecture. "On these roads," he says, "you'd better be fixed up."

I was surprised. But talking with him I found there was a depression and lots of lay-offs and their railroad A. F. of L. union didn't do them much good.

TRIP WITH THE BARTENDER
One August I was in this bar run by some Austrians in Spokane.

The bartender said, "Let's go to the harvest. I've got a car."

It turned out that what he had was a Model T Ford stripped down with no fenders and no top — just wheels and body. He stole 2 gallons of moonshine from the bootleggers that supplied the joint and away we went.

When we stopped in Dakota he brought out the whisky and one of them farmers said, "Great Scott! I'd pay a robber's price for moonshine like this. Have you got any more?"

And to think the bartender could have stole 10 or 12 gallons. Ah! We could have made a killing.

Anyway for me it was more fun to knock around on the freights, dodging yard bulls. So I split up from him at a place called Minnewac. He took the Model T and headed down into Wyoming.

In Minot late in the fall the yard bulls were pushin' 2 or 300 of us, "Get on the freight! Get out of town."

The train was black with men — like locusts hangin' on.

THE OLD DINGALING
I got into a boxcar by myself and an old dingaling came along. He had a long overcoat on. He looked up at me, "Give me a hand up there you dirty old Squarehead!" he says.

I hauled him up.

He pulled out a square bottle with skull and crossbones on it. Milky stuff. Denatured alcohol. He had cut it with something.
"Do you want a drink?" he says.

I says, "Not of that rat poison."

He went over in the corner.

I says to myself, "I better get out of this car. That old ding will maybe die in here and I'll be in trouble."

So I got out. (Laughs) But the brass of him! "Give me a hand up there you dirty old Squarehead."

After 2 months work I got back to St. Maries with $10. My bartender friend hadn't done much better. He told me he drove into Casper, Wyoming on the rims — all tires gone. That's where he left the wreck.

WHISKEY IN CAMP
Big Pete Povich and I went into Spokane on the 4th of July, 1925. Pete used to be tied up with them Austrian bootleggers and he brought back 18 gallons of whiskey to bootleg in Camp 26.

In the bunkhouse he set out a gallon of whiskey and we each took a snort. We went in for supper and when we came out another guy and Jack London, the old barnboss, had found the whiskey under my bunk and they were pretty well organized.

Next morning at the wake-up gong, Jack didn't stir in his bunk. His partner went to shake him and he was stone dead.

Jack had been old and ready to die anyway but it scared hell out of Pete Povich for fear he'd be blamed for poisoning him. Pete rushed around camp, bought a second hand car from somebody and took off.

Pete left all his whisky behind with a young fellow from down on the Troy-Deary Bean Ridge country. This young fellow was night watching the Shay locomotives.

There was a big tank of oil for the Shays on a high platform. It was kind of slow running and thick so it was part of his night job to warm it up with steam and fuel the Shays.

The young fellow got drunk and went to sleep and Holy Mackerel! the crude, black oil filled the tender of the locomotive and run all over the railroad track. It about emptied the 10,000 gallon tank.

Here come Gaffney, the Walking Boss (woods superintendent). He put men shovelling dirt over the oil to hide it. Some of them big shots might come in. Oh! It was a hell of a mess.

McMillan, the camp boss canned a couple of fellows for drinking and they started off down the road with a gallon of whiskey. I got in my Star coupe with another fellow and headed for Clarky. Along the road here set the gallon of whiskey on a stump and the two fellows laid alongside it, asleep.

We hooked the gallon and they never stirred.

So much of this whiskey remained around camp the lumberjacks were stealing it off one another. A little fellow named Handy St. Peter was loading for us. He came into the cookhouse one morning pretty well oiled up.

A woman flunkey brought a platter of hotcakes.

St. Pete bawled, "They ain't fit to eat!" and threw them out the open window.

The flunkey grabbed a pitcher of milk off the table and poured it over his head. Then she made a run back up the aisle toward the kitchen.

St. Pete wheeled after her and hit her in the backside with a hot coffee pot.

We thought it was funny till the whole cookhouse crew swarmed around us with potato masher, butcher knives, a meat cleaver and a pot of scalding coffee.

Then we apologized and pulled Handy St. Peter out of there. He went out to the job with us but he couldn't work. He crawled in under a railroad car and laid there.

It's no wonder logging outfits have an iron-bound rule against whiskey in camp.

PERILS OF BOOZE AND THE BRIGHT LIGHTS, TOO

Gazette-Record items:

9-8-27 — Fred Daniels, employee of Coeur d 'Alene Fire Protective Association disappears after an evening at floathouses along the boardwalk. Hat found floating near one floathouse.

6-23-27 — Napoleon LaBombard, 46, veteran woods worker who had survived dozens of dangerous situations, fell out of a rowboat below the mouth of the Maries river and drowned. He had never learned to swim.

BOHUNK BOB

Roaring Ed Roach, a Potlatch Push, called all Montenegrins, Austrians and Yugoslavs, Bear Dancers because years ago one of 'em used to go around Spokane with a bear on a chain. The name stuck.

But the Montenegrin on our crew got mean if anybody called him Bear Dancer. He always said, "Just call me Bohunk Bob."

Bohunk Bob busted Big Red Pete and I in a quiet poker game in camp.

I said to Big Red, "We better keep an eye on the bugger. If he makes a sneak for town we'll waylay him and go along to help him spend our money."

We started to work one morning. A half mile out, Bob says, "By God! I forgot my gloves."

It was two hours before it came to us he'd ditched us, got his time and beat it for St. Maries. We never got to help him spend his winnings.

The three of us worked together on the donkey. When Bohunk Bob broke his thigh bone we grabbed a skinner with a lumber wagon — the only thing we could get in a hurry. It was awful how that 3 hour ride over a corduroy road shook poor Bob. Big Pete and I almost carried that wagon over the roughest spots to ease his pain.

We had sent word to camp to phone for a truck to meet us at the warehouse on the Clarkia side. Told them we had a man bad hurt with a broken leg.

When we reached the warehouse there was no truck in sight. The skinner turned his team around and went back with the wagon to camp. We stayed to make sure our man got hauled to the doctor. Time was going by and still no truck — and him hurting.

There was a meathouse at the end of the warehouse. Red Pete went in there and he come out with a meat saw three feet long.

Pete says, "Let's take and saw the leg off this Bohunk bugger," he says.

Bohunk says, "I believe you would, you sons of bitches!"

But you can't cheer up a hurt man very long with kidding. It was a long 2 or 3 hours we sat there waiting.

WAITING FOR LIVE ONE
In the fall I came into Spokane and stopped at the Globe Hotel. I'd been running donkey all season and had about $1200 stake. I looked out the hotel window and here I see Bohunk Bob and Big Red on the sidewalk waitin' for me.

I said, "How did you two scavengers find out I was in town?"

But I knew well enough. Guys hung around the Union Depot waitin' for a live one. When you got off the train, Ah Ha! The word spread.

I gave 'em each $5.

That's the last I ever saw Bob but I heard he quit the woods and went to work in the mines in Kellogg. Then later I read in the paper where he was up before the judge.

The judge says, "You've been up before me maybe 15 times already for being drunk. I don't know what to do with you, Bob. How much time do you think I should give you?"

"Oh!" Bob says, "Make it 30 days."

Later, he fell down in the union hall at Kellogg and broke his neck.

PEGLEG DRAKE
The barber in Clarkia, they called him Pegleg Drake. He had lost his leg in woods work and took up barbering and bootlegging.

He used to peddle the barber shop and the tools once or twice a year and go on a drunk. Yeh! My God! He was a fright. He'd go till he got the shakes — delirium tremens.

In about 1925 or '26 he was on a big drunk and he run out of whisky and there was a fellow workin' in his place in the barber shop.

I was in the next room and I overheard him tell the young fellow, "I need a drink, bad! That roothouse back of the Elk Hotel — it's got a built up apron over it covered with sawdust. There's two kegs cached in that sawdust!"

I thought to myself, "Not if I get there ahead of you, there's not two kegs."

THE SEARCH
I got up late that night. Six feet of snow. I went prowling over behind the Elk Hotel. It's a wonder somebody didn't shoot me floundering around out there and scaring the cats. I crawled up under the roof of the roothouse and started pawing around in the dark. The sawdust had got wet and was frozen. I couldn't do anything barehanded. I felt around in the dark and as luck would have it I found an old grass sickle

to break up the sawdust. Pretty soon I hit wood and came out with a keg.

Fella name of Cranky Jack McGuire lived in a shack behind Frank Tom's store and restaurant. He had sold a claim up on Marble in the early years — bought a saloon in Clarky and run it till he went broke.

I come into his kitchen with a keg in my arms. "Get up, Jack! I got a present for you."

He come out of the bedroom in his droop bottom long underwear. 'What the Blue Blazes!'' he says. "You can't leave that here."

I says, "Cover the windows while I get the other one."

When I brought the second keg he says, "We got to get rid of them infernal kegs! Somebody that hid 'em catches us, we'll get shot."

I says, "We got to empty them first."

We filled up every pot and kettle and dishpan with moonshine. Oh! The fumes in that shack. And it was so awful tasting we couldn't drink the stuff.

I said, "What are we gonna do with it?"

He was bustin' up the kegs and feedin' the wood into his heater. "You can take care of it. I don't want any. The smell is enough for me."

CELEBRATION
I was stayin' at Frank Tom's ROOMS UPSTAIRS. There was a bunch of fellows: Fred Ross, Ed Corne and Bert Tofte dingin' around in Frank Tom's store and restaurant waitin' for things to open up in the woods.

I went down and says, "You boys want something to drink?" and set out a whole gallon on the restaurant table.

The fellows tied into it.

Mrs. Frank Tom had invited all the school teachers into her parlor for a society gathering and these fellows got drunk and the racket they put up!

Next morning, Mrs. Tom said, "Mr. Johnson! I thought you was a gentleman. My God! What kind of a party did you have last night.? It drove all the ladies away."

Frank Tom says, "Good thing! We don't need them snooty haybags here."

PEDDLING BOOZE
Well, a couple of gallons went to the Idaho Hotel across from Shorty Wades and it was full of pimps and whores and dope. Jack Mason ran it the last I know of.

And there was a whore, Big Ethel, had a place where Mary's restaurant is now. I went down and says, "Do you want some whiskey?"

Big Ethel says, "I could sell 10 gallons if you got it."

So I brought it down there. Ethel peddled only herself. She had no girls.

Denny Currin, Jack McPhee and I were in there drinkin' and havin' a social time and her pimp showed me a Winchester automatic rifle and a .38 pistol he'd robbed from the punchboard at Peg's joint a coupla nights before.

Her pimp got drunk with us. Then he looked kinda surly at us and left.

THE MAD PIMP

Ed Dorne says, "There's something wrong with that no good pimp," he says. "I think he's jealous."

All at once here come a shot through the back window. Ashes and pieces of cast iron come flying out of the heater stove where the bullet hit.

Denny and Jack McPhee dashed out the door to the road.

I dived behind the daveno.

The back door kicked open. I peeked out and the pimp was standin' in the doorway with the Winchester in his hand.

"I'm lookin' for that Jack McPhee. I'm gonna kill the good for nothin' rat!" he says.

Then he come on in. "I know you're in here, Johnson," he says. "I got nothing against you."

So I got up and walked out into the road. The road had been plowed and there was a bank of snow on the other side 6 feet high. Denny and Jack McPhee peeked out from the snowbank.

I said, "I believe I can go back and take the gun away from that rattle brain. I think he'll let me close to him."

I turned around and the pimp was standin' in the doorway with the rifle half raised. "I heard that. Don't come any closer. I'll let you have it!"

I took his word for it. I kept my distance and talked with him which gave McPhee time to run back toward Frank Tom's under cover of the snowbank.

It's a wonder I didn't go to jail over all that rotgut moonshine. It created a regular scandal in Clarky.

Of course, Peg heard about it. He come to me and says, "You owe me a hundred and fifty dollars for that whiskey."

I said, "You hold your breath till you get it. It's a good thing I stole it. You'd have poisoned the whole population of Clarky."

PEG AND THE CUSPIDOR

There was a big truck driver worked for Richard Johnson — an axe handle and a half wide across the shoulders. He went into Clarky and got drunk and stayed at Peg's place. He had 90 bucks when he came in. When he woke up next morning he tackled Peg about it.

"My God!" Peg says. "I wouldn't know a thing about it. Maybe you mislaid it. Let's go up and look in your room."

They looked in the room. Nothin' there.

So the truck driver went back to camp. He began to brood. He said, "I'm gonna get my gun and I'm gonna go back to Clarky and I'm gonna shoot the other leg off that pegleg pole cat!"

People busted themselves to bring the word to Peg. "That truck driver is mad. He says you rolled him when he was drunk."

Old Peg got so he jumped everytime a door slammed. He started lookin' back of him when he went outside.

When the truck driver came in Peg got long faced and said, "I can't believe anyone staying in my rooms would steal! Are you sure you didn't mislay your wallet someplace? Let's go back up in the room and look again."

The truck driver afterwards told us, "When we went up to the room here was a big spittoon — the kind you can take the lid off. There wasn't any spittoon in that room at the time I rented it."

Lo and behold! Peg pulled off the lid of the spittoon and here was the truck driver's wallet.

Ah! Peg! That slippery devil.

BARBERING IN THE WOODS

Peg moved into Camp 22 on the Incline and was night watching for $250 a month and in the daytime trimmed the hair of the girl flunkies in his barber shop in a railroad car. All girl hashers in the camps at that time. The men could make big money at sawing logs and other piece work with the gypo system and with girls around they spruced up and got their hair cut every week. Peg had a goldmine.

Last time I saw Peg was in Spokane. He used a dull razor when shaving you. He didn't bother with hot towels. The whiskers, he pulled out by the roots. Left you feeling like a scalded pig.

I says, "Hell's Delight! Don't you ever sharpen that damnable razor?"

"Aw!" Peg says, maybe thinking of when I stole his moonshine. He give my whiskers an extra hard yank. "You lumberjacks are tough!"

**Pete and Molly Austad
1930**

THE SLEIGH HAULS AND MOLLY
In 1922 they sleigh hauled burned logs from Camp 6 a mile and a half up Big Bear Creek into the pond at Camp 18 on Bussel Creek and then drove the logs down into the Marble. Molly Austad was one of the hashers there. Her family were pioneers in Trail, B. C. and had a dairy farm and orchard there.

Molly hashed there again in 1926 when they sleigh hauled green timber. We were married July 17, 1930 and had a son, Pete, born in 1931 and a daughter, Louise in 1934.

Another woman hashing there with Molly was Marble Creek Jerry Conroy. She was born over in Washington and was only a stripling of a girl when she come into the woods. Didn't weigh over 110 pounds.

She got to following a fellow named Dick Broderick around, waiting on him, washing his clothes.

I said to her, "He's only making a sucker out of you, Jerry. Using you for what he can get out of you."

"Well," she says. "I don't mind."

You didn't have to watch your language around Jerry. You could say what you meant. I said, "Well! Why don't you wash my clothes then?"

Jerry just laughed. She had a wonderful disposition.

CAUGHT ON A CENTER
In 1926 me and a fellow named Ed Carmody and Ernie Brossed were out in the middle of the Marble at the mouth of Hobo Creek trying to pick a center. Some logs had lodged against a bunch of old cedar stumps out there.

There's a sharp bend in the river above there. As we worked we were watching for the overflow from the Camp 4 dam upriver. As a rule the dam overflowed a half hour before they opened the gates and this little extra wave of water gave you warning to get out.

The flood was already upon Ed Carmody and me when Ernie Brossed yelled, "Flood!" He had already jumped into the overflow and was wading with all his power for shore.

The big flood caught Ernie Brossed in boiling water up to his armpits and more or less threw him on shore and he scrambled out to safety.

Ed Carmody was kinda slow movin'. He just froze, peavy in hand, there on the logs with me. "What'll we do?" he shouted in my ear.

Over the roar of the water I yelled, "To hell with it!"

We could feel the logs under us raising up with the flood. The canyon below was rock walls on both sides. Not a Chinaman's chance to come out alive if our logs went.

It shook under us. "Oh God! She's goin'!" Ed hollers.

I said, "Let 'er go!" I knew it would be our finish.

Water roaring past with logs pouring down from Camp 4 dam. Our logs raised higher and shook. Then they stopped raising and after what seemed a long time they began to lower again. Our wad of stumps had held and we knew we were safe.

That was the most interesting 15 minutes I ever spent in my life.

ED COULDN'T WRITE

Ed came to me one time and says, "Will you write a letter for me to the missus?"

I says, "Can't you ?"

"No," he says. "I can't write. I never went to school."

So I wrote letters for him. He lived for a number of years on Capitol Hill in St. Maries.

About 1940 they was movin' a jammer down the highway just west of Flat Creek. They had the boom up and it came in touch with the powerline.

The jammer puncher yelled, "Don't touch the guyline!"

The boom was a pole but the guyline running up to its end was steel cable and could transmit electricity.

But Ed touched the guyline and it killed him right there.

BUTTERFLY PETE AND OLD BROOMFACE

There at Camp 18 Dam we had the pond filled with white pine logs and this little Frenchman, Butterfly Pete could run over a string of little 6 inch diameter logs and hardly make them wiggle. He didn't weigh over 120 pounds.

This was at the time Strawn, the boss, had hired a bunch of these Palouse farmer fellows to come up and take over the jobs of the Wobblies that was talking strike. Strawn knew the mayor of Spokane and brought him to camp to make us a speech. The mayor's main subject was The Bohunk and how the Bohunks were radical. "You Americans don't want to mix with these foreign anarchists," he said.

One day Strawn, the boss, undertook to travel over the pond. He made it across the big logs but when he hit a run of little ones — in he went!

KNOCK HIS HORNS OFF!

Strawn went down and came up with the water streaming from his whiskers. Three of these Palousers ran out to save him. When they reached out to help him, they all went in. He went down again and came up spouting like an old walrus.

The whole crew was lined up on the bank grinning and watching.

Jimmy McDonald yelled, "Knock the horns off Old Broomface!"

Strawn bawled out, "Who said that?"

Everybody but the Palousers was laughing. We had been calling him Broomface for months behind his back.

Of course Broomface wasn't in any real danger. When he managed to wallow out under his own power he proved he had a sense of humor. He said, "If one more of them damn Palousers had come out to save me we'd have all drowned."

PUT THE WOBBLY TO WORK!

When a Wobbly delegate came into camp one day to help with the negotiations, Broomface said, "By God! I'll find out if that foreign agitator, anarchist will work."

He put the delegate buckin' wood for the camp stoves and the delegate worked hard all day.

Broomface says, "I guess he's all right!"

FELLOW WORKER

I got a kick out of Broomface. He had a big dog, tall as a half grown calf. It was the custom of the Wobblies to address one another, especially at meetings, as "Fellow Worker".

I happened to be behind Broomface goin' out of the dining room one evening and this big dog always waited for him at the door.

"I'll feed you, Fellow Worker," he said, and gave the dog a big hunk of meat.

CLIPPING BUTTERFLY'S WINGS

Somehow Strawn got wise that it was little Butterfly Pete that had nicknamed him Broomface. He caught Butterfly alone out in the middle of the river and held his head underwater.

Afterward Butterfly said, "That old bastard almost drowned me. And he said he's not through with me yet."

In the evening as the driving crew came filing back into camp, Broomface always leaned against the bunkhouse with his arms folded. He didn't say anything, just stood there lookin' whiskery and maybe adding us up. He knew every one of us was a Wobbly.

Butterfly was gettin' more jumpy all the time. He always hurried past Broomface without looking or speaking so as not to attract any extra attention.

One evening we was marching by and Broomface waited till Butterfly got past him far enough to think he was safe.

Then Broomface said,"Hey! You there! Back up here! You're fired!"

LAW OF THE HUNCH
The drive on the Marble was bull work. Mostly you went behind the flood and rolled or dragged the high rear logs back into the channel again. Wade in ice water all day long. Stand in the middle of the river and piss your pants. What difference did it make? Clean water goin' through.

On the lower end of the main Marble Creek when they just had the Camp 11 dam, the logs didn't go all the way through to the Joe. So the last dam they built was at Camp 7 and it splashed them all the rest of the way.

Then above Camp 11 dam was number 4, then 8 and last of all number 15 below the mouth of Freezeout.

Then they had dams on the feeder creeks like the Camp 18 dam on Bussel, Camp 5 dam on Hobo, a dam up Cornwall and Eagle and one I never saw, away up Homestead.

In that spring drive of '26 Jim Grindl's cousin, a big, skookum man come to work. When we dragged a log off the bar, he'd throw a peavy on one side against 3 of us on the other side like he was gonna carry each log all by himself. So we ganged him.

Back in Maine they used to say, "Canada against the world!" Them old timers learned to cool off them young Canadians in a hurry with the hunch. Even with only one man on each side, one man can hunch ahead of the other man and strain the other man's back muscles or break his arm.

So the three of us picked out a log that had maybe 700 feet in it. Just at the moment this Grindl's cousin was beginning to lift, we hunched in unison. It threw the whole weight of the log against him and brought him to his knees.

Ah! Sometimes they've got to be made work-wise. He learned in a hurry.

MUNDY BAR

We worked down past Mundy Bar which is near Camp 3, named for a river driver that drowned there at an earlier time.

Jack Murphy who drove for Herrick had a couple or three men and they followed behind us in what we called a **witness drive**. Herrick had dumped his logs in ahead of the Rutledge logs and we had to drive them all together. Once in awhile we'd catch a Herrick log and leave it lay but that was harder than driving them. Murphy's crew would sit and watch us roll the logs in and smoke and visit and chew and spit.

After awhile they got ashamed of sitting around while we did all the work and started working with us.

RIVER FULL OF MEN

Down below the mouth of Bussel Creek I was with some others in the center of the stream trying to work some logs out of a tangle of cottonwood trees that had lodged there. There was a gut of water running past on each side of us.

Upriver from us was a bar. Sometimes when the flood came down Bussel Cr. from the Camp 18 dam there wasn't enough water to force the logs out into the Marble and they'd pile up on that bar. The other men were rolling logs off that bar into the Marble.

Everybody kept one eye upstream for the overflow coming down the Marble from the Camp 4 dam at the mouth of Cornwall. Remembering how I got caught out on a center up there I kept a special sharp lookout.

This time there was no warning. The flood had caught up with the overflow. They always opened 2 gates at the Camp 4 dam for plenty of water. Here come a 5 foot wall of water, bank to bank.

The men on the bar were caught. Christ! There was no chance for 'em to scramble ashore.

We were below there in the flowage. We had nowhere to go. We climbed like rats up the limbs that stuck up from the cottonwoods. We got barely above the flood and hung on for our lives. I could see a couple of heads bobbin' past in the water.

I said, "My God! The river is full of men."

JOHNNY McDONALD

An old timer I'd worked with on many a job, Johnny McDonald. Here he come riding a log down the gut or channel on the Bussel Creek side of our cottonwood island. Johnny McDonald could ride any log in almost any current with perfect balance. Here he come flying. He didn't see the sweeper ahead of him, a big cottonwood limb sticking out. It knocked him off — stunned him, I suppose, because the water swallowed him and he never came up.

WHITEY ARBEAU TRIED TO SAVE RED

Here come Whitey Arbeau riding two logs into the channel on the other side. Ridin' that flood he reached down and grabbed a fella named Red and had him laying across the logs at his feet. Red was brakeman for Rutledge. He didn't have the first idea about drivin' logs but was doin' this while waitin' for railroading to start.

Frank Norman Arbeau, Silverton Nursing Home, 1975. Born Dec. 28, 1897 at New Brunswick Canada. Died April 24, 1976.

As they went past I could hear over the rush of the water — Whitey was yelling at Red to get on his feet so they could each spear the other man's log with the point of their peavies and ride 'em together like a raft.

Red panicked and slipped off. As they went on down Red was pawing at the side of a little chunk of log and it was rolling and his head was going under. He might has stayed afloat if he'd got hold of the end of the chunk and hung on.

Pretty soon he went down. Away down the river I saw the top of his head come up and go down and that was the last.

THE MAGNIFICENT RIDE

But Whitey Arbeau! He rode the crest of the flood a half mile right into the flowage and stepped off on the Camp ll dam. Son of a bitch! If that man never did anything more in his life than make that beautiful ride it was a wonderful accomplishment.

They hollered "CLOSE THE GATE! MEN IN THE POND!" The gate in the Camp 11 dam had been open to let the flood carry the logs on through. Then we drained the pond and found Red washed up against the dead wood on the apron of the dam. We tried to resurrect him but it was no use.

We went up and down the shore a coupla days lookin' for Johnny McDonald. The boss paid for the time we looked. The flood had taken him down to the Camp 11 dam and through the spillway. Thirty days later they found his body caught in a cottonwoood sweeper down below Zane on the St. Joe River.

I had seen a fellow name of Bill Johnson swept downstream and thought he was a goner. He showed up at the dam as soon as the flood was gone. He had grabbed a'hold of a willow that was hanging out over the water. Mind you! It flipped him out on the bank.

"Screw this!" he says. "That's as close as I'll ever be to meeting the Old Man With The Horns."

Camp 11 Dam, 1977. Center left: drift logs piled against wrecked dam. Foreground spillways through which water and logs poured. Upper left and upper center looks up Marble Creek toward the mouth of Bussell a half mile away, from which Whitey Arbeau made his ride on the flood and stepped out on the dam in 1926.

He never stopped to collect his pay or his belongings. He took the path over the hill to civilization and Floathouse Nellie. He was her man but he didn't use the name Cottingham when he worked on the drive.

After that the Company put a watcher 2 or 300 feet above where we were working to holler if he saw the flood coming.

THEY DIED OTHER WAYS, TOO

Gazette-Record items:

6-21-21 — Joe Strzelecki 36, Polish, struck by falling tree on Mica Creek near Camp 8 of Kelly Yarnell.

2-21-24 — George Pearson killed by snapping cable of a donkey engine near Fernwood, working for Blackwell.

4-15-26 — Louis Olson, 60, drowned on Fishhook drive. Was blasting a log jam. His brother, Martin, had opened the flood gates above the jam before it was broken.

5-20-26 — Edward McDermott struck and killed by a log that jumped chute on Mica Creek.

5-5-27 — Harold Morris, 24, killed by rolling logs on rollway at Hobo Creek, Rutledge Camp 5.

8-11-27 — Albert Johnson, 17, killed when log jumps chute at Rutledge Camp 20 on Marble Creek.

9-6-28 — Manthly Miller died from being struck by a falling tree at Rutledge Camp 5 on Marble Creek.

FIVE DOLLAR FRANKY

They had been paying $6 on the drive. Spring of '27 Frank Daman replaced Gaffney as Walking Boss and The Rutledge cut the pay to $5. There was no strike but Frank Daman couldn't get anybody to work on the drive. Finally they raised the wages back to $6. But after that the lumberjacks called Daman **Five Dollar Franky**.

In the next year or so they cut day wages from 50 cents an hour to 40 cents or $3.20 a day in the camps. So we elected from then on to cut two inches off the shovel — **Take it easy! Don't get in a hurry!**

The last drive on the Marble was 1930. The logs were trailed down Hobo to the Camp 5 dam and splashed down into the Marble. Charley Sweeney took the drive out to the St. Joe River with a small crew.

THE INCLINE

I worked on the Incline from the beginning in 1922 until they shut it down. It was built to get out burned timber in a hurry from the 1922 fire. On the Bussel side of the ridge, the Rutledge Company built main lines up Norton Creek and Toles Creek and used a couple of Shay locomotives to haul trains of timber to the foot of the Incline.

Then a donkey engine threw a cable choker around one log car at a time and hauled it halfway up the 18 percent grade and another donkey reached down and hauled the car the rest of the way to the top where it was lowered down the still steeper 45 percent grade on the Clarkia side.

From there a Shay — what they called a rotor — took the cars 5 miles to Clarkia. Two trainloads a day. The train went past the roundhouse and shop at the Rutledge Ranch where there was a cookhouse and a big bunkhouse and over a long trestle on pilings across the meadow to the railroad siding at Clarkia. You can still see the remains of the trestle.

The Milwaukee Railroad took over from there and hauled them down through St. Maries to the unloading dock on the St. Joe River at Ramsdell, across from Mission Point. Then tugs boomed and towed them to the sawmills in Coeur d'Alene.

I had been in Spokane and come back to Clarky to find that Kavarney's place, the Spokane Hotel which used to be on the other side of the bridge on the right hand going into Clarkia, had burned. Along with it, my suitcase, brand new suit, a new overcoat and all my pictures had gone up in smoke.

A Frenchman named Art Dubois and I started walking back to the job on the railroad from Clarkia toward the Incline. The railroad went

No. 1 logging railroad trestle spanning a canyon leading to the Incline. Trestle is exactly 2 miles up the West Fork of Merry Cr. from its junction with the main Merry Cr. road. 1976

up the West Fork of Merry Creek and where it crossed the first canyon we came to Trestle Number 1 which is 75 feet off the ground in the center.

I was walking the squared timber along the edge of the trestle.

Behind me Art said in a strained voice, "Don't do that!" But I didn't think anything of it.

When I got out in the middle I looked around and here was Art down on his hands and knees crawling toward me over the ties in the center. His face was pale. He stopped moving and waved but his hand was shaking.

I said, "What's the matter with you, Art? Stand up! You can't possibly fall through between the ties."

But Art peered down between the ties at the 75 feet of air between him and the ground and come right on crawling.

INCLINE SHUT DOWN
They shut the Incline down in 1923. They had been having a hell of a time. For one thing, that practice of throwing a cable choker around the whole carload of logs had often pulled the whole load crossways. And it didn't work, using two different donkeys to pull each load up the hill.

REMODELED
So in 1927 they set two big Willamette donkeys at the top of the hill, joined their boilers together and made one unit of them. Then they

spliced their 1⅝ inch cable together to allow it to reach down 6,040 feet on either side. They had to extend the Incline track another 5 or 600 feet out on the flat on the Clarkia side to make the distance even with the Bussel side.

This time — 1928 — they operated with green timber. And instead of hooking the donkey cable around the loaded car they hooked to the drawbar. We didn't think the drawbars would hold but the Milwaukee guaranteed the drawbars and had a man down in St. Maries that inspected all drawbars before they went over the Incline.

The Incline crew always kept a loaded and an empty car at the top. When you brought a load up from the Bussel side another loaded car was going down the Clarkia side to counter weight it. When you brought an empty back up from the Clarkia side it was being counter weighted by an empty going down the Bussel side.

To prevent the logs from sliding off the car going down the 45 percent Clarkia side we put chokers around the load and fastened to the stake pockets of the car. We cinched the cables till the bark flew, using what they called a gilly with 2 drums run off steam from the donkey boilers.

Pete Johnson and Slim Ichwald about to send another loaded car up the Incline. 1930

It was scary hooking cars on either bottom of the Incline at night. You'd hear that rumbling on the mountainside above and you didn't know if it was the car you'd just sent up or a runaway coming down. We used to move off to one side just in case.

And if you rode a car up the Incline or down the other side you made sure you rode one of the uphill corners so you could leap overboard if the car broke loose.

WILD CAR
The boys at the top of Incline always held the cable snug on the loaded car and pinched the wheels by hand over the brow to go down the Clarkia side. But one day they were horsing around and let 10 or 12 feet of slack develop in the main line. When the car went over the brow it took up the slack in a rush and snapped the main line.

The runaway car roared off down the steep track. About halfway down the hill it left its trucks. The Italian and Greek section crew workin' on a switch near the bottom saw this loaded flat car coming. There was no time to get away. They threw themselves belly flat in the ditch and it sailed over them so close one fellow got some slivers in his back. And the logs went end over end and flew all over the place.

STEEL RAILS IN THE GROUND
Another time they were pulling a car of steel railroad rails up the Incline and the car broke loose near the top. The car roared off down the track went end over end and drove the rails deep into the ground. There are still some of those rails sticking out of the ground down near the bottom. The crumpled car lays up on the mountainside.

FREAK ACCIDENT
Frank DeMan (pronounced DeMane) had carried a Wobbly card a long time. He said he was born in Chicago. He went over to Russia to help them out after their revolution. In Russia he might have spoken out of turn because they told him, "Go back to your own country and your own revolution. Why come here and get the fruit of our struggle?"

Frank was broke and had a hard time getting back to the U. S. He stowed away in a ship in Yokohama. And when he got back he didn't talk much about his experience in the Soviet Union.

Frank didn't get picked up in the Palmer raids of 1919 and deported like two Swedes I had worked with. In that hysteria after the Centralia incident a lot of foreign born were picked up and dumped on a boat and sent across.

Pretty soon Sweden got tired of it and said, "You accepted our men and wore them out and now you throw them back at us." They passed a law that they would not accept these deportees unless the U. S. government sent along a couple thousand dollars for a year's subsistence.

That cooled down the deportations.

But it might have been better for Frank DeMan if he had got deported.

He worked at the bottom of the Incline on the Clarkia side.

One day the donkey at the top of the Incline started pulling an empty up from the Clarkia side. The track was uphill only a little at the bottom. For some reason the donkey stopped pulling for a few seconds and the empty car coasted ahead and rolled its wheels over the cable. Then when the donkey tightened the cable again it caused the pin to pull out that connected the cable to the car.

The empty car coasted back and hit a loaded car where Frank DeMan was taking off the big cables that cinched the logs on the car. It struck so hard that a log fell off onto the plank walkway alongside. The plank hit Frank in the chest.

He died shortly after reaching the hospital.

Gazette-Record 8-7-30 — Frank Domain, working on the Incline, August 5, was hit at the foot of the Incline by a runaway flat car, plunging down after breaking loose. Died of injuries.

DEPRESSION ENDED THE INCLINE 1930
1929 and '30 were the two biggest years for the Incline. They were planning on putting a short Incline into Elk Basin, but the Depression stopped everything. They left thousands of dollars worth of rail, locomotives, cars and donkeys in there and it was eventually cut up in scrap and sold to the Japanese to help them get ready for war. They threw it back at us in World War 2.

HERRICK PUT ONE OVER
Fred Herrick slid in on Cranberry Creek ahead of the Rutledge Co. and bought the Hubble Claim which was one of the finest, almost 100 percent, stands of white pine on the Marble. He paid the highest price for a claim — $22,000. He also bought the Ole O'Dean claim.

The road from Rutledge Camp 1 at the head of Bussel Creek to Camp 20 went through both claims, and a half mile up the hill from St. Joe Crossing near Camp 3, the road also crossed the flat where Theriault had his Halfway House.

Everett & Kelso logged both claims. They flooded their logs down Cranberry Creek along with stumps, rubble, brush and chunks of logs. Cranberry Creek is just a trickle down a hillside.

Jim Grindl, drive boss for the Rutledge said, "I've seen logs driven down lots of streams and rivers but this is the first drive I ever saw come down a ridge."

Herrick is rumored to have sued Everett & Kelso for the loss of 8 million feet of white pine buried in the mud at the mouth of Cranberry Creek — probably an exaggerated story.

MOVING DONKEY

In the spring of 1928 we moved a donkey 2 miles from Camp 20 on Cranberry Creek in six feet of snow down the trail and over the ridge into Hobo Creek. We had to move in snow to be able to melt water for the donkey. The name Hobo came from the shortened name of a homesteader named Hobart.

I got a souvenir of that trip, (displaying a scar in the middle of his left forearm). I was holding the throttle and I had neglected to put a screen around the waterglass. I felt a sting and here was a 2 inch long piece of waterglass stuck into my arm. I pulled it out and it spurted blood like I was stabbed.

Jerry Titus used to run that donkey before I took it over. In June 1961 it was brought from Hobo Creek to St. Maries and stands now at the fairgrounds. Another donkey like it still stands on display by the Forest Service at the Camp 5 dam on Hobo Creek.

Anyway, in '28 we had a fellow by the name of Ernie Gore helping us move. Fred Ross was in charge and the crew was always ribbin' Ernie Gore.

We had the holds to a big stump so we could wind ourselves ahead and Ernie had forgotten his riggin' mittens — heavy mitts for handling cable. They was laying in front of the donkey.

"Hold 'er!" Ernie says.

Fred Ross yelled, "Go ahead!"

I pulled the throttle and we slid ahead and buried the gloves.

After the donkey had passed, Ernie shovelled like a madman but couldn't find the gloves.

Next day we had the donkey ready to pull again and there was a snow shovel in front of it.

Fred Ross yells, "Hold 'er there till I get that snow shovel!"

Ernie Gore Says, "You'll stop for a Rutledge owned snow shovel, you devils! But you wouldn't stop for my mittens!"

He put so much feeling in it that we all laughed and kidded him for days.

DONKEY TRAILING IN HOBO

We set up the donkey for trailing logs on the Hobo chute. Stonebreaker was packer at that time and he brought in exactly 5,000 feet of 1 inch cable from Clarky on a string of the biggest packmules he could find. They put it on each mule looped in a figure 8 and dragged 25 feet on the ground between each mule to bring it all in one piece.

Stonebreaker dumped it in one pile and it looked like a bunch of pea vines. We had to be careful we didn't get a knot or kink in it when we rolled it on the drum.

On our donkey line we had what you call tags and each would haul about 5 logs and push 3 logs ahead of it down the chute. We'd move a total of maybe 30 logs. Since the chute curved down the canyon we used side rollers along the chute to hold the line in and braces holding the rollers.

Alongside and close to the chute we ran 2 bare whistle wires on insulators. If something went haywire you could jump over and lay a piece of wire across to short the two wires and blow the whistle that was powered with about 8 dry batteries, at the donkey.

Then when we got the logs as far as the first donkey could move them, we'd hook them onto the donkey below and take them the rest of the way. Then we skinned the rigging all back to the starting point.

The whole business was a foolish boondoggle, like using a giant to handle toothpicks. The logs could have been moved faster and cheaper by teams of horses.

POKER AND STICK-UPS

When young Blackwell took over the management about 1925 of their railroad camps, he turned everything gypo. There wasn't a day job hardly except the bull cook. Everybody wanted to gypo. Gypo! Gypo! That's what made the I.W.W. fall apart altogether. Who could think of unions and wage scales when they had a chance to work their heads off and get more money. And besides the Wobblies had already forced the camps to clean out the lice and bedbugs, put in clean bedding, good chuck, showers and all the rest. What was there to kick about?

That's when poker games came into the camps. Almost every night a big game up on Blackwell Hump. Why, one night they must have had a couple or three thousand dollars in the game.

That big money got noised about and a couple of stick-ups came in and took cash, checks and everything. But the stick-ups had a heart. They left a billfold with all the checks in it on a switch down at the siding.

Some of the lumberjacks figured these good hearted stick-ups was local men who didn't like to be too rough on their friends. But they couldn't prove who it was.

After that the big king gypos, that cleared from five to eighteen thousand dollars a summer, hired an ex-cop from Spokane to stand guard at the game.

That didn't stop the stick-ups from moving in on other games at other camps. And it didn't stop professionals coming in to hoosier up on the boys. The averge man had no chance against them.

SUCKER BAIT

Fred Ross was running Camp 17. They had a pretty good game going there every night. Fred left the office one evening and got into the game. That night they let him get $500 ahead. Sucker bait! They knew Fred had plenty of money.

Every night after that they tried to get him back into the game.

"Hell No!" he says. "I know enough to quit when I'm ahead." And he never did come back. That's one time their sucker bait back fired.

ROOSHIAN PETE

Down at Camp 20 Rooshian Pete come in and got a job greasin' chute for $4 a day. He was just an ordinary looking little man with a ragged shirt and hair on his hands. He took it easy and only won $10 or $15 a night, which with his $4 a day wages made a pretty nice income.

George Hill, he went to Mike Mahoney, the camp boss and squawked.

Mike says, "What the hell can I do? You fellows went into the game, didn't you? I can't fire Rooshian Pete for winning a little money, can I?"

After Rooshian Pete piled up $800 he left camp. For a souvenir or maybe just to stir up the boys he left behind a deck of marked cards.

They found out afterwards that Rooshian Pete was barred in Seattle from games around there.

BLACKLISTED

By the middle thirties the I.W.W. had lost most all of its backing from the ordinary lumberjacks and was no longer feared by the lumber outfits. Worse than that, when some of us Wobs took action we got flattened.

I was walkin' down the street in St. Maries past the Oak Hotel and here was Louie Larson sitting next to the window inside.

He motioned me to come in. Louie was in partners with Richard Johnson and they had a camp up Thorn Creek just outside St. Maries.

Louie had a big grin on his face. "Ah Ha!" he says. "I hear you fellows got blacklisted by the Rutledge. Now maybe I can get some good lumberjacks. Come out to camp in the morning and I'll put you to work."

Until I retired I worked for Louie and also for John Strobel and Cochran up around Rose Lake.

Interviewed 4-4-75, St. Maries, Idaho

Anna Krone

Bear at the garbage dump

Teacher

Ben and Anna Krone 1975

I was born Anna Johnson in 1899 on my dad's farm, about 3 miles from Coeur d'Alene on the road to Worley. Dad was a stone mason and worked on the Spokane courthouse. Dad and Mother were married in the year of the 1890 panic.

BECAME TEACHER

I went through the grades at Meadowbrook and high school at Coeur d'Alene. Then I attended Lewiston Normal in 1919 and taught at Rockford on the Idaho side. I started at $70 a month. I rented a little house for $10 a month and cooked for myself. Then at Christmas time they raised my wages to $90.

The next summer I attended Normal again to renew my teaching certificate and could earn $100 a month. I could live well and save money for further education.

I taught at my old school, Meadowbrook, and earned enough to go back to Normal for 2 years.

I received my life certificate in 1923 and signed a contract to teach that fall at Clarkia.

UPTOWN CLARKIA NOT WILD

Maxine Dawdy met me at the train. She was to teach the upper grades and I the lower. A big general store stood on the left hand side as you enter Clarkia. From there to uptown was a sidewalk only two planks wide.

When we stepped on a plank the other end flipped up. Maxine said, "Oh! This is the friendliest town. Even the sidewalks come up to meet us."

Clarkia wasn't too wild to me. We kept our work and our school separate from the downtown. They called that place by the depot, Hollywood. That's where all the rough stuff was. I think it was before I came that Frank Strand was killed. I heard about it.

Clarkia had 2 years of high school and the grades with about 31 students and pupils. We had 4 teachers altogether.

Lillian Thompson taught primary but by Christmas time she said she couldn't stand living in such an isolated place and resigned. She later married and went to live in Burke, Idaho of all places! So after Christmas I took over the primary and Pauline Hodges came to teach the intermediate grades in my place. The principal of the high school and only teacher was named Standeford.

We organized a lot of social life at the school: card parties, plays and we had a group called the ONO Club. That was Our Night Out group for young people. I never had any trouble with my pupils. They were all really good kids.

A medicine man came to Clarkia and to attract an audience he had a movie. When the reel went blank he'd say, "You know! Reels are like old shoes. They wear out."

Then he'd tell the rest of the story.

At one of our socials, I met Bill Currie. He was an engineer on a logging locomotive over the ridge in Bussel Creek. He brought carloads of logs to the Incline where they were pulled over the ridge by donkey engines and lowered to a train that brought them into Clarkia.

The next year, 1924, Bill Currie and I were married in a ceremony in Coeur d'Alene.

Shay engines plowing snow in Bussel Creek below the Incline 1923

Bill Currie's Shay locomotive bringing logs to the Incline 1924.

Donkeys hooked together at top of Incline 1927

Clarkia side of the Incline

WASTED TIMBER

The first time I went up to where they were logging there were big cedar logs laying all around. I said to one of the fellows there, "All the logs cut and left. It seems so wasteful."

He said, "You must live where they don't have any trees." As much as to say that when we had all those trees why was I worrying about those cedar logs.

Once riding the passenger train from St. Maries to Clarkia, I saw Josy Gaskill and I remember thinking, "Is that the gal they talk about?" She was a very beautiful woman.

RIDE OVER THE INCLINE

Herb Richey, who had replaced Gaffney as superintendent for Rutledge, invited another teacher and I to go with him over to the Marble Creek side one day. We ate with the lumberjacks at Camp 26 where Molly Austad, Pete Johnson's wife to-be, and Marble Creek Jerry worked as flunkies.

Then we rode my husband's train to the foot of the Incline, talked with Pete Johnson — no relation to Pete Johnson, my father — and rode a carload of logs up to the top of the Incline and down the steep Clarkia side.

Logs decked in the St. Maries River 1924. Picture taken from the train window.

Tent where Bill and Anna Currie lived summer 1928.

Bill and I bought a house just behind the store in Clarkia where Mrs. Mathes lives now. I'd go up in the woods to stay with Bill during my summer vacation. One year we lived in an old homesteader cabin near Camp 26 and another year we lived in a tent.

FALLING SNAGS

During 1928, a storm came up. There were dead snags all around the tent and I heard one fall that sounded very close. I ran out in the pouring rain.

It had hit right beside the tent.

I sent word to Bill and Fred Ross, Rutledge boss came down and he said, "There'll be a man down here in the morning to cut those snags down. Don't worry! There won't be any more of them fall here."

Another morning I walked past the garbage dump and here was a bear. I had a little dog with me and I thought, "Oh my gosh! If the dog runs after the bear then the bear will take after the dog and the dog will come running to me for help and the bear will get both of us.

I ran back to the tent.

FOREST SERVICE BURNED CABINS

The old road ran from Rutledge Ranch and swung over into Merry Creek. It crossed Merry Creek at the Foolhen cabin and went on up toward the Incline. The cabin was not over 2 miles from the Rutledge Ranch. It was the cutest cabin with one room and an overhang.

My cousin's husband was Dean Harrington, ranger for the Forest Service at Clarkia. During those years the Forest Service burned all those little cabins like the Foolhen cabin and the Hubbard cabin that had the beautiful built-ins, over in Marble Creek.

ELECTRIC STORM

In 1932 after the Incline and the camps had closed down in Marble Creek and my husband was off working somewhere else for Potlatch, Nita Wineman and I drove our Chevvy coupe over into the Marble to pick huckleberries. Nita's husband was alternate ranger at Clarkia.

We set up our tent and the first day we picked at least 5 gallons apiece by hand. It was August and the berries were big and ripe and gorgeous.

That night a lightning storm with a high wind was whipping the tent around so much that we decided to get out before the tent blew away. We loaded our blankets and cooking pots and the tent into the Chevvy and away we went.

But not for very far. The wind had blown trees over the road.

We went back to where we had camped and a man who packed supplies to sheep camps came along. He took us to his little one room cabin and told us we could stay there for the night. He could camp outside.

We said, "No! We're not going to send you out in the rain. If you don't mind we'll sleep in one corner and you in another."

He stretched a canvas across the room so it was divided into 2 bedrooms and gave us privacy. He was so nice.

We were worried about getting back home but next day some campers who had been further over in Marble Creek came along and sawed out the trees. Of course, we really had nothing to worry about. Nita's husband, Atlee Wineman knew where we were and would have soon sent somebody for us.

Gold Center Schoolhouse 1924

ALMOST AT GOLD CENTER

I had been teaching in Clarkia 9 years from the fall of 1923 to and including the school year of 1932. I decided I wouldn't teach anymore.

Then the school board told me the teacher of the Gold Center school was leaving and asked me to take the job. But before I signed the contract, the former teacher decided to come back.

I said, "No harm done. I don't particularly care for the job anyhow."

Well, the former teacher started to teach and families started moving away because it was Depression time and no jobs for their men. She ended up staying up there the whole term and the only pupils she had were her own 3 children.

I was lucky I didn't take the position. I'd have been teaching to an empty building.

Forest Service survey crew at Homestead Creek, October, 1938
Doug McLeon, cruiser; Vitus Isaacson, cook; Doug Wahl, cruiser
Bill Currie, axeman; Ralph Miller, cruiser; E. E. Ahler, cruiser;
Pip, Bill Currie's dog. Neil Fullerton worked on this crew, too.
He probably took the picture.

A BABY GIRL

In 1935 our little girl, Lorraine was born. She was spastic.

Jobs were scarce. Bill found short jobs with the Forest Service.

Then he found work unloading logs from trucks at Cats Spur for Walt Darry. Darry had a crane for re-loading the logs on railroad cars.

From our house in Clarkia I used to take our lunch up to Cats Spur, a short distance above Clarkia, so our little girl could be outside. She was such a bright, intelligent little thing and enjoyed it so much.

When I saw how hard my husband, Bill, had to work I thought, "He's too intelligent for that. He should be using his brains instead of his muscles." So I said, "Let's go up to the mine district this winter and buy some cabins to rent — or something."

—312—

But we felt too shut in to stay in Wallace. So we waited another year and Bill worked again for Darry.

A CLOSE ONE!

I went up to the job one day and Walt Darry was laughing. He said, "You came very near being a widow yesterday."

Bill had come home the night before with a big scratch on his shoulder. When I asked him what happened he said he had bumped into a branch on a log.

I said to Walt, "Oh! My! What happened?"

Walt said, "A log fell off the load. Bill jumped but it was so close it touched his shoulder."

I understood why Bill hadn't told me. We had this girl and we were both feeling badly that she could never be well. Bill hadn't wanted to add to my worries.

I thought, "We must get Bill away from this job!"

We went to Spokane and bought a little store out on Broadway.

The fellow who took over Bill's job was killed the next year so somebody was doomed to get killed there. I'm glad it wasn't Bill.

Our spastic daughter was so intelligent and cheerful and wonderful to be with, it became our constant worry that she might outlive us and have no one to take care of her.

Bill died in 1954.

I married my childhood friend, Ben Krone, in 1956.

Lorraine lived 22 years. She died in 1957.

Anna Currie Krone's family. Ann, Amerlia, Clarence, George, her twin Clara, Josephine. In front, father Pete Johnson born 1867 and mother born 1865.

Anna Krone interviewed in Spokane, June 26, 1975

Sadie Brayton Lindstrom

Lady With a Heart

Sadie Brayton Lindstrom 1979

I was born Sadie Brayton, April 2, 1905 in St. Johns, Oregon. When I was 3 years old we moved to Leavenworth. Then we left there riding in a hack with one horse for Coeur d'Alene. It must have been cold weather because I remember sitting between Dad and Mother on the seat with a blanket over our laps and a coal oil lantern on the floor so the heat came up under the blanket and kept us nice and warm.

At Coeur d'Alene Dad worked in the woods and I finished the 1st and 2nd grades.

DAD CORRECTED ARITHMETIC
Then we moved to a cute little place right on top of the hill at Ford, Idaho where we could see all around. We took our school work home every night and Dad would correct the arithmetic problems and if they were wrong he'd make us do them over. I don't think Dad had too much education but his father and mother had both been teachers.

While we lived at Ford, Dad and my brother Jack cut logs together with a crosscut saw over on the Harrison Flats during the week. Weekends they rowed a boat across from Harrison and we met them with horse and buggy.

FLU ON HARRISON FLATS
When the flu epidemic came they both had flu at camp. As soon as Jack could get away, he come home. I was one of the last at home to

come down with it. Mother was working all around the neighborhood helping people who were sick.

I went up to the 8th grade at Ford. I never got any more education.

When I was 16 in 1921 we moved to Alder Creek where Dad was logging with horses.

MARRIED A WELL DRESSED LUMBERJACK.

In 1924 my sister Tillie and I were married at the same time. She married Dave Stonas. I married Lawyer Asbury from West Virginia. Lawyer was his first name and it suited him. He came out to the woods dressed like a Philadelphia lawyer — vest, tie, a good hat.

Bert Randall used to laugh about it. The lumberjacks said Lawyer couldn't handle woods work but he did. But he never got over dressing up. Even in 1942 when we were living in St. Maries, he wouldn't go up town unless he had on a suit and tie.

He didn't go often because he was sick. Then he died.

TAXI BUSINESS

My second husband was Dan Curtis in 1955. He was a little, bitty guy. He worked at the sawmill. We bought a little house and started the taxi business. He got where he couldn't breathe and he had blood clots in his legs. He died in 1959, April 2nd, on my birthday, mind you. The kids planned a party for me and had to cancel it.

RUNNING THE ELITE

After Dan Curtis died I didn't give up the taxi business and in 1961 I took over the Elite Hotel. (**It is locally pronounced like it's spelled — Eeelight.**) **I was running them both.**

I just rented the hotel. but I had to buy the furniture and everything from the old lady that couldn't run it anymore and couldn't sell it to anybody else. There was no water in the rooms. Toilet down the hall. A batching apartment with a little kitchen upstairs and another downstairs and two rooms with hot plates. The rooms rented for a dollar and a half a day. Right in the center of town. I had nice tenants and kept the place clean.

In 1962 I married Dick Lindstrom. We kept the taxi business going and ran the hotel. We ran the Elite 7 or 8 years and the taxi business 15.

NELLIE COTTINGHAM

Nellie Cottingham came and rented the apartment downstairs so she could cook for herself. I felt sorry for Nellie. She didn't deserve to be looked down on — the men that went to her didn't get looked down on. It's not right to blame one for it all.

And look at it another way: She did a good deed for the men who had no place to rest. She would feed 'em at her floathouse. If they were broke she'd give 'em money. That's why she had a good name among the lumberjacks.

OBJECT OF DERISION
A lot of the townspeople made fun of her on the street and I thought that was terrible. Even my own kids did till I found it out. Afterwards, they got acquainted with Nellie and liked her.

And another thing. You wouldn't see Nellie a'walkin' down the street with a cigarette in her mouth a'puffin'. She smoked but not on the public street.

One sister and her husband drove over to see Nellie once a year — two times while she was staying at our hotel. I don't remember that Nellie wrote any letters and she'd get one only once in awhile.

We got along real good together. At the Elite we had Christmas parties and she come to them along with the others.

BOARDED NELLIE
Her health was failing so I watched her pretty close. When I found she wasn't cooking anything for herself I talked her into giving up the apartment and taking a room and boarding with us. I boarded 2 or 3 of the old fellows. You don't make much off of it and it's extra work but then...

Then Nellie got so she couldn't even sit up if I helped her.

WATCHED OVER NELLIE
She didn't want to see the doctor but I had the doctor come and check her out.

He said she had some kind of stroke or other and we'd have to put her in a home where she could have nursing. So we took her to Coeur d'Alene. I went in and checked her as often as I could.

As soon as Valley Vista opened I went down and brought her back to St. Maries. I wanted her close so I could see how she was doing.

NOTIFIED RELATIVE
When Nellie got real sick I phoned her sister.

Then I phoned her again when Nellie passed away.

Nellie had only $275 left of the money I'd been keeping for her. The bank had been charging a little each month on Nellie's account so I told Nellie to just draw it out and I'd look after it for her and give her money from it whenever she wanted it.

DECENT BURIAL
I told Browning, the undertaker, "I don't want to see Nellie buried by the county. She don't deserve that!"

He said, "I'll tell you what we'll do. Give me that $275 and we'll give her a nice burial."

There was no one at the service but Mrs. Lawler that lived over in

Milltown and I. I bought a wreath for the casket and Mrs. Lawler brought a bouquet of flowers.

ACCOMPANIED NELLIE'S BODY TO THE GRAVE
The minister gave a short talk and there was soft recorded music and a prayer.

Gazette-Record 6-5-69 — Mrs. Nellie Cottingham, 86, died last Friday at Valley Vista. She was born Jan. 2, 1883 at Moscow, Idaho, the daughter of Flora Shirts and Ovarly Scott Clark. She had resided in St. Maries over 40 years. She had engaged in prospecting and mining for several years. She was married to William Cottingham who died here in 1932.

The Rev. Frank Meyer of the Community Presbyterian Church officiated at the funeral service. Interment was in Woodlawn Cemetery.

Then another sister wrote me that I could have Nellie's clothes but they would like to have her jewelry.

Nellie didn't have any very good jewelry left. She'd take it down the street and sell it wherever she could for money to get by on. But I sent the jewelry to them.

LAST DUTIES FOR A FRIEND.
Nobody was interested in the whole suitcaseful of worthless mining stock and papers.

I gave Nellie's clothes to the Goodwill. The mining papers went to the garbage.

Valley Vista called me and said, "Nellie still has $50 up here. Come up and get it."

I took the $50 to the funeral home.

They said, "You don't have to pay that!"

I said, "No. But I want to! You buried her."

Dick Lindstrom: The reason Nellie got by so long in St. Maries was because she never had anything to do with married men. Also, the cops weren't always having to be called to take care of trouble at her place like happened at some of the other floathouses.

Nellie's husband, Bill Cottingham got killed by a log that jumped the chute. 1932.

Sadie Lindstrom continues: Dick is 75. I'm 74 and we've been retired for 11 years just living on our pensions. I had 6 kids — 1 boy and 5 girls, so I visit with them. I bowl. I play cards. Dick and I help down at the Senior Citizens Center. We run the bingo game on Monday nights.

Interviewed at St. Maries, 1979

Wade Onthank

River Driver   Teamster

You can't drive logs on pea soup!

Wade Onthank at Russell & Pugh's Fitzgerald Cr. camp, 1929, with the horse that had killed a man.

My dad was a miner at the Gold Hunter in the Coeur d'Alenes. He was active in the big strike of 1899. He escaped being put in the bullpen but he used to curse "them Niggers". (**The miners thrown in the bullpen at Kellogg felt doubly humiliated because they were guarded by black troops. The 1st Cavalry from Fort Wright, composed of white officers and black soldiers, was assigned this duty by Gen. George Merriam when the district was declared under martial law.**)

I was born at Wallace in 1905. Dad was blacklisted after the strike. In 1910 he gave up trying to ever find a good job in the Coeur d'Alenes and we moved to the St. Maries country.

Then in 1924, at the age of 64, Dad ran off and left our family. After that, we had some tough sledding.

Ruth Brickle says: They lived in Ferrell at the time. There were 2 boys and 4 girls. The oldest boy, Joe, went to work in the mill at St. Joe and brought all his money home and as soon as Wade could work he also spent all his money on the family. The youngest girl got hurt in a car wreck and was partly paralyzed for a long time. Wade spent a lot on her.

Wade's bones were brittle. We had to watch out at school sleigh riding so he wouldn't break a bone. He already had a silver plate in one hip. He did break a leg later and always walked with a limp. If there was a collection for anybody who had bad luck, Wade was the kind that would always donate five or ten dollars.

Mamie Dittman says: Wade was such a good kid all the way along. I think he couldn't have been more than 15 when he started supporting the family.

Wade continues

HONEY JONES

The story is that Honey Jones was in the Civil War and ran away from it to come to the mouth of Falls Creek to live. He just hid out and didn't talk to people at all till about 1915. That was when Jack DeLys come to live on the Brown place on the point downriver from Jones' house.

It was DeLys' wife, Maggie that kind of brought Honey Jones out of it. Maggie was Annie Eckman's mother.

One time down toward the town of Ferrell, my brother rode a horse into a barbed wire fence. The horse cut himself, threw my brother and got away.

My brother told me to chase him back up the meadow and "We'll doctor him a little bit".

We caught the horse near Honey Jones' house. He saw the barbed wire cuts on him and gave me the devil.

FISHHOOK DRIVE

I worked on the Marble drive the last year they drove it. I think it was 1928. Then me and George Pentland went up to work for Thompson Brothers who were logging for Ohio Match.

Their main camp was 4 miles up Fishhook Creek and their splash dam was a little ways above the camp and below Outlaw Creek. Their logs came down steep chutes in draws on the right hand side.

At that time there was no road up through the rock cliffs of Fishhook Creek so we waded up to the camp.

The boss said, "I'll pay $6 a day and board."

That was fair wages so we went to work wading ice water down that crooked creek.

There was one guy on the crew that I really took a liking to. He was an easy going, tall coal miner from West Virginia and he didn't know anything about using a peavy or driving logs.

I worked along with him and told him every move.

He wore those dashboard (bib) overalls like a milkman. He'd pick the darndest deep places to cross the creek. I'd grab the back of his overalls and float out behind him as he pulled me across.

We were supposed to get a hot meal at noon to thaw us out. The bullcook brought down big kettles of pea soup on a packhorse. Every day it was pea soup and pea soup and more pea soup.

One morning Thompson told us he was cutting the wages to $5 a day.

That noon me and George Pentland cornered Thompson right there when the bullcook was settin' big kettles of pea soup out on a gravel bar.

George says, "We can't take any more of this pea soup. A man can't do a day's work on nothing but pea soup!"

The rest of the crew, maybe 20 or 25 men, gathered around.

Thompson said, "I don't see anything wrong with pea soup."

"We just can't take it!" George says. He lifted his peavy and punched it right down through a kettle. Then he grabbed the pikepole and smashed down through the rest of the kettles. The pea soup run out over the gravel.

"We want our time!" George says.

We followed Thompson to camp. He was still raving when he made out our checks for $6 a day.

THE NICEST GUY

The nicest guy I ever knew in the woods was Glen Dittman. No matter what camp we went to he'd always go to work with us. He couldn't do his job very well, he was paralyzed in one hand and had a club foot. But he wouldn't be there any time at all till they'd give him some kind of job like greasing the chute.

And comical! You never saw a man that could carry on a conversation and be comical like he could. Nobody ever said anything to him about being crippled up and he didn't talk of it, either. When he died he was over in Montana feedin' pigs on a farm.

HORSES

You never know for sure what horses will do. We were up at the logging camp back of Sly Meadows and our horses ran away and went down to visit Lee Carpenter at St. Joe. They had been at his place although he didn't own them.

We went down after them and they threw up their tails and ran away from us. Lee had to come out and catch them for us. Oh! That tickled Lee.

Best horses I ever drove was Molly and Queen. Earling Moe owned them. Weighed 1500 apiece. I'd ride 'em in the wintertime and haul freight with 'em into the camp on Bond Creek.

There's only one team in a thousand that will pull good on a truck that's stuck. The big problem is that they give it all they have in one great pull and if the truck don't move, they give up. I remember one time going up to Earling's ranch with a truckload of hay and it got stuck in the mud. Molly and Queen eased in and got right down and pulled.

That gave us a chance to get the wheels churning and to throw dunnage under the wheels and pretty soon Molly and Queen had it moving. I think Molly and Queen would pull their gol' darn heart right out.

Men used to sometimes tie a horse to a tree with a big rope and then take a blacksnake whip and whip him till their arms ached. That was to teach the horse a lesson. I could take a horse out and beat him and all I'd do was make that horse nervous of me. I never did whip very many of 'em because I soon found out I was only doing them harm.

I drove a horse at the Fitzgerald camp that had caught a man in the manger and pawed him to death. You couldn't go in the barn alongside this horse. He'd tromp you right down. I think he was locoed. After a week I told the boss, Len McCrea there was no use monkeying with that crazy horse. Just as well go get a good one.

LAST LOGS IN THE FITZGERALD FLUME

I was down at the lower feeder dam turning water into the flume in 1930 or '31. A gypo logger I was working with was a mile and a half further up and he was supposed to allow me 15 minutes to get down there and another 8 minutes time to run water into the flume.

He didn't wait long enough and here came the logs pouring down . 300 yards below me the logs outran the water and was grinding to a stop. Other logs were coming down and hammering into them.

I ran up the flume to tell the logger to stop. But before I got there a quarter mile of the flume had filled with logs and collapsed. That was the end of the Fitzgerald flume.

Interviewed at St. Maries, Idaho, October 1972

Ed Ramey

Compassionate Man

Hazel Ramey

Bachelor Girl

I fed

the

Wobblies

Ed and Hazel Ramey 1978

The mountains of southeastern Kentucky are full of Rameys — Appalachia, they call it, with people starvin' half of the time. Dad was a wanderer, criss crossing the United States. First he came to Newport, Washington in 1905 and did pretty good there cutting cordwood. After 2 years he pulled out and went back to Ohio and bought a farm next to my mother's folks. He bought it in December, plowed and planted corn in the spring and sold it.

1908 he pulled out for the West again and ended up in a little town called Eatonville about 30 miles from Puyallup, Washington. He did carpenter work, bought some land and sold it and landed back in Ohio again in about 2 years.

This time he left the family with Granddad and took a trip down into Kentucky, his old stamping ground. He came back to get us in about 10 days. He had bought an operating sawmill and a store.

TO ST. JOE 1911
But in two years his sawmill had cut itself out of timber. In 1911 he sold the mill and store and we came West from Minneapolis on the Milwaukee Railroad and landed at St. Joe. I was born in 1900 so that made me 11 years old.

In St. Joe the snow was so deep you could just see a horse's ears sticking up when he passed on the street. There was absolutely no

James R. Ramey, Emery, Tom, Orie, Jim, Ed, Effie, wife Minnie 1910 shortly before leaving Kentucky for St. Maries.

housing so in 4 or 5 days we came to St. Maries where the snow was just as deep and the housing just as hard to find. We stayed at the Lumbermans Hotel run by a Frenchman, Joe Bouchard.

Dad bought 2 lots down where Schumaker, the jeweler now lives. We shovelled the snow off, got lumber and built a board and tarpaper house. It was about the first of March so we put in a big, heater stove and managed to keep warm.

Dad was a sawyer and he started sawing somewhere at a mill. But in only a little while he bought some teams and started logging, sold the property and built a big nine room house up Mutch Creek about 75 feet south of where Davis lives now. Mutch Creek was named for George Mutch who homesteaded near the mouth. A lot of people lived up Mutch Creek. Barden was probably the best known and has the most descendents.

GENEROUS RASTUS BARDEN
The story in 1911 was that Barden had his third wife and 27 children by this time. Everybody called him Old Man Barden. He was probably about 50.

In the spring of 1913 I was in the 4th grade. Us kids walked from Mutch Creek about a mile and a half to the Lincoln school. Where the City Hall is located at College and 6th, there was a 2 story building with 4 rooms used for overflow pupils from the Lincoln school. I attended 5th grade there. All the playground we had was across the street where the federal building is now, where Fred Haas had a barn and corral and a bunch of work horses.

PASSED OUT

One evening on the road home from school I passed out. The other kids went home and told Mother. Dad was away sawing at the little Henderson mill above Marble Creek Station. I was a pretty good hunk of a kid but Mother came down and packed me home. The doctor said I had pneumonia and typhoid fever. He said all I could eat was milk. In those days they thought if you ate any solid food when you had typhoid you were as good as dead.

There wasn't a cow up in that country except Barden's big, black Jersey that would kick you out of the barn when you started to milk her. Old Man Barden come over and said to my mother, "I want you to come every day and get milk for that kid!"

I think I drank milk for 9 or 10 weeks of the 13 weeks I was in bed. Barden was a Democrat and Dad was a Republican. They argued every time they got together. But still when I got sick Barden kept me alive with milk from that kickin' old Jersey cow.

HOME BURNED

The next spring our house burned down. I think there were 6 of us kids in school. Lost all our clothes and had no place to go.

Here come Old Man Barden, "Come on! You can stay at our place."

He didn't have a very big house and he had 6 or 8 of his own kids at home at the time. But we got by there till we fixed up an empty woodcutters' cabin on the place. And here come Old Man Barden with wagon loads of furniture and cookstove and dishes for us.

That's 55 years, or more, ago but I've never forgotten what that man did for us. His daughter was Della, who married Mansfield Shepherd.

THE SHEPHERDS

Around 1913 Mansfield Shepherd's dad and Barden had a circular sawmill up Mutch Creek. Mansfield was driving team skidding logs off the mountain to the mill. He was the happiest guy I ever met. Always singing. The mill didn't last long, probably sawed out all their timber. When Mansfield Shepherd was 55 years old, he was still a happy person. He'd take a chair and set it out on the floor at Grange and stand flat footed and jump plumb over it. Just for entertainment.

THE KROLL MILL

The St. Maries mill started in April of 1913 but the winter before that, Mike Bogel and Callahan drayed logs for it out of Mutch Creek. They used single bobsleds and let the back end of the logs drag in the snow. In front of Oscar Brown's barn at 233-13th Street, mud dragged them to a stop. Oscar Brown was in the draying business. He'd hook on one of his six mule teams and pull them down and then over to 10th Street and then across to the riverbank where they rolled the logs in the water. Charlie Kroll was the man who put the money into the mill. His

Kroll's St. Maries sawmill 1920

brother, Arthur came up to run the office. They were businessmen from Spokane.

HIGH SCHOOL CORNERSTONE 1913

I was there when they laid the cornerstone of the St. Maries High School in April, 1913. They dedicated it and sealed in the papers.

Where the Heyburn school is now was a brick yard that dug clay from the bank. Many of the buildings in town were built of brick from here. Coeur d'Alene Avenue which comes into the main drag just west of the Heyburn school runs on the old Coeur d'Alene Indian Reservation line.

CUTTING CEDAR

My first job away from home was in 1915. We got off the train at Ethelton and walked a trail 11 or 12 miles up Slate Creek along about where the road runs now. The 1910 fire had burned the country and it had been logged off. We cut fire killed cedar for the old Jim Miller Shingle Mill at St. Maries — that was Glenn Miller's dad.

I worked about a week and rolled up my blankets — you carried your own bedding those days — and walked out. There was no train till evening so I walked up the track to Marble Creek Station where there was a saloon, a hotel and a big store. That was my first contact with real lumberjacks. Most of them were from Wisconsin and Michigan.

I came home and went to work for a fellow with a sawmill in Hells Gulch below the little cattle guard near where Yerian lived. John Diehl had a little sawmill on the same flat over on the other side.

BIG MAUDE AND BRONSON

Big Maude owned the Olympia Bar which was across the tracks from Raleigh Hughes' log house and practically in the St. Maries railroad yards. The railroad roundhouse was west of it where the concrete plant now stands. That made it pretty handy for the night shift to come up to the Olympia. Maude was wife of Bronson, a logger. When he was logging up Big Creek she'd sometimes take the girls up to Herrick at the mouth of the Creek so the lumberjacks could spend all their money without going to town.

Roy Brickle says: At the Maries, Maude had 7 girls and a saloon alongside. And Lousy! Had a guy that tended bar there for years. They named him Lousy. That's the only name he knew. Skinny son-of-a-gun! Nothin' to him. Finally died of leprosy or something like that. Maude would send you to Bronson — that's who Bronson Meadows was named after. He'd put you to work. Then when you went down the road he'd give you a slip good for a drink at Maude's bar and you'd have to go to the Olympia to get your money.

Pete Johnson says that between Bronson and Big Maude they whipsawed the lumberjacks and screwed them at both ends. Her joint in the railroad yards was single story and had 4 rooms or cribs and women sitting on the porch to coax the lads in.

In the summer of 1916 I worked in the roundhouse at St. Maries for $2.04 for 12 hours a day. 17 cents an hour. Charlie Boyce was working there as hostler at the time.

PACKING MAIL
I got out of school in 1918. I took a Civil Service examination that called for a physical from Doctor Smith. He remembered my bout with typhoid and pneumonia in '13. He said, "I find it left you with a bad heart."

I said, "I didn't know that."

He said, "I see you're smoking cigarettes. You shouldn't smoke. I'll pass you, providing you quit smoking."

I said, "O. K. I'll quit." But I probably never missed a cigarette. I went right on smoking. I got tired of packing mail and hanging around St. Maries so I quit after a few months.

HAZEL RAMEY

I WAS A BACHELOR GIRL
I was born March 25, 1900. Hazel Ogden. I was 7 years old when we come West. My dad, Dan Ogden did carpenter work and worked in the woods at Coeur d'Alene. We were living in a tie camp across Hayden Lake when the 1910 fire broke over the hill. We hurried down the creek to the lake and a guy took us across and we went back to Coeur d'Alene.

DAD BUILT MILLTOWN
Herrick hired Dad and a man named Barr to build Milltown in St. Maries. Then Dad worked as a carpenter on buildings up and down the Main Street in St. Maries.

But above everything, Dad liked to build big barns and wooden bridges. He built the Kinsolving barn, the one on the Hughes place where Procopio lived, Landeryou's barn, Mashburn's, Miller's, Heikkila's.

He'd frame a barn over an acre of ground. Pieces here. Pieces there. Then he'd hire a crew and have a barn raisin' and the pieces would all fit together.

Hazel Ramey & father Dan Ogden 1952

Heikkila Barn

Swendig & Mashburn Barns built by Dan Ogden

THE O'GARA JOINT

I was only 14 but I'd heard so many wild stories about the O'Gara joint I was curious. Danny Curtis was staying at the Jim Walters place on the Harrison Flats. He was a good many years older than I was. I pestered him to take me there.

Finally he said, "All right! I'll take you. But you can look and that's all."

We went down to O'Gara Bay 4 miles out of Harrison. Above where the highway runs now they had a restaurant and bar and a big dancehall.

Of course I wasn't legal age but Danny took me in to see those girls and the dancing. But he hung onto me every minute and soon got me outa there.

This must have been about the time the O'Gara sisters were closing it up to move to St. Maries. Danny Curtis married Sadie Lindstrom.

My folks lived out on the Harrison Flats. I had worked some for Mrs. McMillan who was running Herrick's boarding house in Milltown but I had made up my mind I wanted to work in Hughes' Laundry. In order to work there you had to be either 18 years old or have finished the 8th grade. When I was 16, Dad and Mother moved to St. Maries to work and I stayed on the Sharp place and fed the stock all winter so I could finish the 8th grade at the Powerline school and take the State examination at Harrison. My 8 year old sister Edith stayed with me.

Then I got my wish. I took a job at Hughes Laundry, 20 cents an hour for 9 hours a day. The Builders Supply occupied that building later .

Hughes Laundry Crew 1916. Josie Gunderson, Dad Hughes, Ruth Caswell, Mrs. Munn, unknown, Mrs. Lilly, Hazel Ogden Ramey, Mrs. Dorsey, Leifan Jones, driver, Ernie Hughes, boss. Raleigh Hughes, Fireman and Washer.

BACHELOR GIRL
In those days for a girl to live alone wasn't the thing to do. You was always supposed to have a chaperon, especially you weren't supposed to entertain any male in your own home without a chaperon. I lived in a garage behind the laundry. It belonged to Ernie Hughes and I lived not far from his door where he could watch over me.

FEEDING THE WOBS

The Fairgrounds were on the St. Joe road just past Lee Carpenter's house — the last house on the right hand side before you reach the hill. In 1917 they put a picket fence around the Fairbuilding, reinforced with barbed wire to bullpen the Wobblies — the Industrial Workers of the World — I.W.W.

A lot of the Wobblies were local lumberjacks and people knew they were hungry and took food to them. When I walked across the valley to visit my folks, people at the laundry gave me big baskets of food to take to them and a fellow at the bakery gave me leftover cookies and rolls to take. Of course, he liked to go along and help carry the heavy baskets — but that didn't get him any place with me. I already knew Ed Ramey.

When the Wobblies saw me coming they'd wave. The soldiers patrolling the fence were friendly and didn't make any effort to stop me from talking to the prisoners. One guard was a big, husky guy that said he should be inside the fence — that he didn't know how come he was on the outside.

The Wobblies sang a lot of Wobbly songs but I can't remember any of them. They made up a song about Tom Hay — something about he should be hanged for a one armed bandit. That Mrs. Hay was a rough character — a tough old gal.

There is a persistent story that when the vigilantes were about to confront the Wobblies up on First Street, Tom Hay built a barricade and Mrs. Hay sat behind it holding cartridges in her apron in readiness to reload Tom's rifle like in pictures of the Revolutionary War. Ed.

For more about the Wobblies see JoJane Hammes "Living World War 1 1917-1918, St. Maries, Idaho". The Corporation 127 S. 7th Ave., St. Maries, Idaho, Publishers.

Ed Ramey continues: Pete Madison was one of the well known Wobblies locally. Pete told the lumbermen, millmen and employers that if they done certain things the Wobblies would go back to work.

Some of them said, "How do we know they'll go back to work?"

Pete said, "Well! I'm a'tellin' you they'll go back to work."

And they found they could depend on his word.

MISSED THE ARMY

World War 1 got me as far as Camp Lewis where the doctor told me, "The first bunch of immunity shots would kill you. You might outlive some of these other fellows but I can't take you."

Hazel: I worked at the laundry 2 years, then in 1918, Ed and I got married. I didn't work out no more. Ed worked for the railroad awhile and then in the woods.

Ed continues the story:
PETE JOHNSON — TOP MAN
I run skidding jammer on different jobs like at Falls Creek, Elk River and the Little North Fork of the Coeur d'Alene and Trout Creek. I was always glad when Pete Johnson did the hookin'.

With other guys I've tore up jammers a'pullin' on logs that was stuck crossways between two stumps or hooked around a tree. But when Pete Johnson hollered, "Go ahead!" a log came out of there. Then when the tongs or the choker got back he had another log ready to go. With Pete we'd always get out more timber.

POKER DAVE
At the Richard Johnson camp on the Little North Fork, Lovell Wood, Lee Perry and my brothers and old Poker Dave was there.

After supper the guys in the bunkhouse would be shaving or playing cribbage or reading magazines and Poker would start tellin' a big story. We'd already listened to him half the summer so we'd get up one at a time and walk out and leave him talking to himself. Old Poker had wore out his welcome.

JAKE POAGE AND IRA HORNE
Jake and I and Pat O'Reilly and some more was out on a party in town one night. Next morning Jake was gone when I got up. I never seen him for 4 or 5 months and when I did see him, he'd had that accident on the runaway train at Emerald Creek and one leg was missing. Ira Horne worked on that same train.

Afterward when Ira Horne was sheriff, the Federal Prohibition officers was heading for St. Joe to pinch Jake Poage for bootlegging. They came to the sheriff's office and told Ira Horne to come with them.

Ira Horne unpinned his star and took off his gun and laid them down on the desk. He said, "I'll quit this job before I'll help arrest Jake Poage. Maybe bootlegging is the only way he can make a living. When Jake Poage lost that leg, he saved my life."

LIFT FOR A TIRED MAN
Late in the fall I took a long deerhunt from the highway down to Cardwell Spur. I came home tired and ate supper and went down with Hazel to the Legion Hall. Pete's Electric at College and 5th is in the old Legion Hall.

After one dance I said to Hazel, "There's something wrong. Either me or that music is plumb dead."

She said, "It's you!"

I singled Wallace Daniels out of the crowd and I said, "Let's hunt up a drink."

Jake Poage was bootleggin' in the old Skelton-Warren building.

Went down there and climbed the stairs and told Jake we wanted a bottle.

He pulled out his own and poured us a drink. He said, "I can't keep liquor here. The Law is giving me a bad time. But give me 5 minutes."

When he came back with the pint we paid him. He gave us another drink out of his bottle and we left. Down at the bottom of the stairs Wallace and I pulled the cork on our gypo pint. During prohibition there were lots of bottles made that cheated on the amounts. I think I took first drink because I'd paid for it. I put my finger on the bottle and drank down half. Wallace drank the other half and we went back to the Legion Hall. The moonshine didn't make me the least bit drunk and I had a good time.

Hazel: Ed was a real good dancer. Still is. But that night he couldn't dance at all.

SKELTON-WARREN HAD CUSPIDORS
People called the Skelton-Warren store the little Sears and Roebuck. In the early days it carried everything. The boat landing was right in front of the store and their supplies came in by water. In the store they had a big, potbellied stove with spittoons clear around it. The fellows would stand there and chew tobacco and spit. Sometimes they missed.

Old Skelton used to get awful drunk and Roe Warren didn't. Especially on New Years Eve, John Skelton would go through town hollerin' "Happy New Year" and wake up everybody at 2 o'clock in the morning.

GOOSE HEAVEN RANCH
We bought the ranch at Goose Heaven in the spring of 1929 and built a log house in 1931. Elwood Hollingsworth was an expert axman and did the notching and the joints. Fred Herrick gave us lath for nothing so we could finish the inside with lath and plaster — —only Herrick didn't know it. When the big flood came in Christmas of '33, Herrick's whole mill and lumber piles were flooded out. Ed was working. Another woman and I took our rowboat and picked up bundles of lath floating down the river.

Ramey Ranch Home 1931

Ed continues:
DRIVING LAUNDRY WAGON
I drove laundry wagon for Ernie Hughes, 1928-1932. I'd see Togo, the little old Chinaman driving that one horse and rickety wagon around town every day to pick up garbage for his pigs. One time his horse ran away and turned the wagon over and bruised him pretty bad. When

they took him to Doc Platt's hospital and undressed him, he had on more clothes than any 3 men: 2 or 3 pairs of overalls and pants, two or three suits of underwear and shirts. Around his middle he had about a dozen of them 50 pound flour sacks like a big pad. They called me down to take this pile of clothes to the laundry and get them washed. The bill was something enormous but nobody complained. Togo had cooked in logging camps for Fred Herrick.

FLOATHOUSE ROW
Picking up and delivering laundry I knew all the red lighters on floathouse row like Josy, and Nellie and Molly and Giggles, and a lot of others that stayed as little as a week and moved on. I would say at least 50 came and went during the 3 ½ or 4 years I drove laundry wagon. I remember one very lively French girl who went to dances out at the Brown Jug on the Harrison Flats. she could do step dancing — something like jigging. She was well liked. One of the local boys married her and they moved to California.

I didn't look down on them. My belief is that a man who goes to a prostitute is himself a prostitute.

BROWNIE
One day I was going down the waterfront walk past Old Lady Bell's — she was a red lighter, too — and old Brownie hollered up at me. "Hey! Come down." Brownie was old and stayed with her.

I went down to the back porch of the floathouse and he hauled out a jug of moonshine. He took the cork out and handed it to me.

I tasted it. What it was, some guy had run his still down till he should have throwed it out but he didn't and run 2 or 3 gallons more. No alcohol hardly in it at all.

I said, "I don't like it."

Brownie talked with a lisp. He said, "I do. I can dwink it and it don't make me dwunk!"

NELLIE COTTINGHAM
I owned some apartments on Center Street between 13th and 14th. Torn down now. One of them was empty and without saying anything at all to me, Nellie moved into it. She said, "I had to get away from that damp river."

Part of the time she was so mentally confused that I handled her financial affairs for her, like when she sold her floathouse and property just above the mouth of the St. Maries River and running over east to the hill, for $2,000.

Then she wanted to go to Vancouver, Washington to live with her sister. Jake Shanks and Rusty Johnson's sister Doris loaded her stuff into a pickup and took her there. But in 3 or 4 months she came back and lived with Mrs. Lee Lawler over in Milltown.

CATCHING LAKERS

Along in the spring of 1937 I sent word to my brother-in-law, Wilford Rushing that the lakers were running up Hells Gulch Creek to spawn and to meet me on the little bridge Sunday morning.

We started fishing off the east end of the bridge. I had an old willow pole with line and hook.

Wilford had a good fly rod with an automatic reel that belonged to his uncle. That was a pretty expensive rig for those days.

What we was doin' was strictly illegal: fishing without a license, fishing in a closed stream and fishing out of season. As soon as we caught a couple of nice 14 inchers we carried them over to the west end of the bridge and buried 'em up in leaves.

We had a couple of trout apiece and Wilford put another away in the leaves. He come back and put a big gob of worms on his hook. He was kind of a clown anyway. He spit on it and threw it out. "This is gonna be good!" he said.

Right then, Shep — Mansfield Shepherd, the game warden, stepped out of the bushes over at our side of the bridge. He walked up behind us. "How's the fishin', boys," he says.

Old Wilford went paralyzed. He held the pole out stiff in front of him with the line dangling in the water. "Oh. OOOOOH! Not very good!" he says.

PINCHED

Shep walked over to the west end of the bridge and dug our fish out of the leaves. He said, "I hate to pinch you boys but that fellow livin' on the hill called me up and I had to do something."

Then he took our outfits and our fish. Told us to show up in court next morning.

We did. They fined us each $25 and $4 costs.

I didn't have any money but I had plowed some land for Ed Kinsolving the week before and had $25 coming to me. I went over and got that. Then I went down to the poolhall in town and hunted up a guy that owed my wife for eggs he'd bought from us. That gave me the $4 costs.

RAZZING SHEP

Mansfield Shepherd and I had always been friends. After this fishing incident we were going to dances together down at the Eagles or different places. I was always razzin' Shep, tellin' him the only reason he took our fish was that he wanted some to eat and couldn't catch 'em himself. Everybody knew he was one of the best fishermen in the country.

One night we was drinkin' a little bit down at a dance in the Oddfellow's Hall. I rubbed it into him so bad that old Shep got mad.

"Damn you!" he said. "I'll go out next week and I'll catch you a mess of fish."

I said, "You can't do it! You can't catch fish!"

Come home from camp Saturday night and Shep had been there that day and left 12 of the nicest 12 to 13 inch trout you ever saw. He told my wife, Hazel, "You tell that Ed, now maybe he'll shut up about them fish I took away from him."

KNOCKED DOWN — ROLLED OVER
I only got hurt once and that was when I was logging for myself at the ranch. When you're skidding a log on the sidehill you always stay on the upper side of it. This time I got careless and walked on the lower. If it hadn't been for a stump the log would have rolled plumb over me. As it was, it knocked me down and rolled over my left leg and broke the bone just above the ankle.

When Bob Hustler come up with a peavey and rolled the log off me, my foot was twisted plumb around and pointing straight backwards.

Old Doc Platt probably was the best loved doctor that ever hit St. Maries. Platt took me over to his hospital and straightened the foot up.

He said, I can't put a cast on it because it's goin' to swell to beat the band." He knew I didn't have any money so he said, "You'd just as well go home. You can stay there as well as in the hospital."

I laid on my back at home 26 days.

Elwood Hollingsworth come up from Carlin Bay to visit and he was settin' by the bed eyeing that foot. Elwood was a droll guy. He grinned and said, "I believe that foot of yours is goin' crooked."

I said, "At first it was straight like my right one but I'm sure it's turning further left."

He said, "What does Doc Platt say?"

I said, "I hate to say anything about it to old Doc."

"You mean you haven't told him?" Elwood jumped up, "Well, by God! I don't hate to make a noise." I never before heard Elwood swear.

CROOKED FOOT
In about 30 minutes he was back from town with Doc Platt. I could guess from Doc's face that Elwood had given him a bad time.

Doc got down at the foot of the bed, got a'hold of that foot and gave it a twist. I could hear the new formed bone breaking. "There!" Doc said. "That foot's not crooked!"

It hurt like everything. I said, "No, Damn you! You just straightened it."

He put a cast on it and rigged a block and tackle on the end of the bed with a rope and a bucket of sand hanging on it.

He wasn't gone 4 hours before I couldn't stand the pull and tore the whole outfit off.

It's been crooked ever since. I walk with it at about a 45 degree angle so I stumble once in awhile. Otherwise it don't bother me. But if I'm walkin' in the snow it's easy to trail me.

DOC STUCK

I never held it against old Doc. Not long after that, Doc Platt knocked on my door at about two o'clock at night. Wanted to know if I had a tractor or a truck.

I said, "No! All I have is a pickup."

He said, "My car's stuck down the road. I need a pull."

Platt 15 bed hospital opened '23.

Dr. Owen Platt with
adopted daughter

He'd been out in the night lookin' at his cattle. What had happened, he tried turning around in a mudhole and backed off the road and the differential of his car was settin' on a big boulder about 2½ feet in diameter. Both hind wheels was up in the air turning free.

My pickup couldn't pull him out. We tried shoving posts under his wheels for traction but as soon as he put the power to it the wheels kicked the posts out.

Doc says, "We've got to get more help."

I said, "There's always another way. If we can't get the car off the rock, let's see if we can get the rock from under the car." I had a grubhoe and shovel with me. The ground was steep below the rock. I started diggin'. It took awhile but finally the rock dropped down, the car rested on its wheels and Doc drove out.

OWE ME NOTHING

Doc got out his pocket book and pulled out a ten dollar bill. "Here!"

That was about 2½ days wages at that time. I said, "You don't owe me anything."

He stood there lookin' at me and chewin' tobacco. He shoved back the $10 and pulled out a five.

I said, "I don't want that either. You don't owe me anything."

He said, "Why should you come down here in the middle of the night and get me out of this mudhole?"

I said, "Why should you go out in the country in the middle of the night to deliver babies or take care of somebody that's hurt or sick? And half the time you don't know you'll get paid. If you can do that all of the time, it's not going to hurt me a bit to help you this once."

He looked like he didn't know what to think. He rolled the bill up and stuck it back in his pocket and drove off.

We always sold chickens and eggs over at Platt's little hospital. Hazel come back from a delivery one day and said, "Doc Platt wants to see you."

I couldn't imagine why he wanted to see me but I went over.

BUYING STUFF FROM DOC

Doc said, "I'm going to California for the winter. I've got 3 cows and 3 horses down on my place" — he owned the land where Hartman now lives — "and a brand new set of harness, a steel wheeled wagon and some other stuff and a pile of tongue and groove flooring and 2 or 3 tons of grain. I don't want to leave that stuff there for somebody to pack off and I can't leave the stock roaming the roads or the neighbors will holler. You can have the whole works for $175."

I said, "That's a give-away price but I haven't got any $175."

He said, "I know you haven't. But go get the stuff and the stock. When you get around to it you can pay me."

I paid him off as soon as I could.

BUYING LAND FROM DOC

A couple years later Doc had 30 acres of land in the meadow for sale. A half dozen neighbors wanted to buy it and I knew one neighbor was offering him cash.

Doc Platt come over to our house. "Can't you use that land?"

I said, "Yeah! I could use it but — "

"Well, you can have it," he said.

I said, "Doc! I haven't the money to buy it."

He said, "Pay down whatever you can. Pay the rest when you get it." He set the price at $1500 which I thought was about right. He never even wrote up a contract. I paid him off in a few years.

RENTING FROM DOC
Later I rented that Hartman place from him for two or three years. Then I had to go to him and say, "I can't handle it anymore, Doc. I'm, milkin' too many cows and have more work than I can do."

He said, "If you don't want it, it'll stand vacant. I won't allow nobody else there."

I said, "I'll get you a good renter. Somebody that won't tear the place up and will improve it."

And I did.

But old Doc Platt. He was gonna get even with me for helping him that time in the middle of the night. And he sure did. Many, many times over.

TOUR OF GOOSE HEAVEN ROAD FROM HELL'S GULCH TURNOFF TO PETERSON GULCH — WITH ED RAMEY
Set your speedometer at zero where the Hell's Gulch road turns off Highway 3.

5½ tenths — Dave Wallace's old place up the slope to the right. Dave was an eccentric old bachelor. He had an orchard and cut wood to sell. He had a lot of Washington Water Power stock. A very independent man. He got diabetes about 1930 when he was in his early 60s. One morning after he'd taken a bath and shaved and put on his best clothes, he came down to this mailbox here. Took a rusty revolver and blowed his brains out.

He willed his place to Mrs. Elwood Hollingsworth. She had diabetes, too.

6½ tenths — An old house over on our left is where Tom Boyce lived — Charlie Boyce's dad.

On our left where the trailer house sets with a shelter over it is where Packsack George Sypal lived. He was part Cherokee Indian. For years and years he walked in from Hells Gulch to St. Maries almost every day with a packsack on his back. People in cars used to pick him up. He had been a signal maintainer on the Milwaukee till his craft went on strike and some scab took his job. He lived on the money from 3 floathouses he rented to women. He wasn't able to go back to work for the railroad again for years and years till World War 2. Then when he finally went to the job again he had the drinking habit. They didn't want to fire him after those years of credit he'd built up so they advised him to retire on a pension.

1 mile — We're crossing Hells Gulch Creek. 200 yards down the creek, there used to be a service bridge for people owning land. That's where Wilford Rushing and I got pinched for poaching trout in 1937.

1.3 miles — A hump in the road. This is where **Doc Platt** backed off the road onto a big boulder. During the time Doc Platt had cattle they ran the road and about drove everybody nuts. There was no fence on the lower side then.

Most of the timber ahead and on the right has grown up since I left here in 1952. There had been a fire that burned most everything out and left only a few dead trees standing.

1.6 miles — The driveway road swinging upgrade slightly and to the right goes to the **log house** where Hazel and I lived for 21 years. **Duncan** owns the house now.

1.9 miles — On our left is a 36 inch diameter **yellow pine tree** on the edge of the road. It was only 14 or 16 inches when I moved here 44 years ago.

2.2 miles — On our right is the big house where **Ed Kinsolving** lives now and his father, **Doctor Kinsolving, M. D.** lived before him for 25 years.

We enter the oiled highway at the mouth of **Peterson Gulch** named after a homesteader, and turn left toward St. Maries. On our right a channel comes in from the river into which loggers like **Bill Tucker** dumped logs from the Harrison Flats, hauled on Mack Trucks, in the early 1920s. I worked for Bill Tucker a few days.

The channel makes a turn into the marsh and on this turn, when we came here in 1911, you could still see the old **willow fish traps** the Indians had built, though they were not in use. Fish came into the marsh at spots further down and couldn't get back out this end without getting into the willow pens.

This **dike** was built in 1919, using horses. While they were putting a road on top of it, it got so muddy they had to shut down. I hired a team from the contractors and hauled logs from where **Ed Murphy** lives now.

Interviewed at St. Maries Oct. 27, 1975

HOMESTEADERS DAUGHTER

Florence Bruun Reynolds

Mica Halfway House

I was named Florence after my mother, Florence Alderman. How she and my dad, George Bruun happened to meet in the first place: He was in Muscatine, Iowa, along the Mississippi River. It was spring of the year. My mother's brother got acquainted with my dad and brought him home. My mother had to go down to the river after a bucket of water and she had to climb over ice that was breaking up and my dad helped her. Dad was 27. Mom was 17. Just a little while later they was married.

Florence Bruun Reynolds 1974

Mother played harmonica and Dad the fiddle. They lived in floathouses along the Mississippi and played for dances.

MOTHER BRUUN WAS LIVELY

From an interview with Mrs. Bruun, age 90, by Sarah Rosenbaum, 11-2-69, staff writer of the Lewiston Tribune:

To learn the harmonica Mrs. Bruun said, "I had to steal my brother's harp."

After watching a daring lady parachutist drift to earth in a holiday exhibition, young Florence "got Daddy's big umbrella", clambered to the top of the woodshed and jumped. The umbrella turned "inside out on me!"

Mrs. Bruun said, "People have asked me what I laid it to to have lived such a long life. I've always had a song on my mind when I've been a'workin' and I always knew that God was with me."

Florence Bruun Reynolds continues: Mother lived to be 97.

PARENTS CAME WEST 1901

Dad and Mother came west to St. Maries in 1901 when my brother Edward was 4 years old. Perhaps a year later, they went up to Ferrell or St. Joe by boat and packed back to a homestead on Mica Creek.

Some of the hazards of early day boat travel are related in a reprint from the St. Joe Budget, placed in the Harrison Searchlight of July 22, 1904:

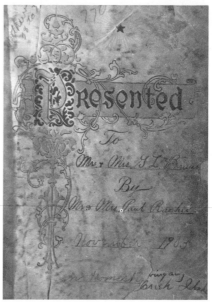

Flyleaf of Bible presented by Mr. and Mrs. Paul Rochet to Mr. and Mrs. G. L. Bruun, Nov. 1903, on homestead at Mica Creek.

Last Monday as the steamer Spokane was nearing Wm. Ferrell's place, one of the passengers, contrary to the rules of the boat, and regardless of surroundings, fired a rifle at a duck that was flying ahead of the boat. As might be expected, he missed the duck and killed one of Mr. Ferrell's best cows. The man paid for the cow and expressed his intention of observing the game law in the future.

I was born January 30, 1907, at Huetter just outside Coeur d'Alene, when my folks had come off the homestead for the winter.

HALFWAY HOUSE AT MICA MEADOWS

Our homestead took in the upper end of Mica Meadows. We were 18 miles from St. Joe City by trail and something of a Halfway House for many homesteaders who had settled further up Mica Creek and in branches of Marble Creek.

Mother served meals on the main floor. I remember as a toddler, the table in the dining room seemed awfully long. My mother had a small table in the kitchen for the family. We ate some wild meat but mostly cured meats like ham and bacon and salt pork. My brother Edward was quite a hunter so we had lots of grouse and he used to catch trout almost every day.

Dad packed homesteaders to our house, they slept in the second story, then next day they'd eat breakfast and go on to their cabins.

PULLED BABY SISTER OUT OF THE WATER

My folks had this wooden walk going down to Mica Creek and they had dug a deep hole where they dipped up water. Mary, who was born at the homestead, Nov. 10, 1908, and I were still very small.

1909 at Mica Meadows. George Bruun 41, Mary, Edward, Florence and mother Florence Bruun 31.

Mama said pretty soon here come Mary and I up that walk and I told her Mary fell in and I had to get in and pull her out!

DAD PLAYED WITH US KIDS

Dad played with us kids a lot. He sang ditties to us, especially when Mother was gone to St. Maries or taking care of Mary. He built us a swing 25 feet high. He always fixed a little piece of ground for each of us to have our own garden. We planted and cared for it any way we wanted to just so we stayed out of his garden.

Then before the snow came he built us a sled so we could climb the hillside and slide down into the meadow.

DAD BUILT A LOG SCHOOL

Two or three other settlers had children. My folks wanted a school for my older brother, Edward so my dad built a log school further up Mica. There weren't enough children for the district to furnish a teacher so my folks brought a boy from St. Joe to stay with us and attend school and sent me too, though I was only five. By the time I rode horse about four miles I slept most of the time in school and didn't learn much.

The settlers together paid the wages of the man teacher.

BEAR IN THE NIGHT

A man and his nephew lived up Mica Creek. They heard a noise one summer night. They thought a bear was getting into the cabin. Woke 'em up. The boy jumped up and grabbed the gun and evidently, the uncle had woke up first because he went out and was coming back in and the boy was so scared he shot him.

The next day my dad and some of the other men brought the body out horseback to St. Joe and before they got to St. Joe — it was hot — he commenced to smell pretty bad and my dad was the only one that could go on with him because my dad had no sense of smell.

BOY PACKER

My brother Ed was only 14 but during the 1910 fire he was helping my father pack supplies to the firefighters. Once he came back from leading a packstring of supplies with his shoe soles cooked black from walking through hot ashes in burned over ground.

Then in August when the fires got bad they wanted Mother to go out to St. Joe. She was heavy with child then and she couldn't stand riding a horse so she walked while we rode the 18 miles to St. Joe.

When the fire was all over with we went back to the homestead. On the day, Nov 24, 1910, that my brother George Junior was born, Ellen

Engstrom happened to come in to our Halfway House and she helped Mother. Ellen Engstrom was one of the single women that homesteaded. She played the piano real well.

In summer Dad cut natural hay from the meadows with a scythe to feed the horses. The snow got so deep in the wintertime that the horses never got out of the barn.

Bringing in a load of wild hay at Mica Meadows, 1911. Young Ed Bruun driving and the rest of the family riding.

BUILT TOWNSITE STORE

I don't know how much money Dad got when he sold the homestead but he gave my mother $500 so she could take all us kids back to see her folks in Muscatine, Iowa. We was gone all winter while Dad built the Townsite Store in St. Maries.

We came back in the spring and lived upstairs. He run that store six years.

In the spring of 1917 Dad decided to move to St. Joe and sold the Townsite Store. Mother stayed in St. Maries visiting my brother Edward and getting our household goods packed.

Us kids were staying with Aunt and Uncle Bill Bruun at St. Joe while just down below the hill, Dad was using a mill team to clean up a plot of ground to build us a house.

Shortly before noon my aunt fixed a lunch and gave it to my cousin and me to take down to Dad.

Dad took the lunch bucket and set off with the team for the mill — that's where he fed them hay and oats at noon and he'd eat his lunch down there.

8 YEAR OLD DOLLY McKINLEY FELL IN RIVER

Dad was only part way when he heard some women screaming down toward the river that a little girl had fell in. It was eight year old Dolly Mc Kinley from Harrison who was visiting some folks in St. Joe.

See, the high water had flooded some houses and people were living upstairs in those houses and went out from land on a floating walk. The women had been gathering some dandelion greens and were washing them on this walk when the little girl fell in.

Dad had already saved two people from drowning that year.

DIVED IN IN HEAVY WORK CLOTHES

When Dad heard the women screaming, he threw down the reins and dinner bucket and ran for the river. Dad always wore a tie, generally a long black tie, even when he was packing. Like many men those days, he wore a vest, too. It was a warm day so he wasn't wearing a coat. He had on calked boots and must have had a wool shirt and heavy work pants.

Dad dived in and reached the girl.

She grabbed him around the neck and was strangling him.

He tore her arms loose and had her little cap under his arm when the current carried them under some logs and brush.

I think Father and Dolly would have made it all right if it hadn't been for the logs and brush. Dad was a powerful swimmer.

They got Dolly out first.

When they pulled Dad out they found something was holding him and his shoe lace had caught on some brush down under. The little cap was still under his arm. He was only 49.

CARNEGIE MEDAL FOR HEROISM

Someone must have sent our names in to the Carnegie Foundation. We received a posthumous medal for heroism for Father. Then the people of the Foundation visited us in St. Maries and started sending Mother a small pension. We managed to make out with it, along with sewing for people and taking in washing and ironing.

My husband, Russell Reynolds and I lost our boy in the river here at Potlatch. My sister lost her boy in the ocean and my grandchildren's father drowned in the Salmon River.

So I don't like water!

George Bruun in 1917

Interviewed at Potlatch, Ida. April 22, 1974

Bill Robinson

Old Time Teamster and Logger

Bill Robinson at 88 in 1973

I was a runaway kid!

I was born in Oxford, Indiana in 1885. Dad left my mother. I never knew him. I had a brother and sister that was adopted out. I was 6 years old when my mother and my brother, Ed and me moved to Dayton, Washington.

That's where my mother met my stepdad, a butcher. We went down to Arlington, Oregon and across the river on the ferry where they both worked at Peters Sheep Ranch. Stayed there a few months.

Then with 2 horses and a buckboard and me and Ed ridin' in the back we went down through the sagebrush to where we could cross on the ferry to the Dalles. My stepdad sold the horses and outfit and we got on the Dalles City boat to Portland. Went to Oregon City and rented a room up over a store.

RUN AWAY

My stepdad got drunk all the time and beat my mother and us kids just for nothin'. I ran away from home.

Next day I was going down the street in Oregon City and I see him a'comin' up the street. I slid around a telephone pole because I was afraid he'd beat me to death if he caught me.

A crew was buildin' an electric line from Oregon City to Portland. One of 'em said, "Lad! You want a ride?"

LOOKIN' FOR A BUTCHER JOB

I climbed on their wagon and rode the 18 miles. I had heard my stepdad say that at Troutdale was a big outfit that butchered cattle for all of Portland. I asked a man how to get out there.

He said, "You can catch the streetcar right here. That's where I'm goin'."

I was standin' there in knee pants talkin' to him and here come a policeman. He said, "What's your name?"

I said, "Willie Robinson."

He said, "You fit the description of a boy that run away from Oregon City name of Bluerock." That was my stepdad's name. The policeman eyed me awhile. "Where you goin'?"

I says, "I'm goin' home. I live in East Portland."

The policeman stood there and watched to make sure I got on that streetcar.

The man I'd been talking to sat down beside me. He said, "How old are you, Willie?"

"Seven."

He said, "They won't hire you at Troutdale. You're too young."

I told him the only other place I knew to go was Peters Sheep Ranch at Arlington.

He bought me an Arlington ticket.

HERDED SHEEP AND CHORED
Peters let me herd sheep and do other work. I could drive team as good as anybody. Every year at shearing time they loaded wool in them big sacks on a wagon. I'd take it across the ferry over to Arlington.

When I was 12 a young guy was standin' on the front of the ferry when it came over.

"Hello Will!" he hollers.

I said, "Hello."

He says, "Don't you know your own brother? I'm Ed."

"Yep!" I says. Hell! I hadn't seen him in 5 years. I didn't know him from nobody.

My mother had sent him up. She was at Cottage Grove below Eugene.

HALF OWNER IN A SAWMILL
Ed says, "I've got a little sawmill down there. If you'll go down with me I'll give you half interest in it."

I'd never seen a sawmill let alone havin' anything to do with one. I could just see myself important and ownin' a sawmill. So I took him to Peters and says, "My brother's got a sawmill and I gotta go down to Cottage Grove and help him run it. He's givin' me half interest."

So I rolled my extra pair of overalls around my spare pair of boots, shoved 'em under my arm and went over to Arlington with Ed.

Ed says, "We'll beat our way down on the freights and save money."

I could see that was a good idea because we could use that money to run the sawmill.

We rode the rods which wasn't easy them days. The trainmen throwed you off every time they caught you.

Got down to Cottage Grove. The sawmill was a 7 foot crosscut saw. I got on one end and him on the other cuttin' 2 foot wood. The trains all burnt wood then. We'd saw the wood and take turns splittin' it and haulin' it over to the Southern Pacific railroad. In that country it rains mud up to your neck.

RIDIN' & BREAKIN' BRONCS
I didn't last long at that sawmill. I took off for Arlington but I didn't go back to the sheep ranch where they paid nothin'. I went to Condon. A cattle, horses and sheep outfit took me in. General ranch work. Breakin' broncs. I rode all over the country — Canyon City, Prineville....

When I was 15 I left Condon and worked for Art Whitmore and his brothers big racehorse ranch at Pomeroy. I took care of chores and broke horses to ride. I got top-hand wages $30 a month and they feed and sleep you. I stayed there till I was 20.

SKINNER AT HARRISON
1905 I heard about the timber and mountains around the Coeur d'Alene lake. Got as far as Harrison and it looked pretty good. I got off the boat and went to work for Grant Lbr. Co., driving logging team at O'Gara.

Later, I went to St. Joe. Milked cows and did chores for Al Reed's big dairy.

SAWMILL STIFF
I don't know how it happened but my brother, Ed came to St. Joe in 1908 as master mechanic when they built the mill there. Meantime, I went down to Salem to see my mother. Got stuck on a girl down there an' married her. Came back and we lived in an old log house in Reed's Gulch. Every day I'd row up to the mill in an old rowboat. Worked 10 hours for $1 a day.

LUCKY IN THE 1910 FIRE
They sent a bunch of us to the head of Bear Creek to put out spot fires. All that saved us was the wind blowing hard out of the northeast.

Never burned at all at the head of Bear Creek but about 6 miles away a whole bunch of fire fighters burned up.

HOMESTEADING & LOGGING AT PEEDEE

1914 I bought a relinquishment from a man and took over his homestead up Peedee Creek. I had never gone to school a day in my life. That's where my second wife that died, the mother of my kids, taught me to read and write. She was well educated. (When he said this his eyes filled with tears. He had difficulty going on.)

I logged for Walters at the rim on the north side and drayed logs all the way down the hill to Round Lake with a 4 horse team. A log rolled on the hillside and pinned my leg down. I managed to work out from under it but it hurt so much I had to sleep on my belly with a pillow around my leg.

When it didn't get any better I rowed a boat to Harrison to see the doctor. May have been Busby. When I stepped out of the boat on the beach I slipped and fell down hard on the rocks. When I crawled to my feet there was nothing the matter with me a'tall. Must've been my knee was out of place and the fall threw it back in. I got into the boat and rowed home.

Bill and Willia Lee Robinson at Peedee homestead with Myrtle, Joe and Aaron. Leonard (Skip) was born later.

Bill Robinson cross hauling a yellow pine onto a wagon 1914

RUNAWAY SLEIGH

I was sleighing logs down the Peedee Gulch with my fine team of sorrels. I had rigged up a brake that was a wood bar with iron on the tip end which went down through the sleigh runner and this would hold the load back. It broke one day. The load pushed the sorrels faster and faster. There wasn't a thing I could do. On a turn the breeching broke. The loaded sleigh dived over the bank, pushing the horses ahead of it. One horse ended up with a log across him, dead. The other

Skidding logs with his sorrels into Chatcolet Lake landing 1916

one, Pete, wasn't hurt at all. I was mighty glad that it was the best one that was saved.

I went to Coeur d'Alene and got advance money from the lumber company and bought another sorrel to match Pete.

BIGGEST TROUT

You can't believe the trout that used to be up the Joe river above Avery in the early days. Along about 1912 a fellow and me was fishin' above the S Bend and he caught a 14 incher. Right then I caught a fish — I honestly believe he was 30 inches long. We didn't have no net or nothing.

I hollered, "Come and help me!"

He says, "I haven't got time to monkey with you! I got a fish!"

I was following that pole downstream and I fell off into a deep hole. The water was cold but I floundered around and got hold of the fishpole again and got bottom under my feet and I kept playing him up and down and everywhere.

Finally I got it in the shallows close to shore. I got down on my knees on the rocks and leaned over.

He gave a flop and broke the line.

I jumped right on top of him. Do you think I could hold the slippery son of a bitch!? No! He got away. God! He was a big trout. Bigger than anything I ever caught in my life.

We fished up the river to the Quartz cabin. In that cabin there was some 5 gallon cans. We soaked the trout in salt water overnight. Then in the morning we put in one layer of fish, some leaves and ferns, then another layer. We each had a 5 gallon can of fish. All we could pack downriver.

THE MOST POWERFUL TEAM

My team of blacks, the most powerful I ever owned weighed 4125. I weighed 'em after I bought them and the collars and harness in 1920 for $1,075. I put up $500 that no 4 horses could outpull them. Nobody took me up on it. 'Course you couldn't get 4 horses that could pull together like them two.

We was draying long cedar poles down the mountain to Cardwell Spur. Floyd Gregory got loaded up and he unhooked from his load near camp. It was too late to go on down to the river.

DRAYING, a favorite practice on steep ground, means the poles (or logs) were loaded with only the front ends resting on a single pair of sleigh runners with the other ends dragging to hold back the load.

Charlie Gregory and me went up and loaded the next morning and drove down. Here was Floyd still in the road by camp froze down. I had a big load on with double top chains.

I yelled at Floyd, "Get out of the way and let somebody haul poles that can!"

It made Floyd too mad to answer. He got Charlie to hook his team on in front. By God! They dug into it and couldn't pull it with the four horses.

Floyd looked kinda sheepish, "Why don't you hook on with us. Maybe 6 horses can move it."

Theirs were pretty good horses, too, but I was about half mad that he let his outfit freeze down and set there in the way.

I said, "I won't hook my good blacks on with that outfit! Take your horses off and I'll show you how a good team can pull it out."

I had special double trees because the blacks could break any doubletree you could buy. I hooked onto it and stood on his load. The blacks dug in. Next thing we was goin' down the skid road and all we had was the bunk and chains and the cornerbinds. The rest of the poles was laying back there with the dray runners still froze down. I'll never forget that.

Floyd looked at his whole outfit tore apart and his eyes bugged out and he said, "God Damn!"

But the night before if Floyd had throwed a stick down to drive the runners up onto, you see, he could have swung the team sideways and broke it loose.

SKIDDING A BIG CAMP RANGE

I took my team of blacks up to skid for Everett & Kelso at Cranberry Creek on the Marble. They wanted me to help set up camp. We had a big cookstove down at Marble Station and Talbot, the packer, said, "I can't pack that great, big thing up there on my mules even if you strip it down."

I figured you could pull a big load like this same as you would a plow. I sawed a 16 inch log in two, hewed a turn-up on one end for the front, bored some holes and put big stakes V fashion in the holes. Then I put in two stakes stickin' out behind like plow handles. Then we loaded the stove in this V and hooked one horse onto the front.

You'd be surprised how easy it was for one man to hold the handles and balance it while the other led the horse. Of course we took our time and we changed off. I don't know what one of them stoves weighed but I'll bet it was never moved again. I suppose it's settin' up there yet.

THE INCLINE WAS FOOLISH

That Rutledge Incline was the foolishest thing I ever saw. Pull carloads of logs up one side of the ridge and let them down the other with them 2 big Wilamette donkeys. They could have come up Merry Creek and through Davies Pass into Bussel Creek and run all over Marble with the railroad. Look how high Blackwell went with their railroad out of Fernwood.

Bill at Cd'A Fire Protective
Ass'n cabin-Marble Mt.
About 1920

I used to think about that when I was blading all those roads for the Forest Service. I worked 33 seasons for the Forest Service — never the year around. I'd work a month and maybe they'd be out of money. Then I'd come home and log. I laid off in 1926 and never went back till 1933. Stayed '33 till 1952. Last job I done was build those creosote timbered bridges in Marble Creek.

Interviewed at St. Maries 1975

Bert Russell

& *Author Fill-Ins*

Bert Russell 1979
Courtesy Lewiston Tribune

Andy Knutsen & Bert Russell
on flume pond.

FLUME TIME

When I worked at Fitzgerald Creek in 1929, flume time after supper always livened things up.

Len McCrea, the boss, stuck his head in the bunkhouse door and called, "Come on, fellas!"

Five or six lumberjacks who weren't afraid of water wheeled for the pond. Andy Knutsen and I grabbed a pikepole apiece and ran out across the logs in our calked boots, feeling catty, showing off because a lot of these lumberjacks hadn't been raised around the Coeur d'Alene lake and trained from childhood to run logs like ourselves. And the ones that came to the pond worked mostly from floating walks. (I learned in later years that some of these same guys like Lee Carpenter could ride circles around me. They knew they were good men on the round stuff and didn't need to show off.)

Len McCrea paced back and forth on the shore of the pond, watch in hand. "**Open the gate! Open the gate!** I want that flume brim full. Ten minutes from now be ready to shove logs."

This is the curse of fluming logs on a steep flume. You have to let the flume fill far ahead with water before you start feeding in logs or the logs sliding downhill on the water will outrun the water and come grinding to a halt in a dry flume.

On the other hand if you run water into the flume too long there won't be enough water left in the pond to send down all your logs and the pond must be emptied to make room for more logs the next day.

The Fitzgerald flume tipped steeper the last half mile before reaching the river and made logs race so fast they scooped water out of the flume. A feeder dam had been built at the beginning of this steep pitch and a man stationed there to dump extra water into the flume.

Steep part of the Fitzgerald Flume nearing the St. Joe River.

So Len McCrea yanked at his mustache and paced the shore and looked at his watch. Although nobody had made a move to feed any logs into the flume, he yelled, "Hold 'em back there! I say, **Hold 'Em Back!**"

Then he hurried to the cedar tree just below the dam. He cranked the phone there and shouted, "The water get there yet? What's that? I can't hear you. This damn water makes too much noise."

Len hung up the receiver and galloped back to the edge of the pond. "God damn it! She's down two feet already. That fellow at the feeder dam never talks so anybody can hear him. Anyway the water should be over halfway there by now."

He paced back and forth even faster, eyeing his watch.

Suddenly at 7 minutes he couldn't stand the suspense. He ran out a floating walk, grabbed a pikepole from the nearest man and shoved a log ahead where the roaring water caught it. The log dived through flying spray into the flume and took off rolling and bobbing around the bend with its wet sides shining.

"Shove 'em in! No God damn it! Hold back. There went two at once. Space 'em! Space 'em! Now shove 'em faster. That's too much space."

Logs crowded ahead in the pull of the current like racehorses at the gate.

"Damn it!" Len shouted. "They're jamming!"

I knew Len regarded me as a punk kid who ate like a horse and didn't know beans about skidding logs but here I thought I was king. I ran across the logs close to the spill off and started breaking them loose.

"Hold back there. Let the lad break that jam!"

Five minutes of frenzied activity and Len rushed to the phone, shouting to the man at the feeder dam, "Turn your water in! Turn your water in!"

Another five minutes and someone furthest from the sound of rushing water hollered and pointed, "The phone! The phone!"

Len rushed down, came back bawling, "Hold up! Hold up! The logs got ahead of the water. Close the gate."

But we had already emptied most of the logs out of the pond. The floating walks rested on the mud and water running out the gate was dying to a dribble.

CLEARING THE FLUME

Next morning Len took a crew of us down the flume. Alongside and below the feeder dam the logs lay touching nose to tail in a string a half mile long extending down the steep pitch toward the river.

But the logs had not outrun the water. Len had misunderstood.

The feeder dam man was explaining, "You shoulda seen it! Them first big tamaracks come around the bend pushin' water in a geyser 50 feet high till there wasn't a drop of water left behind 'em. Not a damn drop. When the big ones come to a stop down below and the others come around the bend and started hittin' 'em, like pile drivers...Jesus! I thought they'd knock the flume off its stilts and smash — "

Len interrupted. "Here now! You fellows grab every fourth log and roll it out of the flume. Then space the ones left maybe 4 feet apart."

It took a good half day.

Then Len cranked the feeder dam phone. "You at the camp dam! Give us a little water. Only a little, ay? Watch it!"

Les Darrar & Len McCrea driving the Fitzgerald logs on down the river. 1930

Pretty soon the water was gurgling among the logs and Len was shouting into the phone, "A little more, now. Easy does it."

Then after timing with his watch, "One of you boys there. Give me water out of the feeder dam."

After a bit he shouted down the flume to a man standing at the bottom end of the stranded logs. "Has the water worked down there?"

The man waved that it had.

Then to the feeder dam man, "Give me a little more water now."

Then he shouted into the phone to camp. "Open the gate more, ay? I want the flume half full."

In the flume the little logs stirred first, then the big ones began to float. They began to move slowly, bumping one another, the big ones scraping the sides of the flume.

Murphy Driving Crew below mouth of Fitzgerald Cr. 1931 Val Neff, George Salchurt, Pete Madison, Jack Murphy, Les Darrar, Len McCrea and Walt Darry.

Then the whole long line was in motion.

Suddenly the water from the camp dam came racing around the bend and slid in among them, churning up froth, carrying them faster.

Everybody yelling, "Hey! She's goin'! God damn!"

When the first of the long black line began disappearing where the flume went beneath the Milwaukee railroad track a half mile away, little jets of white spray rose one after another as the logs dived into the Joe river.

DANCE AT FERRELL

About all that was left of the old town of Ferrell in the summer of 1929 was the old schoolhouse in the field and Kreuger's house up the road with some tired looking trees in the yard.

Some St. Joe lumberjacks that we worked with at Fitzgerald Creek steered my friends Andy Knutsen and Bill McCrea and I into Kreugers where we all loaded up on his ether needled homebrew.

Smelling a chance to sell more beer at two-bits a bottle, Kreuger was promoting a dance in the old schoolhouse. Kreuger said, "I got corn-meal to slick up the floor. I'll send word over to the joints in St. Joe. It will surprise you what a crowd we can get. Have another brew!"

Someone had stored hay in the schoolhouse and the bunch of us dragged what few bales were left and threw 'em outside. There was an old piano there with a couple of dead keys.

About dark, Kreuger hung a gasoline lantern in the ceiling and I started playing the piano — if you call what I do playing. I'm a pounder. The Fitzgerald lumberjacks like Lee Carpenter and Sonny Ditt-man and Wade Onthank and Oscar Moe and St. Joeites like Royal Carpenter and Toad Darling started to dance. Pretty soon a bunch from God knows what other camps were dancing.

Kreuger had 2 little girls about 10 to 12 and along with another 2 little girl friends they were the belles of the ball. If the lumberjacks weren't polite enough they'd stick their little noses in the air and turn their backs. Without enough girls to go around, the floor was filled with lumberjacks dancing with each other or solo.

Bill McCrea and Andy Knutsen whirled round and round till they ended up dizzy against the wall. Once Andy thumped me on the shoulder and said laughing, "There's two guys dancing with calked boots. Look at the slivers fly."

Whenever I stopped between pieces somebody shoved a bottle into my hands. The dancers howled for more like I was the King of Jazz himself.

There comes a time in this kind of a dance when the piano rocks back and forth in perfect time with the beating of feet and the music and the people are all welded together in a kind of rhythm intoxication. It makes your heart swell up. Makes drunks throw their arms around one another and blubber eternal friendship. Makes everybody love everybody else.

It became too rowdy for the little girls. They took hold of hands and ran out.

Maybe about two in the morning I realized in a hazy way the hall had emptied. Andy and Bill came in to tell me the sheriff and deputy had come up from St. Maries to make a raid for moonshine and about 80 lumberjacks crowded around their car and convinced them to go back before they got hurt.

An old lumberjack draped himself over the end of the piano with a jug of moon dangling from his index finger. He pushed it at me.

I took a jolt.

He took a jolt.

I took another jolt. The room dimmed out in a rosy haze.

The lumberjack and his moonshine never left me from then on. I think he couldn't — he was hanging to the piano for support. He leaned over it with his glassy eyes riveted on my fingers.

Every time I stopped playing he'd come to life and say, "My Gawd! How that boy can play! How that boy **can** play!" Then he'd wag his head like he was seeing the wonder of all creation.

My sheet music was strung along the top of the piano. I knew all the pieces by heart but in order to get my bearings and start on a different piece I'd set the music in front of me, put my nose right against it to focus on the notes and away I'd go pounding out ditties like **Three Little Words,** or **Melancholy Baby,** or **Five Foot Two.**

I'd be hammering away, grinning at the revolving dancers in that rosy glow and maybe singing the words. Pretty soon it would come to me I was playing the chorus of **Let Me Call You Sweetheart.** It didn't matter what I started with, I ended up playing **Let Me Call You Sweetheart.** It pleased me like it was happening to somebody else.

The affair roared on. The dancers didn't know the difference.

Without any noticeable passage of time it was morning with daylight coming in the windows. It came to me that my lumberjack friend and his jug were gone. I looked around and all the dancers were gone, too, except Bill McCrea and Andy Knutsen and they were holding hands and whirling slowly round and round in an otherwise empty room to **Let Me Call You Sweetheart.**

I stopped playing and gathered my music and Andy and Bill. At the

bottom of the schoolhouse steps my lumber-jack friend lay snoring peacefully in the dewey grass with his now empty jug hooked on his index finger. A few others littered the yard.

Bill and Andy and I staggered off up the road to Fitzgerald and in the heat of the rising summer sun climbed the Fitzgerald flume, stopping every hundred yards or so to unload some of the needled beer and rotgut. Our mouths were dry as cotton, our heads pounded and we swore weakly after each heave we'd never drink again.

Toad Darling & Royal
Carpenter at St. Joe
1930

NIG, THE TEACHER

When I told Len McCrea, the boss at the Fitzgerald camp in 1929 that I didn't know much about horse skidding, he just laughed and said, "Never mind! Nig will teach you."

Nig was a black gelding owned by Russell & Pugh all his life and he worked without any lines. I was 20 years young and Nig was close to 20 years old. My schooling began when I followed Nig up the skid trail. He came to a log. He turned around and waited till I hooked the tongs on. Then he pulled it down the skid trail a little, stopped for me to unhook and we'd go back and pull another one up behind the first. I'd fasten it on with trail dogs and we'd go back again for a third and a fourth or fifth.

Then he'd pull the whole string down over the hill to the log chute.

Coming back up with me hanging to his tail, if we came to a branch skid trail and he stopped uncertainly, I'd say "Gee" for turn right or "Haw" for left and he'd go on.

Aside from this directing, Nig mostly tolerated me as a servant only, to feed, water, curry and harness him. He didn't care for petting or ear scratching. He just wanted to be let alone to perform his job.

One little problem came up. A tree had blown over and the sawyers had left an eight foot piece of the trunk still attached to the turned-over stump. This piece stuck out beside the skid trail, bright and freshly cut.

To Nig it looked like the end of a regular 16 foot log. Every time we came up the trail he stopped at this spot, turned around and waited patiently for me to hook him on.

I'd explain to him that this wasn't really a log, take hold of his halter and turn his nose up the hill and "Giddap!"him to go on.

One day I got tired of stopping there. I said, "Old Boy! If you think you can pull it, let's see you try."

Nig watched me set the tongs. Then he set his feet into the black dirt and eased into the harness. When it didn't move he dug deeper, got down with his belly low to the ground and gave it his all till sweat broke out on his flanks.

When it didn't move a particle he began to ease up.

I said, "Whoa!" Backed him up and unhooked him.

After that he always gave it the cold eye and kept going.

HORSE DRAGGED

My partner Andy Knutsen and I each had a single horse and skidded logs into a level spot at the top of a chute. We'd skid down maybe a dozen logs and roll them into the chute, space them a foot or two behind one another. Then I'd hook Nig with trail tongs onto the rear log.

Nig started them like a locomotive starts a freight train. He dug his feet in hard, started the log and kept digging harder and pulling with everything he had. The rear log bumped the next one into motion and then it in turn bunted the next one and so on till all were moving.

As the logs slid over the brow of the hill and shot forward under their own weight for the half mile run to the flume pond, we'd yell down the canyon to warn anyone coming up to get in the clear, **"LOOK OUT BELOW!"**

And as their rumbling speed increased, **"LOOK OUT BELOW!"** again.

As the last log went over the brow Nig knew to swing sideways and set his feet. As the log went past Nig, his chain tightened and flipped the trail tongs backward and they clanked free behind him.

But this day we had points on the tongs that a new blacksmith had shaped and the blacksmith hadn't known his business. Instead of flipping out, the tongs only set deeper. The log yanked Nig backwards on his rump down into a wad of bark and limbs alongside the chute. Nig and the pile of trash slid 50 feet before he crashed into the log underpinning of the chute. It stopped him and jerked the log out of the chute. We grabbed our peaveys and pried the tongs free and Nig scrambled to his feet.

Nig knew he'd come damn close to being injured or killed. After that when I hooked him to start logs in the chute he'd begin trembling. To give him confidence I'd take him by the halter and lead him. But often he'd break free from my hand and tear off up the hillside with his eyes white and his tail in the air.

GRUB BOX

It took a full size wooden milk case to carry our lunch and it was so heavy that Andy and I nailed a leather strap to it and hung it over the horse's hames. We filled it with thick beef or pork sandwiches, hard boiled eggs, cans of fruit, cookies of 2 or 3 kinds, doughnuts, several pieces of cake and 3 pies. We always chose pies of different kinds so we could each have say, half a mince pie, half an apple pie and half a peach pie.

The cook watched us load the box one day and he said, "My God! Where do you put it?"

After our noon stuffing all we were able to do was sit in the shade two hours travelling to romantic South Sea Islands where we'd be chased by beautiful, seductive women with dark eyes and long, black hair. (We were both light haired.)

Inside of a month between the high elevation hill climbing and the eating, we could take a deep breath and snap buttons off our blue cotton work shirts. But the work suffered. We were to be paid according to the amount of logs we skidded. At the end of the job Len McCrea added up what logs we had skidded and shook his head sadly. He paid us off at day labor wages — $4 a day — and told us we were overpaid.

He said, "It's a good thing you're leaving. The way you two eat, the cookhouse would go broke."

CLAIM JUMPER BOULETTE

The first time I saw Boulette's grave was in 1939. I was running compass for timber cruiser Bill Schell and we almost walked over it. A syrup can with the front cut out was nailed to a tree and inside the can someone had scratched a corny poem — something about how this man broke the code of the West. I doubt if the can was over 5 years old.

In 1975 the moss covered and fast disappearing chute into which Wash Applegate rolled logs in 1927 almost touched a stump grave marker carved: Ed Bouley Died Aug. 21, '04. The French name is Boulette and pronounced "boolay" with accent on the last syllable. 20 feet southeast of this stump a 6 foot long mound marks the grave although the rock headstone placed there 15 years ago by Charley Scribner has been moved to the foot of the stump. The Mica-Grouse Cr.-Marble Cr. trail which Boulette was following runs due south at this point and passes 30 feet beyond the grave. On a big cedar nearby, now dead, someone long ago carved a cross facing south.

Boulette was probably shot from the trees east of the trail which offered plenty of concealment. Stories differ as to the number of men involved. One fanciful account claims he was felled by a barrage from so many rifles that the volley of lead killed a big tree.

Carving reads ED BOULEY DIED AUG. 21, '04. Johnny Freeman photo.

Boulette's Grave Marker 1975 B. R. photo

Lindsley, who was associated with Boulette, but was not a gunman, testified in court that at least 23 shots were fired and he ran away after begin hit in the arm.

Most all stories agree that Boulette was mounted on a fine horse and wore 2 guns. The horse was killed also and Boulette's body was piled crossways on the horse carcass. Some stories added a dog crossways on the pile, perhaps for artistic effect. But a dog would likely have smelled a waiting man or men in ambush and warned Boulette.

Oldtimers, including my father Walt Russell said Boulette got what was coming to him.

In 1934 I had moved my floathouse up into the Maries river and tied up near the beached floathouse of Ole O'Dean and John Olson. One day Ole mentioned that he had homesteaded on the Marble. But anytime I brought up Boulette in connection with Marble Creek, Ole O'Dean clammed up. When I was about to move downriver to Harrison, Ole asked me over for a farewell drink of homebrew that he and John had made.

It was dusk and they hadn't lighted the lamp in the house. Ole O'Dean was sitting in a wooden armchair with his swelled up feet on a nail keg. After 3 mugs of homebrew he sighed heavily and said, "You been askin' about Bouley. I'll tell you the story I heard.

"He had to be stopped. He had been braggin' around the saloons in Harrison and the Maries about how many homesteaders he had scared off their claims for that son of a bitch lumberman he worked for. Him and Tyler worked together.

"There was eleven homesteaders that trusted each other. These men met at the cabin of a woman homesteader who was gone. (Harold Theriault says the woman homesteader was Elsie Kirk and the Kirk cabin was on the main Marble-St. Joe trail where the trail left Bussel Creek. My father, Frank Theriault packed out the body of Gene Tyler, the second claim jumper, thought to have been killed at about the same time as Bouley.) They put 10 white beans and one black bean in a fruit jar and blowed out the light. Then they shook 'em up and drawed and left the cabin one at a time. That way no one would ever know who got the black bean and did the job."

"Bouley was shot with a .38-55 rifle. He got off his horse to get a drink. He was shot once in the middle of the back as he bent over and again after he fell. Then his horse was shot in the head. They say neither one of 'em suffered."

I said, "How about the other claim jumper, Tyler? Was he shot the same day?"

Gene Tyler's bones were discovered almost a year later by a timber cruiser following the township line between 2 East and 3 East of the Boise Meridian. He had been killed about a half mile north of Boulette on the south side of Eagle Creek. Boulette was killed on a branch of Eagle.

Ole sat looking silently at me through his metal rimmed spectacles. His heavy body seemed to recede into the distance. He slowly lowered his feet to the floor. He set his mug down and creaked upright.

"I don't know a God damn thing about Bouley," he said, harshly. "Nor about Tyler neither. I'm tellin' just what I heard."

Guy F. Russell, who homesteaded near Fernwood in 1902 and shortly afterward worked on a crew with Boulette driving his logs down the Maries river said, "Boulette was one of these show-off men. He wore a fancy sash around his waist and let everybody know what a good riverman he was but when it came to hard work he was lazy."

Henry Morin, timber cruiser for McGoldrick, Herrick and later for Russell & Pugh said, "My oldest sister married Louis Bond from which

Bond creek was named. Bill Theriault packed people up into the Marble country and he rented this hay meadow from my brother-in-law at the mouth of Bond Creek. I was visiting my sister one year and Boulette was hired by Theriault and Louis Bond to help put up the hay. From what I saw of him on the job he was an ignorant French-Canadian, a bragger and lazy.

He was a big eater at the table — crazy about biscuits. I put my sister up to putting epsom salts in the biscuits and he ate a whole panfull. He sure spent a busy day at the hay field.

"Ed Bouley and Gene Tyler was hired by the head of one of the biggest lumber companies to jump claims. Marble Creek was a hard place for homesteaders to stay in winter on account of being a long distance back and with deep snow. The claim jumpers would go to the Federal Land office in Coeur d'Alene and testify you'd been gone more than 3 months from the land and the land office would cancel your application. Then the claim jumper would file on it and would turn around and relinquish his claim to the big lumber outfit which would file Civil War Veteran scrip on it. The government gave civil war veterans scrip entitling them to 160 acres of land as a bonus. The big outfits had picked up the scrip for next to nothing."

YOU NEEDED A FUR HAT
Fred Jydstrup says he saw some fellows rustling for a job with Lavigne one time — Lavigne was French-Canadian and part Indian — and in the line were five guys. Four of them had fur hats which marked them as French-Canadians. In the early days French-Canadian could mean part Indian. Anyhow, Lavigne looked at man No. 1 with the fur hat. "We can use you." and 2nd man with the fur hat, "We can use you." He looked at the third without the fur hat, "I don't believe we can use you." and then to the other fur hats which he hired also. As the minus fur hat one turned away, he laughed and said, "I guess this is as close as I'll ever get to a wigwam."

Gazette-Record 2-13-20 — The body of Louie drowned in Marble Creek in 1913 was brought to St. Maries for re-burial. The creek was washing the bank away exposing the body. A tree nearby carried the name LOUIE carved on it.

From Oscar Blake's
THE LEGEND OF LOUIE
The first drive taken down the Marble was a short one, only about 3 miles from the mouth of the creek. This was a couple of years before my time in that part of the creek. It was on this drive that French Louie was killed. He was buried on the bank of the creek. This man was little known, but became a legend.

Every year when the rear of the drive went by I have seen as many as thirty slough-pigs march by this grave, all bareheaded, to lay their rock on the mound as solemnly as though it were the most delicate flower. Young men and men with snow-white hair...some with tears streaming down their cheeks.

I guess Jimmie Burns summed it up when I asked him why he was shedding tears.

"You see," he answered, "you or me might be the next one.....I'm just glad to be here to put my rock on Louie's grave again this year."

A man, well past eighty, had a cabin up Marble Creek right near the grave. His name was Jimmie Peterson and he made a good grade of corn liquor. One evening just before we started the drive in 1914, I went down to have a visit with him and to buy a gallon or so of his moonshine.

Jimmie told me about the drowning of French Louie in 1912. We sampled his new batch quite freely.

Suddenly Jimmie pointed downstream from his cabin. "See that windfall?" he whispered.

Although it was getting dark I saw the one he meant. It was about a hundred yards from the shack and extended toward the middle of the creek about twenty feet, and fifteen feet above the water.

"On moonlight nights, Louie walked to the end of that windfall with his peavy on his shoulder. I seen him jump straight up, click his heels together and spin his peavy 'round and 'round. The old Mick Spin. Then he throws the Saginaw Flip, the St. Croix.

"Stick around till morning and I'll take you down to that log and you can see Louie's calk prints on it and where his peavy had it all chewed up. Louie always sticks his peavy in it and turns his face upriver; stands that way for a minute with his hands up over his head, then he shoulders his peavy and walks back to the bank. When he does that I know he won't be out again that night."

Oscar Blake describes a log jam hauling:
The first big log jam in 1914 was about a mile and a quarter up Marble from the mouth of Homestead Creek at Dollars Camp 2 — about 3½ million feet.

I have seen log jams haul when the creek was nearly dry in front of them. They were pushed along by the tremendous force of millions of feet behind them. They would start very slowly and the noise was terrific as the jam moved, logs grinding over rocks and crashing together. It went faster and faster as it unraveled, until a man couldn't have kept up with the logs, running his best.

Shortly after we got rolling I saw Beef Mundy drown. He was a teamster, one of three who were breaking up a jam with their teams. At lunch time they started across the creek with their horses. Each skinner was riding a horse wading in water belly deep. There were large slippery rocks on the creek bed and Beef's horse stumbled and almost fell down.

Beef slid off into the water. I don't know why he didn't grab the harness or the horse's tail, but he didn't. The swiftwater took him downstream, and the last we saw of him was just as he went around the bend. He threw up one hand, as if waving goodbye.

We found him under a wing of logs — but he wouldn't be helping to break any more jams.

Homestead Creek, June 29, 1916
Mr. Arthur Olson, Deputy Sheriff
Marble Creek, Idaho.
Dear Sir:
   John Monday drowned up here on Marble Creek last night. He was riding one of the horses he was driving across Marble Creek on his way to camp. The horse stumbled and Monday in trying to get off, lost his balance and fell into the creek and was carried downstream and drowned before anyone could help him. He was about 55 years of age, 5 ft. 10 inches tall, weight 165 pounds. Had brown and gray hair and mustache and the top of one ear bit off. Understand he was devorced from his wife. His people are in Emporium, Penn., I understand and he is known back there. Enclosed please find his cheque and in separate package I will send his belongings.

Yours, Respt.
Carey & Harper
(signed)   W. D. Colburn

BEN STRAALSJOE SAYS:

The mill in St. Joe shut down June 31st, 1926 so I was out of a job. That fall I went to work up at Marble. I worked in Canyon Creek. They started the sleighs way back by Marble Mt. and landed the logs on rollways on that sandbar just before you come to the lower tunnel. They had a dam on Boulder just up in the box canyon and they used that water to splash the logs down Marble into the river.

We heard over in St. Joe about 6 o'clock that two fellows had drowned in Marble Creek and it was Jonas Delyea and Johnny Marquette. Babe Delyea afterwards showed me Jonas' watch and the letters for Jonas Delyea constituted the figures normally on a watch. J was in place of number 1 and O in place of number 2 and so on.

LUMBER PILER
When I was working at the St. Joe Mill I saw an incredible feat. This Swede lumber piler was young. He was 6 foot 3 with tremendous shoulders. He'd take one of those big 9 inch spikes, wrap a handkerchief around his hand and put the point of the spike against the top of a green 2 by 12 inch plank and shove it through. Then he'd take a hammer and bend over the head of the spike, hook his finger under it and drag it out again, slow motion.

We knew the Bruuns very well at St. Joe. Where George Bruun drowned was just back of the depot at St. Joe.

MOES
I knew 'Ling and Oscar and their sister and brother when when they lived in Coeur d'Alene before they moved to St. Joe. Old Albert Moe, their father was a great lumber piler and he got a good contract at St. Joe so he moved up there.

DAD PETERS
Dad Peters lived up Marble below the tunnel. About 1927 when I hiked back to Sullivans camp on Canyon Creek, Dad Peters was sittin' in the house and he hollered at me to come in. He was short and heavy set with a beard and medium brown hair. He had his foot on the table and it was red as a rose. Blood poison. Settin' a trap the winter before and the darn thing closed on his foot. All that summer he wouldn't go to a doctor or anything. So I told one of the fellows at the camp, "Gosh! That man's gonna die."

They finally came and got him but he died on the way over to Wallace.

HAROLD THERIAULT REPORTS:
PYLE'S RANCH
Railroad elevations: Avery — 2195, Calder — 2140, St. Joe City — 2130

Below Big Creek there's a railroad rock cut and below it a curve and then a flat between the railroad track and the river. That flat was the location of Pyle's Ranch. Above where the track now runs, Pyle had built a couple of 2 story bunkhouses.

Pyle was an old timer on the river and run a resort with cabins for tourists and fishermen and homesteaders like the one Randall did at the big hole at Goat Rock. My dad and I stayed at Pyles' in 1907 and kept our pack horses and saddlers in his barn. Pyle had been many years on that place. He brought supplies from Ferrell in poling canoes His wife was a wonderful cook.

When the swiftwater sternwheeler **Shoshone**, powered by two Stanley engines for the paddlewheel and a third for the capstan ran up there sometimes as far as Marble Creek, it stopped at Pyle's Ranch where Mrs. Pyle served dinner. (**The capstan was like a big spool set vertically on the bow of the boat and slowly turning under power to wind in a rope anchored to a piling or tree upriver.**) Generally though, the **Shoshone** turned around at Pyle's and went back downriver.

There were 3 bad stretches of water on the river that often required help from the capstan: Fitzgerald, McCormack's — opposite Mica Creek and Pyle's Chute which lay alongside Pyle's Ranch. Two other spots important enough to name were Honey Jones Riffle below Little Falls and the Jim Dandy Riffle below Moe's Big Eddy resort below Calder where they've built that roadhouse. The men poling the river with swiftwater boats named it that because it was a fast stretch and it took a lot of power on the poles to get up it with loads.

Another swiftwater boat was the **Swastika**. It was smaller than the Shoshone and had a gas engine and two sidewheels. At some time a piling had been driven at the head of Pyle's Chute and when the **Swastika** was loaded heavy and had bad water, it also had a capstan to pull itself through so it could take supplies to the Copper Prince Mine a mile further upriver. The **Swastika** wasn't much of a success. It was a tin boat.

Pyle's Ranch lasted till steel was built through in September of 1908 and then he pulled out. I think Pyle got some sort of settlement from the railroad because the 2 buildings on the upper side of the track were used for section houses afterward for a time.

JIM PETERS
Jim Peters was a water poler who homesteaded near the mouth of Marble Creek on Marble Creek. He poled people and freight upriver before the coming of the railroad.

Whenever Jim Peters came to St. Joe I'd always have his wonderful swiftwater boat at my disposal for fishing or just paddling. I think his boat was built by Slim Inman and Sam Ettings who had a shop on the riverbank at Ferrell. They built the best. Jim's boat with me in the stern is in that picture on page 79 in Ruby Hult's **Steamboats In The Timber**, the picture that shows the Ferrell Hotel.

Jim Peters probably also worked as boatman on log drives to keep busy. It was much later in the 1920s that he moonshined.

BERT RUSSELL CONTINUES:

TITLEY AT CLARKIA
I bought a quarter section of timber ground up a little creek near Mr. Titley. If I met him on the road with his team or walking I'd give him a cheery Hello but he'd only stare and keep moving. Then one day as I

came down the abandoned logging road from my ground I saw his tracks in the frost where he'd followed me a quarter mile and then gone back.

I wondered if he was being merely curious or if he resented me as an interloper and carried a gun.

Next time I walked in I climbed the road bank and lay behind a vine maple and waited. After a bit here came the old man with his head down, following my footprints. He wasn't carrying a gun. When he came to the spot in front of me where I had climbed the bank he stopped and looked puzzled. Then seeing where my prints had changed direction his eyes lifted and we were face to face at a distance of maybe 15 feet.

I said, "Hello, Mr. Titley. Nice day."

He said, "Oh!" and he whirled and walked swiftly down the road. After that he grunted when I spoke to him but he never followed me again.

My cousin, Lloyd Russell stopped one time at Titley's cabin door to ask direction. His knuckles hadn't touched the wood when the door flew open and there was a pitchfork against his belly. Titley backed him all the way out to the gate demanding to know what he wanted. Lloyd had no chance to explain and he didn't dare turn his back for fear he'd get harpooned in the behind.

FRANK TOM AND THE KNIFEE
I went into Frank Tom's place at Clarkia one time and one of those CC kids came in and went over to the counter and pointed his finger down through the glass and said, "How muchee knifee?"

Frank gave me a wink and walked over and he said, "My Lad! That'll cost you exactly a dollar and six bits."

The kid looked like he wished he was somewhere else.

DOC PLATT OPERATED ON HIMSELF
Back in 1917 and World War 1, Dr. Platt was turned down by the army for having a scrotal hernia. He wanted so much to go into the service with his friends that he went into his office, set up a mirror and operated on himself. That night his wife wanted to go to a movie and rather than admit what he had done, he went along. During the movie he fainted and was helped home. Right afterward DeMars, a Frenchman, and his wife went into the dark movie and his wife happened to sit on Platt's seat. When they discovered Mrs. DeMars white dress was covered with blood, DeMars said, "What's the matter old woman. You young again?"

MORE ON FLOATHOUSE

Harry Woodbury: During the time I was partners with Bill Belleau in the Parkline Supper Club, I'd see Nellie Cottingham fairly often. She'd come in with men friends and buy them a meal or stand her turn at buying drinks.

Harry and Pauline Woodbury 1980

I liked her. My wife and I had her to dinner a few times. You didn't have to worry about her doing or saying anything out of the way in front of the kids.

She owed a little bill at the Parkline when we went out of business. A year or two went by and she never mentioned it and neither did I. I thought she'd forgotten it.

One day my wife and I ran into her on the street in St. Maries.

"Say!" she said. "I still owe you a little bill." Then she grinned, "Business is so poor you'll have to take it out in trade."

I laughed, too. I said, "Well, Nellie, that'll just have to be one bill that never gets paid."

And it never was.

Calder packstring 1970. Jack Johnston, Bill Brewer & Mike Clifford

Russian Alec

I was

river hog

I was born 1890 in Russia. Kiev. Big city. I was 22 when I came here. Not here. I came to Canada. I get away from Russian Army. 1913. I stay 3 years and I got to go to Canadian Army. You can't get away. War! I got to go.

WORK HELD OFF ARMY

The czar and the English king is first cousins. And the czar give the king 250 million

Russian Alec 1975 at 85

dollars for build the Grand Trunk Railroad. Then many men go to work on the Grand Trunk. In those days, work by hand. Grubhoe and shovel. Building from Prince Rupert east to what the hell I can't think. Build it for years, you know. So they have a steam shovel and they drill the rocks by hand.

So Jesus Christ! You turn the drill and I hit a one and I turn the drill and you hit a one. Bang! Bang! Bang! Bang! You don't hit the hand. You get so perfect. Hecka yes. I work there 3 years before I come to the United States.

So in United States I can't get away from army. So dumb you can't talk English, you know.

So old country Russian officer come up. So says, "If you don't want to go to war here you go to old country. Gonna fight over there."

But that's why I leave old country. War is a son of a bitch over there.

So I go back to Canada. Work in coal mine. Up above Edmonton. Is bad. Work with pick over head.

So say we go back to United States. We go to see Russian friends in Spokane and we all go together to fight in old country.

They tell me, "You don't want to go to old country. Bad enough to be in war here. Is worse there."

God Damn! We bum around. So don't know what to do. Stay with friends in Peaceful Valley.

SAWING ON THE COEUR D'ALENES

I get job sawing for Winton on Little North Fork country. Above the Lieberg, Picnic Creek. They gotta chute and dams. Hard work but I don't mind.

Good camp after Wobbly strike 1917. Make 'em clean up. Furnish blankets. Before, you sleep on straw on floor like cows and pigs. Everybody sleep in one bed with canvas over. Full of lice and bedbugs. Have tent.

After strike then build camp 1918. Shower baths. Better grub.

Everything come from Coeur d'Alene by boat and then by pack horses.

Before that on Copper Creek drive we been drivin' for two six bits and board. Splash dams there before flume. 10 hours a day.

After this is 8 hours. Seven dollars a day if you stay through the winter. Six dollars if you don't.

I WAS RIVER HOG
I tell you 'bout drivin'. I drive the Little North Fork first and go back drivin' the main river from Pritchard to Cataldo. Bradford was running the drive on the Coeur d'Alene River. Mc Donald too.

Dunc Mc Donald is going to Marble Creek. So I go too. I been young them days. They are afraid water will get away any time after Christmas. Lots of horses too them days. Get logs out from the rocks. Rutledge logs. Nobody else. Herrick have his own drive. Logs go all the way out of the Marble and down the river to Chatcolet. Whole crew is driving Marble all of summers and half of winters. Young Crandall is big, husky guy. Before he die he got rheumatism, you know. Ice Water!

I drive on Marble 1918,'19,'20,'21. I drive with Murphy on the Joe sometimes too.

This last hitch before I been hurt I go on Coeur d'Alene River as far as Steamboat Rock where logs is dumpin' in for Ohio Match. Big Moe logging.

LOG SMASH ME

At Trout Creek landing I send for mechanic at camp to come fix jammer so I can unload trucks. Mechanic don't come so I unload six trucks by hand. Then truck comes in that has hit big rock in road and breaks one chain and logs is all spraddled out.

Jammer still won't start.

Truck driver say, "Why we can't unload by hand?"

Wherever I been workin' I couldn't stand another man with me get hurt. So I trip the chain. 18 foot log come off the face of the load. Hit me on the side of the head. Break 4 ribs and hand and leg and nose. Bends my fingers back on top of my wrist. Push my stomach out of place. Lost my left eye. I doctor 3 years.

WORK WITH CRANKY MAN

1954 I work for John Ankor. I'm carry box of dynamite out for road building.

Ankor he say, "You don't got much to do so you go down and help Three Finger Glover to shake 'em up big stump for bulldozer." Ankor say, "He alone, cranky. Him don't want nobody work with him."

I say, "I don't know him cranky."

So I go there. I'm workin' fine. Helpin' him. He drillin' deep hole down under stump into bedrock.

He send me after 14 foot drill. I don't ask him what he want long drill like that for.

I bring him dynamite too.

He put stick of dynamite in hole and push him with drill.

I say, "Jesus Christ! Don't do that. In old country I know better than that. In Canada, too. It's dangerous!"

He say, "I know it's dangerous but I do it all the time."

I say, "What's the matter with that stick to push it?"

Powder Monkeys carry tamp sticks of varying lengths for packing powder into the bottom of the hole. Steel can set it off from a spark or concussion.

He say, "If I push him with stick the hole plug up."

I say, "Jesus Christ! If I know you do that..." I drop the drill. I start to walk away.

He say, "You goin' stay away all day? We do that all the time. Help me push it down!"

So I get hold to push. Then he get behind me.

DYNAMITE BLAST
When it go off it blow me up the hill in the rocks. Blow off all my clothes. I even have some money in my shirt pocket. I never find that. It don't hurt him. He is behind me, the Son of a Bitch! Nobody ever find the drill.

Give me shot. I want some drink and ambulance bring me, I think, to St. Maries.

Come with straw. Push in my mouth. Give me drink.

Three Finger Glover he say to Doctor. "I hurt, too."

"Where you hurt?" Doctor say. "How far you been from dynamite?"

Three Finger go to bed and stay there 3 days.

Doctor say, "You can go home. You got nothing wrong."

I bet you that Son of a Bitch hide his head behind me. He don't get a scratch.

DOCTOR KIDDIN' ME
Second time doctor come, he kiddin' me, that Son of a Bitch, because I can't see.

He say, "You know the difference between woman and man?"

I say, "Sure!"

He say, "Feel her hand."

I forget name of nurse but I know she is married so I feel hand for ring. I say, "No ring. Is man."

Doctor say, "You don't know difference between woman and man."

They laugh and have hell of a good time with me. That little one is cute. She pick them rocks out of me. Still some rocks in there.

She say, "You come up and meet my husband when you get out."

1951 Log hurt my left eye. Now dynamite hurt my right eye.

Doctor say he got to cut off that cataract and get them rocks. The Xray show rock still in there.

The Specialist in Spokane clean some that time with kind of rubber fork. I see myself in lookin' glass.

I see little bit now. Walk down to Old Town with cane.

Eye Specialist in Spokane gonna operate on me now anytime I go in. But I put it off. I waitin' on my medicare.

Stella Bottrell: Russian Alec was the shiek of the town. He would come in loaded with money. He'd let out a yell and throw the money on

the bar. If I was there he'd grab me and kiss me and Rusty'd come and knock him away.

Fred Jydstrup: Kulchak, that's his name. His cursing don't mean nothin'. I like Alec. He's honest as the day is long.

Alec worked by brute strength. Up Mica Creek in '21 he didn't want to swamp the logs out. He'd go in the brush, drive a dog into the log. Then he'd grab the chain and wrastle the son of a bitch out to the road. He didn't know his own strength.

Big Alec had two Russian pals on the drive. They played a game throwing peavies 40 feet into the end of a log. Good men on the water! One of them I saw take a crap going downriver in the current. He stuck his peavy upright in the log, hung his hat and his jumper on it and finished the job before reassembling himself.

Interviewed at St. Maries 1975

Rutledge Camp 5 on Hobo Creek 1920

Clyde Shay

Gypo Logger & Stull Maker

A verbal contract for 19 years

Clyde Shay, 85 in 1973

Charles White and John P. White right, founder of Whites Shoe Shop in Spokane, Mary White Shay, twin of J. P. and mother of Clyde Shay.

I was born in West Virginia in 1888 and came to St. Maries in 1907. My mother's twin brother, John Porter White, born in 1860 was already here. He come from Bridgeport, West Virginia to Bonners Ferry then Wardner and in 1902 he came to St. Maries with his tools and set up a shoeshop where Robinson's repair shop is now.

I stayed at his house because he was a relative, although he came from a different area in West Virginia and I hadn't ever seen him.

MAKING SHOES

J. P. White had one man in the shop besides himself. His father — born about 1820 — had taught him the White Last which used soft leather in the toe and was easy on the feet. In West Virginia they skidded hardwood logs with horses so he had learned to make calked boots.

He didn't have any machines. Every day, come hell or high water, old J. P. made one pair of shoes by hand besides his cobbling and repair. The repair was his bread and butter. The shoes was his profit. And old man White wouldn't overlook careless work in himself or in a man he hired. He was going to sell that shoe to somebody and it had his name on it and he wanted to be proud of it.

FIRST CALKED BOOTS

Old J. P. told me if I'd go out and help one of the boys cut some wood while I was waitin' around to find a job, he'd make me a pair of calked boots. He measured me and patched up the last with pieces of leather for my high arch. He put another piece of leather on the last and shaved it down for my long heel. He had started the system of keeping people's measurements on file so they could write from anywhere and have boots made and sent to them. As he worked he put my measurements on a paper to go in that file, too.

Say! When I put those new shoes on and started down to the river-bank — I was 19 years old and had never known a shoe could fit like this — I looked back to see if I was making tracks. I couldn't believe I was walking on the ground.

White sold lots of calked boots in St. Maries. In those days when lumberjacks came to town they paid their bills before they went out and got drunk. Then they charged a new pair of boots when they went back to the woods.

J. P. White had 6 kids — 3 boys and 3 girls. Two of his boys, Otto and Orpheus became shoemakers.

About 1915 old J. P. moved to Spokane and established the **White Shoe Shop.**

OTTO BOUGHT OUT THE SPOKANE SHOP

J. P. White's son, Otto, had homesteaded and set up a little sawmill on the southhand side of the Fighting Creek road just off the Coeur d'Alene to Worley highway back in 1907. About 1915 he set up a shoe shop in Kellogg.

Old J. P. died in 1937 but sometime after 1920 Otto sold out in Kellogg and bought his dad's shop in Spokane. Otto had vision. He had some good men and wanted to keep them. He made an arrangement under which men working in the Spokane shop could buy stock and become co-owners. Then in October 1972, Otto died at the age of 91. His wife came around and sold his interest to those men. Must be 15 or 20 men own it now.

Thomas Shay in 1926. Ran the St. Maries Ferry 1907-1910 & 1918-1928   Shay boys Joe, Ed and in the stern Clyde, crossing the Joe 1910.

DAD RAN THE ST. MARIES FERRY

My own family moved to St. Maries shortly after I arrived. There was Ed, born in '85, Joe, in '91, Fred, in '95 and Orpha in '98.

My dad, Thomas Shay ran the ferry 1907 to 1910 and again from 1918 to 1928. Dad and my brother Ed and I all took homesteads at the top of what's now called Shay Hill above Sweeney's Landing. My two brothers and sister were too young to homestead.

I went up into the mine district and worked for the Bunker Hill as miner, motorman and at other underground jobs till 1917 when I went into the service — World War 1. My sister Orpha died in the flu epidemic in 1918 while I was away. After that I'd go to the mine and work again when things were slack. But in 1925 I just couldn't see where I was getting ahead and quit the mine entirely.

HAULING FOR VALENTINE-CLARK

When I came home from the service in 1919 the Valentine-Clark Pole Co. owned a box factory down on 10th Street. They had decked 2 or 3 million feet of logs in the Benewah the previous fall and didn't have snow that winter to haul them out.

Fulton Cook asked me if I'd go out there and take charge. He said, "We'll get some Velie and Diamond T trucks out of Spokane if you'll see to hauling the logs out."

People had been fooling around with those heavy, solid tired trucks but this would be the first time anybody had really tried to haul a lot of logs with them. Some fellow named Morris in Hells Gulch had 4 Mack Trucks. I went up to the Morris job and drove one of them. The trucks were heavy and cumbersome and didn't have much in the way of brakes. To keep them from getting out of control and running away at the top of that steep Hells Gulch hill you'd plow your right hand log into the clay bank and get up on the seat and set both feet against the brake. The Mack had a long handle for an emergency brake.

But it proved you could haul logs with a truck even though they had drawbacks. I remember one of the Macks had only a hundred yards to go to the landing and one of those heavy steel tires ran right off of it.

St. Maries to Fernwood road at top of Thorn Creek Hill lined with big white pine. 1925

So Valentine & Clark bought Diamond T and Velie trucks and I worked for them hauling out of the Benewah to Sweeney's landing below St. Maries. From there the logs were towed up to the box factory. At that time there wasn't any road downriver from St. Maries on the south side.

FINDS A GYPO JOB
Blackwell Lumber Co. had some timber they wanted logged up on the hill by the Halfway House. I asked them if they'd let me log it.

They said, "If you can get Tom Hay to go in with you on the job it's all settled."

I had done some work for Tom and logged some of Tom's timber and he thought I knew my business. So we became a partnership, Hay & Shay. I've got to give credit to Tom Hay for getting me started.

OUR BACKERS
We sat down and listed the banks and people of the town that would let us have money if we needed it. And we listed the merchants. In the early days a good gypo's credit was good all through the towns. You'd charge all the supplies you needed for another year and pay the bills as they came in. That's what kept gypos going like Curly Gaskill, Oscar Brown and Jim Nevins. Maybe we didn't make much more than money to feed our families but we could get any equipment or groceries we needed.

WE HIRED GOOD MEN

To make money logging you've got to think about your labor costs. We built lots of roads so men and horses didn't have far to skid logs. And you've got to use the best men you can find. We never did send to Spokane for men. Plenty of good men lived right around St. Maries: like Johnny Procopio, Albert Larson, Wash White, George Haas — men whose word was good and who could be trusted to scale what they handled. Some of these men could cut or skid or drive truck for you or do most any other job. Like Dave Cardwell. We had a little horse jammer to load trucks with. If it broke a line down in the woods he'd splice it on the spot and in no time be goin' again. And you've got to have men that are easy on horses and riggin' and trucks and careful about each other. You don't want men getting hurt or killed.

FREAK ACCIDENT

We killed one man in a freak accident — Harold Bridgeman of Harrison. He worked on the loading jammer. The truck was backing in to get loaded. We didn't know till later but off maybe 200 feet from the skidway someone had fell a tree that had grazed a hundred foot high buckskin tamarack and loosened its hold on the ground.

I said, "Harold! Let's hook the crotchline on that long log — it was 18 feet — so we won't have to fool with it when the truck gets into place."

He took one end and I took the other. There wasn't a breath of air stirring. As I went to set my hook I saw out of the corner of my eye something coming out of the air. I blinked and ducked. It was that hundred foot high tamarack falling without any warning.

The top struck Harold in the left side over the kidney. His spine wasn't broken. He was conscious and said his arm hurt. I think it was the shock that got him. Nowadays he might have been saved.

Hauling on hard tires in the Benewah 1928. Front truck is a White, 2nd is a Mack. Seats only-no cabs.

Shay trucks loaded with stull for the Day Mines. 1942

STULL BUSINESS

I logged with Tom Hay 6 or 7 years. Then came the Depression and nothing doing. Along about 1936 World War 2 was coming. The mining industry began to stir. I'd sell a few loads of stull to some of the little mines. Stull is peeled logs. Red fir is preferred but some tamarack is accepted. The mines use stull for posts underground. Peeling makes them last longer. Nowadays they chemical treat the wood to make it last still longer.

I had a requisition for 3 loads of stull to the Day Mines. The general superintendent was there when I unloaded the last load.

He said, "You got any more like this?"

"I've got more or I've got timber to make more."

He said, "Just keep hauling. Any size you got."

IF WE CATCH YOU CHEATING!

I stopped at the office to talk to Henry Day. I said, "The superintendent says for me to bring any size, any amount. I've got to put on 8 or 10 men peeling timber. I can't stand to get shut down with a lot of peeled timber on my hands."

Day said, "If we have to slow down or quit, you can bring all the pieces you got and we'll take them."

"What about the scale. Who is to tally my loads?"

He said, "We haven't got anybody on the dump to scale it. Can't you tally it as you load?"

I said, "Sure! I always tally it for my own information."

"Then you tally it and hand the office the slip."

I got up to leave.

Clyde Shay and his two sons, Tom and Fred. 1937

Henry Day says, "If we can't trust your tally we don't want you up here. If we catch you cheatin', you're gone."

We never did have anything in writing. That verbal contract was all I had for 19 years. I hauled to the Dayrock, the Tamarack, the Hercules and the Galena.

HIGHER PRICES IN TWO WARS

When the World War 2 rationing and price regulation came in they raised stull 20 percent right across the board. Then in the Korean War they come up with another 15 percent.

In 1967 everything shut down. I retired in this house with some tree covered lots alongside to remind me of the woods where I spent most of my life.

Interviewed at St. Maries, April 1973.

Rose Tom

Petite and charming

I born San Francisco, 1894. I eighty-five year old. My dad come from China when he was a young guy. I never know what my mother look like. She die when I little one. My dad work in store. He get other woman to raise me in her home. I tell you, I got a good one! That woman no give me enough to eat to get strong or

Rose Tom at 85, 1979

nothing. You know how kids hungry. I nibble a little. She lick me. I don't dare tell my dad because she licking so much I afraid.

Rose spoke only Chinese till she was 17 which prevented her tongue learning to form English Rs and Vs. Her mispronunciation is given occasionally because it is part of her charm.

SHIP TO HONG KONG

When I'm nine years old my dad take me on a big ship. Oh Boy! Got 3 smokestacks — big ones! Long trip on ocean.

In Hong Kong this woman she 18 years old. Got poor father. My dad pay her father dowry $800 Hong Kong dollars. That maybe $200 American dollars. You know how Chinese tie the feet? She can't walk much. Always go in taxi. Lotsa Chinese women can't walk.

My father marry this woman. Bring her back to San Francisco. She get pregnant. Have baby.

We live in 3rd floor apartment. Never see nothing green except in flower pot. My stepmother good to me. Even after I grow up I never tell my father about that other woman that lick me and don't give me enough to eat. It only make him feel bad.

But I never go to school. Old timers that time no care if you go to school or not. Oh No! Terrible. I know banker there he no write his own name. Carry his money in his pocket.

I live with Chinese people. Never talk English. But at least I learn to write my own name.

FRANK TOM VERY AMERICAN

Frank was born in Missoula, Montana. His mother had 13 children. His father worked as a janitor in the bank. Got only a dollar a day. It used to be with old timers all the kids had to work.

When Frank was only 12 years old he was washing dishes in a restaurant. He was so short they had to give him a stool to stand on so he could reach the sink.

My father was a good friend of Frank's father. Every year he loaned Frank's father money to buy vegetable seed for a big truck garden out by the cemetery in Missoula.

GOOD LUCK MONEY

Every year when Frank's father come to San Francisco to get the money he bring Frank and his brother, too. It is Chinese style to give Good Luck money when somebody visit you — like Americans give candy to the kids. My dad give each boy maybe four-bits or a dollar. Every year my dad gives away 'bout $40 to kids. (Laughs) He say, "It good luck for them but not good luck for me."

I know Frank and his brother and his father so one year I go to Missoula. Stay with Frank's family for vacation. I seventeen years old.

MARRY AMERICAN STYLE

Frank ask me American style to marry him. But Frank come to San Francisco and my family celebrate Chinese style. Just my family. Some live in San Francisco. Some in Arlington. Some in Honolulu. Maybe 80 people go to restaurant and have cater meal. My father have to pay for it. Cost lotsa money. Oh Yes!

My husband begin to teach me English and educate me. We go to Chicago to visit his brother. That only time I scare in a plane. Coming into Chicago our plane fly low over the lake big like the ocean.

I look out the window and I think, "Maybe we gonna get wet!" Then I think, "Oh well! You only got to die once."

That time I no work. I pregnant. Frank waiting table. He learn about restaurants.

COOK ON WORK TRAIN

Then we come back to Idaho with our daughter, Myrtle. Frank does carpenter work on a Milwaukee work train and I work in cooking car. Maybe 6, 7 sleeping cars for men. We stay on the train maybe 3 years. Live different places between Spokane and Avery.

We run Club Cafe in St. Mellies (St. Maries) near the depot in 1921. The lumberjacks say I good cook. I tell you how to get pie crust nice brown. Before you put him in the oven you wash the pie face in milk. You take Kleenex and rub it all over with milk. Not cream. Cream is brown too fast.

BURNED OUT

We go to St. Joe. Big mill up there. Have restaurant and rooms and card room. Lotsa work. We burn out. We start again. Have good store — everything. It sets on posts lower side of the street. Part basement below and one end no basement at all. Open.

One night I wake up. I don't know what. Hear crack! Oh God! I tell you fire start where is open underneath. Everything burn up. Frank think someone burn us out. Two times is enough.

Frank and Rose Tom with daughter Myrtle 1921 at Club Cafe near St. Maries depot.

Clarkia in the 1930s

BOWLING LOTSA FUN

We move to Clarkia 1928. Have store and restaurant and upstairs rooms. We have good friends there: Bill and Anna Currie, Mrs. Avery, wonderful ladies. We on bowling team. Lotsa fun. Belle Walker and Roland.

Oh Yes! Call Clarkia Hollywood down below where is wild. (Laughs)

Bowling Team about 1945 in front of Larson's Service Station at Clarkia. Jim Cunningham, Rose Tom, Rhea Cunningham, Belle Walker, Frank Tom, Beulah Larson, Roland "Spike" Walker face almost hidden, Gene Sackwell-depot agent, Paul Larson and Earl Anderson.

Roland Walker 1979 who with his wife Belle, operated the Santa store 35 years.

Frank Tom Store & Rooms Upstairs 1928

I like it go by air. No get tired. I say I feel like going. I got a good husband. He say, "I get ticket and everything ready." Oh! He a wonderful husband. I go to Washington, D. C. to see my daughter Myrtle working there. I go to Honolulu so high in air — can no see nothing — to visit my family. Honolulu O.K. for short time. I get breaking out on my neck and legs. Look like the measles. Too much salt air. Honolulu not good for long time. My brother take strawbelly (strawberry) over there. Won't grow. Too much salt.

I leave Honolulu 11 o'clock at night and over Seattle 5 o'clock in the morning alledy (already). They give you eat. Good stuff.

Frank died 1951. He is buried in Missoula by his father and mother. I will be buried there, too.

Myrtle's boy, Ronnie Kienbalm is 26 now. He is mechanic in Spokane. A fine boy.

DAUGHTER MYRTLE TOM KIENBALM CONTINUES THE STORY:
People say Dad was a graduate of the university at Missoula but he only finished the 8th grade. He was a real bug for reading and this gave people the belief that he had a higher education.

A lot of people think Mother is Japanese because she and I are built shorter and smaller. But Mom came from San Francisco where we have many Chinese relatives.

FEEDING THE TROUT
When Mother and Dad got married they went back east to Chicago where my uncle lived. I was born in Chicago in 1915.

Then, when I was 2 we came back to Avery and Dad worked in the restaurant for a year. I fed hamburger to those big trout in that concrete pond at the depot and people got off the passenger trains to watch them eat.

In about 1918 Dad had the Club Cafe near the depot in St. Maries. Mother worked herself to a frazzle there for years.

ST. JOE AND BURNOUTS
In about 1923 we moved to St. Joe where Dad and Mother had a cafe, hotel, poolhall and barber shop on the same side as Kickbush's store only further down toward the depot. It burned. Then they rebuilt in about 1924. The place was so busy and full you could hardly get in the door. Pinochle, cribbage, pool tables.

The flume came down Bond Creek then. We used to sit on the track and watch the logs dive from the flume into the St. Joe River hour after hour.

Then we burned out a second time. Dad said that was enough for him and we left.

They bought a store, restaurant and rooms upstairs at Clarkia in 1928. Dad and Mother never let anyone go hungry. He'd let lumberjacks have calked boots and wool shirts and mackinaws and let them pay later or maybe never. People came from way over in eastern Washington to buy from him and from Coeur d'Alene, Elk River, St. Maries. Sheepmen came in and spent a hundred dollars at a time. Lumberjacks didn't care about price so long as they got the best quality.

RUNAWAY CAR
The Incline was running then. An old lumberjack that always came to visit Dad worked there as a brakey. An empty car broke loose and ran away. He stayed on and tried to brake it. It went so fast it jumped the curve and broke his leg so the bone stuck right out. They brought him to our place for the ambulance to take to St. Maries.

A lot of tough guys come through Dad's place. If they got drunk and belligerent he'd say, "Here! I'll give you a dollar. Buy yourself a dinner." And that usually got around them.

STICK-UP

One night between 9 and 10 o'clock when the men had gone to bed in the rooms upstairs, a man pulled a gun on Dad down in the store. Mother and I could hear him talking to Dad and I was going to take a .22 Colt and go down. I was afraid he'd hurt Dad. But Mother wouldn't let me. The guy got away with $800. They never caught him.

Dad was almost crushed in a car accident in Seattle in the 1940s and lost an eye so he wore an artificial eye for years. He never was so good after that.

One time in Portland somebody yelled at him, "You're on a one way street!"

A cop stopped the car at the end of the block and Dad shook his head and said, "No speak English." The cop let him get away with it and that tickled Dad.

SWEDE JOHN AND A SHOTGUN

Clarkia had some interesting old bachelors. Swede John was a great, big lumbering guy. He kept a bunch of goats and lived in a tumbledown shack up by Cats Spur landing. He'd sit on the bed and fry everything. Dirty.

When the state wanted to widen and straighten the highway they needed right-of-way through a little point of land that belonged to him.

Dad went up there to talk with Swede John and, as well as John knew Dad, he met him at the door with a shotgun.

Swede John sat on the road bank for days with that shotgun. They finally talked him into giving in — told him he'd go to jail if he didn't.

DICK TITLEY AND HIS MINE

Mr. Titley had a homestead a couple of miles up the road toward Gold Center. He had a prospect hole between his buldings and the road. He didn't want anyone to get near that mine. If you went across his meadow to fish in the river he watched you every minute.

His nephew bought a 40 or 50 foot trailer and moved it in there for Mr. Titley. First thing you know Mr. Titley was back in the old shack again. That shack had the logs rotted out on the upper side and made a kind of a dirt bench inside. His dog had dug a hole right out through the dirt floor under the door. Talk about lack of sanitation! But Mr. Titley lived to a ripe old age in all that dirt and never went to a dentist or doctor.

When Dad got cancer of the throat I flew back from Washington, D. C. to be with him when he started the cobalt treatments. It was very painful for him. He died in 1950 at the age of 56.

Interviewed Coeur d'Alene, 12-1-79

Irene Trummel

Poultices of Navy Beans

Irene Trummel at 84 with son Boyd, 63, in 1978

I was born Irene Scudley, Nov. 2, 1894 in the Indian Territory that later became Oklahoma. Scudley comes from Pennsylvania Dutch. My dad entered the big land rush and took up some land but there was no water. So then he tried Kansas.

I can remember driving from Oklahoma across the line and a cyclone had taken the roof off a two story farmhouse and we could see the beds standing in there.

Then we went to Colorado awhile. It was hard times. All of our neighbors and friends went to Idaho and sent good reports back. Dad went first and sent for us. In 1900 we came by train to Athol, Idaho. I was six years old.

There was a big sawmill at Athol and tall, huge pine trees everywhere. Dad run a butcher shop.

My dad and mother separated when I was 10 years old. My mother took the two of us girls to Davenport, Washington. Dad took the boy. Mother run a boarding house. She did nursing. She did dress making. She worked for the telephone company — any way to make a living for us.

Then she got married to a barber and moved to Valley, Washington. I was 15 and in the seventh grade. At Valley, all of us young girls went down to the depot to meet the trains. That was the highlight of the day. I'd see the 24 year old telegraph operator, Oscar Trummel. He was a tall, good looking man with dark hair and blue eyes. Very handsome.

He played violin for the dances, too. I went to the dances. I was old for my age. He always took time out for one dance — and it would be with me.

We got married in 1910.

Oscar got bumped off his job at Valley by someone with greater seniority. We moved to Oroville. As telegraph operator, Oscar made $80 a month. And we built a house on that. The lumber that was in our

Irene Scudley age 12. 1906.

house was shipped from Albert Culver's mill at Valley. Oscar did a lot of the work himself but he did hire one old carpenter to help. It was a long time before it was finished. But Oscar never would buy anything he didn't have the money to pay for.

I was 16 when Jack was born. It seemed natural to me to have a baby and be responsible for it. I didn't go to school any more but I always did like to read. And life educated me.

A railroad telegrapher with more seniority bumped Oscar off his job at Oroville. We moved to Okanogan. Lost that job. He got another job at Nighthawk right on the Canadian line. After 3 or 4 months he decided we were going to be able to stay there so we moved our furniture up there and rented a house. Just after that, someone bumped him out of his job at Nighthawk.

Oscar said with a family he didn't want to be moved from pillar to post so we went back to Oroville where he could learn the barber trade from my stepfather who was a barber there.

THE MUMPS

Oscar caught the mumps in the barber shop. He kept on riding a bicycle back and forth to work. He wouldn't listen to my mother and he wouldn't listen to me. He was in bed then for a whole month and nearly died.

But my mother helped me and the doctor had us make poultices of navy beans. He had us cook them till they were real tender and spread them between two cloths. We put them on as hot as Oscar could stand it. When we'd take the cloth off, the beans would be just green from poison.

Then Jack and Robert got the mumps, too. I didn't get them — I had them when I was little.

To make onion poultices, you cook 'em so they're not real well done, then put them between flannel and lay them on the chest. You could blister from it if you weren't careful.

Robert had asthma so bad. An old Indian woman told me to put dry mustard between flannel and quilt it in. I made a vest of it and Robert wore it day and night.

The boys never had scarlet fever or smallpox. And they never had shots for those diseases then, either.

One evening when Jack was quite small and it was time for him to go to bed, I went out in the yard to get him. When I took hold to pick him up I found his arm was broken. We never knew how he broke it. And he hadn't been crying or anything.

Oscar worked late and didn't get home till 10 o'clock. We didn't have any horse and buggy. Oscar carried Jack to the doctor who put a cast on the arm. It wasn't long till Jack had the cast pounded to pieces and needed another.

Oscar's brother, Frank, wrote from St. Maries of an opportunity to buy this barber shop with a man named Council. The barber shop also had the agency for the Spokesman-Review.

When we moved to St. Maries, Robert was 18 months old. This would have been the middle of 1915. Boyd was born in St. Maries in 1915.

The Spokesman-Review cost subscribers 75 cents a month. Oscar delivered the papers himself.

When we came to St. Maries, Platt had his big hospital on the corner of 2nd and College. The I.O.O.F. Hall had been built somewhere around 1908 and they had a post office in one part of the street level and an overall factory in another part. The Robinson brothers have made a garage out of it now. 1978.

A little later, Mr. Council sold out to Oscar and moved to Spokane where his girl friend lived.

Frank Trummel ran the Table Supply and then sold out to Otto Moseley.

Then Oscar bought a poolroom that had a barber shop in it where the Husky Service Station is now at First and College. The poolroom burned down and we didn't have a cent of insurance.

Lumbermens Hotel about 1912.

The Lumbermens Hotel across the street had a barber shop. Early pictures show it had 3 stories but when we came to St. Maries the third story had burned and they lowered the roof and it was only two stories high. We bought it about 1917.

FROM WASHBOARD TO WASHER

I had been washing on a board with 2 tubs and a wringer in between ever since I was first married. My 3 boys wore long, black stockings and I'd have to rub the feet because they'd get sweaty and smelly. I didn't know how to rub right. I'd get blisters.

Then the man that sold the electric Maytag Washer with those square tubs brought one for me to try. Oscar bought it right then. I kept it in the kitchen. That way it wasn't so far to carry water from the wood range. And OH! It was such a help. It made quite a pleasant job out of washday.

One summer business was bad. The lumberjacks didn't pay their rent when they come to town. We didn't have any money to pay for laundry so I washed all the sheets and pillowcases for the hotel. And I had to iron them. People nowadays can't begin to imagine what it's like hanging washing out in the dust or in the icy cold.

CHILDREN BORN AT HOME

All my children were born at home. A doctor came to the house. And I nursed all three of them. Robert had asthma. I nursed him till he was 18 months old.

REFRIGERATOR

To keep food from spoiling we had a box with a screen over it in the cool basement. I had to run down the stairs and back up carrying food. Then we bought an ice refrigerator. Hughes cut ice on the river every winter and stored it in a big icehouse at the mouth of the St. Maries River. They delivered it all through the hot season.

DISCIPLINE FOR THE BOYS
One time when my boys went swimming, I said, "Now, the mill whistle blows at 12 o'clock. You come home."

They were 10 or 12 years old. They didn't come and they didn't come. I went down to the barber shop and told Oscar.

So we started out in the car, Cherry Creek way, and here we saw them coming. There was another little boy with them.

I said, "Never again! Don't you do that EVER again!"

And they didn't. They were easy to manage without punishment. I don't remember Oscar ever whipping any of them. But they knew Dad's word was law.

LADIES SEWING CLUB
I joined the Sewing Club in 1925 when my boys were 10, 12, and 14 years old. We met twice a month at one anothers' homes. We limited it to 8 housewives because it was too hard to entertain more than that number. We sewed and quilted. One would find a good pattern and some more of us would make a quilt of that same pattern. At Christmas time we'd make a flour sack dish towel for each member so each one had 8 dishtowels for the year.

One time when I had the Sewing Club at my house — at the southeast corner of First and College — we always had a big garden, I had a tub full of green beans. The other members helped stem them and pack the jars for canning.

The Depression in the lumber industry got so bad by 1928 that we had to close the Lumbermens Hotel. Then the bank uptown failed. We didn't have a lot of money in it but we lost what little we had.

In 1931 Oscar went to Harrison and borrowed $3,000 from Cathcart and set up a service station by making over the old O'Gara restaurant building. He ran it 13 years. It burned in 1944 and the Lumbermens Hotel burned with it. Then Oscar went right across the street where the old poolhall and barber shop had burned and set up another Trummel Service Station with his brother Frank's help. He ran that station for 18 years and it's still there. On the northeast corner of First and College. We sold it in 1965.

In 1962 something happened to Oscar. He'd fall down and he couldn't get up. Dr. Raybuck sent him to Spokane for tests. They told him that he had Parkinson's Disease — the rigid kind, not the shaking kind — and there was no cure for it.

I hated to sell our house with the big garden, but it got to be too much — and all the noise of trucks and traffic. I thought if we could get away it would be better for Dad. So we moved up on Jefferson.

Oscar would go along and then get worse and we'd have to take him to the hospital. Then he'd come home again. Oscar finally had to go to the nursing home the last 18 months. We had financial help from Medicare but after 30 days in the nursing home it ran out and the rest we had to pay at $310 a month. They say it's now $600. We had our savings and a little interest and we got along. Oscar died July 3, 1970.

I still get along. I haven't asked for charity. I get social security but you couldn't begin to live on social security.

I just hope I can go to sleep in my chair like Mrs. Smylie did. She lived up the river. And not have to go to the nursing home. I know I'd just hate it. Because there are so many people up there that don't know anything.

Of the Sewing Club, only Elsie McLaughlin and I are left in town. Mamie Thibault lives in Harrison. Mrs. Aikman in Bremerton. The other members were Martha Rector, Inez Glidden, Anna Berglund, Lena Briscoe and Myrtle Frail.

Interviewed at St. Maries, Feb., 1978

Rolling down logs for McGoldrick drive at Slate Cr. 1912
Courtesy Mrs. Dave Nelson

Wash White

Yellowjackets thicker'n the hubs of hell!

I was born in 1890. My dad was a logger and cedar man at Pestahigo, Wisconsin. When I was 20 or 21 they put me on the driving crew.

My wife and I got married and looked at a house there. I said, "We're never gonna pay any rent. that's out!" I asked the owner how much he wanted.

He said, "$50."

I said, "Where do you get your water?"

He said, "I go to the neighbors."

That was a town as big as St. Maries and no water system. A lot of people there water witched wells. My wife's uncle could do it. It takes a man with a lot of electricity in his system. I had a driller come and we had the best water on that street. 93 feet deep.

THE WOBBLIES

I come to St. Maries in 1919. The Wobblies had struck in 1917 and did every ornery thing they could. One time they asked me to join the Wobblies.

I said, "Shucks, Man! That ain't nothin' in the first place. And nothin' from nothin' leaves nothin'!"

SAWED AND FILED

I sawed with some mighty good men in this country. If a man wasn't a good one I just wouldn't saw with him. Up on the Marble for Rutledge I had a partner named Heinball from Montana. He was a big husky man. Wasn't a lazy bone in his hide. He had a little ranch and needed money. We got a dollar a thousand sawing white pine. We sawed 21,000 a day and the boss allowed me half a day's wages for filing 6 crosscut saws after supper. I got $10.50 for my share of the sawing and another $2, or a half day's wages for the filing. Good money. But they should have paid me $3 for the filing. Doggone it!

I fought fire on the Marble in 1919. Only man that got hurt fightin' fire was a man from Spokane. The yellowjackets was thicker'n the hubs of hell and a bee stung him right on the end of the penis. He swelled all out of shape. That man throwed up all over the place. Sickest man I ever see in my life. They took him out on a saddle horse. I don't know whether he died or not.

I worked for Art Reddekopp's father, Reed Reynolds, Blackwell and McGoldrick and for Tom Hay and Clyde Shay when they was together. I worked on Mica for Cole.

Working in the woods I've had several close calls from limbs that fall when one tree brushes another. Neighbor of mine in Wisconsin he had Oregon on his mind and he was buckin' logs. Limb fell and struck him across the head. He never knew what hit him.

I was sawing with Cecil George. We had the saw buried and a limb hit right across the crack between us.

Cecil looked around and he said, "If that one had hit one of us on the head...! From this on I'm gonna look for limbs!"

SEARCHING FOR THE SECRET

Fellow I worked with in 1934 said he had some relatives that was missionaries in Egypt. When they come back they told him about a woman offering a million dollars for the secret of embalming those mummies. There was a chemist from London, England that was trying to do it but he give it up. I think the Egyptians started on reptiles and then went from them to people. They have to seal them up or they deteriate so if you go to look at King Tut they seal it right up again.

Well Sir! I don't know what I'd do with a million dollars if I had it but I was always curious to know how the Egyptians mummied things. I always figured there was some kind of an acid and it was. But there's an awful lot of different kinds of acids in the world. Here's a fish I mummied for my grandson. And here's a piece of beefsteak. That's 18 years old this summer.

TROUBLEMAKERS

I've run into smart guys in the woods. When they get that way I just walk away and leave 'em. In a camp above Clarkia there was a couple of brothers. We had the first woman to cook in a camp and they said they wouldn't eat grub cooked by a woman.

I forget the name of the woman but she was a good cook. I said, "Fellow! I'll tell you something. You keep still or I'll break your seat with a heavy fall!"

There was two of 'em but they took it. Probably they'd never had a decent meal in their lives till they come there.

The woman appreciated it.

ELK HUNTING

I was up by the Halfway House one time on my way elk hunting and a deer went away from me. I had a 30.06. I shouldn't have shot at it but I did. Hit it in the hip and shaved off the whole side of it. I never touched that gun again.

The biggest elk I ever killed in my life I killed with a little .32.20. Me and Perry Fleming up on Marble Creek. Every time I shot, Perry pumped his bolt and threw another shell on the ground. He was shakin' all over. Buck fever. Never fired a shot.

TOOK MY OUTFIT

My father was one of these honest men. He never beat a man out of a dime but what he'd spend a dollar to get it back to him. And I've told my kids to be honest. Don't take nothing that don't belong to 'em.

I've worked hard all my life. I had a little loggin' outfit and sold logs to the St. Maries mill when Pugh owned it. When I got sick they took my outfit, everything I had.

I kept a quarter section and after I got sick I went out there and piddled around a little bit and I'd be all in. Bad heart! I was 2 days in the Spokane hospital in 1945 and they didn't think I'd make it.

I went back to Wisconsin to see one of the best heart doctors. I wouldn't be alive today if I hadn't gone to him.

He asked me what medicine I was taking and he looked at it and he says, "You want me to doctor you?"

I said, "That's what I come here for."

He said, "Then we'll just take all this in one dose." And he poured it down the toilet. He said, "This heart trouble won't hurt you too much but it will just gradually drag you down. There is no medicine that will help a heart. If you get tired and need something you can take a little drink of brandy. Don't get drunk! But a little drink of brandy is the onliest thing that will help a heart."

He said, "Don't lift anything. A hard lift can send the blood pressure down for a well man and for you it could kill you."

Interviewed March 1973 at St. Maries

Log strikes pond in shower of spray at Big Creek 1911
Courtesy Ruby El Hult

Neil Yager   Veteran

I heard the door open behind me....

Neil Yager at 77, 1976

I was born in Michigan. By the way, there's 4 of us around St. Maries born March, 1899. Lee Swofford the 6th, me the 15th, Clarence Isbel the 21st and Arvid Johnson the 9th. My family come to Wardner, Idaho in the fall of 1901 and Dad bought a shoeshop there. He run it all winter then Carl Renfro found a homestead for him west of Santa on Sheep Cr.

In the spring of 1903 Dad and R. J. Thomas built a cabin on our homestead and we moved out there in time for my brother Harold to be born, July 7th.

Then Dad started a shoeshop in Santa and built a house there so us kids could go to school. The Santa townsite was all on the older Mrs. Renfro's homestead.

My mother had been a schoolteacher in Michigan and she taught us a lot at home and by Golly! We all started to school in the 1st grade and wound up in the 3rd grade the first year.

DRAGGED PIPE THROUGH THE MUD

It was fun living in town. During the gold strike the Tyson Mining Co. freighted all their pipe through Santa. They'd use 8 or 10 head of horses fighting one pipe from the steel bridge which came across the river just below that little campground and then up the muddy main drag along the river past Perry Hugh's store, the Hendershott Hotel, the Renfro Livery Barn and past the two log houses that set on the flat below Walker's store. They were old Carmen's saloon and his bar from in the early 1890s.

The Hendershott Hotel had dining room and office on the ground floor and rooms upstairs. When I was 9 or 10 years old 3 of us boys worked in the kitchen washing dishes for that dining room. They served meals there for years.

Hendershott Hotel built before 1902

Harvey Renfro Livery Barn

School drill 1907 at Santa: Lyle Stowe, Frank Stowe, Adolph Schuder Neil Yager, Wesley Renfro, Norman O'Donnell, Sidney Yager

O'Donnell Hotel

Santa Grocery & Post Office

SOLD PAPERS IN THE CAMPS

The three saloons was busy places with 16 or 17 logging camps not too far away and 40 to 100 men in each. My brother and I used to walk out to the camps to sell the San Francisco Examiner, Saturday Globe, Saturday Evening Post and Ladies Home Journal. We'd stay overnight and come back to Santa in time for school next morning.

There was a weekly Santa Gazette but we didn't sell that. Old Dursland was editor and owner and his building was down below the O'Donnell Hotel on the right hand side of the street and about 150 yards before you reached the old bridge.

BLOOD TRAILS

In the morning when we went down to the saloons to peddle papers, by Golly! If there had been a fresh snow during the night we'd see a trail of blood going down the sidewalks from some joint or other. A lot of Finns and Scandinavians carried knives.

When my cousin came in late years to visit the cemetery I'd give her the history of some of the graves, like my Uncle Tyler that got shot in the Marble Creek wars.

Or Bert Erb. Bert was pretty drunk one night and he was pickin' on Denny LaFurnia. Denny was a little bit of a Frenchman and a gambler. Denny had cleaned Bert at the poker table.

Pretty soon Bert Erb got rough and took Denny down on the floor.

Denny told him, "If you don't get off me I'm gonna shoot you!" and pulled out a .32 automatic.

Bert Erb took the gun away from him. He stayed sittin' on Denny while he took the clip

Fred Tyler 1869
Aug. 7, 1904

out. He was too busy to notice Denny sliding another .32 out of his other pocket. So they buried Bert Erb. The tombstone reads, A. BERT ERB 1877 — October 24, 1906

TOO BIG FOR MY PANTS

I always had a little money from selling papers and I had a .22 single shot pistol and some fishin' tackle so I felt pretty damned independent. I'd get a lickin' at home and I'd take to the brush like a wolf for a week or two. By the time I was 12 I left home to drive work teams on February plowing down in the Palouse country.

I don't like to take orders from anybody. That's why I didn't get along in Fort Lewis in World War 1. I was sick in the army hospital for a couple of months. They told me, by Golly! My division was moving to

France and I couldn't go along. I was gonna be transferred to a casualty batallion.

I said, "That's for the birds! If I ain't goin' to war I'm goin' bye bye."

They never caught me even though I worked in the woods around St. Maries part of the time under my own name. Six years after the Armistice they granted amnesty to all military offenders.

When they sent me the questionaire for World War 2, I told 'em my record. I was 43 but they grabbed anybody with previous military training. So they drafted me anyhow.

SHOOTIN' MATCH
But the worst shootin' match I ever went through was right here at home in 1975. My veteran's check come the 1st. of January and when I got my social security on the 3rd, me and my neighbor Jess Gardner went into St. Maries with the mailman.

I had decided before long I'd leave the winter behind and go stay with my brother in Arizona so I went to the bank and bought $600 in traveler's checks and stuck the other $200 in my pocket. Then we went to the bar to drink and visit.

After awhile the daylight run out. I said to Jess, "It's gettin' late. Why not sound around amongst these guys and see if somebody will take us home?"

So he worked his way down the bar and finds this guy, Dolphin Bergland that will take us home for five bucks.

We rode out to my trailer, 7 or 8 o'clock, pitch dark and snow stormin' bad. Bergland had a bottle of vodka and I had some gin and whiskey. We had a few drinks.

Then Jess said he had to take his box of groceries home to his family. Grover Blevins lives next door about a hundred yards away. His son-in-law come over with his snowcat and went off with Jess.

Me and Bergland was chewin' the rag, wonderin' if Jess would come back. Finally decided he wouldn't.

Bergland got up and went out, he said, to start his pick-up warming. Instead of that he got a .30 .30 rifle.

I heard him open the door behind me but didn't pay no attention. I was settin' bent over in the chair because my back was achin' damn bad after bein' up all day downtown.

Neil Yager has 20 percent disability for injuring his back in the World War 2 airforce, lifting boxes of 50 caliber ammo into planes at an airfield in England.

The chair that Bergland had been settin' in was just about in front of the door opening 6 feet away. I don't know if he sat down or if he shot from the doorway but the gun went off twice. Those two shots are the ones my two neighbors heard: Grover Blevins on my side of the highway a hundred yards toward town and Pruett that has a trailer directly across the highway from where my driveway enters it. The door must have been open so they could hear those two shots.

The first bullet went through the sleeve of my jumper and never touched me. The other went through my left shoulder from behind and came out with a piece of bone from my arm through another hole in the jumper.

I took a nose dive.

When I woke up I was rollin' around on the floor. I couldn't figure out why I couldn't get up.

Bergland's feet was almost touchin' me while he was sittin' up in my chair cussin' about not bringin' enough cartridges. I don't know whether he went out and got some more or not. I was havin' lapses of memory.

When I couldn't seem to get up I rolled on my back under the table.

Then the rifle went off right in my face and blinded me and knocked me out. Maybe he shot twice then. There is 4 bullet holes in the floor.

The neighbors didn't investigate because I'm shootin' nights around here at skunks or rodents — you name it. It could be that after the first two shots Bergland closed the door and my neighbors couldn't hear.

I hadn't had any argument with the man. So it must have been the money. Somebody must have told him I had cashed $800 in checks. With that money and his pick-up and camper maybe he figured he could travel quite a ways.

But he didn't find the money. I had a billfold layin' there with several cards in it and no money at all. He didn't find the $600 in travelers checks in the flat folder in my shirt pocket.

But afterwards, everybody that knowed him told me he gets to drinkin' and he just goes plumb nuts.

After awhile I woke up. It took 2 or 3 minutes to orient myself. Then I thought, "What the hell is that?" I could hear snorin'.

I thought, "By Gosh! I get another chance!" That's exactly what I thought.

I was layin' in a lot of blood. I took my time and rolled out from under the table. Then I got my good hand ahold of the cupboard and got on my feet, hangin' onto it.

The bottle of vodka was still settin' on the table, drained down a lot more while I was knocked out. He had left his overshoes — he had a pair of slippers in 'em — sittin' right beside my chair and walked into my bed in the other end of the 14 foot trailer in his sock feet. Laying there and snorin'.

A loaded 12 gauge shotgun that I'd kept ready for a bobcat that had been killin' our kittens set against the corner of the bed but his .30 .30 was leaning against it. If I fumbled around gettin' the shotgun it would knock over the rifle and wake him up. I had a .22 magnum rifle in the clothes closet but I didn't think I could stand up while I swung the door open because I had to hang onto something to stay on my feet.

I started to move along the wall supporting myself with my good hand. If I tipped my head I got dizzy and I'd blind so I had to wipe my eyes with my arm so I could see. The way I staggered you could have knocked me over with a big feather. I knew then I couldn't hope to hold up either a rifle or a shotgun with one hand.

My only chance was a .357 Smith and Wesson six shooter. I had sorted out a bunch of clothes to take 'em in to wash and I had 'em piled right at the head of the bed. He laid his head down on them clothes and underneath them was that pistol.

I worked along the wall till my knees hit the bed. Soon as I stooped over to fish under the clothes I got dizzy and I'd blind and have to wipe my eyes with my arm so I could see. Then I'd go fishin' again. Every time I disturbed the clothes, he'd stir. I'd stand there and wait till he snored again.

Then by Golly! I touched the pistol butt, got my fingers around it. I pulled a little. It wouldn't come. The sight had hung up on the clothes.

He stirred, startin' to wake up. I couldn't wait. I jerked hard and pulled the pistol out. The front sight come draggin' a shirt sleeve that flopped across his face.

He raised up on his elbow facing me.

I had just wiped my eyes and straightened up so I could see. He wasn't a foot away from the end of the muzzle. That's when I shot him. Twice. One shot in the middle of the forehead and the other above the temple.

Now I was free to call help. I slid along the wall to the door and pushed it open with the gun barrel and fired 4 times in the air. I knew Grover Blevins and Pruett would hear it.

Grover said afterwards he went out his door and looked. He could see somebody standing in my trailer door. Thought I'd shot at a skunk or maybe that bobcat.

When 5 minutes passed and he didn't show up, I set down and got out a box of cartridges and reloaded the pistol. I'd have to go over closer to Grover's and shoot some more.

I went out in the snowstorm and got as far as the lightpole across the yard and fell down. I got up and next thing I run into the corner of the little bunk shack where I've got a heater and TV and fell down again. Laid there till the cold got me to my feet. Got up and went across toward Grover's and run into the old bus and fell down again.

When I got up this time I seen I wasn't gonna make it any closer to Grovers. The snow was pert near knee deep and I still hadn't made it through the fence. I guess it was 9 or 10 o'clock. I still had the gun in my hand but I forgot all about shooting it.

I staggered back to the little shack and made it inside and flopped on the bed. I worked my jacket off to see what damage was done by that bullet. I couldn't tell much except I was bleedin' heavy and my arm hung like a dead weight. About then I keeled over.

When I woke up it was daylight. I was layin' in a lot of blood. I knew I'd better find help.

I got outside and the driveway that had been plowed yesterday had only a foot of loose snow. I headed out that way to the highway and across. On the other side I was so weak I had to get down and crawl over the berm thrown up by the snowplow. I got to Pruett's door and hammered on it. When he opened I told him, "I'm shot!"

He helped me inside and set me on a chair and his wife got a blanket and put around me. He's got a CB radio and telephone. I don't know which he used. I wasn't very interested in what was goin' on about that time.

The ambulance and the sheriff's car come out and took me to the St. Maries hospital. They give me a shot and put a bandage on my shoulder — after the sheriff arrested me. I don't know what made him think I could get away. I couldn't navigate alone.

The doctor told me the upper armbone was shattered and I'd have to go where they had facilities. Did I want to go to the Vet's hospital in Spokane or Seattle?

I said, "In this blizzard I doubt if the ambulance could get through."

So they sent me to Coeur d'Alene. The sheriff there arrested me, too. Then they give me another shot and started to clean up the wound. The doctor told me my heart was weak. It wasn't pumping hard and that's the only reason I hadn't bled to death overnight.

I asked the doctor what the chances were.

He said, "They're practically nil." The last thing I heard before I passed out, "If we'd have got him within an hour or two at most.....the amount of blood he's lost and the shock..."

I woke up in the intensive care room. For 3 or 4 days it kept snowin' and blowin' so they gave up trying to send me to the Vets hospital. Didn't figure I could make the trip anyhow.

Kept me in intensive care 25 days then stuck me in the nursing home. I damn near died there one night. They got the doc out to look at me at two in the morning. He said, "It's your heart."

"Listen!" I said. "At home I've been pert near livin' on vodka and gin and here they won't let me have it. That's where the trouble is."

The doc examined me. He said to the head nurse, "We've got to give him back some liquor or he's goin' into delirium tremens."

After that they gave me beer whenever I woke up. And vodka too. Whichever I wanted I got.

The trial was Sept. 21-25, 1975. The jury: Herb Anderson, Dan Reid, Reuben E. Marquardt, Juanita Loe, Dean Marty, James H. Jensen David G. Slead, Rick Neimeyer, Lorraine F. Dugger, Henry W. Sindt, Erle H. Wheeler, and Bradley Sullivan found Neil Yager not guilty.

But one thing had been bothering me and that was how a man could shoot twice at me at 6 foot range and then only a foot away another couple or three times with a .30 .30 rifle and hit me only once — especially that shot where he fired the rifle right in my face.

During the trial, Walker, the deputy, brought me out with others to the trailer to figure out what happened.

Bergland's glasses was layin' there on the floor.

Walker examined them and said, "I can see now why he missed you when he coulda poked the gun in your ear. Once he dropped his glasses he was practically blind.

Neil Yager place. Trailer house right where he was shot.
Old bus left where he bogged down in snow trying to make it to Grover Blevins house 100 yards left, shack where he lay all night is behind the log building. Center front is driveway which he came out to cross highway to Pruett's trailer.

Interviewed at his trailer 6-7-76

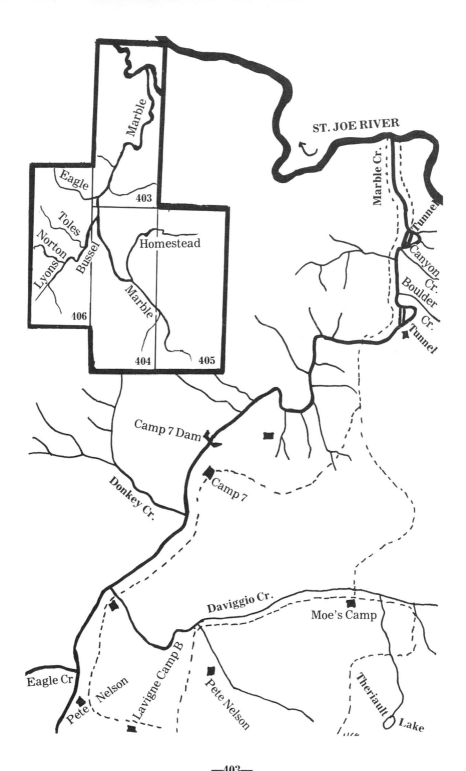

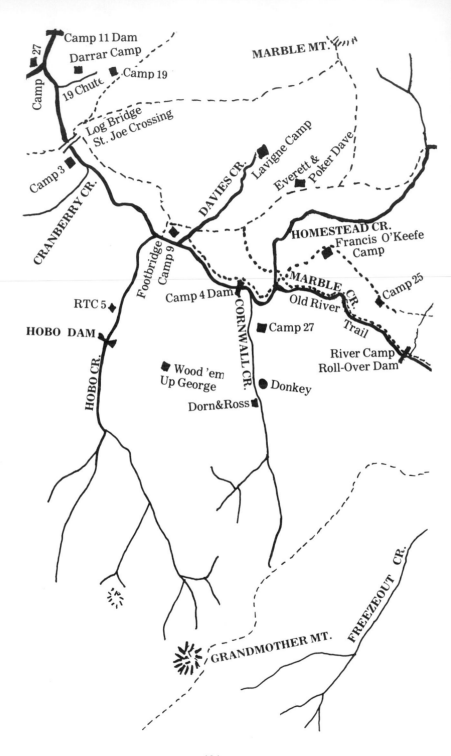

Camp 27

Camp 11 Dam
Darrar Camp
Camp 19
19 Chute
Log Bridge
St. Joe Crossing
Camp 3
CRANBERRY CR.

MARBLE MT.

DAVIES CR.
Lavigne Camp
Everett &
Poker Dave

HOMESTEAD CR.
Francis O'Keefe
Camp

Footbridge
Camp 9
RTC 5
HOBO DAM
HOBO CR.

Camp 4 Dam
CORNWALL CR.
Camp 27
Wood 'em
Up George
Donkey
Dorn&Ross

MARBLE CR.
Old River
Trail
Camp 25

River Camp
Roll-Over Dam

FREEZEOUT CR.

GRANDMOTHER MT.

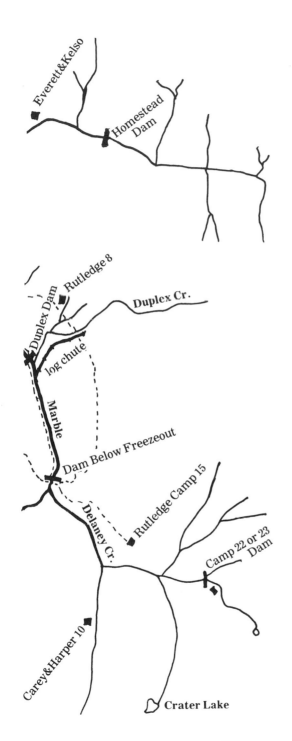

Everett&Kelso

Homestead
Dam

Rutledge 8

Duplex Dam

Duplex Cr.

log chute

Marble

Dam Below Freezeout

Rutledge Camp 15

Delaney Cr.

Camp 22 or 23
Dam

Carey&Harper 10

Crater Lake

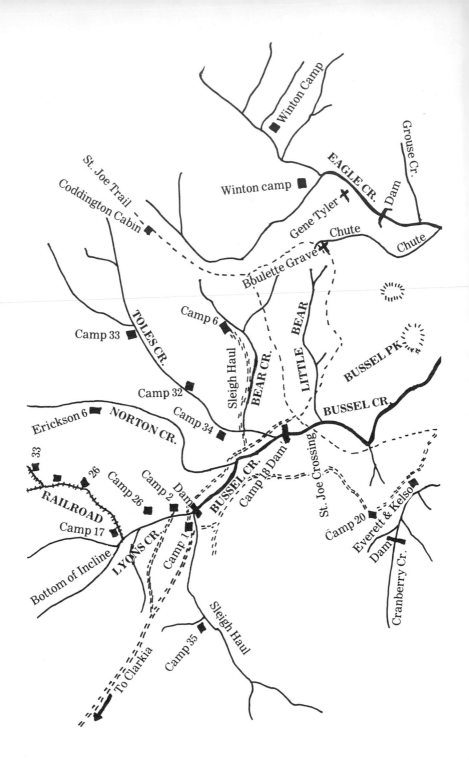

Winton Camp

Grouse Cr.

EAGLE CR.

Winton camp

Gene Tyler

Dam

St. Joe Trail

Coddington Cabin

Chute

Boulette Grave

Chute

Camp 6

LITTLE BEAR

BEAR CR.

Camp 33

TOLES CR.

Sleigh Haul

BUSSEL PK

Camp 32

Camp 34

BUSSEL CR.

Erickson 6

NORTON CR.

33

26

Camp 26

Camp 2

Dam

BUSSEL CR.

Camp 18 Dam

St. Joe Crossing

Camp 20

Everett & Kelso

RAILROAD

Camp 17

Bottom of Incline

LYONS CR.

Camp 1

Dam

Cranberry Cr.

Sleigh Haul

To Clarkia

Camp 35

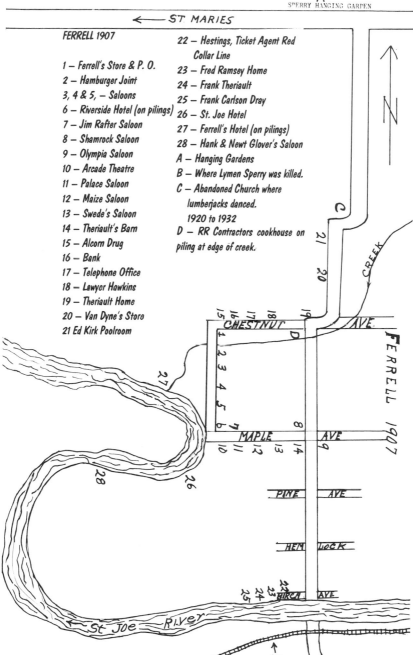

← ST MARIES

FERRELL 1907

1 – Ferrell's Store & P. O.
2 – Hamburger Joint
3, 4 & 5, – Saloons
6 – Riverside Hotel (on pilings)
7 – Jim Rafter Saloon
8 – Shamrock Saloon
9 – Olympia Saloon
10 – Arcade Theatre
11 – Palace Saloon
12 – Maize Saloon
13 – Swede's Saloon
14 – Theriault's Barn
15 – Alcorn Drug
16 – Bank
17 – Telephone Office
18 – Lawyer Hawkins
19 – Theriault Home
20 – Van Dyne's Store
21 Ed Kirk Poolroom

22 – Hestings, Ticket Agent Red
  Collar Line
23 – Fred Ramsey Home
24 – Frank Theriault
25 – Frank Carlson Dray
26 – St. Joe Hotel
27 – Ferrell's Hotel (on pilings)
28 – Hank & Newt Glover's Saloon
A – Hanging Gardens
B – Where Lymen Sperry was killed.
C – Abandoned Church where
  lumberjacks danced.
  1920 to 1932
D – RR Contractors cookhouse on
piling at edge of creek.

N

CREEK

CHESTNUT AVE

FERRELL 1907

MAPLE AVE

PINE AVE

HEMLOCK

BIRCH AVE

St Joe River

OTHER REGIONAL BOOKS

CALKED BOOTS & OTHER NORTHWEST WRITINGS
HARDSHIPS & HAPPY TIMES
-By Bert Russell
Lacon Pubs. Harrison, Id. 83833

STEAMBOATS IN THE TIMBER
NORTHWEST DISASTER
LOST MINES & TREASURES OF THE PACIFIC NORTHWEST
TREASURE HUNTING NORTHWEST
-By Ruby El Hult
Binford & Mort Pubs.
2536 SE 11th.
Portland, Ore. 97202

THE WAY IT WAS--a book of photos.
-Compiled & edited by Robt. M. Hammes & E. Mark Justice.
Western Historical, Inc. St. Maries, Id.

LIVING WORLD WAR 1 1917--1918 ST. MARIES, IDAHO.
-By JoJane Hammes
Pub. by the Corporation
127 South Seventh, St Maries, Id. 83861